T0121709

# THE
# TEN-YEAR CAREER

*The Fast Track Guide to*
*Retiring Young, Wealthy, and Fulfilled*

## D. M. Lukas

iUniverse, Inc.
Bloomington

THE TEN-YEAR CAREER
The Fast Track Guide to Retiring Young, Wealthy, and Fulfilled

Copyright © 2013 D. M. Lukas

iUniverse books may be ordered through booksellers or by contacting:

iUniverse
1663 Liberty Drive
Bloomington, IN 47403
www.iuniverse.com
1-800-Authors (1-800-288-4677)

Because of the dynamic nature of the Internet, any Web
addresses or links contained in this book may have changed
since publication and may no longer be valid. The views
expressed in this work are solely those of the author and do
not necessarily reflect the views of the publisher, and the
publisher hereby disclaims any responsibility for them.

Any people depicted in stock imagery provided by Thinkstock are
models, and such images are being used for illustrative purposes only.

Certain stock imagery © Thinkstock.

ISBN: 978-1-4759-7012-8 (sc)
ISBN: 978-1-4759-7011-1 (e)

Library of Congress Control Number: 2013900452

Printed in the United States of America

iUniverse rev. date: 4/5/2013

# Praise for the Ten Year Career

This is a super book, loaded with great ideas for success that everyone can learn and apply, in any business, at any age.
- Brian Tracy, Author, Maximum Achievement

Very few people live long enough to be themselves. Perhaps, they should pick up this great read and avoid that unfortunate sequence of events. After all, the only thing you can control is your attitude and whether or not you purchase this superb book.
- Daniel Moneypenny, World Famous Branding Expert and President & CCO of Emaginit

You may not get rich because you read this book. But, you will be smarter, more competent, and understand a lot of things that can make you more successful (and life more employable!) Finally, if you take Dave's advice, I believe it will also lead to more happiness—and that alone is well worth the small investment! I wish I had a book like this when I was starting my career. It is easily worth as much as a college education in terms of career success.
- John L. Marriotti, Former President of Rubbermaid Office Products, Former President of Huffy Bicycles, and Founder & CEO of The Enterprise Group and Award Winning Author

Dave Lukas has delivered a brilliant and highly relevant, principled roadmap to achievement and success that few have achieved. His successful and energetic track record of entrepreneurial accomplishment elevates Dave to the top as a transformational, innovative and marketing leadership that many of us are seeking to accomplish. "Fasten your seat belt", you're in for an unforgettable journey in transformational thinking and results.

- Miguel A. de Jesus, Founder & CEO
of Purpose & Action, LLC

The Ten Year Career delivers everything someone needs to put them on the path to success...and keep them there. Dave gives an incredible amount of top-tier advice and a clear set of actions to get any reader to their next level all in an easy, concise way. The principles that Dave teaches are timeless and should be passed down from generation to generation!

- Doc Severson, Founder of Options MD

The Ten Year Career should be required reading for everyone at some point in their life!

- M. Erik Mueller, Founder and CEO of Grasp
Technologies and Creative Computer Resources

# Contents

# FOREWORD:
## LEARNING FROM LUKAS

I want to start by introducing you to Dave Lukas. He is an exceptional young man who has earned multiple successes through his initiative and hard work. He has also done it at a much earlier age than most people. Part of that is because of his active and inquisitive mind; a larger part of it is because of this proactive, determined and optimistic ("can do") perspective. There, that's a thumbnail. I'll close with more about Dave, but first I want to tell you why this book is so valuable.

Through most of my lengthy career, I have always believed that it was best to learn from someone who has "been there, done that." As I got older, and more experienced, I also discovered that the best learning comes from listening to someone who has not only "been there and done that" but has done so fairly recently, and is intimately familiar with the current reality and today's challenges.

That's why I was delighted to see that Dave Lukas organized his learning and is sharing it with thousands of others who will benefit from it. At first glance, you might mistakenly think that this is a book for "young folks, just getting started." That is true; but it is not just for young folks.

This book is a treasure for anyone who needs to "get started" regardless of their age. Millions of Americans are currently unemployed or underemployed and need to "get a new start." This book is every bit as valuable for them to do that as it is for younger folks, just starting out for the first time. But that's not all. Dave also imparts some wisdom that belies his youth when he writes down to earth advice about getting "financially smart," and about "managing your time," or "becoming a lifelong learner."

Bottom line is that at a very early age, Dave learned by doing, by observing, by studying, by reading, and then applying that with an aggressive and intuitive attitude that led to success. And we all know "nothing succeeds like success." In his relatively brief career to date, he has worked with big companies and small ones, with well-known experts and business neophytes. Who better to provide ideas on how to build a plan for starting a career and a life than someone who has been doing it—and living it.

Thus I encourage you to read Dave's book and share its messages with your family, friends and loved ones. Everyone will be smarter, better prepared to face life's challenges, and most of all, to find success built around a sensible "ten year" plan.

Now, to go back to Dave personally: I've known him and worked with him for several years, including working as co-authors of a book—my tenth and Dave's second. It's probably a bit unusual for co-authors of a complete book to have forty years difference in their ages, who share such similar viewpoints.

In my business, consulting and executive career of almost 48 years, I've had to evaluate a lot of people. After a while, you develop a "sixth sense" about young people who are what we used to call "go-getters." You want to be around them; and you want to have them on your team. That's how I see Dave.

He is well known to many of my colleagues and their reactions to him are largely the same as mine. This book is full of solid advice from a young, but surprisingly experienced man, who has discovered what works (and what doesn't) and chosen to share it with others.

Don't hesitate! Read this book. Don't stop part way through it. Read a chapter every week, and discuss it with those close to you: what have you learned, and most important, how can you improve your life and your "fortunes." Mark up your copy of the book; make notes about what you plan to do. Then set out to do it.

You may not get rich because you read this book. But, you will be smarter, more competent, and understand a lot of things that can make you more successful (and life more employable!) Finally, if you take Dave's advice, I believe it will also lead to more happiness—and that alone is well worth the small investment. Good luck on *your* T*en Year Career.*

**John L. Mariotti**
**Former President of Rubbermaid Office Products, Former President of Huffy Bicycles, and Founder & CEO of The Enterprise Group and Award Winning Author**

# WHY YOU NEED THIS BOOK

This book is a culmination of over five years of hard work and study (and, as a result of that study, hundreds of years of ideas and information from the greatest thinkers in history). It took over five years because I had to find, learn, perfect, and execute flawlessly all of the principles I am going to teach you.

*We live in exciting times!*

As I write this book, the United States and the world are going through extraordinary economic times. Most people of the Gen X and Gen Y generations (of which I am part) have never seen or gone through a time when there wasn't economic growth. The word of the day seems to be *crisis*.

So, why do I say "exciting"?

Because no matter what type of economic situation exists, there is always opportunity. Even during the Great Depression, people became very wealthy. Now, I won't say that people have not fallen on hard times—because they have. And even if you are wealthy and successful, in today's world, one wrong move can really change that!

That is why you need this book. Since 1971, the dollar has lost over 90 percent of its value. The United States' current unemployment rate is hovering around 8 percent, our national debt stands at over $16 trillion, and in just a short time, our government has promised, guaranteed, and voted to print billions more! Just to put that in perspective, the entire US output—that is, what we make and produce as a country—is about $15 trillion per year. The interest to pay this new debt alone is almost $1 trillion per year going forward.[1]

All of this makes a few things likely to happen. First, world markets and economies are going to continue to go through wild fluctuations. Second, some industries (automakers, for example) are going to go through radical changes and may never be the same. Third, in order to pay for our new debt, taxes will likely continue to have to go up in future years. Lastly, with so much new money being printed and financed primarily with debt, we are headed for a time of inflation (as can already be seen by food prices reaching twenty-year highs around the world in 2011)[2]

The good news is that those who are prepared, who have the skills to succeed and the wherewithal to stay logical, and who learn to harness the power of their minds to *think* outside the proverbial box have an incredible chance to seize opportunities, gain wealth, and reach their goals and dreams.

*The Ten-Year Career* and its accompanying website, www. TheTenYearCareer.com, were written and developed to

---

1    http://www.treasurydirect.gov/NP/BPDLogin?application=np
      and http://www.bea.gov/national/index.htm#gdp)
2    http://www.reuters.com/article/2011/02/24/us-usda-forum-
      foodprices-idUSTRE71N4TT20110224

give you everything you need to get on the path to wealth, success, and ultimately personal fulfillment. Success is a process, and the following pages offer you a concrete process for obtaining the success you desire.

*D. M. Lukas*

# INTRODUCTION

"It is so easy to get rich in America—because almost nobody is trying!"

I know, I know, the first time I heard this statement, from an incredibly wealthy mentor, I thought, *What are you talking about?* At first it made me angry, but then, after some thought and about five years spent in the "real world," I realized that it is absolutely true.

Most people get up, aimlessly go to work, come home, watch some TV, go to bed, and then get up the next day and repeat the process all over again. They go to work dreading it, just wanting to get it over with—and rightfully so, because for many, there is no incentive to work harder, to go above and beyond, or to strive for the next level. The reason lies in the way that many people are paid.

## Results versus Time

Most people are paid for their time, meaning they go to work, make sure they get eight hours on their time card, get the hourly wage for those hours, and go home. For many, the incentive to do much more is just not there.

Let's take a look at the average situation.

You have Jim and Barry. They both work for the same company, doing exactly the same job, and sit in cubicles right next to each other. Jim works extremely hard, takes short lunches and no breaks, and does twice the daily work of Barry for the department. Barry, on the other hand, comes to work, walks around and talks with everybody for the first hour of the day, does a little bit of work, goes to lunch, comes back, and takes a couple of breaks in the break room before calling it a day and going home.

This cycle of Jim and Barry goes on every day until the end of the year comes and it's time for the annual review. Since Jim and Barry work in the same department, the company looks at how the department does as a whole as part of the evaluation. In this case, the department has done very well (no doubt thanks to Jim's extra efforts!). But the company looks at them and the rest of the department, says "good job," and gives everyone a 3 percent raise (barely beating inflation).

Jim cannot believe it—all of his hard work for what? The same measly 3 percent that Barry got? Jim goes back to his desk and vows never to have this happen to him again.

So what does he do? He works just enough to get his basic work done and takes breaks as much as possible, maybe a little longer lunch, just like Barry.

Sadly, this happens all of the time in today's world. *People do just enough to* not *get fired*. It happens frequently with people being paid for their time, because there is no incentive to do more than the bare minimum. Even worse, many times it is the Barrys of the world who get the promotion.

*So, how do you prevent this from happening to you? It is simple. Be paid for your results.* This does not mean that you do not have an hourly wage or salary, but it does mean that you need to have some aspect of your pay or income come from your hard work and your ability to be more productive than your peers.

If your work in some way has impact on the company's bottom line, you are not as expendable and you will be paid more. Similarly, if you own your own business and are not spending every moment on results-based activities to help your bottom line, you are losing.

The previous few statements are fundamental principles in this book. Our competitive human nature pushes us to further ourselves and gain better results for ourselves. It is this competitive edge that drives us to excel, attain more, grow more, take on new challenges, and keep life and work interesting.

Ask yourself, "Do I want to spend forty years working without a chance to truly grow myself and have a realistic chance to reach my goals and be fulfilled?"

You should probably ask yourself another question: "Why does it have to be forty years?"

That is the standard we all hear about, right? Work forty years and *save, save, save* for retirement, and you just might be able to live comfortably in retirement, barring no major economic crashes like the one we have experienced recently.

But, "comfortable?" Do you want to be just "comfortable?"

Not me!

I want to be wealthy, rich. I want to play, travel the world, start a foundation, give my family everything they always wanted, and beyond. Furthermore, I don't want to wait forty years to do it. I want to be doing it now!

*Do you want to be doing it now? I bet you do.*

But then you think, "I can't do it now. I don't have the money, time, or freedom."

Okay, okay, so maybe not right now, but how about five years from now or even ten? That still sounds a lot better than forty!

This book was written to help you create the life you want, faster and easier. It will show you how, just by doing a few things right early on in your life and career or just by changing a few in your current situation, you can make exponential strides in reaching your goals and getting what you want. In short, you will be on the fast track to a ten-year (or less) career!

Now, you are probably saying, "But I don't know how to do that! What is he talking about?" Well, first, I want you to understand one thing very clearly. Pay attention now.

*Anything can be learned. Right now, if you are not sure how to reach your dreams or not getting what you want, all it means is that there is something that you have not learned or don't know—yet!*

That's pretty comforting, right? All you have to do is figure out what it is that you don't know, and you will get yourself on the ten-year career path to anything you desire.

I have done this for you. I have done the research; I have spent the time. I have succeeded and I have failed while learning how to get on the ten–year career path, and I have taken all of this knowledge from my own experiences, as well as from top executives, successful entrepreneurs, industry icons, famous teachers, top athletes, and many others, and packaged it all in the pages to follow. They will give you a rock-solid foundation on which to build your future.

Think about this: There is not much difference between you and Bill Gates, Donald Trump, Henry Ford, and others, except for two things. First, they figured out and learned the things that they didn't know; and second, they all are paid or were paid in direct proportion to the results they delivered. That is it. As you read on, keep that in mind and have fun getting on *your* ten-year career path!

*Author's note: Throughout this book you will be asked to complete certain tasks as you navigate through each chapter. Please read each chapter carefully and complete each task as you go. Studies show that if you read the entire book and do none of the tasks, the chances of you revisiting the book and doing them are small. Also, be sure to visit this book's companion site, www. TheTenYearCareer.com, for materials to help you complete these tasks. Bottom line: Before you read further, make yourself a promise to actively participate in each chapter and take the time to do each task!*

"If you fail to plan, you plan to fail."

*—Unknown*

———

## CHAPTER 1

# WHO ARE YOU AND WHERE ARE YOU HEADED?

———

In order to get where you want to go, you must first know where you are. You can tell a lot about people by just observing them. Their habits, traits, actions, and views of their surroundings, and how they talk about their goals, desires, and dreams tell you a lot about where they are and where they are going.

The same holds true for you. Look at yourself, your habits, traits, actions, and views of your surroundings, and how you discuss your goals, desires, and dreams with others. Where are they leading you? Take five minutes to write down the answer to that question, how you see yourself, etc., and then go a step further. Ask yourself three additional questions:

- Who am I?
- What is my world view?
- Most importantly, where do I want to go?

Your answers to the above questions are very important because they help to shape your life and its outcome.

*Most people do not get what they want.* It is a sad thing, but it is true. A large majority of people do not reach their full potential. *The biggest reason they do not is that they simply do not know what they want.* Many times they do not know themselves, and even more importantly, they have no idea who they want to become.

The truth is that it is not who you are today that matters (although you must have an idea where you are starting from). *What matters most is realizing who you must become to get where you want to go.*

Let's stop here for a second. What I just said can be confusing.

*It is who you must* become *that matters most in getting where you want to go.*

What does that mean? Well, someone who truly wants to be successful and wealthy must make changes and sacrifices in his or her life to become the person that he or she aspires to being. If it is a millionaire, great! An Olympian, go for it. Success and wealth can mean many different things to people. Everyone must define success and wealth in their own terms.

There is one thing that holds true in almost all cases of those who reach their dreams and become what they aspire to be. It is that they knew that they did not know everything or had every talent, but sought out the people, knowledge, sources, and skills to get them there. ***They had to become the people they wanted to be at the end of their journey before they got there.*** You have to become that person as well, way before you reach the end of your success and wealth journey.

**Everyone *Wants* to Be Successful**

Everyone, if asked, wants to be wealthy and successful. So the question is, if so many want it so much, why do only a few make it? Why is it that you can have a room full of people who have the same skill sets and learn exactly the same information, but only one or small handful of them will take those skills and information and become successful?

You know people like this, people who have all the talent, ability, and information in the world, but go nowhere. Author John Maxwell wrote a book about this. It is called *Talent Is Never Enough*. It is the perfect description for these types of people.

So, what is the difference between those who make it and those who do not?

Let's do a short exercise, and I think you will understand. If I told you right now that there were $100 million sitting in a briefcase somewhere in the world and you had twenty-four hours to find it and it was yours, would you want to go after it?

When I ask this question to just about any audience, their response is always "Yes!" Of course you would; almost anyone would. The next thing I would tell you and them is, "Okay, go get it."

At this point, many people, probably as you are right now, look at me with confused faces, deer-in-the-headlights looks, and crinkled noses. I'll ask you the same thing I ask them, "What's the problem? I just told you there was $100 million out there for you. Why are you still here?"

People sit staring until finally, someone asks the question, "But *how* are we supposed to find it? We need some direction."

Ah! There it is. It is direction that people need—the map to get them where they want to go.

In short, as author and speaker Brian Tracy says, "Clarity is the most important, essential part of success."

You must be crystal clear on what you want and have clear plans to reach it. That is a critical difference between those who reach their success and wealth and those who have the same skills, talent, knowledge, and so on, but do not. Along with seeking out the knowledge and resources they need to become whom they aspire to be, the former have a clear plan, a map. As John Maxwell put it, "Talent is never enough." It is the crystal clear plans that you combine with talent that get you to where you want to go.

This is an area where this book can and will help you the most. It will help those people thirsting for the missing link between where they are now and where they want to be in the future—those who are looking for the map.

The rest of this book is devoted to helping you create your map and getting you on the road to your personal success, wealth, and fulfillment. Of course, I can only get you so far. There are much wiser, smarter, more talented people than me out there. The later chapters in this book will help you find them and continue your journey. You must have a clear plan or, as stated at the beginning of this chapter, "if you fail to plan, you plan to fail."

"Perhaps the only limits to the human mind are those we believe in."

—*Willis Harman*

————

## Chapter 2

# Harnessing the True Power of Your Mind

————

All of the chapters in this book are designed to build upon each other as you read them. Think of it as the order or process through which you will work toward your desired success, wealth, and fulfillment. As far as I am concerned, these first two chapters are interchangeable.

You must know where you are starting from and have a clear plan to get you where you want to go, but you will never accomplish anything without harnessing the true power of your mind.

In the last chapter, we talked about who you must become to reach your desired level of success and wealth, as well as the need for a concrete plan to get you there. This chapter is devoted solely to helping you start the journey to become that person and, most importantly, to how you will think yourself to success.

Yes, I said "think." Now, I do not mean that if you think hard enough about a million dollars that it is suddenly going to appear in front of you, because it won't.

But I will tell you this: thinking will get you 50 percent of the way there. There is one more ingredient to getting what you want, and that is *action*. More about that in a later chapter.

*Your mind can be your biggest obstacle to success, wealth, and fulfillment.*

In the last chapter, I asked you to look at yourself and ask who you really are. Many people do not realize that who they are ultimately is a product of the influences that have been around them all of their lives. Your current success and wealth path is a product of the different people, events, media, culture, and so on that you have been around your whole life.

Write down the immediate first thoughts that appear in your mind to the following questions in the spaces provided. Do it quickly.

What is a lot of money to you (in terms of what one can make in a year)?

_____

When I say "six figures," what number comes to mind?

_____

*What were your answers?*

About 99 percent of the time when speaking to people, the answer I get to the first question is between $30,000 and $300,000. Occasionally, I get $1 million.

Almost 99 percent of the time when I ask the second question, I get—you guessed it—$100,000.

Now, why do I do this exercise? It is an indicator. It tells me where someone's success and wealth path is taking him or her. If people *believe* that $50,000 is a lot of money, guess what they are going to make or are making? Yep, $50,000. No wonder they haven't reached their desired success or wealth level. Their mind is set to a $50,000 path, and that is what it is holding them to!

Don't believe me?

Go back to the second question I asked you. Look at your answer.

Why does it not say $999,999?

If it does, great! You are already ahead of the game, but do you know why you gave that answer? If it doesn't say $999,999, it's okay, but we've got some work to do.

**Changing Your Path**

The question you may be asking now is, *How do I change my path?* Well, first you must realize where the way you think originated or came from. Then, you must decide whether this is really the way you want to think or not.

So, where did your thoughts come from? As stated above, your thoughts are influenced by many areas: parents, friends, relatives, media, culture, religion, teachers, and so on. All of these sources influence who you are and how you think through time, starting all the way back when you were just a kid.

Raise your hand (if you are in public, just say "yes" or "no" to yourself) if you heard things like, "Money doesn't grow on trees" or "Do you think I am made of money?" or maybe a description of a wealthy person as "evil rich."

Chances are that you did hear all of these things and many others from a variety of sources. If that is the case, do you think it affects your view of wealth and success? Especially if the things that were said were negative?

If the above statements were the type that you heard and were said to you over and over again for all of those years, do you think that they may affect you or influence you? Do you find yourself saying them today in your life?

*Subconsciously your mind may be holding you back from the path that you want to be on.*

The last statement may be the most important statement you will ever read. Why? Notice that I said that *your subconscious mind may be holding you back.* You must understand that the subconscious mind is the most powerful part of our brain; it runs everything in us without us being "conscious" to it. For example, in school, when you are taking a test, you have to be conscious and think of the answers to the questions. You are using the conscious part of your brain. But how hard do you really think to drive a car? Or throw a baseball? Or take a shower? Or brush your teeth?

The answer is that you do not really have to think about these things; they are automatic reactions. Your subconscious mind has been conditioned to do these things. It is the same with many of your views on wealth and success. Most of the time that a success or wealth situation comes up, your subconscious mind uses its automatic responses; it reacts without you even knowing it.

## An Example

Let's look at an example of how our minds have been conditioned or trained. Many of us, me included, do things a certain way because "that is how I was taught!" or "that's how my parents did it." In fact, I have to wash a car a certain way because "that is how my father taught me," and anyone helping me has to do it that way as well. My wife has even coined the nickname of "car wash drill sergeant" for me and salutes me anytime I ask her to help wash the car. But, is it really the most efficient and best way? Probably not, but "that is how I was taught." Can you think of any examples like this in your life? You are probably chuckling at a few examples right now.

*What really matters is that if you can realize that you have the ultimate control of what you put into your mind and make "automatic," you can do almost anything. You can change your success and wealth path from being set at $50,000 per year to $1 million per year and beyond just by what you choose to think every day.*

I will say that this realization that you can choose and decide how you think and where you want your mind to drive your path is not new, *but it is absolutely crucial.* It has been said in many different ways over hundreds of years.

In fact, the latest way it has been said is the book and audio phenomenon that is sweeping the world as I write this, called *The Secret.* There is, however, one book—a timeless classic—that should be in every single individual's personal library. It teaches these principles more effectively than anyone else. It is called *Think and Grow Rich*, by Napoleon Hill. This book was written in the 1930s and is the mind-set gospel. In this book, many of the greatest quotes of all time were written, such as "Whatever a man can conceive, he can achieve" and "Thoughts are things." Take a moment to think about the significance of those two quotes and what they really might mean to you.

Now think about this; it is very eye-opening. Robert Kiyosaki, best-selling author of *Rich Dad, Poor Dad*, states something extremely interesting about the title of Napoleon Hill's book. He says, "Notice the title of the book is **Think and Grow Rich** not Work Hard *and Grow Rich!*"

I think this is very important, because money itself is just an idea. It can come in many different forms and can be many different things to different people, so the way you think can give you much more control over your success, wealth, and desired outcome than just working hard. If you have the right mind-set, *one of choice and control of your own conditioning, and* are willing to work hard, there is nothing that can stand in the way of getting what you want.

## Money Is Just an Idea

Above, I stated that money is just an idea and can come in many forms. What do I mean? Well, if you think about it, money is not the paper currency you hold in your hand. That is the end result. Money is really the idea(s) or way of creating the source of that paper currency. For example, a book such as this is a collection of thoughts and words. But when put together and then purchased by somebody, it becomes money. Money can come in tons of different forms—from a book to a product you create, to advice people are willing to pay for, to even the "pet rock"! That is why your mind and your ability to harness its full potential are so critical. Remember that as you begin to create your ten-year career plan; take note of all the ways you can "create" money.

## A Realization

Nobody is born with a success and wealth path already set. No one said to your parents when you were born, "Beautiful baby! Too bad it will never make more than $35,000!"

I know it is funny, but it is true. The good news is that since we now know that we have been taught and conditioned on how to think and act when it comes to wealth, success, and really anything, we have the ability to change ourselves. We can learn to have and create the mind-set of success that *we desire*, not a subconscious one made from other sources' beliefs and thoughts.

## Start with Your Attitude

Much of what we have discussed so far in this chapter has to do with things in your subconscious that have been part of you for a very long time. It will not be easy to change them, and it will not happen overnight. As the saying goes, "Rome was not built in a day."

*But I do believe this: Awareness is the catalyst of change.*

The goal of this chapter so far is to make you aware, so that, if you want to, you can change. You can change your outlook, your path—your whole life.

Most people, after thinking about what I have said above, understand that much, but their next thought is, *Where do I start?*

Well, the first place I started when I became aware was with my *attitude*. Your attitude is a reflection of your subconscious thoughts and is what you project to your surroundings. Have you ever met people who had what you thought was a "poor" attitude?

If you think about it, that poor attitude is just their conditioned mind on the outside—*their* inner game *showing in their* outer game.

After being around people with a poor attitude, did you want to stay around them? Probably not—and people wonder why they cannot get ahead.

Once we are aware that our daily attitude is something that we have control over, we can decide to have a great, fair, or poor attitude every day. What we choose gives us the power to create our lives and our path that day and every day.

Have you ever noticed that if you are in a bad mood, everything around you seems to be down or bad as well? Our environment is a mirror of our attitude and what we expect from ourselves and from our surroundings. If we do not expect much, we do not get much. If we expect to succeed, we will.

The average person does not think about controlling his (or her) attitude every day. He gets up, goes to get paid for his time, and lets his surroundings and subconscious affect him, dictating how the day will go.

*If you remember from Chapter 1, we talked about who you must become. Well, in order to become the person you want to be, you must have the attitude to think, act, and carry yourself as that person every day,* even if you are not there yet.

If your *inner game* is what affects your *outer game*, then you must become who and what you want mentally (on the inside) before it will happen on the outside; otherwise, it will not last.

A perfect example is the young sports star who, at a very young age, gets millions of dollars, but years later after squandering everything, is working for peanuts. Or the lottery winner who goes broke in five years. We have all heard similar stories before. These people simply did not develop their inner game enough to grow themselves to hold onto and increase their sudden wealth; instead, they lost it all—and probably are still scratching their heads, wondering why.

A simple exercise that I started doing years ago and still do every day is this:

> Create a system to automatically keep a great attitude. Take a sheet of paper and type or write the following sentence: "What attitude will I *choose* to have today?" Below that, put the following three words with spaces between them: Great, Fair, Poor. *I have put an example on the next page.* Make 365 copies. Every day, right after you get up, take a sheet off the pile, read the question, and circle the attitude you will have.

As rudimentary as it is, this exercise does two things. First, it forces you to *choose* what attitude you will have for that day; and second, after you have circled your choice, it holds you accountable to that choice for the entire day. I have been doing this for almost six years at this point, and I can say that never once, after looking at that sheet of paper, have I chosen "Fair" or "Poor." It has made a huge difference in my entire life, even on days when not everything necessarily goes my way.

I have also put a sample of the Daily Attitude Sheet for you online at www.TheTenYearCareer.com.

**What type of attitude will I *choose* to have today?**

**Great**  **Fair**  **Poor**

Before moving onto the next chapter, create your attitude sheet and take some time to think about all of the things that were said to you about wealth, success, and personal fulfillment growing up—good and bad. Take a moment to write them down and ask yourself if they are driving you toward your desired path.

Then, *write down the thoughts you want to have and believe.* Resolve to *choose* your attitude every day. Keep what you write about the thoughts you *want to have and believe about success, wealth, and personal fulfillment* in a place that you can take a look at it at least once or twice a week.

*Author's note: A great deal of this chapter is spent talking about money as a measurement of wealth and success. First, because it is easy for someone to relate to and see in an example; and second, money whether directly or indirectly is a result of increased wealth and success. I do want to stress that success and wealth does not have to mean just money. Know that this chapter's ideas can be used in many other ways—from strengthening relationships to changing the way you think about yourself, or even how you interact with your loved ones. Many people have seen great success in these areas just by changing how they think in their lives.*

"If you're bored with life—you don't get up every morning with a burning desire to do things—you don't have enough goals."

—*Lou Holtz*

––––––

## Chapter 3

# Goals, the Key to Your Map

––––––

Now that you have begun to plan and harness the true power of your mind, you must figure out where that plan and mind-set are going to take you. This chapter is critical to putting you on the path you desire because goal setting is the one thing that separates most people from those who truly become great.

The realization of the importance of goals and the effect they have on mankind has literally been around for thousands of years. Aristotle, the great Greek philosopher, once said,

*"Man is a goal-seeking animal. His life only has meaning if he is reaching out and striving for his goals!"*

Throughout time humankind has had goals, whatever they may be, and those goals are what have propelled us to create all that we have. It really is amazing! If you look at even just the last hundred years, at the turn of the last century, people were still on horseback. Today we are running entire businesses with just a cell phone and traveling to the International Space Station—and it is no big deal! None of these things could have been accomplished without goals.

If you think back to what we discussed in the last chapter and to the last paragraph, you may see something in common. That "something" is really more of an epiphany or what I consider one of the great realizations of a person's life.

The realization, as I alluded to at the beginning of this book, is the fact that whatever you want to do, become, have, and so on, *can be learned*! Throughout time, we have learned to create whatever it is that we want—from flying the first plane to virtual networks.

I think that author Brian Tracy said it well in his book, *Goals!* when he said,

> One of the greatest discoveries in human history is the fact that there are no limits on what you can accomplish, except for the limits that you place on your own imagination.

And

> Since there are no limits on what you can imagine, there are no limits on what you can achieve.

*You can learn to do anything!*

Goal setting is an innate ability within all of us. Many of us just do not realize it. Whether you have goals or not, you subconscious mind will always be driving you toward something—it may just not be what you want.

The best part is, as we discussed in the last chapter, once you become aware of the fact that you can have control of your subconscious, and thus control over just about everything in your life, including your goals, you can then go to work and *learn* to accomplish whatever you want.

*Setting goals is a process.*

Most people have never had someone sit down and seriously discuss the importance of goals and the effect that having properly set goals can have on their lives. Furthermore, they have never been taught a concrete process that will increase their chances for a successful outcome for each goal.

As discussed above, goal setting is a process, and like anything it can be learned. For you to reach the true potential that you are capable of, it must be learned!

When asked, the average person may say that she has goals, but when asked to show them, she will usually say, "Oh, they are in my head."

Much has been studied about goal setting, and the evidence is conclusive: If you do not write down and plan for your goals, your chances of reaching them are very low. Author, speaker, and motivational master Dennis Waitley sums this up perfectly when he says:

> "The reason most people never reach their goals is that they don't define them, or ever seriously consider them as believable or achievable. Winners can tell you where they are going, what they plan to do along the way, and who will be sharing the adventure with them."

In this chapter, we are going to go through a basic goal-setting exercise I have used for many years. It consistently has produced the results that I desire and helped me to reach my goals. There are many goal-setting programs out there that are available to you. Many are much more in depth than the exercises we will do here and can take hours to complete. Our program should take you about one hour.

I suggest that, after reading this book and getting your initial goals set, you do take some time to look at some other programs to further define and develop your goals. My suggestion is to check out Zig Ziglar's goal-setting program. It has a lot of the elements of what we will do in this chapter, but takes them to the next level, further building upon them and giving you more insight into the goal-setting process. I suggest this program because it is tried and true and the first program that I learned to use.

**Let's Get Started**

When going through my goal-setting program, I first separate out the three areas of my life in which I have goals. I have found that these three areas hold true for just about everybody.

- The first area is Personal.
- The second is Professional.
- The third is Discretionary.

From there, I begin to plan and set the goals for each area and then further develop them.

I am often asked, "Why three areas?" This is very common. Most people want to just lump all of their goals into one "goal list" and then go from there. If you remember Dennis Waitley's statement above, you must be able to tell where you are going, what you plan to do along the way, and who you will be sharing it with. It is extremely important that your goals be specific to each area of your life and that you plan accordingly for each area. This avoids having a bunch of unfocused, jumbled goals on a piece of paper that may not be in line with each other.

If you separate the goals and put them in a specific area of your life, you will find that many of the goals for each area overlap and that working on one in that area may help you in reaching others in that area. This is important because it keeps you and your subconscious mind (remember that little guy?) focused!

For example, if your professional goals include getting promoted to management and making $120,000 per year, and you are working hard at getting promoted, an unintended result may be that you end up making more money and getting to $120,000 much faster, maybe even before getting the promotion. This happens because your goals are focused by area. So each day, depending on where you are, you can focus on that particular area, such as during work hours you can focus on just your professional goals.

On the contrary, if you have all your goals in one goal list and not separated, it can lead to problems. For example, if you are at work looking at your goals and one says to "get promoted and make $120,000" and right underneath it, the next goal says to "take more time off to learn to surf better," you are giving yourself conflicting messages from two different areas of your life, professional and personal, and this may slow your ability to reach them—especially if you are taking your lunch breaks to go surf.

I want to point out something that is very important and that you have probably experienced. This especially can affect your goals if they are not focused.

*When your subconscious mind must choose between emotional decisions and logical decisions, most of the time emotional decisions will win.*

This greatly affects your goals because many times the logical things are the things that are not as "exciting" as the emotional things, such as working harder to develop yourself versus surfing. This is a kind of inner struggle that we all must go through and we will touch on greatly when we get to the next chapter on becoming financially smart. Money is a very emotional subject.

If you think about it, though, the struggle is very real. We all have examples, myself included. Do I really need the Aston Martin DB9? When I talk to audiences, many times the ladies will break down and say that they really do not need the twentieth pair of shoes or that fifteenth purse. The men are even funnier. I mean, guys, how large of a grill do we really need to cook a few steaks? You know the one I am talking about too! It has got the huge grill surface, fifteen extra burners, a warming center, an iPod hookup, and granite surfaces just to round out the look. Yep, the best $1800 I ever spent!

You probably can think of many other times in your life where you said, "Why did I do that?" or "Why did I buy that?" and almost all are probably centered on emotional decisions!

*There is nothing wrong with this!* We are all human and we will continue to do it, but we can set some things up in our lives to give us a little bit of an edge of thinking logically over emotionally. One way to do that is to separate out the areas in our lives and focus on the goals for those specific areas.

## The Three Areas

Let's quickly define the three areas of goals in our lives.

The first is "Personal." Personal goals are very important because they are focused on such things as our family, friends, relationships, and so on. This area is always first because how we are doing from a personal standpoint affects the other two areas. For example, if you have an unhappy relationship at home, it will directly impact your professional and discretionary areas.

The second area is "Professional." The goals in this area are very important because they are focused on your career and work life. Whether you are a student, whose "career" right now is to get the degree, an employee who wants the promotion, or a business owner trying to grow your business, you must have goals that are specifically focused and driving you to where you want to go in this area.

The third area is "Discretionary." This area is important because it is focused on all of the other pursuits that you have outside of your personal and professional goals. It may include things like starting a home-based Internet business, learning to scuba dive, writing a book for people to get on the fast track to a ten-year career, or buying a vacation home. This is my favorite area for creativity and dreams in goal setting. The other two areas help to give you the means to reach these goals!

## Setting Your Goals

Now that you have the three areas, take out three sheets of paper; at the top of each page, write down the specific area for that page. So you should have a sheet for Personal, Professional, and Discretionary.

You can find examples of these goal sheets with everything on them to go through this exercise at www.TheTenYearCareer. com.

Now, there are four questions that you must answer for each area.

### *The First Question*

*The first step is to ask the question, "What do I want to be, do, or have in this area of my life?" This is the first step in defining your goals.*

Write down your answers on the sheet of paper for each area, planning to take about ten to twenty minutes to answer.

*But before you start writing, read the following:*

This is personal to you. No right or wrong answer exists. I am giving you permission to be extremely selfish if you want! This is about *you* and *your* goals. And, since this is personal to you, do not put down, "I want to give $10,000 to charity," just because it sounds good to others when you tell them, if that is *not* something you actually feel that you can or will do! (We will talk about giving in a later chapter.) Like I said, be selfish. If you want the Ferrari or a yacht, write it down and do not feel one ounce of guilt!

The previous paragraph may be controversial, as it goes against a lot of what people were taught, namely, to not over-want, or go for excess. While in some ways I agree with that, I do believe that things are relative; if you do things correctly and are successful enough that you can responsibly purchase and emotionally handle purchasing a Ferrari or a yacht, you should go for it! If you are at this level, then it is not excess; it is sufficient for the success level that you have reached. Buying a Bentley to Donald Trump is like buying a Honda Civic to someone else. They are just at different success and wealth levels, and what they can do at those levels is relative to those different levels.

Other examples of *be*, *do*, and *have* include: be the manager (professional), have a bigger home (personal or discretionary), do a special thing for a loved one to let him or her know how much you care (personal), or have the ability to take a trip to Hawaii (personal or discretionary).

Now take ten to twenty minutes and write down what you want to *be*, *do*, or *have* for each area.

### The Second Question

The second question is very simple and is a yes-or-no question. Write this down on your sheet of paper for each area:

"Can I explain why each of these 'be, do, or have's' is important to me and my life in thirty seconds or less?"

Please take no more than thirty seconds to actually explain each one's importance out loud. If you are in a crowded place like a Starbucks or bookstore, go ahead anyway. It is actually very liberating and will get you outside of your comfort zone, an important part of reaching your desired success, wealth, and fulfillment. Besides, you never know when someone may be listening who can help you reach your be's, do's, or have's!

Take that time now for each "be, do, or have" you wrote down. Then, write yes or no down for each one to indicate whether you could explain its importance in no more than thirty seconds.

Why do this? *Because if you cannot explain the reason why each goal is important quickly and concisely:*

*1) You probably have some thoughts conflicting around it, which makes it hard to be a focused goal.*

*And*

*2) If you have to think so hard as to why it is important, it probably isn't. This will help you eliminate goals that are actually not priorities.*

Now, once you have finished, go through and put a line or an X through anything that you wrote down if it has a "no" next to it.

### The Third Question

The third question requires a little bit of writing. Please write this down next on your sheet of paper for each goal.

"How will reaching this goal affect me and others involved?"

Please take the time to write two or three sentences for each be, do, or have goal. If you achieved it, how would it affect you and those who are involved in your life and therefore may be involved in reaching this goal? Examples include family, friends, coworkers, and so on.

Why do this? You want to make sure that the outcome of going after this goal and reaching it will have a positive effect on you and those who may be involved around you.

Go ahead and write the answers for each goal now.

If any of your answers for a certain goal come up negative, eliminate it right away. This is where many people get into trouble, especially when the goal is "in their head." They do not take the time to ask and reflect on if the goal will actually have positive or negative consequences on them and those whom they care about in their lives.

### *The Fourth Question*

The fourth question is another yes-or-no question. The question is as follows:

"Can I achieve this goal?"

A quick note on goal achievement: *Everyone is different, and therefore their goals are different. In fact, individually your goals are not just different from others, but also different from each other, not just by the area of life they are in, but also by the time it will take to accomplish them. Some goals may take only a few months, while others may take six months, a year, or even several years.*

This is important because many goal-setting programs will tell you to set "realistic goals" that you can achieve. They do this simply because they know you must achieve your goals in some form or fashion; otherwise, you may get discouraged and stop using a goal program.

While I believe there is great validity in looking at your goals this way and asking, "Can I realistically achieve them?" I also believe that truly great things happen when you set goals that may, at this time in your life, seem to be out of reach. I feel that there is a lot of truth in the statement, "If you shoot for the moon and miss, you will still fall in the stars!" It is for this reason that I personally set goals that I feel may be a little out of reach at the time. Now I also set goals that are definitely within reach and realistic, because

I know that it is the smaller goals that can help me get to the larger ones the fastest. So my goals are comprised of both types.

The point I want to stress here, and this is totally up to you, is that there may be some goals on your sheets of paper that seem, at this time, totally out of reach and unachievable. You do not have to take them off the list just because you feel you cannot reach them now. You may want to make a separate page for "Shoot for the Moon Goals" and put them on it. These goals may not happen for five or ten years, but they still can, so do not eliminate them if you do not want to.

Go ahead now and answer question number four for each goal, and remember to create a "Shoot for the Moon Goals" page if you want.

For any goals that cannot be achieved, for whatever reason, eliminate them.

### *The Final Step*

The final step in setting your goals is going to take you another twenty to thirty minutes. In this step, you will need to take each sheet of paper with your goals and:

1. First, make sure each goal is clearly defined.
2. Second, set a deadline by which you plan to accomplish each goal.
3. Third, write a short plan of minigoals or subdeadlines leading up to reaching the final goal.
4. Create your Goal Sheet.

### *First, Further Define the Goal.*

Take the time now to further define each goal to get it exactly how you want it. You must pay attention to detail in this stage and be specific. For example, if your goal is to graduate college, do not just write down, "graduate college." Instead, write specifically what you are graduating with and so on. So, instead of "graduate college," the goal becomes "graduate college with a degree in business management, a minor in economics, and a GPA of 3.5." This is where the focused part comes in that we talked about in the beginning of this chapter.

Why do you need to be specific and focus? Remember the subconscious mind, which chooses emotion over logic most of the time?

Well, if you do not define for your subconscious exactly what it needs to do, it will make its own rules.

If you are not specific, then you may not get the minor in economics or the 3.5 GPA, and your mind will justify it by saying, "Well, you graduated." I cannot stress enough how powerful this influence is in your life and how with practice and doing some little things right, you can have more control and get more than you ever dreamed of!

Take the time *now* to specifically define your goals.

### *Second, Set a Deadline.*

Look at each goal and set a deadline for achieving it. Again, be specific; do not say six months, one year, and so on. You need to put a date on it. For example, using our graduating example from above, if you plan to graduate with a degree in business administration, a minor in economics, and a 3.5 GPA, you need to say exactly when you want that to happen, so the goal becomes "graduate with a degree in business administration, a minor in economics, and a 3.5 GPA by May 10, 2015." The date has to be specific.

Taking things a step further holds you more accountable because you have that date locked into your mind. You have a deadline. It is important to note that I use "deadline" instead of "time frame." A deadline is "set in stone," while a time frame is expandable. For example, if you say, "I will reach the goal in the 'time frame' of six months to one year," that leaves a lot of leeway to put off the goal and keep expanding that "time frame." But if you put an exact date as your deadline six months in the future, you will hold yourself to it, and so will your subconscious.

Take the time *now* to put a deadline on your goals.

### *Third, Write Your Mini-Plan.*

Now that you have clearly defined your goals and set deadlines around them, you need to take a few minutes for each one to write a miniplan and set minigoals or subdeadlines for reaching them.

This is the "how" of reaching your goals.

For example, if your goal is to save $1000 in your savings account by January 15 and it is October 20, you will need to set minigoals and plan to reach the end goal. As an example, you may look at the time you have to reach $1000 in your savings account and, after doing the math, you can see that you roughly have eighty-seven days or about twelve to thirteen weeks. You could then take the end result, in this case $1000, and divide it by 12, or $83 per week. So now you know you would need to save roughly $83 per week to reach the goal. This can be your minigoal, to save $83 per week. Some people may choose to stop there, while others will take it further by looking at a daily goal. Daily, you would need to save about $12.00 per day to reach the goal.

How far you take your plan and how in depth is your choice. Everyone has different abilities to hold themselves accountable. Just know that the more defined your miniplan and minigoals are, the better your chances of reaching your end goal.

Write your miniplan and minigoals *now* for each goal.

### *Fourth, Create Your Goal Sheet.*

Once you have completed your miniplan and minigoals for each goal, there is one last step. You must take your new goals, separated by category, and put them on one sheet of paper. You will keep your minigoals and miniplans separate. Once you have them on one sheet of paper, go to any office supply store or copy store and have the sheet laminated.

You may choose to shrink the sheet and put your goals on a wallet-sized card (front and back), so that you can carry them with you wherever you go.

This step is important because, after you have defined your goals, you cannot just set them on a shelf or leave them in a drawer. You must constantly remind yourself of your goals and where you are going. Having a laminated goal sheet or card that you can take with you wherever you go and look at multiple times per day will keep you focused and train your subconscious mind to go after those goals. Think about it:

you will "touch" your goals all throughout the day. That is very powerful.

Remember, I have put the steps that we just went through into concise worksheets to help you in your goal setting at www.thetenyearcareeer.com under the "resources" section.

**Congratulations!**

You have just succeeded in doing something that a great majority of people never, ever do, "defining and setting your goals." It is a big accomplishment. Give yourself a pat on the back.

Now it is time to help you go after them. The rest of this book is dedicated to working with your plan, your abilities, and the power of your mind to reach these goals in some very important areas. To give you a little motivation, I think the following Harvard study will really open your eyes and get you excited.

Mark McCormack reported in his book *What They Don't Teach You at Harvard Business School*, that there was a study conducted on students in the 1979 Harvard MBA program. In that year, the students were asked, *"Have you set clear, written goals for your future and made plans to accomplish them?"* Only 3 percent of the graduates had written goals and plans; 13 percent had goals, but they were not in writing; and a whopping 84 percent had no specific goals at all.

Ten years later, the members of the class were interviewed again; and the findings, while somewhat predictable, were nonetheless astonishing. *The 13 percent of the class who had unwritten goals were earning, on average, twice as much as the 84 percent who had no goals at all.*

And what about the 3 percent who had clear, written goals? They were earning, on average, <u>*ten times*</u> *as much as the other 97 percent put together.*

Congratulations, you are in the 3 percent!

"Money is one of the most important subjects of your entire life. Some of life's greatest enjoyments and most of life's greatest disappointments stem from your decisions about money. Whether you experience great peace of mind or constant anxiety will depend on getting your finances under control."

—*Robert G. Allen*

---

## CHAPTER 4

# BECOME FINANCIALLY SMART

---

We go to school to learn, and we do learn a lot. We learn skills. We learn concepts. We learn trades. Our curriculums in schools and colleges are very rigorous, giving us a great foundation on which we can build for the rest of our lives. One thing that we do not learn as part of the curriculum, although sometimes by an elected course of our choosing, is the basics of personal finance and financial responsibility.

For some reason, we simply do not teach the fundamentals of money management and investing in most school curriculums as a general subject. Maybe it is because schools feel it should be left to the parents or families in the home, or worse, up to the students themselves.

Another, more probable reason, as I stated in the last chapter, is that money is a very emotional subject. It takes a lot of self-control to manage money logically and subsequently teach it.

The sad thing is that many people have to learn the fundamentals of money management on their own and have to go through some hard times and setbacks before they really understand them.

As Robert Kiyosaki, investor and best-selling personal finance author of the *Rich Dad, Poor Dad* series, states, "Academic qualifications are important and so is financial education. They're both important and schools are forgetting one of them."

School and college are important in today's information age, but I believe that it is even more important to learn to utilize and put to work as much information as possible.

I believe that *information is the new currency in today's age.*

What I mean is that because information travels so fast now, those who know how to keep up and harness information better than others will be more successful. Why are Facebook, LinkedIn, and other social networks such a hot topic today? Because they have the information, and people and companies will pay enormous amounts to have access to that information. In this way, information is currency; it is a new form of money. You must go to school, get every piece of information you can, and be on top of your game, because the competition is fierce and the world is changing much faster than it used to, especially with respect to money.

The Internet has changed everything and has made things move much faster. Money moves much faster over the Internet and changes hands faster than it ever has. A perfect example is how fast the current economic situation deteriorated. Within just a few months in the fall of 2008, the stock market lost about half of its value, and subsequently we have continued to experience major market gyrations since. You must be prepared to deal with such extremes.

School and college will give you the basic knowledge to play the game (make money), some of the basic structure needed to succeed at it (learning to live on your own), and some of the basics of accountability. From there you will need to educate yourself on personal finance, money management basics, and beyond.

This chapter is about the basics. It is about the essentials for getting a solid financial footing and preparing you for your own "Ten-Year Career."

As stated above, it is about the basics. We will not be going into anything more sophisticated than fourth-grade math. We will use a couple of more complex concepts for example purposes only. We will focus on basic concepts, as I am not a financial planner and am in no way giving you financial advice. A competent financial professional should be consulted when making any major financial decisions. I am simply asking you to consider some basic financial concepts.

*D. M. Lukas*

## The Basics

When looking at your financial situation, there are a few basic things that you must consider to either get yourself on the right financial path or make sure you continue on that path.

The first is to find out where you are. The way that I always do that is to look at a few things. The first thing I look at is my cash flow and budget. I simply add up all of my monthly expenses and then compare that to the income that I am bringing in. I typically use a budgeting tool like the one below to make sure I do not forget anything. Please take the time to fill it in for yourself.

**Expense Calculator:**

Rent/Mortgage
Property Taxes
Education/Tuition
Credit Card Minimum Payments
Car Payments
Other Loan Payments
Car Insurance
Home Insurance
Life Insurance
Health/Dental Insurance
Telephone
Cable/TV
Heating/Electricity
Water
Gasoline
Public Transportation
Groceries
Eating Out
Subscriptions (Online and Offline)
Memberships
Miscellaneous

Total Spent for Month:

Once I have taken the time to see what my expenses are, I multiply that number by 1.1 (or 110%). I do this to give me a buffer in case I go a little over. If I stay under, that is great—more money to invest. But I always budget with the extra 10 percent. From there you will want to take the expense number with the 10-percent buffer and subtract it from your income.

For example, if your expense number with a 10-percent buffer is $2200 per month and your income is $2600 per month, you have a *budget surplus* of $400, meaning that you have an extra $400. On the reverse side, if your expense number with a 10-percent buffer is $2200 per month and your income is $1800 per month, you have a *budget deficit* of $400, meaning you are in the hole for $400—not a good situation.

This chapter is going to discuss concepts around both situations. If you have a surplus, great! What you probably want to know is what to do with it and how to get a larger one. If you have a deficit, you are probably asking, "How do I get to a point where I break even or can have a surplus?"

### Getting a Surplus

First we will cover some things to do to get you a surplus. If you already have a surplus, these concepts might just help you get a little more, and if you do not, then they should definitely help you get closer, if not to a surplus.

> *Author's note:* While the following examples and ideas will help you to save money and get a surplus, know that they are things that must be done to get a budget surplus in the *short term*. Your goal should always be to have a budget surplus, but not because you are so cheap that you eat on $10 a month. Life and the fruits of

our work are meant to be enjoyed. Besides, who wants to be cheap anyway?

Your goal should be to, yes, take a step back in spending and do what needs to be done to get a surplus. But, *once you have done that, figure out what you need to do to* expand *your means and create more income so that you do not have to live below your means.* Trust me; life is a lot more enjoyable living at a higher level and continuing to expand that level. For now, read on, get a surplus, and I will help you expand your means with it throughout the rest of the book.

The first thing we need to do is look at where you are spending your money. Take the time to look at the expense calculator that you filled out above. There are some things that are a must every month, such as mortgage/rent, tuition payments, car payments, insurance, electric/gas bills, and so on. There are also some that you can have more control over, such as groceries, gasoline, eating out, miscellaneous, and even your cell phone. We are going to focus on these expenses because they are the easiest to control.

### Groceries

First, if you really want to save money when you go shopping, use this simple little tip: *Make a list.*

It is very simple, but studies have shown that people who shop with a list spend less on average than those who just go to the store and fill up their cart. The reason this works is very logical. If you shop with a list, you have something to hold yourself accountable to and, thus, do not buy extra things that you do not need. Try it next time you go shopping—I bet you will save at least $10. If you shop weekly, that is $40 per month. Not much, but it will add to your surplus or start to eat away at your deficit.

A couple other things that you can do to save a few bucks:
- Buy store brands instead of national brands. Many times there really is not a difference except the cost.
- Sign up for a frequent shopper card at your local grocery store. These are typically free and save you a ton of money when you shop at the store.

As stated earlier, the above example and the following examples are ways that you can really save money to get yourself on the right financial track. In the latter part of this chapter and upcoming chapters, we are going to focus on how to grow your surplus and expand your horizons so that you do not have to worry about saving $1 on a can of spaghetti sauce. For now, though, we need to first "right the ship."

### Gasoline

Saving on gasoline at $4 a gallon or even $2 a gallon is pretty crucial and simple. Stop driving as much!

Now, how do we do that? There are a few ways. First, you can carpool with others as much as possible. You can also choose to do activities that are closer to home and walk, jog, or ride a bike to them. (As you will see later, exercise is a very important part of your wealth and success plan.)

If it is possible to arrange your schedule to work at home at least part of the time, this will help a great deal. Many employers are now allowing employees to work more and more from home. Ask your employer, as it may be easier than you think.

You can also look into some incentive programs that offer money off or cash back on gas. For example, many of the grocery stores are giving points off toward gasoline when you use that frequent shopper card we talked about above. In fact, I have seen a few that offer twenty to thirty cents off or more per gallon just for shopping at their store. That can add up over the course of a month.

### *Cell Phone*

Cell phone providers are in heated competition, and the services are getting less expensive every day. One of the easiest ways to save money is to just ask! You have heard before to "ask and you shall receive." It is absolutely true, and one of the most overlooked things that you can do when you want something in life. Many people miss out on some great deals just because they do not ask.

Remember, EIN—everything is negotiable!

Many cellular services will reduce your rates if you just ask. Also, if you are nearing the end of your contract period, you have a great deal of negotiating power. Shop around and look at some other services and their plans. You will find better deals. Go to your provider and tell them that if they want to keep your business, they are going to have to do better and use the examples you found. The first time I did this, I saved almost $100 per month on my cell phone bill.

Another thing you can do is reduce your plan. If you are one of those who have five hundred to a thousand minutes left over every month, then it is a sure bet that you will probably not use that number of minutes. Go to your provider and reduce your plan to the next one down or less. Many times this can save a great deal for you.

### *Credit Cards*

Hmmm ... How do you save money on credit cards?

First, if you are in debt on one, *stop using it!* Credit cards are one of the biggest financial traps that destroy wealth. I do not think that I need to go into too many statistics here, as the problem of credit card debt is pretty well noted in our society. Unhinged credit and lack of financial education have both helped to get us to our current economic situation.

Let me say this. I use credit cards. I like them and have a few. I also *pay them off in full every month.* I never carry a balance. If you are going to have a credit card, you must do this. When you carry a balance, the interest rates will eat you alive, and it takes you years to pay off a $100 iPod.

Many of the interest rates today are 20 to 30 percent. Yes, that means for every dollar you have as a balance, you are paying an extra twenty to thirty cents. Since the average family in the United States has about $9000 in credit card debt that means that they are paying $1800 to $2700 before they even touch the initial principal of $9000.

To me, it is insane if you average that or more every year like many people do in the United States. The credit card issuers (banks) do everything they can to keep you in this cycle and are very good at it. They are some of the wealthiest companies in the world because they are banking—yes, literally banking—on you being ignorant!

Well, you are not ignorant, so here is what you need to know about credit cards. First, if you have one, pay it off in full every month. Second, if you are in debt on a card or cards, stop using them *now*.

*Stop and really take responsibility for your actions in getting to this point. If you are in debt on credit cards, it is your fault and no one else's. One of the greatest things that you will ever do for yourself in your life is take personal responsibility for your actions and choose to not act like a victim. Once you do this, you will find that you will accomplish more, people will respect you more, and you will get to your goals much faster. Oh, and most importantly, as T. Harv Eker says in his book* Secrets of the Millionaire Mind, *"There is no such thing as a rich and successful victim!"*

Now, if you do have some credit card debt, here are your next steps. You need to call each creditor and tell them that you want a reduced rate. Stay adamant about it. They will do everything they can to coerce you into paying more, so do not believe their lies that they will not lower your rate. You can and will get a lower rate if you stay tough and do not back down. Once you have a lower rate, take the surplus you have gained from other areas of this chapter and use it to pay the card with the lowest balance off first. You will still have to pay the minimums on any others that you have, but once you get the ball rolling and pay off one, it is easier and easier to pay off the others. It is like a snowball rolling down a hill—the longer and faster it rolls, the bigger it gets. Same with paying off the debt: It gets easier and easier to get out of debt by starting with your smallest and paying that one off, and then using the money you were putting toward that plus the money you are saving from not having that debt, to pay off the next smallest debt, and so on.

Once you have the credit card(s) paid off, you can use the larger surplus toward other debt, such as student loans or car payments or start investing it. If you want to learn more about how to get out of debt, there is a book called the *Total Money Makeover* by Dave Ramsey. I consider it one of the best books for beginners and people struggling with debt.

### *Eating Out and Miscellaneous*

There is a reason I left these two for the last part of this section. You probably guessed it. This is where you can save the most money. This is where our emotions win over logic almost 90 percent of the time. Take a good look at the number you put down for eating out and for miscellaneous. "Where did all the money go?" is usually the question I hear people ask out loud. Many times it is probably on that credit card.

Believe me, this is the hardest part of the expense area to keep track of. It is our social lives, our fun, our rewards to ourselves. Notice that all of those are emotional reasons. That is why this area is also where we can save the most money!

### *The Latte Factor*

David Bach, author of *The Automatic Millionaire*, has a wonderful concept in dealing with this emotional side of our spending. He calls it "the latte factor." It is pretty much what it sounds like.

As he says in the book, "The Latte Factor is based on the simple idea that all you need to do to finish rich is to look at the small things you spend your money on every day and see whether you could redirect that spending to yourself. Putting aside as little as a few dollars a day for your future rather than spending it on little purchases such as lattes, fancy coffees, bottled water, fast food, cigarettes, magazines and so on, can really make a difference between accumulating wealth and living paycheck to paycheck."

In the book, Bach asks people to add up how many times they go to a place like Starbucks and spend four to five dollars to get a coffee or drink, morning muffin, and so on per week. The results are astounding. Many people are spending hundreds of dollars per month on these types of products.

In fact, here is an example he gives:

> $5 per day (the average cost of a latte and a
> muffin) x 7 days = $35 per week
> $35/week = $150/month
> $150 per month invested at a rate of 10 percent
> annual return =
> 1 year = $1885
> 2 years = $3967
> 5 years =$11,616
> 10 years = $30,727
> 15 years = $62,171
> 30 years = $339,073
> *40 years = $948,611*

I find it pretty amazing that at the very basic level, if you just put away $35 per week, you could become a millionaire in forty years.

But this book is not about waiting for forty years. It is about the ten-year fast track to your first million, so use the example above as a basis from which to build. Throughout this and the following chapters, you will learn the skills, traits, and secrets that you can utilize to accelerate the growth of your wealth.

A good foundation for that growth is to have control over those miscellaneous and latte-factor-type expenses because as you begin to acquire wealth, there are other larger categories of the latte factor. I call them the "Lexus factor" or the "Mercedes factor," and sometimes the "I can afford it factor" (this is the worst)!

The wealthy have their own financial issues as well. The more money you have does not necessarily mean you are smarter with it. I have met many people who drive a fancy car and live in a big house, but underneath, they are one little financial issue away from disaster. There is a lot of pressure on these people from an emotional or ego standpoint. That is where the phrase, "Keeping up with the Joneses" comes from. The problem is that most of the Joneses are going broke.

As I put in parentheses above, the worst is the emotional "I can afford it factor." This is the one that traps the middle class. It comes in the form of credit cards or, worse, the words "nothing down" or "low monthly payments." The reason that these things trap people is because they can have the low payments, but on the back end, they are paying a huge amount of their wealth out in the form of interest or hidden charges (remember our credit card example from above).

### *Groupon and Similar Sites*

As I write this, Groupon and similar coupon sites have become very popular. These sites allow you to save a tremendous amount on everyday purchases from dining out to spa services. It is easy to become a member and receive daily alerts for products and services in which you are interested.

Using these types of sites can save you a great deal on the "Eating Out and Miscellaneous" areas of your budget. Visit www.groupon.com or www.livingsocial.com and use these tools to help you enhance your budget surplus!

### *The Concept of Delayed Gratification*

There is a concept that you must become familiar with and embrace if you want to reach your ultimate goals of wealth, success, and fulfillment. It is the concept of delayed gratification. Delayed gratification simply means having the ability to forego an immediate pleasure or reward in order to gain a more substantial one later.

In other words, it means when all of your friends are buying fancy new cars, you keep the one you have had for the last few years and continue driving it, knowing that the extra money you would be spending on the new car you are saving and investing to help you reach your wealth and success goals.

*Commit this thought to mind: "It is not how much you make, but how much you keep that matters!"*

So if you can go a few years, put away a ton of cash, and invest it correctly, there will come a day when you can have much more than a fancy, new car.

This one single concept, along with constant learning, was one of the biggest factors that allowed me to put away over

$100,000 in savings before I was twenty-five and use it to help me invest in my first few pieces of real estate.

The statement, "It is not how much you make, but how much you keep," along with the concept of delayed gratification, should be fundamental to your financial strategy.

Stop here and write down a few things that you are willing to delay gratification on so that you can either get to a surplus or add to your surplus. Write them on the lines below or on a piece of paper if you need more room.

I am willing to delay gratification on the following:

_____

_____

_____

_____

## Develop Your Financial Plan

As with everything else in this book so far, we must plan for future wealth and success in the area of finance as well. It is vital in helping us to reach our goals. I think it is important that we have certain plans for certain stages of our financial growth. Yes, there are stages. There are actually three stages. The first stage is the Survival Stage. The second stage is the Growth Stage. The third stage is the Wealth Stage.

starting stage. In this stage, you have to be good at budgeting
yourself from the beginning, so that you can start to act on
your success and wealth plan.

*If you are in this stage, make sure that you go over your budget at
least two times per month! You have to get to know your expenses
and income very well.*

It is also in this stage that people are introduced to the
wonderful concept of taxes, and for many it is a rude
awakening. You may have already experienced this when
you got your first paycheck. Many of us have. In fact, I
remember a funny conversation I had with my brother just
after he had graduated from college. He had just graduated
with a degree in a very technical computer-driven field with
high demand.

He was hired on with a good salary. He was also given a
signing bonus of $5000, at which I was amazed! Just a short
while earlier, there was no such thing as a signing bonus for
college grads! By the way, don't get the idea you are supposed
to get one. If you have to ask, then there isn't one, and many
times it is an interview killer, so watch out. At any rate, he
called me after he got the check and was amazed at how he
only took home half of it. Wow, 50 percent—that was it.
Yep, welcome to the world of taxes.

66

This is why budgeting is such an important skill. If you are spending like you are making $5000 per paycheck and end up only bringing home $2500, you are in trouble.

The basic concept is called gross to net. Your gross is what you make before everything is taken out. Your net is what you actually get to bring home after everything is taken out.

Budget yourself based on your *net* income.

### *Pay Yourself First*

The survival stage is probably the most crucial stage in your financial life because it is here where you will set the groundwork and develop the habits needed for success in the other stages.

One habit that you must develop as early as possible is to pay yourself first. Many people ask me, first, "What does that mean?" and second, "How do I do it if the taxes and other things are coming out before I get my check?"

I am going to explain this as simply as possible. By budgeting, you will know your surplus, if you have one. If not, use some of the examples above and do whatever else it takes to get one as fast as possible. (I will be giving you some ideas to make more money later on, so do not worry.) When I say pay yourself first, you must put this surplus into savings to invest.

The other way—and a very important way—*if you are an employee* to pay yourself first is to participate in a company 401(k) plan or equivalent. 401(k)s are retirement savings programs. Most major companies have these programs, and you have no doubt heard of them before. Here are the important things to know about them:

1. The money that you put in goes in before taxes, meaning you pay no taxes on it, and it grows in the account tax free.
2. The company typically will match some of the amount that you put into the account. This helps to give you extra and grow the account even faster!

It is critical to consider participating in such programs if you are an employee simply because there are not too many tax breaks that you get as an employee and this is one of the biggest. Also, since the money is pretax, you really are paying yourself first! The bonus is the match from your employer. It helps give you some leverage, an important ingredient in your success and wealth plan that we will spend more time on in Chapter 8.

*Author's note: There are many ways to earn money. Unfortunately, the way that most people end up earning the bulk of their money is by being an employee. This is because our school system and society in general are set up to make you an employee. I say unfortunately because most of the tax advantages are not given to employees, but to business owners and investors. I started out as an employee and still derive some of my income from this area, but I quickly learned about the other areas and the advantages of them. I spend every free moment that I have expanding my ability and bank account in those areas.*

*If you are interested in learning more about the different areas of earning money and the advantages of them—and you absolutely should be—I would go as fast you can after reading this book and get Robert Kiyosaki's* Cashflow Quadrant. *I read it over a decade ago, and it helped to greatly boost my ten-year career path.*

*For now, back to things you can do as an employee ...*

At the minimum, you should consider putting in as much as the employer matches from the beginning, or you are leaving free money on the table. I suggest that you investigate putting at least 5 to 10 percent of your income in these programs when starting out for three reasons:

1. Because it comes out pretax, you actually do not see it come out of your check. You can just set your budget according to the "net" that you have left from the beginning and base everything off of that.
2. You actually save some on taxes as well as have 5 to 10 percent of your money being invested right from the start.
3. Since you will do this from the beginning, you will be used to it; as you make more, more will be put into retirement, and it will grow faster.

   *Note: Please take the time to consult with your employer and a competent financial advisor when making decisions such as those above. I, again, am just providing a concept and not "financial advice."*

So, to recap, when paying yourself first, consider participating in the company 401(k) or equivalent from day one, and make sure you are putting any surplus into savings to invest. One last tip I can give you, if do invest in your 401k, is be prepared to manage it, either yourself or with a competent financial advisor. We live in age where there are more frequent and wilder market swings and you must be prepared to make changes in your investments, so as to mitigate losses from these types of moves.

I am often asked, "What if my employer does not offer a retirement program?" or "Are there other ways to save and invest?" There are other ways to invest money and get some tax-free advantages. Depending on what you make, you can also have what is called an IRA—an Individual Retirement Account. The one bonus to an individual retirement account is that you have more control over how the money is invested.

In most 401(k)s, you can only invest in mutual funds, which are by far not the best investments in the market for someone who has taken the time to learn and study the markets.

For someone just starting out, they will do, but remember, as happened in 2008 to 2009, if the market gets beat up, so do mutual funds because they are typically a basket of many stocks and have more exposure to the entire market. That is why many employees' retirement accounts got destroyed by the quick market downturn.

I like IRAs, if you have studied, because you can invest in individual stocks and do more advanced investing techniques in them. For people just starting out, a 401(k) is a good start to set up a base for your retirement. You can then take the time to learn about investing, and typically by the time you are in the growth stage, you can have an IRA set up and working for you. There are different types of IRAs, and depending on your situation, one might be better than another. Again, as with any investment, consult a competent, trusted financial advisor.

An important thought that I want to leave you with from this section is that a 401(k) or equivalent should be only a part of your overall investing and retirement strategy. As discussed above, if you put all of your eggs in this one basket, you have the potential to lose a great amount in a large market swing or downturn.

If you are an employee, take advantage of some of the tax savings you get by being in this category, but always be looking for other ways to add to your overall retirement plan. To give you some idea of what is available to you, we will discuss some other examples for you as this chapter goes on. You need to be prepared and not have all of your retirement in one vehicle, as you never know what the future holds or what can happen because of changing markets, societies, or even legislation.

### *Financial Advisors*

I am going to stop here and discuss financial advisors for a second. I am probably going to anger some of them. Good! Maybe it will encourage some of them to do better. First off, many financial advisors are salespeople and are really not true investors. In fact, many of them may make less than you. They are simply selling mutual funds or other investments, and they get paid from the sales whether they make money for you or not.

I have been contacted by many financial advisors and have met ones that are fairly good and others that are very bad. I caution you in picking one. As of right now, I do not use one. I have a couple of very good friends who are advisors (CFAs and CFPs) and are very good at what they do. I bounce ideas off of them and ask for advice, but I make the decisions and investments on my own.

Why?

Well, for a few reasons. First, I have found that I can educate myself and do more sophisticated investing techniques to make a great deal more money. Most retail financial advisors either would never recommend or have absolutely no experience in these techniques. Second, I learn very well by doing. Third, if I want to make a million dollars in the stock market, I am not going to do it with someone who either:

1.) Has never done it themselves,
or
2.) Is making less than I am, trying to sell me a product, and hardly invests.

Here is what you need to do if you want a financial advisor, and you should start doing this in the survival stage. You need to identify a great financial advisor. This would be one who personally invests every day and can prove that he or she has made money in the same ways that he or she is advising you. In fact, a question I ask any person who wants to get to "my money" is "Do you invest in these investments yourself?" If the answer is yes, I follow up with questions like "Why do you choose to invest in these vehicles? How much have you made in them? How much have you lost? What are the biggest lessons you have learned about investing in these vehicles? What type of returns can you show on a consistent basis, and can you prove it?"

You will need to interview many advisors to get one who can honestly answer the above questions, and you will learn that once you find someone who fits the profile, he or she is probably not going to work with you—yet.

These people *are* very good at what they do, but typically will not work with someone until he or she gets to a certain size of account or income level. They will be very useful to you as you reach the end of our next stage and progress into the third stage, the wealth stage. Many will talk to you, though, and keep you in the loop until you get there. All you have to do is ask.

Does that mean that there aren't some great advisors just getting their start on their own ten-year career path as well? Of course not—there are some very promising people getting their start every day. But if they truly are getting on their ten-year career path and are destined to be a great financial advisor, you will notice things like they self-educate in their field on everything from conventional to unconventional investing methods. They will admit that they are just getting started, don't know everything, and are working hard to get a surplus to invest. They will have goals and know exactly the types of investments they want *their* money in.

These advisors are great to know, and maybe after getting to really know them and their business values, you will give them a little bit of your money to invest. This is how I found the couple of people with whom I discuss ideas—they were getting their start. It took me a few years of getting to know them and watching how they work and what they invest in before I began to work with them in any capacity, even for ideas. They are smart, because they know that at some point, I will not want to manage my entire portfolio, maybe just a smaller portion, and they will be there to take care of the rest.

One other piece of advice—I got this from my father, a great mentor and savvy investor. Beware of someone who tells you he or she always makes money or has never lost. *"If it sounds too good to be true, it usually is."* Just ask anyone who invested with Bernie Madoff.

## *Your Rainy Day Fund and the Power of Interest*

The last thing you want to do in the survival stage is to put away a rainy-day fund or emergency fund. There are many theories on how much this should be. I always use six to eight months' worth of expenses as a good number.

I feel it is important to stop here and discuss compound interest. It has been called the eighth wonder of the world and rightfully so, as it can help greatly as part of your wealth strategy! Interest is simply a type of return that you get on taking a risk with your money. As with any investment, the bigger the risk, typically the more return. I will note that *as you learn more about the investments available to you on the ten-year career path*, there are abundant ways to get a great return without much risk. Many of them are too advanced for our discussion here. However, later in this chapter, I will provide a few examples of what I am talking about; and in later chapters, I will give you some resources to learn more about these advanced investing strategies.

Now, I talk about interest here, because if you are putting aside all of this money in the bank for your rainy day fund, you would probably like to earn some money for leaving it sitting in a bank account, right? Well, an average savings account pays you almost one-half of a percent on your money or nothing in today's low interest rate climate. But there are accounts out there that will pay you more. They are sometimes referred to as high-interest accounts, money markets, and so on. Some of these accounts pay 3 to 4 percent or more on your money (even in the current economic downturn).

Let's say that your six-months' expenses amount is about $20,000. Well, $20,000 at 4 percent will pay you an extra

$800 a year in interest with very little risk—just for keeping your money in the account. I know that it is not much or very exciting, but it is better than nothing just for changing the type of account you have. You will have to pay tax on the money you make, but it keeps compounding on itself and growing every year. It will eventually turn into a larger sum of money. Hey, you were going to have the emergency fund sitting there anyway, right? Might as well let it grow too.

Remember the latte factor example of just putting away $35 a week at 10 percent and what it would be worth? Well, same thing here, just not as large of a scale. Three to four percent interest is not a very flashy return, but the risk is low in a high-interest account. Make sure you find one of these accounts. If you go into Google and type "high-interest checking," you will find banks that are paying 4 to 5 percent. They usually have a couple of strings attached like using your debit card with them a certain number of times in a month, but it beats earning only half a percent! This is a basic first step in *having your money work for you,* which is a secret of the wealthy. We will discuss it more in the third stage.

Once you have put away six months of expenses, have it earning interest, have your budget concrete, are putting away your surplus, and have your company retirement plan or retirement account going, you are ready to move on to the next stage.

*Just remember to delay your gratification.*

## *The Growth Stage*

The growth stage is a very exciting stage. This is where you start to put away a little bit of money and really get control of your finances. It is also the most dangerous of the stages. Why? Because this is the stage that you have more spending money, or disposable income, and those emotional purchases can rear their ugly heads and get you into trouble.

This is the stage when you start to notice "No money down!" or "No interest until four years from now!" and you say, "Hey, no interest! I can afford that low payment over four years in my budget." The problem is that many people also say, "Oh, I have four years to pay it off. I will just pay most of it in the final year. It is such a nice couch!"

As I said above, my father taught me something at a very young age, and it still holds true today—"If it sounds too good to be true, then about 99 percent of the time it is!"

Believe me, it is tough to not upgrade the furniture or get that big screen—I have been there. Just hold out a little while until you've either created the income to pay for it or paid off a little more of that student loan debt, credit card debt, or whatever debt you already have.

## *A Quick Word on Debt*

There are two types of debt: good debt and bad debt. Good debt is any debt that *puts* money in *your* pocket, and bad debt is any debt that *takes* money from *your* pocket. Ninety-nine percent of people are deep in bad debt. You want to keep as little bad debt as possible and learn to acquire good debt.

Before you add more bad debts to your budget, get rid of what you already have first.

Good debt comes in many forms, such as a loan you make to someone in which you get paid interest or a rental property that you own for which the renter pays the mortgage and puts money in your pocket. We will discuss good debt further in the pages ahead.

### Back to the Growth Stage

In the growth stage, you should have everything working and growing from the survival stage. You should be rock solid and know your budget by heart. You should have your company retirement plan working for you. Lastly, you should have a nice emergency fund going. This is the secure portion of your portfolio.

The growth stage is all about learning—hence the term "growth." This is the time when you need to start learning about other investment vehicles and spending as much time as possible developing your skills to use them. Investment vehicles that I am talking about may include investing in individual stocks, CDs, mutual funds, ETFs, real estate, gold, silver, other precious metals, commodities, setting up IRAs, and potentially any side businesses you aspire to.

If you remember, this book started with discussing finding a way to have some of your income come from results and not time. It is in the growth stage that you can really begin to have this happen for you. Whether you create income from the results of learning new, leverageable, investing skills or just learning to have your money work for you and grow, you will start to be paid for your results and not your time.

In this stage, I suggest that you read at least two books on each of the subjects you are interested in and take one seminar. I am not going to go into detail of how to invest in many of the things mentioned above, as that is for you to find out for yourself and talk with a great financial planner about. (You have to do a little of the work!)

## *Taxes*

Remember when I said before that it is not necessarily how much you make, but how much you keep that matters? The other thing that you need to study in this stage is taxes and the legal ways to utilize the rules about them to your advantage. For example, the 401(k) or IRA talked about above gives you a tax advantage. It saves you tax money.

There are many tax advantages and deductions, such as business expenses. Your job or business may allow you to have deductions on your taxes, saving you money. Please take the time to get with your employer or a competent tax professional to see if there are some of these available to you.

As I write this, there are also a few standard tax advantages that I want to highlight. These can be changed, based upon government legislation at any time (as current proposals are being debated), but as I write they are still in place.

The first is the capital gains tax. This tax is useful for any investments, such as stocks, that you hold longer than one year. *So, if after doing your research, reading two books, and taking a class on stock trading,* you decide to invest in some stocks and hold them over one year, any money or gains that you made are taxed at a flat 15 percent federal tax rate (if you make less than $400,000 per year), instead of the higher income tax rates.

For example, let's say you invested $2000 in a stock and the stock went up 30 percent in that year. Then, you sell it after holding it for one year; you would have made $600 ($2000 x .3). Under the capital gains rule, you would pay only 15 percent, or $90, in federal taxes. (Depending on where you live, other state and local taxes may apply, but the fed is usually the largest; thus, getting a significant savings in that area is a major advantage.)

Compare that to if you made $600 in your high-interest savings account or your job. After social security and Medicare, federal income tax, state taxes, local taxes, and school district taxes (if you live in a state with them), you'll pay a lot more than $90 in taxes.

How do you want your money to work for you? Remember, being financially smart is about how much you keep.

Another tax advantage is in investment rental real estate. I will stress that real estate is one of the best investments for tax advantages, but also one that requires the most skill. I have made some good investments here and some bad ones and have learned some hard lessons, but I enjoy it so I continually learn and get better.

Investment rental real estate has many tax advantages, of which I will talk about two.

The first is called "depreciation." The simple way to explain this concept is that for any rental property, the government will let you write off, or deduct, a portion of the value of the property each year to offset against your earnings.

For example, if I have a $100,000 rental property, my mortgage and expenses for the property are $650 per month, and my renter pays me $800. After expense deductions, I have an income of $150 per month, or $1800 profit per year, that I would have to pay tax on. Now, because of depreciation, the government lets me deduct an additional $3700 off on that property (like an expense), which once I apply it toward the $1800, it looks as though I have a loss of $1900 ($3700-$1800). In fact, I actually put $1800 tax free in my pocket, plus I have the $1900 "loss," which can be used to offset other taxes I may have paid throughout the year.

It is hard to grasp, but the depreciation is almost like free money. Many times it is often referred to as "phantom income." There are many rules regarding this, and the above is just a basic example of how I can make $1800 tax free. There are actually rules that take this deduction away when you hit a certain W-2 income, and believe me, if you can get there, you are doing just fine. Besides, if you do get there, there is a whole new set of rules you can play by. But for most people, they would have to make double that, or $3600, in a job to take home $1800. I do not know how much you make, but for many people, that is an extra month's take-home pay. What would you do with an extra month of pay?

Another real estate deduction that exists is a legal way to take all of the profits from selling an investment rental property and pay no taxes on them. It is called a 1031 exchange, outlined in section 1031 in the tax code. Basically it works this way: If you sell an investment property, you can "roll" those gains (profits) tax free into another investment property without paying taxes on them. There are rules governing this, but that is the basic concept; it is one big secret of wealthy and successful real estate investors. Many investors never ever pay taxes on the gains they make—ever. They just keep "rolling" them or trading up into bigger real estate investments.

### Start Learning

I cannot stress enough how the above examples are just that. In the investing world, there are many other things that must be considered and many other types of investments that you can do. I just want to open your eyes to some of the rules of the ten-year career path and the fact that you can have some control over your income.

Now it is up to you to start learning. If you are in this stage, great! It takes some hard work, good self-control, and dedication to get here. Now you can really take the time to start studying and learning how to grow in areas that you aspire to.

### The Wealth Stage

In the wealth stage, you have mastered control over your emotions when it comes to money and finances. You have probably doubled your emergency fund to a year's worth of expenses, you have your budget so memorized you can recite it in seconds, and you have started investing in some sort of way, whether it is in a few pieces of real estate or in a stock portfolio or starting a business.

It is at this point that you will really start to realize something funny. Getting wealthy and successful is not really that flashy. It is a process, a system, and all you have to do is learn and then keep growing and expanding the system to your abilities. Ultimately at some point, you will have your money, businesses, and so on not only work for you, but pay your expenses, give you a surplus, and allow you to do whatever you like!

As I said above, in the survival stage, learn to let interest grow your money. As you can see, the wealthy and successful go way beyond basic interest and have learned how to manipulate money so that it is constantly working for them. This can come in more sophisticated stock trading techniques, such as options and credit spreads, or in more intricate real estate investments. It can come in the form of a website that generates income without you even having to be there, or a small business that you own. It may also come in the form of starting a company and taking it public on the stock exchange or being part of an IPO (initial public offering) as an investor—what some call the richest game in the world.

No matter what it is you do, you are on the financial fast track and may already be semiretired at this point. All you have to do is expand your knowledge and keep growing and expanding the system. This is where I am now, and I am still probably in the early stages. In fact, writing this book was one of my goals once I got to a certain level in the wealth stage.

Some of the things that can be accomplished in the wealth stage are as follows. You may be able to quit your job, if you choose to; as your bad debt will be low and good debt high and your money will be working for you. You may be accomplished enough to become an accredited investor. This is defined as someone with over 1 million in net worth or who individually makes over $200,000 per year or $300,000 if married. Accredited investors are invited to invest in IPOs and investments that the public is not allowed to and thus can make more money and get better returns.

At this point, you will need to have a solid team of professionals, from a good banker to a good CPA, a good attorney, and a great financial advisor or team. You would have most likely started working on this in the growth stage, but it really needs to come together in the wealth stage. You can never start too early on building your team, so no matter what stage you are in, start today.

If you are in the wealth stage, congratulations! You are part of an elite group and have a lot of responsibility to help teach others and give back. You will need to continue to grow and find better, more sophisticated mentors to guide you.

No matter what stage you are in, I wish you the best of luck. Keep working hard, and you will be in the wealth stage soon. In fact, you may want to revamp your goals as to what dates you want to be in each stage.

"Don't say you don't have enough time. You have exactly the same number of hours per day that were given to Helen Keller, Pasteur, Michelangelo, Mother Teresa, Leonardo da Vinci, Thomas Jefferson, and Albert Einstein."

—*H. Jackson Brown*

———

## CHAPTER 5

# MANAGE YOUR TIME— DO NOT LET IT MANAGE YOU

———

Ahh … time management. We hear about it constantly and that we need to practice "good time management." What we do not hear is the "how" of managing your time correctly. Because of this, many people do not actually know what time management really is or means. Many people get so bogged down in trying to practice time management that their time "flies" by and they do not even know where it all went. Have you ever had a day where you were "busy" the whole day, felt exhausted at the end it, but had nothing to show for it—no measureable results? I think we all have at some point. This is a case where our time manages us.

I think it is important to note the quote by H. Jackson Brown at the beginning of this chapter, "Don't say you don't have enough time. You have exactly the same number of hours per day that were given to Helen Keller, Pasteur, Michelangelo, Mother Teresa, Leonardo da Vinci, Thomas Jefferson, and Albert Einstein."

This is good to note because, when you think about it, "Time is the great equalizer." It is the one thing in which everybody has the exact same amount. Time does not discriminate. No matter what country you are in, where you were born, how intelligent you are, or how much money you have, it is always the same for everyone.

So, the question becomes, why are some people, such as Mother Teresa, able to get so much more done and accomplished than other people? Harnessing the true power of your mind has something to do with it, but the main answer lies in a few concepts.

Just like everything else that we have talked about, there are some things that you can do to give yourself an edge. These simple things can boost your productivity to incredible new heights!

Many great concepts surround time management. In fact, there are far too many to go into in just one chapter. For that reason, I have narrowed them down and picked the five principles that I use daily, that have worked throughout the ages, and that the most successful and wealthy use to manage their time.

**Principle 1: Plan Your Day.**

One of the simplest and most effective pieces of information that I ever received was to "Plan Your Day." If you remember, we started this book with the importance of planning and talking about even writing miniplans to reach your goals. So it only makes sense to plan each and every day as well! If there is one thing that I can say that I see consistently with successful and wealthy people, top performers in their industries, athletes, and so on, it is that they plan each and every single day. They plan what they are going to do, when they are going to do it, how much time it will take, and whom (if anyone) they will be doing it with.

As noted above and in our first chapter, isn't it amazing how planning carries through into everything?

Absolutely! In fact, one of Zig Ziglar's most favorite quotes was "Success is not an event, it is a process—a plan!" He usually coupled that with, "Failure is an event, not a person."

Those are two great quotes to keep in mind because, as we will discuss in more detail later, "failure" is part of getting ahead. If you are not failing at doing things, then you are not pushing yourself hard enough. The best thing about failure is the lessons that you learn from going through it and getting back up and resolving to do it again. At the same time, you can help yourself to be more successful and fail less often by having a good, solid process or plan.

The first step is to plan your day. This can actually be hard for people. Many times people get so excited about this concept that they try to plan way too many things all at once and jam-pack them all into one day.

*Planning your day is about simplifying things.*

We need to keep it simple—that way we can get things done. Remember the example from earlier about being "busy," feeling exhausted, and having nothing to show for it? Many times when this happens, you are not keeping things simple. In fact, you keep adding things to your plate all day as it goes on, and you never really get to what it was that you wanted to do. You were "busy," but accomplished nothing.

There are four components to planning your day.

The first is to *take the time to do it*! Set aside fifteen minutes each day in your calendar, cell phone calendar, or tablet/PDA. (If you do not have a calendar or way to schedule yourself, *stop* reading right now and go get one, and then continue!)

You can schedule it in for the last fifteen minutes of your day at work, later in the evening after dinner, or even better, first thing in the morning as you eat your breakfast!

Whatever time works best for you, just put it in, and make sure it is a recurring event, if possible with a reminder each day. Many phones/tablets/PDAs and online calendars, such as Microsoft Outlook, will do this. You can also set your cell phone to remind you each day. Remember, we want to make this an automatic reminder, so we do not have to "think" or "remember" to do it. We cannot remember everything, and a good reminder takes the stress out of things.

Once you have done that, you need to do the second component, your *to-do list*. Notice it is called your *to*-do list, not your *try to* list. You are going to write down the things that you will *do* for the day. You can either type your list or write it by hand. It is up to you.

I simply take out a sheet of paper and at the top write "To *do* for 'x' date." Make sure you put the date. Remember from our goal-setting exercise before, we want to be focused and hold ourselves to a deadline. The date is your deadline to accomplish the tasks you will put down.

Once you have made your to-do list, you will go on to the third component, *your priorities list*. Divide the paper into three sections across, like the diagram on the next page. Next, write the following:

In the first section, write "Absolute Priorities, things I must do by 5:00 p.m. today" (or whenever your work or school day is over).

In the second section, write "Secondary Priorities, things that I will do when I have accomplished the first section by 5:00 p.m. today."

In the third section, write "Other Priorities, things that I will do, if possible, after accomplishing sections 1 and 2 by 5:00 p.m. today."

Now, you do not have to write all of that, as I was describing each section for your knowledge, but each section should say something like, "Absolute Priorities, by 5:00 p.m. today" and so on.

# <u>To Do for (date here)</u>

## Absolute Priorities:

## Secondary Priorities:

## Other Priorities:

Once you have done this, make copies like you did with the *daily attitude sheet*, so that you can just fill them in every day. Next, you are ready for the fourth component, *writing your priorities*.

*It is very important* that you keep this as simple as possible. You should only have two or three things for each section, *no more*! This will help you to *focus* and get them all done. It should look like the example on the next page.

You will find that if you do it this way and check off each priority as you go, you will sometimes get things done so fast that you will have everything done for the day by lunchtime and be sitting around, saying, "What do I do now?"

Well, that is the beauty of it. You could then make another to-do list and get even more done in the afternoon and really get ahead ...

Or ...

You could use some of that time to further educate yourself on things that can help you reach your goals. For example, if you have an interest in investing in real estate, you can take some time to read a book about real estate investing or do some research.

Planning your day will help you get any task done and help you reach your goals exponentially faster!

## <u>To Do for (date here)</u>

## Absolute Priorities:

1.)

2.)

3.)

## Secondary Priorities:

1.)

2.)

3.)

## Other Priorities:

1.)

2.)

3.)

*Here is a tip that I started using: Combine your to-do list with your daily attitude sheet so they are both on one piece of paper and you can grab one each day, as on the next page.*

You will find samples of all of these sheets at the companion site for this book, www.TheTenYearCareer.com.

## <u>To Do for (date here)</u>

**Absolute Priorities:**

**1.)**

**2.)**

**3.)**

**Secondary Priorities:**

**1.)**

**2.)**

**3.)**

**Other Priorities:**

**1.)**

**2.)**

**3.)**

**What type of attitude will I *choose* to have today?**

**Great**       **Fair**       **Poor**

**Principle 2: Get Thirty Extra Minutes in Your Day.**

Many people after reading or talking about "planning your day" will say to me, "I don't even have fifteen minutes to do that" or "I am too busy." I usually tell them two things: First, the choice is all in your head, your mind-set. If you wanted to do it, you would. Second, the fact that they do not have fifteen extra minutes is the exact reason they need to plan their day!

For all of you who are still saying, "That's nice, but I still do not have the time," here is one thing that you can do that will guarantee you the time to plan your day—and maybe do more. Ready?

*Get up thirty minutes earlier in the morning!*

This one thing will help you out tremendously, and it is not like we aren't really awake at that time already. How many people hit the snooze button a few times before they get up, or actually wake up but lie in bed for an extra half hour? We all have done it.

If you can get yourself to just get up when the alarm goes off or when you wake, and get going just one time, it makes it easier to do it tomorrow, and the next day, and the next, and on and on. Even setting your alarm fifteen minutes earlier will help you do this.

If you get up a half hour earlier, it will change a lot of things for you. First, how many mornings do you rush around to get showered, dressed, grab the "to-go breakfast," and get out of the house? Pretty stressful, isn't it? Wouldn't it be nice to have some extra time to relax, eat a nice breakfast, do a little reading, maybe "plan your day" and get started on it, even getting going a little bit earlier? Of course it would! Starting your day stressed like that is bad for you. Have you ever had the stress of being rushed or being late cause things to compound throughout the day and make them seem to stack on top of each other, giving you more stress? I have, and it sucks! This one thing has made my life so much easier and less stressful. I get up a little earlier, make a nice breakfast, plan my day, and get going on it. It is great!

Okay, so there may still be some die-hards out there who cannot, for whatever reason, get up any earlier. I still have a solution for you:

*Be on time.*

Being on time will not only help to save you time, but also help you to get ahead in your career, school, business, or whatever.

Don't believe me? Well, if you were five minutes late to every appointment (or class) you had each day and let's say you had five appointments (or classes), that would mean that you just lost twenty-five minutes from your day (it only takes ten to fifteen to plan your day). Also, if you are late to your appointments, classes, or other meetings, what type of impression does that give the people who are waiting for you (clients, peers, teachers, professors, or bosses)? Some people never know it, but they lose the job before they ever get into an interview just by being five minutes late!

I had a college football coach who used to have a great saying: "To be early is to be on time, to be on time is to be late, to be late is to be forgotten!" Incredibly true.

You do not want to get labeled as someone who is not timely. Many things come with this. People will question your reliability or maybe even question your sincerity.

Of course, there are times that we have circumstances that we cannot control, and these circumstances prevent us from getting somewhere on time. Just have the common courtesy to call and let someone know. It will go a long way and prevent you from getting any negatives associated around you in this area.

Getting up a little earlier and being on time are just tiny little things, but they can make such a difference in your productivity, your career or school results, and ultimately your life.

## Principle 3: A Lesson from Mr. Pareto

The next two principles are musts for getting control of your time and your life! There is a principle, although well-known to people on the ten-year career path that is not so well-known among the masses. Many times they have heard about it or been taught the principle at some time in their lives, but it does not seem to sink in. It is called:

*The Pareto Principle or Pareto's Law.*

This law was first developed by an Italian economist named Vilfredo Pareto and is widely used in business and many other areas.

The law simply states that "80 percent of effects come from 20 percent of causes." It has also been called the 80/20 rule.

When used in time management, it means that 80 percent of the results that you generate are coming from 20 percent of your efforts (your time).

So the question is, what are we doing with the 80 percent of our time that is generating only 20 percent of our results? You guessed it—we are wasting it! This is where planning your day can help to give you a concrete set of activities and prioritize them so you can get more done!

Still, what are we doing with the 80 percent of our time? Try this idea. How many of you do the following:

- Check your e-mail fifty times per day?

- Surf the net out of boredom?

- If you are in an office, how many days do you come in and shuffle some papers on your desk, check your e-mail, stare at the screen, take a break to talk to other coworkers, and do other nonproductive tasks just to pass the time by?

- Take "extended" lunches?

I think everyone has been guilty of this at some point. This is where the 80/20 Pareto principle can change your life.

All you have to do is find the 20 percent of your activities that generate 80 percent of your results and go spend your time in those activities, focusing on them, and finding other activities like them.

If you do this, your results and productivity will at least double!

Don't stop there. You can apply this rule to all parts of your life. What are the 80 percent of activities at home you're doing that are keeping you from learning more about what you must do to accomplish your goals? If you want to learn to scuba dive or fly a plane, what is keeping you from having the time for lessons, or more importantly keeping you from making the necessary money to take those lessons?

The rule is simple, and we like simple. So keep it simple!

Here is an exercise I would suggest to help you. Take a blank sheet of paper, make seven columns on it, and write the name of each day starting from Monday through Sunday at the top of each column (like on the next page).

For one week, record what you are doing from 8:00 a.m. to 8:00 p.m., writing it down for each half hour. Do it, just one week. You will be amazed at how much extra time there is that you didn't know you had. It will also show you where you are wasting large amounts of time.

As with everything in this book, you can find the Weekly Time Tracker at www.TheTenYearCareer.com.

Once you are done, you can use the techniques in this chapter to make yourself more efficient and focus on your 20 percent activities!

# D. M. Lukas

| | Monday | Tuesday | Wednesday | Thursday | Friday | Saturday | Sunday |
|---|---|---|---|---|---|---|---|
| 8:00 | | | | | | | |
| 8:30 | | | | | | | |
| 9:00 | | | | | | | |
| 9:30 | | | | | | | |
| 10:00 | | | | | | | |
| 10:30 | | | | | | | |
| 11:00 | | | | | | | |
| 11:30 | | | | | | | |
| 12:00 | | | | | | | |
| 12:30 | | | | | | | |
| 1:00 | | | | | | | |
| 1:30 | | | | | | | |
| 2:00 | | | | | | | |
| 2:30 | | | | | | | |
| 3:00 | | | | | | | |
| 3:30 | | | | | | | |
| 4:00 | | | | | | | |
| 4:30 | | | | | | | |
| 5:00 | | | | | | | |
| 5:30 | | | | | | | |
| 6:00 | | | | | | | |
| 6:30 | | | | | | | |
| 7:00 | | | | | | | |
| 7:30 | | | | | | | |
| 8:00 | | | | | | | |

## Principle 4: A Lesson from Mr. Parkinson

There is another law that goes hand in hand with Pareto's Law.

It is *Parkinson's Law.*

First developed by Professor Cyril Northcote Parkinson, the law simply states, "Work expands to fill the time available for its completion."

It is the ultimate definition of a huge success and wealth killer, procrastination!

Let's use an example. For those of you who are working, and even for students, I want you to take a minute to think about your last vacation. Maybe you went to the beach for spring break, went skiing in Colorado, traveled through Napa Valley, or just relaxed at your favorite hideaway.

Now, I want you to think about how freakin' hard you worked the week, a few days, and even the day before you left to get every last little thing possible done before you went on that vacation. Do you remember that feeling of gratification when you got the last little thing done before you left and got on the plane or road with a clear conscience and not a care in the world?

Well, you were using Parkinson's law. It is the ultimate time manager. As it states, you will expand the work that you have to do for a project, task, or whatever, for the time allotted to get it done. You will procrastinate to the very last second! Think about the day before you left—why was it so busy? Why wasn't it a very relaxed, easygoing day? Well, because just like I used to do, you put everything off to the very last day or minute and then had to scramble to get it all done.

That is the essence of the law. What if you worked every day as if it were the day before you were going on vacation? How much more work could you accomplish? I suspect it would be a lot.

So, the question becomes "How do we use this law to our advantage?" Well, we must take action on things when they come up and not let a time frame dictate when we will "get to it." We must use the concept of planning our day and Pareto's Law to set our own *deadlines* for things and get them done faster and more productively.

For example, if you are a student and you get an assignment for a paper due in one month, start working it into your daily plan now. Maybe it starts as an "Other Priority" in the first week and you get a small start, then moves to a "Secondary Priority" in the next week and you get a good amount of it done, and then moves to an "Absolute Priority" in the third week, where it is finished one week or more before the deadline and you can then keep working on your other goals. The due date comes and it has been done for a week, you have had plenty of time to proofread or tweak it, and you are not stressed at all. In fact, because you were able to get it done so early, you were able to get ahead on some other assignments or tasks, or even get started on those scuba lessons you hadn't previously had time for!

Conversely, the same example can be used for an assignment at a job or in your own business. The simple thing to note is that if you plan right (plan your day), prioritize correctly (focus on tasks each day in each area), and spend your time in the areas that generate the majority of your results

(80/20), then you will always be ahead of the game (defeating Parkinson's Law).

## Using Pareto's and Parkinson's Laws Together

I had been using both Pareto's and Parkinson's laws for some time in my life and getting great results from them when I picked up Tim Ferris's book *The 4 Hour Workweek*. The title was too catchy not to! Tim is a pretty incredible guy. He does more in a week than most people do in their lifetime. Whether being the first American ever to win the Tango World Championships to jet-setting around the world and living abroad wherever and whenever he chooses, Tim is the "Jedi master" of time management and leverage.

And, yes, he has set things up in his life so he only has to work about four hours per week! I am not going to spoil the book for you as it is a must-read, but two of the things that Tim focuses on that allow him to do what he does are Pareto's and Parkinson's Laws. Since he is so good at utilizing them, I am going to let him fill you in on how to use them best together. Below is an excerpt from his book:

> Parkinson's Law dictates that a task will swell in (perceived) importance and complexity in relation to the time allotted for its completion. It is the magic of the imminent deadline. If I give you 24 hours to complete a project, the time pressure forces you to focus on execution, and you have no choice but to do only the bare essentials.
>
> If I give you a week to complete the same task, it's six days of making a mountain out of a molehill.

If I give you two months, God forbid, it becomes a mental monster. The end product of the shorter deadline is almost inevitably of equal or higher quality due to greater focus.

This presents a very curious phenomenon. There are two synergistic approaches for increasing productivity that are inversions of one another:

1.) Limit tasks to the important to shorten work time (80/20).
2.) Shorten work time to limit tasks to the important (Parkinson's Law).

The best solution is to use both together: Identify the few critical tasks that contribute most to income and schedule them with *very short* and clear deadlines.

Tim makes a very good point in saying that the two laws are inversions of each other. In short, this means that they feed off of one another—the better you get at one, the better you get at the other, and vice versa. He also makes a statement about "scheduling *very short* and clear deadlines." This is the focus of prioritizing your tasks in planning your day and why you must keep your to-do list short and concise, with only two or three things for each area of priorities. It keeps you focused and allows you to accomplish more and more.

**Principle 5: Eliminate Clutter.**

There are so many interruptions in our lives that take up precious amounts of our time. We live in an instant society.

Everything has to be right now! Most of us can't even wait for the microwave to finish; we stop it with one second left! I know you do it. Whether it is e-mails, phone calls, text messages, meetings, talking with friends around the water cooler, or playing nine hours of *Madden*, there are a lot of things "stealing" our time.

I call these things "clutter." Now I must admit that "clutter" can mean different things to people and *be* different things in their lives, so I do not know what your clutter is. What I do know is that, ultimately, everybody has some. In order to "take back" our time, get more done, and reach our desired results faster, we must get rid of our clutter.

This is a must to put yourself on a ten-year career path, so I have taken the time to create a short exercise for you to:

1. Figure out what your clutter is, and
2. Remove as much as possible from your life!

First, we need to identify our clutter. I define "clutter" as anything in your life that you feel wastes time or that you spend too much time on out of *habit*.

Notice that I said, out of *habit*. Yes, back to our mind again. We have conditioned it to attract clutter. So what we have to do is train it to get rid of clutter out of habit.

The first thing that we need to do is identify those habits or activities taking time in our lives that we could do less often or eliminate altogether. Look at the diagram on page 107. An exercise that I suggest to help you in this area is the following:

Get out a sheet of paper and write at the top, "My Clutter."
Take a few minutes and separate the sheet of paper into two
sections, Habits and Activities. Now, take five minutes for
each section and write down what in those areas (Habits or
Activities) is taking your time that you could spend less time
on or get rid of altogether. Remember, a habit is a behavior
that is part of your life such as "waking up late every day"
whereas an activity is something that you choose to do such
as "watch too much T.V." The next step is to write down
next to each one how you are going to eliminate or greatly
reduce each item.

Examples include: "Stop checking e-mail every five minutes,"
"Start checking voicemail only once per day or every other
day," "Shorten my *Madden* time to four hours twice per
week, instead of every day," "Stop spending an extra thirty
minutes socializing in the gym," or "Use my drive time in
my job more effectively and get priorities done via phone
instead of waiting to get to the office."

# My Clutter

## Habits                    ## Activities

As I said, everyone has different "clutter" in their lives, so take the time to figure out what yours is.

After this exercise is done, take the time to review and start making the changes. Tim Ferris gives some wonderful examples and suggestions on how to do this. For instance, if you want to reduce the number of times you are going to check your e-mail to only twice per day, simply put a nice, cordial autoresponder that sends an e-mail to the sender that states something like this one I got from Tim's website: www.FourHourWorkWeek.com

> Hi, all.
>
> In an effort to increase productivity and efficiency, I am beginning a new personal e-mail policy. I've recently realized I spend more time shuffling through my inbox and less time focused on the task at hand. It has become an unnecessary distraction that ultimately creates longer lead times on my ever-growing to-do list.
>
> Going forward I will only be checking/responding to e-mail at 11:00 a.m. and 4:00 p.m. on weekdays. I will try and respond to e-mail in a timely manner without neglecting the needs of our clients and brand identity.
>
> If you need an immediate time-sensitive response, please don't hesitate to call me. Phones are more fun anyways.
>
> Hopefully this new approach to e-mail management will result in shorter lead times

with more focused & creative work on my part.
Cheers & here's to life outside of my inbox!

*The beauty of setting things up like this is that it is automatic and trains people to know when and how to best get hold of you and for what type of needs.*

There are many other ways to reduce your time-wasting habits and activities. As I said, everyone is different and their "clutter" is different, so take some time and be creative about how you will eliminate some of these "time stealers" in your life. It will do you wonders.

If you learn to utilize all of the ideas in this chapter, you will not just manage, but *take complete control of your time* and find an abundance of availability to spend working on *your ten-year career.*

"Everyone lives by selling something."

—*Robert Louis Stevenson*

---

CHAPTER 6

# LEARN TO SELL AND NEGOTIATE

---

So, how long have you been in sales?

Many times I ask this question and get the response, "Who, me? I am not in sales!" Well, I hate to break it to you, but that is not true! Everybody is in sales in some form or another. Even if you are a student, you are selling something. Remember that last date that you went on? Did you spend some time working on impressing that guy or girl? Well, you were selling yourself to him or her.

The most innate ability in humans is to sell—whether it is selling ourselves and who we are to the one we are with so he or she will like us (i.e., buy what we are selling), or selling a product or service. Even when students write a paper, they are selling the teacher or professor on their knowledge so that they get a good grade. Babies and kids are the best salespeople. Think about it—they have about a 100 percent closing ratio. Anytime babies or kids want something, what do they do? You guessed it—they whine, cry, throw a fit, or most often just keep asking for what they want until someone, usually their parents, gives it to them. It may be a diaper change, a feeding, or the latest toy, but almost always, they get the "sale."

You have to realize that in your life, you are selling something. It may be selling your boss on your ideas, selling your spouse on why you should *not* clean up the house because the "important" game is on, selling a future employer in an interview, or selling your business as the solution. Whatever it is, you are selling it.

Most people do not realize and are not conscious of the fact that they actually are selling something. If you are in the workforce, did you somehow "end up" in sales? In fact, author and speaker Chris Lytle wrote a great book about it. It is called *The Accidental Salesperson*. If you *ended up* in sales, then it is a must-read for you, as it will help you take yourself from being there accidentally to having a purpose and a plan.

So, *if we are all in sales in some kind of way*, we must learn how to use this innate ability to our advantage. Do you think, if you were conscious as to *how* to sell, that you would get more of what you want?

This chapter is going to teach you some basic sales skills so that you can have an advantage in sales situations. It is also going to teach you the basics of one more skill, negotiating.

Negotiation is one of the most underutilized skills in our society. By learning how to properly negotiate, you give yourself an advantage anytime you are looking to buy something or sell something. This one skill will help you to become more successful and wealthy, get you to your desired results faster, and save you large amounts of money and time throughout your life.

## Selling Is a Process

Selling is a process. You must be disciplined when selling anything and follow a few key rules. Once you get to know them, they become automatic, and the process becomes automatic.

The first thing you must do in your process is your research. I say this, and people say to me, "But, how do I do research when I am not selling a product or service, just myself in some way or another?"

To put it bluntly, you must *think*. You need to put yourself in the shoes of your "prospect" and ask yourself what would cause him or her to "buy" what it is that you are selling. For example, if you are in school and you have to write a paper selling your ideas to a professor, do you think it would be a good idea to research the professor's background, looking at what it is that he or she is focused on (e.g., areas of study, hobbies and interests, passions, etc.)? Is he or she pursuing some sort of PhD right now in a certain field? Would it help you to know these things so that you can appeal to them in your paper?

Or ...

If you land that big date, wouldn't it be nice to find out a little bit about him or her (basic stuff—do not be a stalker!) from the friend who introduced you? Maybe what type of food he or she likes or hobbies and interests, so that you can plan a nice date? Of course it would, and it would make things less stressful.

Why less stressful? Because you are *prepared*. When you do your research, whether it is for an example above or for a meeting with a new customer for your business, job interview, or selling a product, service, or idea, you are more prepared and know your prospect better from the start. This makes you more comfortable, more confident, and more likely to get what you want.

That is why no matter what you are selling, you need to do your research. It is pertinent to the foundation of your sales process. You do not have to spend days on it, though.

You may take longer on something of extreme importance, but most of the time you can get what you need in about ten to twenty minutes. For example, talking to the friend who introduced you to your date should take about ten minutes. Hopping on your school's website and looking up a professor's areas of interest and additional study should take five to ten minutes.

For those of you who are fortunate enough to own a business or are in professional sales—and I do mean "fortunate," because you are in one of the best situations in the world, being paid for your results, not time—your research is very easy as well. Google has just about everything you need to know about a company, an individual, or a type of product or service. It has everything about your competition, its weaknesses and strengths, and the info you need to win the sale. The prospect's website will also give a ton of information about them, their philosophies, and how they work.

For those of you who will be interviewing for any type of position in any company, these skills are priceless, and I promise you that they, combined with the rest of this chapter, will not only help increase the chances of getting the position, but maybe get you paid a little bit more as well.

This is very valuable information that you will use to your advantage to be more prepared and confident, and you will apply to one of the golden rules to selling. We will touch more on this rule later in the chapter.

## Information, the "Currency" of Our Time

I remarked earlier, in the chapter on getting financially smart, that I believe information is the new currency of our time. I would like to discuss that more in depth here.

*In the last few years, we have moved from the Industrial Age into the Information Age. In the Information Age, "The one who has the* information *makes the rules!"*

It is no longer just about having tangible assets (things you can touch and see), such as a product produced by a business, a piece of real estate, or a big bank account. What matters today is how much information you have and how you use it.

The word *currency* means to be in constant motion, like a current. That is what we must do with our skills and investments and how we operate in today's world. The Internet has changed everything about how we operate, and we must keep up with it. For example, the barriers to start a business in the Information Age have gotten very low. You can take an idea, create a website, and presto, you have a business that has access to the whole world in minutes. Many times you do not need an actual product—just the right information.

This book is an example of needed information, but the accompanying website for it allows me to go far beyond the book, offering ten times more information to help you build on the concepts in the book! Unlike this book, the website can be changed and updated daily, offering you new information and tools, in seconds.

There are many examples of millionaires and billionaires being created with just information. What is Google's actual product? Do you order something from Google, and the Google Widget ends up on your doorstep? Of course not; Google and its founders are masters at dealing in information. Facebook, Twitter, and LinkedIn are the same way. Companies pay them millions of dollars to have access to *you* and your information.

*I want to stop here and let what I just said above sink in. In recent times, the above concept is probably one of the most important things that I have learned and that will be a major part of my personal goals and success going forward. If you can grasp the concept that information is money in your hands and learn to utilize the tools out there to make that a reality, you will be able to accomplish any goal you desire on your ten-year career path.*

So, how do you use this to your advantage for sales in the Information Age?

Here is an excerpt from one of my recent sales talks about a success trait of top salespeople. I think it will help you to understand.

*Successful sales reps know* a little about a lot.

*Unsuccessful sales reps* specialize … expanding on the law of the Information Age. While successful reps are specialists in their product or service, when it comes to working with clients, they also strive to know a little about a lot, instead of a lot about a little. Why? Because in the Information Age, unless they are doctor, attorney, or in a specific trade, people do not specialize in the traditional sense. A purchasing agent for a prospect you meet with today that makes textbooks could leave the office at noon, check his stock trades, look at one of his for-profit websites, put up a quick post on his blog, check out his LinkedIn or Facebook profile to see any new contacts or leads, and check his eBay auction account to see how it's going—all on his one-hour lunch break.

*Successful sales reps realize they have to know a little about a lot in all environments to keep up with their customers and to separate themselves from the crowd!*

The concept of knowing a little about a lot in the Information Age is very important, because you never know what little tidbit you read about on Yahoo! Finance, concept from a book, or piece of research you did on a prospect might separate you from your competition and get you what you want.

*One of the added benefits of this book is that it was one of my goals to give you basic knowledge, a foundation, of a lot of concepts so that you are prepared to learn and grow in whatever path you take. I want to help you gain the basic knowledge to follow what more experienced mentors are telling you. In other words, I want to teach you a little about a lot and open your mind to the world of abundance and unending possibilities around you.*

## The Outside Salesperson Is Dead!

A statement that grabs everybody's attention is, "The outside salesperson is dead!" Figuratively speaking, this is true. The outside salesperson used to be the liaison of information between his or her company and the prospective customer. The salesperson *used* to have all of the information, thus giving him or her the upper hand. In the Information Age, this is not true. For just about any product, you can jump online and check on pricing, product, service stats, and specs, and get reviews—in seconds. What is it that I cannot find out on the Internet that a salesperson is going to tell me?

For most salespeople that I meet, the answer is nothing. There are, however, the few who realize that there are some things that only they can give, and cater to their prospects with those items, thus creating some curiosity for the prospect to meet with them on their product or service. In reality, they follow the 80/20 rule regarding information on their product and approach prospects with the 20 percent that is most important or unknown to the prospect.

For example, a good mortgage broker or lender will get my attention by looking at a deal I brought her, with financing options I found through my own research, and tell me there are better options for this particular project that can put more money in my pocket. Obviously, she has the information, and I am willing to listen.

You must learn to be the *total solution* and look for other ways in which you can help a prospect that are not found just in pricing, reviews, and specs. These ways may come in the form of tax breaks, time savings that turn into monetary savings, areas for greater efficiency, access to information he does not have or cannot currently have access to, or many other forms.

*In essence, today's top salesperson has to be more of a consultant looking for benefits in all areas rather than just the area of his or her product or service.*

Do you see that you need to know a little about a lot of topics to set yourself apart?

In doing this, you will realize one thing, and this one thing can make you very, very wealthy: prospects ultimately buy *you*. They buy you first and your product second.

It is a proven fact that one in six buyers is a true price shopper, meaning that no matter what, all he or she cares about is price. That leaves the other five to you and your skill. If you are in sales, do you close five out of six times? Chances are you don't, and if you do—awesome job. Pay attention to the rest of the chapter as it will help you get number six.

So far in our process, we have covered a few things:

- First, we need a process.
- Second, we need to do our research as the first step in the process.
- Third, we need to know a little bit about a lot and not specialize, so that we can work in just about any situation our customer throws at us.
- Fourth, we need to understand that ultimately people buy us.

## What Makes People Buy You?

So the question becomes, "What makes people buy you?"

As you probably have heard, you never get a second chance to make a *first* impression. This is very true in all cases, from meeting with a prospect to an interview. You must be on your game at all times. I have been in many different first impression situations in different ways and have learned a lot.

In one case, the prospect purposely made salespeople wait and bought on how well the salesperson treated their assistant. I was later told the reason I got the sale was because I had done my research, knew the assistant's name, and had a polite conversation with her about the office! She liked me best.

You never know what will win you the sale, and that is why research and preparation is a key to sales success. Have you ever heard a story about a musician coming out on stage and saying good evening to the *wrong* city? Or worse, forgetting the words? I have heard that a few times. How embarrassing.

How do you think the people of that city or the audience feel about that musician?

### *Dress for Success*

Another thing that you must do is dress for success. I once had a mentor who was fond of saying that he would rather be the best dressed in a room than the worst dressed! I think there is a lot of wisdom in that statement. If you want to be taken seriously, you must dress and carry yourself seriously. In business, especially the sales and corporate word, this is a must. Make sure that you have a clean look. Yes, guys, this means being clean-shaven, and no earrings, sorry. You must make sure your suit (ladies and men) or appropriate attire is cleanly pressed or dry-cleaned. Lastly, make sure any accessories, necklaces, watches, shoes, belts, and so forth match the outfit well and are in good condition. It has been shown by numerous studies that the way you dress correlates to the size of your income, so make sure you take the time to find the right attire to set yourself apart.

### *You Must Believe in Yourself and What You Are Selling*

Since your prospects do buy you, your attitude about your product, service, and yourself is very important! You must believe in yourself and what you are selling! If you do not, it will show through very quickly. You must have conviction for yourself, your knowledge, and your ability, as well as your product or service.

If you do not believe in what you are selling, stop now, and go find something that you do believe in! It will make you happier, and you will sell more of it just by having a better attitude.

If you are not sure about your product or service, you maybe just need to find out more about it. You can do this by asking your superiors or other, more experienced, successful sales reps why they are passionate about it—or even better, ask your customers why they like it so much! This will really help you when you encounter similar situations with new prospects.

### Never Prejudge a Prospect

As your attitude is important, so is the way you think toward your prospects. If you go into a meeting with a prospect thinking that she is not going to buy, chances are she is not going to. This is because your attitude, your subconscious mind, won't allow it, and even worse, this attitude will show through to the prospect.

You must never prejudge a prospect.

This is a good rule to keep in mind when in sales. Some of my biggest sales have come from prospects who some would think 1) did not look like they could even afford a cheeseburger, let alone the product or service, and 2) did not *seem* as though they had a need for the product or service. Of course, I found the exact opposite in all of the cases, but if I had gone in with the attitude that these prospects didn't need me or couldn't afford it, I probably would not have gotten the sale. The same goes for cold-calling or phone conversations as well. Do not prejudge them.

One of my earliest "big" sales was in college, where I was working as an intern for a stockbroker at a prestigious firm. My job was to telemarket. Talk about starting at the bottom! Every evening, I was given a four-inch-thick stack of leads.

My job was to call them to see if they would be interested in sitting down with the broker/advisor. Needless to say, my closing ratio wasn't too high, and I definitely learned to handle rejection.

One night, as I was getting particularly frustrated with being told to "stick it," I came across a young lady who seemed as though she had no money but *actually* wanted to listen.

So instead of using my "canned script," I used the *information* I had gained from sitting in the office and listening to all the brokers to pique her and then her husband's interest. As it turned out, they were unhappy with their current broker, and a couple of things I said made sense. As a result, the gentlemen that I worked for got the account, and it ended up being a multimillion-dollar brokerage account!

If I had just gone through my canned script and believed that the young lady had no money, I probably would have not have gotten the sale. It was from this example that I realized two powerful things:

*Don't prejudge, and information = currency.*

### Never Bad-Mouth Your Competition

*Do not ever* bad-mouth your competition. It makes you look unprofessional and desperate, like you do not know how to beat them. This is always a big problem with new salespeople because, many times, they don't know how to beat them. Even if you are new, take the high road. Instead, compliment the competition on their feature or selling point, but then redirect your customer on your benefit or how you make up for this issue. Then go learn more and do your research on your competition! You must know them better than they know you! As a result, you can identify ahead of time what a customer might perceive as a difference between you and your competition and have an answer for it. Again, preparation is the key.

### *Your Personal Touch*

If people do buy you, then you need to separate *you* with some special personal touches. It may be something like a handwritten "thank you" to each sale. You could find out what your prospects' and customers' interests are, and if you see something (magazine, book, newspaper article) that appeals to these interests, get it for them.

I once was working with a few companies that were pretty exceptional and cutting-edge. They were run by some really strong entrepreneurs who had a thirst for knowledge. As a result, we got along very well. Anytime I saw a book that looked interesting to me and really focused on growing a company, I would get them a copy as well. They loved it, and I loved talking about it with them!

As a result, I got more referrals from those few companies than any others that I worked with! Set yourself apart; add your personal touch. Remember, in sales you are paid for your results, so you are in control of your business and your destiny. Take ownership!

## A Few More Steps in the Process

Okay, so you now know you need a consistent process, you've done your research, you have taken the time to know "a little about a lot" in many areas, and you know that people buy *you*. What else is there? Well, read on.

### *The Biggest Selling Secret*

Do you remember earlier in the chapter when I said that there is a sort of golden rule in sales? Now, it is not an end-all, but I will tell you that if you figure out how to use this correctly, you will get more sales and definitely increase your results. Ready?

*People rarely resist their own ideas.*

Read it again and think deeply about what the above sentence means. The fact that people rarely resist their own ideas is a golden rule for top salespeople with a good process. It simply means that through research, asking the right questions, and understanding how your prospect thinks and does business, you can *use their ideas and ways of thinking* to sell your product or services to them.

It is a profound idea to have your customer sell herself your product or service, and it is not easy to grasp, especially for beginners. The power of the rule is that if you have done a good enough job and your prospect uses her own ideas to sell herself, then it is very hard for her to argue against herself and her ideas. We will not be able to go into all of the details here, but I'll give you a quick example.

*A Brief Example of People Rarely Resisting Their Own Ideas*

Let's say I sell document shredding services and I am meeting with a customer who is concerned only with what my cost is. If I ask him the right questions, such as "Why are you concerned only with cost?" or "When you choose to do business with a partner, what do you look for in him?" it does two things. First, I take control of the conversation; and second, I still keep their concern of cost in the mix, but get them talking about their ideas and philosophies.

The customer might respond with, "Well, we have a tight budget to meet." In that case, I make a mental note that I need to know what their budget is. Tight to them may mean my most comprehensive service fits in his price range. They may then go on to say, "When we do business, we look for someone with integrity, a good service record, and a quick response time." Well, if I know my company has the fastest response time in the industry, I make a mental note to use "their idea" as the selling point.

I am going to stop here because this example can go on for a while with everything that you can do. That is why, for our company, this is almost a whole-day seminar. The point is that in the beginning of the situation above, I have found that "their ideas" line up with some of the best abilities of my company—the ability to have the fastest response time and work with any budget. I would simply restate his ideas back to them asking if they are important, to which they would say "Yes," and then show them how my company fits into those ideas. The customer has sold themself.

This is an extremely basic example of this way of selling. Many people actually do some of it without even knowing it, but if we are aware of how to do it correctly and use it to our advantage, then we can really sell a lot more.

## Get Your Story

It has been said that one of the most powerful forms of selling is to tell a story. I would agree. Some of the best sales pitches I ever received were not from salespeople but a satisfied customer telling the story of how "awesome" a job a company did or how it went above and beyond.

You need to use this form of selling along with your prospect's ideas. First, know the story of your company. Many companies have a wonderful story of how they got started. Think of companies like Microsoft, Disney, or Starbucks. They all have amazing stories that get the emotional side of a customer involved. That may be the reason that stories work so well—they appeal to the emotional side of the prospect, and for you are exciting to tell!

Remember that your attitude and the way you are perceived are a big part of sales. I have never bought a product from an Eee Ore with a ton of product information (they specialized and seemed less than thrilled to be talking to me), but I have bought from an excited Tigger with a lot less product information (they knew a little about a lot and were excited to work with me).

Your story is just as important. If you are a salesperson, how many times have you been asked, "So, how did you get with this company?" or "What are you doing selling for XYZ Company?" I will bet it has happened a few times, and having a compelling story will only help you with your prospect.

If you are a student in an interview, you probably will get questions like, "Why did you choose XYZ School?" or "What made you choose your major?" Again, a compelling story with passion and personality will show the interviewer what an asset you can be!

### *Testimonials: The Secret Weapon*

No matter if you are a student, sales professional, business owner, manager, or in some other role, you must have testimonials about you, your products or services, your skills, and anything else that will help you. Testimonials are the third-party proof that you, your product or service, or your business will do what you say.

Brian Tracy, renowned sales expert and author said, "As a general rule, the prospect will discount anything that you say about your product or service. After all, you are a salesperson. You are expected to speak positively about what you are selling. But if someone *else* says something good about your product or service, especially in writing, that is considered to be a valid statement. Third party proof, in the form of testimonial letters, is a powerful way to convince people of the goodness and value of what you are selling. This is why it is said that 'salespeople who don't use testimonial letters have skinny kids.'"

Brian has a great point! Why should you do all of the work? Just as you should utilize your prospect's ideas and way of thinking to sell your product or service for you, you should have your customers do it as well! No matter what you do, a couple good testimonial letters of your hard work, great service, and personal integrity will help you get ahead.

## *Always Follow Up and Follow Through*

The last step in your sales process should always be to follow up on your work, your prospects, and the results. It can be done through e-mail or handwritten notes. You should also make sure that anything else that has been promised or that you said you would do is followed through with and done. Your credibility is something you can only establish once, so do what you say.

It is suggested for most sales to follow up after thirty, sixty, and ninety days. Many times it is taken a step further to follow up at one year as well. No matter what you choose, make it a point to have some type of follow-up program. It may be an e-mail at 30-60-90 days or a stop in at the customer's, but remember, "out of sight, out of mind." A customer can quickly forget about the great job you did for her, unless you take the time to cement that feeling. Make sure you have a good reason when you follow up, even if it is to just remind him about the great work you did together. It will last. The follow-up is also a great time to ask for referrals and testimonial letters.

For prospects that maybe choose, for whatever reason, not to do business with you, a strong follow-up program should be used. "No" many times just means, "Not yet." It is amazing how having a strong follow-up program for prospects you did not sell when you met with them can later get you the business.

*People who know me have often heard me say, "The fortune lies in the follow-up!" I can say that being strong in this area definitely has had a large impact on my sales success, my companies' success, and the success of teams that I have coached.*

I cannot count how many sales I have gotten just by following up after a meeting and reiterating why our two companies were such a great fit. Sometimes it was an immediate sale, other times it took a few months, but just by staying on top of things, keeping myself and my company in front of them, they eventually came aboard.

Do not make the mistake that many salespeople make: once you have gotten a "No," to forget about a prospect or take them off of your prospect list, especially if you know that they are a great fit. Some of your best customers will come from initial "no-sales"!

Lastly, a little tip for interviewees: Make sure you follow up with your interviewer within twenty-four hours with a handwritten thank-you note. Many times people just send an e-mail thank you. Setting yourself apart with a good handwritten note will leave a lasting impression.

## Negotiating

The final part of this chapter is going to cover a few small basics of negotiating. I am going to give you two things you must do in any negotiation. Those who know me or have seen me speak have heard me talk about a dear friend and business associate—author, speaker, and trainer S. G. Lewis. S. G. is what I consider the authority on negotiating. He has studied more than anyone I have ever come across and gives arguably the best talk on negotiating skills and how to implement them. It is titled *The Ten Keys to Negotiation*. This simple, two-hour seminar has saved me thousands of dollars and helped me make more sales than I ever thought possible. I am going to cover two of the keys here. You can visit the resources section at www.TheTenYearCareer.com to learn more about him and tips for negotiations.

*Key 1: Do not let someone else establish the baseline from which you will begin the negotiation.*

This is the number-one key for a reason. It means that *you* need to control the negotiation. You set the baseline. If your prospect or the person you are negotiating with "reestablishes" the baseline, you must reestablish it back and keep control.

S. G. gives a wonderful example of this in his talk. He tells about while he was coming up with the seminar and the ten keys, he would go out and spend hours testing them everywhere he could. One time specifically, he was at a car dealership and going out on a test drive of a new SUV. He tells the story of coming to the exit of the dealership, getting ready to pull out onto the street, and he asked the salesperson, "So, what are these things going for anyway?" The salesman, beaming with pride, answered, "Oh, these are so 'hot,' we are not selling them for a penny below sticker!" (establishing the baseline).

They sat there for a second, waiting for the light to change, and the salesperson said to S. G., "Just go ahead and make a *right* out of here onto the road."

Well, S. G. immediately made a *left* turn, and the salesperson said, "What are you doing?" S. G. then said, "Turning around and going back to the dealership." The salesperson said, "Why?" and S. G. replied, "Because I don't pay sticker for anything!" (reestablishing the baseline).

Ha! Classic. I bet you can tell me what the salesperson did next. Yep, he started stammering and saying things like, "Well, maybe I can talk to my manager, uh, and I am sure we can do something … uh … uh."

S. G. had won. He had reestablished the baseline and controlled the negotiation.

If you can master this one technique, it will not only save you thousands in your purchases, it will also help you to get more of what you want and get you more sales in your career.

*Key 2: You must be willing to walk away.*

This is a critical key to learn and where I see salespeople get into the most trouble. The scenario goes like this: The salesperson gets done with his "awesome" presentation, highlighting all of the wonderful things about his product or service and how it is worth the price. And then comes the price. The salesperson gives the price, and the prospect says something along the lines of, "Oh, that is way too much" or "Your competition is offering a substantially lower price for the same service."

What happens? The salesperson panics and goes into "super discount" mode, discounting the product or service for the customer.

The problem I see is that if you are the salesperson and you just spent all of this time explaining how "awesome" your product or service is and how good of a deal it is, don't you really think you devalue yourself and everything you just did by discounting it by 25 percent?

First, you have not reestablished the baseline. The negotiating is just beginning at this point. You need to reestablish the baseline and show the prospect why your product or service is worth the cost. If you have done things right, you should have their ideas to use here.

Second, you need to have a mental limit at which you will walk away. It may be that you will not discount lower than 10 percent. If that is it and you get to that limit, simply thank the prospect for his time, reiterate one more time why he should buy your product, and walk.

I have done this many times—and guess what happens as I am about two steps out the door? I get the call back. The prospect follows me out or calls me later on the phone and says "we should revisit" or "we can work out a deal."

She does this because of fear of loss, among other things. If you have so much passion and conviction about what you are selling that you are willing to walk out on someone because you will not devalue yourself or your product or service, it really makes people think about what they may be losing—and by the way, sets one heck of a baseline.

In conclusion, selling and negotiating are two of the most useful and powerful skills you will ever learn to help you on *your ten-year career path* and your life. This chapter is just a small sample of what is available out there. I suggest you learn more about the sales process, skills, and techniques available to help you succeed, especially if you are in a sales profession. It can be through our site at www.TheTenYearCareer.com or through any other programs that interest you. Just make sure you get the training. Here's to the rest of *your sales career*, in whatever it may be!

"You only have to do a very few things right in your life so long as you don't do too many things wrong."

—*Warren Buffett*

CHAPTER 7

# THE QUALITIES AND TRAITS OF THE MOST WEALTHY, SUCCESSFUL, AND FULFILLED

Would you like to know the qualities that the most successful, wealthy, and fulfilled people on the ten-year career path have and use every day?

There are so many qualities out there that people can possess to set them apart from the crowd. Some people, like Sir Winston Churchill, are great speakers and orators. Others are amazing at making decisions at the right time like Warren Buffet. Still some just have the ability to walk into a room and everybody will stop and listen, such as a Bill Gates or the late Steve Jobs.

While many wealthy and successful people have one trait or quality that sets them apart, they also have a great deal of others that make them who they are. The bad news is that I do not know *your* one great separating trait or quality. The good news is that I have taken a tremendous amount of time to study up on some of the most successful and well-respected leaders of our time and have narrowed down ten traits that almost every one of them does possess and that you can learn to have too!

This chapter will give you each one of those traits or qualities and a few examples that embody them so that you can study up on each trait and work to make sure you embody it in your ten-year career journey.

## Quality 1: Integrity

Integrity is the foundation of your success. It is so important that without it you cannot succeed. Webster's defines integrity as "to have a strict adherence to moral and ethical principles; soundness of moral character, and honesty."

I would like to add a little bit more to this definition. Integrity also means that you will do what you say you will do. If you make a promise, you must do everything possible to keep it. Your word and integrity are one of the most important things that you have. If you lose someone's trust, it is almost, if not impossible, to repair.

That is not to say that people do not make mistakes. We are not perfect, and believe me, I have made my share of mistakes, but if I say that "I will not do that again" or "I will make it right," I always follow through. You must do the same.

There will always be situations where people may choose not to care for you, but if you are someone of great integrity, they will have to respect you.

A great example of a man with impeccable integrity is author and billionaire owner of the Huntsman Corporation, John Huntsman. John is an amazing example of integrity. As it says on the cover of his book *Winners Never Cheat,* he built a twelve-billion-dollar company from scratch the old-fashioned way: with integrity.

His accomplishments are so many that I cannot name them all. I will highlight just a few. He was a special assistant to the president in the Nixon White House, and six months before all of the trouble in the presidency happened, John got wind of it, voiced his opinion of how amoral the dealings were, and promptly left his position. He was the only West Wing staff member *not* brought before the congressional Watergate Committee or a grand jury! In addition to building a twelve-billion-dollar company, John has given millions to different causes all over the world. One of his most notable is the Huntsman Cancer Institute, a world leader in the prevention, early diagnosis, and humane treatment of cancer.

He also is the chairman of the board of overseers at the Wharton School at the University of Pennsylvania, which some argue is the best business school in the nation. Oh, one more thing about John: it has been reported that many of his dealings, contracts, partnerships, and so on, are done on a handshake—no lawyers, no 150-page agreements, just a handshake and his word! How's that for integrity?

## Quality 2: Passion

You cannot reach your goals without passion. Whether it is a passion for life, your work, your family, a hobby, or an interest, you must be passionate about what it is you want in order to get it. This one quality can show through and set you apart from everyone else.

In my career, I have had the chance to hire or have input in hiring people in a multitude of businesses, and I can tell you that some of the best hires were not because of sheer talent. The best hires and most successful people that I have had the privilege of working with and learning from are the most passionate people that I have met. It may not have always been a passion for the business we were in, but it was about something, whether life or their children or just the ability to have what they considered a great opportunity. This passion and excitement would rub off on you and get you excited as well.

I define passion as a strong conviction or compelling desire for something or a cause.

A great example of people with tremendous passion were our founding fathers, the signers of the Declaration of Independence. The fifty-six signers of the Declaration of Independence knew that they were signing their names in blood. They knew that the moment they signed, they would be considered traitors, hunted down, and ultimately put to death. But they were so passionate about their cause and so committed to ending the tyranny placed on them by the British that they were willing to sacrifice everything for a chance at freedom. In my view, these were some of, if not *the* bravest men in history. They were willing to give up everything for an idea—an idea of what we now have in this country today.

We citizens of the United States are extremely fortunate to have had these men of foresight and passion. Actually, they in some way or another embody all of the qualities in this chapter. If you really want to understand passion, take the time to read the Declaration of Independence. The beginning basically says that when there is great harm and wrongdoing, those with the ability must act to abolish it. It is not a choice, but their duty. Give it a read—it will take you about ten minutes—and afterward you will understand why passion is a must for you on the ten-year career path.

## Quality 3: Vision

Vision is the ability to see what others cannot. It is the ability to believe without physically seeing what you will accomplish and achieve. All those who have been successful in some way or another have vision. You may have been part of a team that "won it all," or you may have worked so hard at your grades in school knowing full well that you would not stop until you got that scholarship. Whatever our situation, we must have vision to see where we are going and to reach the goals we set out to achieve. If you think about it, many times a goal is a vision.

I can think of no better example of someone with vision than Bill Gates and the story of Microsoft. It all began with one man's belief that the "computer would be a valuable tool on every office desktop and in every home."

The story goes like this: Bill Gates and Microsoft cofounder Paul Allen studied together in high school. In Lakeside Prep School, they had their first dealings with computers. Both of them had a great interest for computers and programming. They would spend hours in front of the computer.

The turning point in their lives was when they came across an article about the Altair 8000, a small computer. Gates and Allen approached the manufacturer, MITS (Micro Instrumentation and Telemetry Systems) to launch a programming language for the computer even when they did not have the program ready.

In a span of eight weeks before the demonstration, Gates and Allen developed the interpreter. The interpreter worked at the demonstration, and MITS agreed to distribute Altair BASIC. It was a great achievement.

Talk about vision! At seventeen years of age, a young man was promising to deliver an operating system to a company that had not even been created yet!

Skip forward a few years; Microsoft had been created, and IBM came knocking on Bill's door. Gates first had success with the MS-DOS operating system. In 1980, Microsoft joined hands with IBM. Under this agreement, Microsoft's operating system was bundled with IBM computers. This worked out well for Microsoft. Five years later, IBM wanted Microsoft to write a new operating system for their computers called the OS/2. Microsoft created the OS/2.

However, Microsoft managed to get the rights to market MS-DOS separately besides the IBM deal. The Microsoft version emerged successful. It raked in fortunes for the company.

In another visionary move, Bill recognized that the software was the future of the computer, and even with behemoth IBM coming to his little company, he managed to negotiate to keep the rights and ability to sell it—a great example of how important negotiating skills are. This may be one of the greatest moves in business history because it is what allowed Microsoft to grow at such a rapid pace and as a result become even bigger than IBM!

From there, you pretty much know the rest of the story, but it really is amazing how much vision played a role in the formation, growth, and success of Microsoft. What started off as an idea became arguably the greatest technology company in history.

Whatever you may aspire to, create your vision, set your goals, and go after it!

## Quality 4: Commitment

Commitment is one of the biggest things that people lack in going after their goals, desires, and dreams. It means to devote oneself unreservedly. It means to not stop until you get what you seek. Committing to something is a very big step in reaching your desired outcomes, because once you commit, there is no turning back. It is not an option.

For me, this book was a commitment. I had told my wife for over a year that I wanted to write it and had still not put pen to paper. Knowing me all too well, she simply said, "You will when you commit yourself."

So it began, with those words resonating in the back of my mind. I had to truly commit to putting in hours upon hours and days of writing, researching, and editing to get this book done. On top of that, I had my own work, businesses, and endeavors to complete and stay sharp on, as well as coming up with and doing the work on the website for this book.

Once I started, I knew that there was no turning back. It is scary at first to commit unreservedly to something, but once you get going, the passion and vision take over. You are so excited that it almost becomes addicting to get more and more done and to see your progress every day. It makes you want whatever it is that you desire more and more.

Another great example of commitment is Mother Teresa. Her story is so remarkable and her commitment to her cause is so great that I do not believe that there has been anyone ever more committed than she.

She earned a Nobel Peace Prize. Below is a short synopsis of her biography from their website, www.NobelPrize.org.

> Mother Teresa was born Agnes Gonxha Bojaxhiu in Skopje, Macedonia, on August 26, 1910. Her family was of Albanian descent. At the age of twelve, she felt strongly the call of God. She knew she had to be a missionary to spread the love of Christ. At the age of eighteen she left her parental home in Skopje and joined the Sisters of Loreto, an Irish community of nuns with

missions in India. After a few months' training in Dublin she was sent to India, where on May 24, 1931, she took her initial vows as a nun. From 1931 to 1948 Mother Teresa taught at St. Mary's High School in Calcutta, but the suffering and poverty she glimpsed outside the convent walls made such a deep impression on her that in 1948 she received permission from her superiors to leave the convent school and devote herself to working among the poorest of the poor in the slums of Calcutta. Although she had no funds, she depended on Divine Providence, and started an open-air school for slum children. Soon she was joined by voluntary helpers, and financial support was also forthcoming. This made it possible for her to extend the scope of her work.

On October 7, 1950, Mother Teresa received permission from the Holy See to start her own order, "The Missionaries of Charity", whose primary task was to love and care for those persons nobody was prepared to look after. In 1965 the Society became an International Religious Family by a decree of Pope Paul VI.

Today the order comprises Active and Contemplative branches of Sisters and Brothers in many countries. In 1963 both the Contemplative branch of the Sisters and the Active branch of the Brothers was founded. In 1979 the Contemplative branch of the Brothers was added, and in 1984 the Priest branch was established.

The Society of Missionaries has spread all over the world, including the former Soviet Union and Eastern European countries. They provide effective help to the poorest of the poor in a number of countries in Asia, Africa, and Latin America, and they undertake relief work in the wake of natural catastrophes such as floods, epidemics, and famine, and for refugees. The order also has houses in North America, Europe and Australia, where they take care of the shut-ins, alcoholics, homeless, and AIDS sufferers.

The Missionaries of Charity throughout the world are aided and assisted by Co-Workers who became an official International Association on March 29, 1969. By the 1990s there were over one million Co-Workers in more than 40 countries. Along with the Co-Workers, the lay Missionaries of Charity try to follow Mother Teresa's spirit and charism in their families.

Mother Teresa's work has been recognised and acclaimed throughout the world and she has received a number of awards and distinctions, including the Pope John XXIII Peace Prize (1971) and the Nehru Prize for her promotion of international peace and understanding (1972). She also received the Balzan Prize (1979) and the Templeton and Magsaysay awards.

With no funding and no immediate help, Mother Teresa set out on her own and committed herself to her cause, never looking back or quitting.

You must be committed to reaching your goals and getting yourself on the ten-year career path.

## Quality 5: Perseverance

Perseverance goes right along with commitment, in that in order to commit, you must be willing to have the perseverance to get through the stumbles, roadblocks, and rough times that you will encounter on the way to your desired outcomes on your ten-year career path. Almost all successful and wealthy people have had setbacks at some point in time. Trump went bankrupt more than once; it took Thomas Edison over ten thousand attempts to create the light bulb; and even J. K. Rowling, author of the Harry Potter series, faced serious adversity. What matters is not that these people faced adversity, because everyone does in some way or another, but what they did to overcome that adversity. How did their perseverance get them through these tough times?

Well, I think you know the answer. Trump came roaring back and is now wealthier than he ever was.

Thomas Edison handled his perseverance with one statement. He said, "I have not failed 10,000 times. I have successfully discovered 10,000 ways *not* to make a lightbulb!"

J. K. Rowling was basically on skid row when she started writing the Harry Potter series. She was going through a divorce, living in a tiny little efficiency apartment, and taking care of her daughter, while living off of government subsidies. Her mother had just passed away from multiple sclerosis, and the book was initially rejected by twelve different publishers. Despite all of that, she used her writing in her "spare time" to persevere through it all. Of course, you know the rest of the story.

If you want to succeed and reach your desired results, you must develop a "thick skin" and be willing to persevere through any obstacle that comes your way.

## Quality 6: Desire

Author and speaker Dennis Waitley says this about desire: "Out of need springs *desire*, and out of *desire* springs the energy and the will to win." Your desire to achieve your goals and dreams must be at its highest all of the time. Your desire will determine how you act toward your goals and the ferocity and speed in which you will reach them.

Desire is simply the mix of passion, vision, and action. It is the burning sensation deep within you that propels you to get things done.

An example of someone with incredible desire to reach her goals is Helen Keller. Many know Helen and her accomplishments, but have not heard her story. Helen was born with the ability to see and hear in 1880. At nineteen months of age, she fell ill and was for many days expected to die. She came out of the sickness only to be permanently deaf and blind. Her early years were very rough, with Helen throwing fits every day and many people considering her a terrible child. After a while, Helen's parents decided that they had to do something. They made some connections and found a young woman by the name of Anne Sullivan. Anne had lost most of her sight at age five and as a result had trouble finding work. Then she was asked to work with a deaf-blind mute named Helen Keller. Anne started out simply, teaching Helen to finger spell, and then progressed from there. Slowly Helen's behavior started to get better and she showed signs of promise, but she did not always understand the words. Then, it happened.

When Anne led Helen to the water pump on April 5, 1887, everything changed.

> As Anne pumped the water over Helen's hand, Anne spelled out the word water in Helen's free hand. Something about this explained the meaning of words within Helen, and Anne could immediately see in her face that she finally understood.

Helen later recounted the incident:

> "We walked down the path to the well-house, attracted by the fragrance of the honey-suckle with which it was covered. Someone was drawing water and my teacher placed my hand under the spout. As the cool stream gushed over one hand she spelled into the other the word water, first slowly, then rapidly. I stood still, my whole attention fixed upon the motions of her fingers. Suddenly I felt a misty consciousness as of something forgotten, a thrill of returning thought, and somehow the mystery of language was revealed to me."

Helen immediately asked Anne for the name of the pump to be spelt on her hand and then the name of the trellis. All the way back to the house Helen learned the name of everything she touched and also asked for Anne's name. Anne spelled the name "Teacher" on Helen's hand.

Within the next few hours Helen learnt the spelling of thirty new words.

Helen's progress from then on was astonishing. Her ability to learn was far in advance of anything that anybody had seen before in someone without sight or hearing. It wasn't long before Anne was teaching Helen to read, firstly with raised letters and later with braille, and to write with both ordinary and braille typewriters.

From there, Helen's desire to learn propelled her to go on and go to college, travel the world, and become a huge advocate for those with disabilities. She was an inspiration to all whom she met.

Without the desire to keep trying and learning, we might not know of Helen Keller today, but because of this one quality the world was changed.

Your desire will give you an edge in reaching your goals and dreams as you further your journey.

## Quality 7: Accountability

Holding yourself accountable is vital to long-term wealth and success. Being accountable to yourself, your actions, and your commitments will not only help make sure that you get to your desires, but also help you in all of your dealings with others. It is sad in our society today, but much of the accountability of individuals has disappeared. Many people do not feel it necessary to follow through on their commitments or, worse, procrastinate on them continuously.

Notice that I said you must hold *yourself* accountable. You cannot and should not rely on others to do it for you.

A great example of someone with a very high standard of accountability is Warren Buffet. One just has to read an annual report from Buffet's company, Berkshire Hathaway, and they will understand what accountability means. Where most CEOs of companies spend their time highlighting all of the good things about their company in these reports, even when it is in a down slump or performing poorly, Buffet does exactly the opposite.

While Warren Buffet does have a lot to praise (he is the wealthiest investor in history and has been ranked the single wealthiest person in the world), he also holds himself to the highest degree of accountability, even when delivering what most investors consider great returns. He is not shy to take responsibility for slower returns (although still crushing the market) and is quick to praise and deliver compliments to those responsible for success in Berkshire Hathaway.

What's more is that Buffet practices what he preaches. He believes, as I do, deeply in giving, whether monetarily or with your time, efforts, resources, and so forth. He still lives in the same house he bought in 1958 for $31,500, and for being the wealthiest investor in the world and CEO of an enormous company, pays himself a modest salary of $100,000.

Now, as you have learned in this book, there are many ways through his investments that he takes home much more, but by salary and living standards, he's just the average Joe, a neighborhood billionaire. Even more impressive is the fact that he recently donated the bulk of his wealth, $31 billion, to the Bill and Melinda Gates Foundation. Talk about being accountable to yourself, your actions, and your commitments; there is no question that Warren does this every day.

If you want to move even quicker on your ten-year career path, learn to *hold yourself accountable*, every day.

## Quality 8: Tenacity

Tenacity is one of my favorite qualities. It separates those who talk a big game from those who actually walk the big game. Tenacity is persistent determination. It is the raw grit and steadfastness to get something done at all costs. People with true tenacity do not stop until they reach what they are after and will not let their course be deterred in any way. If they are knocked off course, they work even harder to get back on. People with great tenacity are winners. They have a fire that cannot be extinguished.

Some of the best examples of tremendous tenacity are athletes. There are so many examples, from people like Michael Jordan and Jack Nicklaus, to Peyton Manning, Lance Armstrong, and the tennis domination of the Williams sisters.

One particular athlete comes to mind. As I have been writing this book, I have watched one athlete with so much grit and tenacity that I do not think that anyone will ever be better than he. It is the number-one gold-medal-winning Olympian and US swimming sensation Michael Phelps. Michael is incredible. He not only won eight gold medals in the 2008 Beijing Olympics, but he set world records in every race except one and even in that one he set an Olympic record. That is seven world records in one Olympics! He then followed that up in London in 2012 to become the most decorated Olympian of all time!

What's not as well-known about Phelps is his behind-the-scenes workout routine. Phelps started swimming at seven years old. His heart pumps thirty liters of blood each minute to his muscles, which is double the amount of the average adult male. He also produces only one third of the lactic acid that the average swimmer does, meaning that he does not suffer from muscle burn during intensive exercise like his competitors do. He says that after a race, his lactic acid levels are the same as a person who is at rest.

Michael trains for six hours a day, six days a week, without a miss. Even if holidays fall on training days, he does not miss. He swims fifty miles per week (eight per day) and takes in a staggering twelve thousand calories a day! Not bad, since the average male takes in two thousand calories a day. It is Michael's incredible tenacity to train and devotion to his exercise, training program, and diet, without fail, that have determined his success. He is a tenacious machine that sacrifices everything to win. His favorite quote is "Actions speak louder than words."

It could not be said better. You must be fiercely tenacious about your process and the way in which you go about reaching your goals.

## Quality 9: Boldness

Those who have taken a huge risk and gotten either a huge payoff or major disappointment know what it means to be bold. Boldness is a quality that many people do not naturally have, but thankfully it is a quality that can be learned. Boldness means to take risks, to stand for something even though it may not be popular, to get up when you get knocked down, and to keep pressing forward in the bleakest of times.

Think of some of the greatest leaders, athletes, philanthropists, and heroes in your life. I am willing to bet you that all of them are examples of tremendous boldness in some form or another.

Arnold Palmer, world-famous golfer, said, "You must play boldly to win." Robert Frost, the great American poet, said, "Freedom lies in being bold."

If you are not bold enough to take the risks to get on a ten-year career path, you never will. And taking it one step further, as Robert Frost hinted, the *freedom* you get from getting on the ten-year career path lies in being bold and acting boldly.

Perhaps one of the boldest survival stories in history is that of Louis Zamperini. Louis is the subject of the best-selling book "Unbroken" by Laura Hillenbrand. It may just be of the greatest stories of boldness, survival, and redemption ever told. I will not spoil the whole book for you as it should be part of your library, but I will give you a short synopsis.

Louis Zamperini was a former Olympic athlete who was one of the youngest and fastest distance runners ever during his time. He had even captured Hitler's attention at the 1936 games in Berlin. In fact, he came very close to breaking the 4 minute mile well before Roger Bannister and most likely would have if he had not had to serve in WWII. Louie's story is gut-wrenching, but incredibly remarkable. He was an airman for the US Air Force and on a fateful day in 1943, his plane went down in the middle of the Pacific Ocean. There were only 3 survivors including Louie. Thus began one of the greatest survival stories in war history. For the next 47 days, Louis and the two other survivors, one of which died, would drift over 2000 miles with no food or water and sharks circling their tiny little raft.

They survived only by Louie's clear thinking and ingenuity in creating fishing lines of materials from the raft, eating birds that landed on the raft, and finding ways to catch and retain water when it rained. It is the longest anyone had ever survived at sea. But the story didn't end there…

On that 47th day, Louie and the other survivor, pilot Russell Phillips, were picked up by Japanese sailors.

For more than two years, the two men were held in a series of prison camps, where they were repeatedly beaten and starved. As an ex-Olympian, Zamperini was considered a propaganda tool by the Japanese and saved from execution; at the same time, however, he was singled out for particularly vicious forms of torture. In fact, there was one crazy Japanese prison guard, who for over two years, took pleasure in finding as many ways to torture and try to beat Louie into submission on a daily basis. But he never broke. Defying all odds, Louie managed to survive and was released after the war ended in 1945.

Louie Zamperini should have been dead from 47 days on the ocean. He should have been dead as his body wasted away from being adrift and then from multiple years in prison camps with daily beatings and little to no food (a bowl of rice). In fact, the government had pronounced him dead. But, through it all Louie's boldness shined through, along with his perseverance. As the quote from Robert Frost said earlier in this section, "Freedom lies in being bold." Louie's boldness ultimately kept him alive to regain his freedom.

Your boldness will help you get to much higher levels than you think are imaginable. Be bold, be willing to take risks, and remember, your "freedom lies in being bold."


## Quality 10: Humility

Of all of the qualities I have mentioned in this chapter, I have saved humility for last. We have talked about believing in yourself and its importance in reaching your goals and dreams, but reaching them cannot be done with blind cockiness.

It is those who *think* they are better than everyone else and put no effort of study or work into *making* themselves better that never really get on a ten-year career path. They get stuck because of their own blind ambition and are left for years scratching their heads as to why they are not where they want to be—all the while thinking that they have everything they need.

These people are very dangerous and many times destructive to themselves and those around them without even knowing it. It order to get onto and stay on a ten-year career path, you must remain grounded. You must never forget where you came from or the basic principles and hard work that we have covered this far that will get you there.

You are not entitled to anything; therefore, what you are able to accomplish and achieve should be celebrated but also be kept in perspective. In short, you must practice humility and remain humble and thankful toward your success.

One of the best examples of true humility is a simple story that you have heard many times, "The Tortoise and the Hare." The story goes like this:

There once was a speedy hare who bragged about how fast he could run. Tired of hearing him boast, Slow and Steady, the tortoise, challenged him to a race. All the animals in the forest gathered to watch.

Hare ran down the road for a while and then paused to rest. He looked back at Slow and Steady and cried out, "How do you expect to win this race when you are walking along at your slow, slow pace?" Hare stretched himself out alongside the road and fell asleep, thinking, "There is plenty of time to relax."

Slow and Steady walked and walked. He never, ever stopped until he came to the finish line. The animals who were watching cheered so loudly for Tortoise, they woke up Hare. Hare stretched and yawned and began to run again, but it was too late. Tortoise was over the line.

The story is very basic, yet powerful. The hare, with no humility and blind cockiness, thought that no matter what, because he was who he was, he would win the race. Of course, Slow and Steady, the tortoise, not saying a word, just working very hard and being humble, came out the winner.

We can learn a lot from this story. Keep yourself grounded, keep your humility, never lose perspective, and be thankful for your success.

These qualities will help you to excel in all that you do in your life. Each one of them is extremely powerful standing by itself. But to put all of them together will make you unstoppable. You can use them in everything that you do. Make it a point to glance over them at least once a week and put them into practice. You can get a copy of all of them on one page at www.TheTenYearCareer.com. Utilizing these qualities daily, you will be amazed at how much more you will accomplish and the speed with which you will accomplish your goals.

"It is time for us to stand and cheer for the doer, the achiever, the one who recognizes the challenge and does something about it."

—*Vince Lombardi*

## CHAPTER 8

# TEN CRITICAL CONCEPTS YOU MUST MASTER

Aside from embodying the ten qualities in the last chapter, there are ten concepts you need to master to help you reach the highest levels of success, wealth, and fulfillment. As you study this chapter, keep in mind that many of these concepts can be used in all aspects of your life and not just professional areas. Each one of these has helped me in one way or another and helped me to succeed for years.

## Concept 1: Resolve to Step Out of Your Comfort Zone Daily.

You must make the commitment to push yourself out of your comfort zone daily. You cannot let yourself become complacent in any way. The moment your start to feel "comfortable" is the moment you should get worried, because it is when you stop pushing yourself that your growth, and thus your success and wealth, will become stagnant or, worse, go away.

There are many examples of people who stopped stepping out of their comfort zone, got complacent, and as such lost ground and sometimes much more. A perfect example as of late is Starbucks. It shows what happens when you stop stepping out of your comfort zone, realize it, and then start stepping out again.

For many years, the company's growth rate was incredibly successful. But if you looked at the stock of Starbucks over the last few years, you would notice that about two to three years ago, it had gone way down. In fact, in those years, Starbucks chose to close over six hundred stores.

Now, as with all stocks, there are fluctuations, but I find it particularly interesting that Starbucks's stock started to have trouble after the founder, Howard Schultz, stepped down as CEO. So what happened? Well, as you are probably guessing, for many years, Schultz was the driver, the inspiration. He challenged all those around him to step out of their comfort zone every day. In fact, the story of how Starbucks came to be, written by Schultz and called *Pour Your Heart Into It*, is one of just that: constantly pushing the limits of what was thought possible. The title alone gives his attitude away.

Whether it was raising money for expansion or trying things like iced coffee, Schultz was there to push his people to make it go further faster. I suspect that when he stepped down, some of that constant challenge to go further, outside the boundaries, was lost.

And that is the thing: it only takes a little bit of complacency or being comfortable to drastically change a situation. Because of the issues, recently Shultz has come back to run the company. Already, with small changes, like their new VIA product, their stock is reaching new heights. In fact, Schultz recently wrote a new book called, *Onward, How Starbucks Fought for its Life Without Losing its Soul.* Watch the company over the next few years, as it most likely continue to regain it swagger and continue to impress.

*Winning is all about being just a little bit better.* There is a video produced by Simple Truths (www.simpletruths.com) called *212.* The premise of the video is very interesting. It illustrates the fact that at 211 degrees, water is still water, but at 212 degrees, water becomes steam.

Why is this important? Because in your life you will find that to get ahead and become more successful, reach your next levels, or acquire more wealth, you do not need to be head and shoulders above your competition—you just need to be a tiny bit better. Often, it is called "winning in the margins." It is a large component in pushing yourself to new heights.

Think about it: how many things are won or lost just by a tiny, tiny margin?

Olympic races are won or lost by just a fraction of a second. Major business deals are done by people who brought one more little thing to the table that their competition did not. Sometimes sales are made simply because the salesperson got there first. Valedictorians can win by just a fraction of a GPA point. Some of the best real estate deals that I have done were because I was there twenty minutes before someone else and was prepared to go out of my comfort zone to lock it up. I am sure in your life you can think of an instance where being just a little bit better helped you.

Resolve to step out of your comfort zone daily. It is a must to keeping yourself on the path to higher levels. Whether it is a promotion you seek, a business deal that is just out of reach, or getting better grades, stepping out of your comfort zone makes you have to think and find a way. Here is a suggestion:

*Put a reminder in your calendar or phone, tablet, or PDA to go off every morning at 10:00 a.m. Put in this question, "Am I stepping out of my comfort zone today? Am I acting to elevate my success level?" It will remind you every day to go a little further, do a little bit more, and risk where you may not have before. Take some risks, look for ways to win in the margins, and get out of your comfort zone today!*

## Concept 2: See Yourself as the Owner.

See yourself as the owner. In order to get ahead and reach your desired levels of success, wealth, and fulfillment, you must take ownership of your life, your actions, and your results.

You may be saying, "I do that already."

Do you? If you have a job, do you see it as a job? When people talk to you about your "job," do they come away thinking that you own the company? Students, do you look at school as something you need to do to get a job or are you so passionate about learning and getting the knowledge to take you ahead that people think you are already in your chosen field?

For most people, this is not the case. As the example showed in the beginning of this book, most people just go to work, put their time in, go home, and dream about having a better life. Many people sit around waiting for something to happen for them.

Not us! As you have learned thus far, we take those dreams, put a plan around them, prepare for them, accelerate the rate in which we get to them, and make them a reality. You must have control of your life, taking ownership of it and where it is going.

I am reminded of a great quote: "You never work for someone else. Someone else might sign your check, but you are the one that fills in the amount!"

Flipping the switch from just "being there and doing" to "being the owner and doing" will do many things for you.

Most importantly, it will give you more pride and ownership in what you pursue and help you to hold yourself accountable to getting there. Secondly, it will help you to elevate your thinking and creativity. The reason that this is so important is that if you do not take ownership of something, then your vested interest to put time, effort, and thought into it is low. If you take ownership, then it causes you to think of all the ways possible to make whatever you desire better and get it to the next level—and beyond. Not taking ownership is debilitating to thinking and using your mind. This kills ingenuity, passion, and drive—three important qualities and ingredients in attaining your desires.

A great example of taking ownership is the pride people take in their country. In the United States, almost everybody has tremendous pride and will let people know how great our country is if challenged on it. It is as if most people act as though they "own their country." We all can relate to that, but if someone says something bad about the company you work for, do you challenge back or just let it go? Or if you are a student, do you take pride in your area of discipline or your school? It is easy to flip the switch and accelerate your success by thinking like the owner. Remember: elevate your thinking and creativity. Take ownership.

**Concept 3: Ask for What You Want.**

As we have talked about, most people do not get what they want because they do not know what they want. They don't have goals or a plan. I want to take that a step further and say that even those who have concrete goals and a plan many times still do not get what they want unless they *ask* for what they want. Everyone has heard the phrase, "Ask and you shall receive." But very few actually do it.

It is amazing, because many times we want to; it is right on the tip of our tongue, but we shy away or are scared to ask. That is one of the reasons I advocate learning to sell—because it will force you to step out of your comfort zone and ask for what you want, the sale.

It gets easier and easier as you do it too. Some of my greatest deals and successes have come from just asking for them. I once saw a way to help a company I was working for, and thought, "If I tell them about this and take on the responsibility of making sure it works, I should get a raise—a significant one." About that time, the little voice in my head said, "You can't do that. There is no way you will get that much, and you may make the vice president think you are ungrateful for what you currently make, thus giving them a bad impression of you." Well, I didn't listen to the little voice. I put a proposal together and stood firm in asking for a $15,000–a-year raise.

I bet you can guess what happened next. I didn't get the $15,000 raise, but I did get $10,000, and in doing what I proposed and making it work, I opened up doors for advancement that I never thought possible.

You have to ask for what you want. It works with anything. If it is on the tip of your tongue and it is appropriate, ask for it. What I mean is that if you are going shopping for a new car and you walk in and ask for it for free, chances are you probably won't get it. But if you are thinking to yourself, "I would buy it if I got it for $4000 less," then tell them. Ask them to take the money off and use the negotiating skills from earlier in this book to get it.

Remember the phrase you have heard since you were a little kid: "Ask and you shall receive."

## Concept 4: Constantly Practice Building Relationships with People.

Working with others is a skill that you must get good at. It is essential to helping you build the relationships of a ten-year career path that will get you to your goals and success levels. You must treat people right and understand what makes them tick so as to help them and you in your relationships and dealings.

There is one source for getting all the advice you need on working with people. It was written over eighty years ago and still remains the source for this skill. It is a book called *How to Win Friends and Influence People* by Dale Carnegie. What makes this book so special is not just that it is a sort of bible for working with others, but the stories it contains illustrate how to use the book's principles. The pages seem to come alive as you read it, so the lessons stay etched in your mind.

I am going to take two of the lessons and speak to them here, but you *must* get the book and read it yourself.

The first lesson is a very simple one and the one we forget the most: Don't ever criticize, condemn, or complain about others. This is important because it deals with the subconscious mind of others, most importantly the ego. Let me ask you, have you ever been criticized by someone or yelled at? How do you feel afterward? Chances are you do not feel good, even if you were wrong. The reason is that we hate to be told that we have flaws; our ego has trouble taking it. The worst part is that when something like that happens to us, it can ruin our whole day, week, and so on. Not to mention that sometimes, for a little while, we keep repeating it in our head and bringing it up over and over again. It is not healthy and definitely can knock us off track for a little while.

Well, if that is how we feel when these things happen to us, how do you think others feel when we do it to them? The same way, of course.

Now, even though it made us feel good to criticize and get it off our chest, it still is not going to get the person to do what you want them to do or the results you desire. In fact, it will probably hurt your relationship. So the fact of the matter is, do not criticize, condemn, or complain about someone, because it will get you nowhere. Look for ways to praise people when they do well and work with them to help them when they have done wrong. This may be in relationships with your significant other, teammates on your team, or your employees or peers. Criticizing will not help get you closer to your goal.

There is a great story that has been told over time about an employer who sent a salesman to handle a huge $750,000 deal. The salesman botched the deal, lost it, and was pretty sure he would get fired. When the salesman got back to the office, ready for the worst, he went into the boss's office. The boss simply went through the deal with him talking about what they could have done to make it work, and much to the salesman's surprise, he did not get fired. In fact, the salesman said, "I am surprised at your reaction. I thought that I would be fired for sure!" The boss just chuckled and said, "Fired! Why would I do that? I just spent $750,000 training you and know that you won't make these mistakes again!" With that, the salesman smiled and said, "You're right," and went on to become one of the best salespeople in the company.

Now, I tell the story to illustrate the point that if the boss had not fired him, but instead criticized him, yelled at him, or threatened him, he probably would have left the office and immediately started looking for another place to work on his own; but because the boss treated him with care and respect and did not criticize, the salesman ended up one of the company's greatest assets.

The second lesson from Dale Carnegie is simply just to smile. Smile when dealing with people, talking about them, or on the phone to them. It will show through in all ways and almost always elicit a warm and receptive smile from those you are smiling at! You have heard that a smile can be worth a million dollars, and it is true. Your first impression on someone can mean a lot. In fact, Dale Carnegie says it best: "Actions speak louder than words, and a smile says, I like you. You make me happy. I am glad to see you." Sometimes that is all it takes. Besides, smiling makes *us* feel good as well. So when dealing with others, be happy to see them, smile at them when you are asking for the deal, smile when you are complimenting them, and most importantly, smile to show that you care.

Use these techniques and read *How to Win Friends and Influence People* to practice building better relationships with people and increase your speed down your ten-year career path.

**Concept 5: Remember the Self-Fulfilling Prophecy.**

The self-fulfilling prophecy states that what you believe to be true becomes your reality. Or as T. Harv Eker states in his book *Secrets of the Millionaire Mind*, "The Universal Law is that what you focus on, expands in your life."

This goes straight to your attitude. If you have a bad attitude or one that is not set on getting you to your goals, desires, or success levels, you will not get there. If you believe that you cannot reach your goals, desires, or success levels, you cannot get there. It is the essence of mind over matter.

In order to get where you want to go, you must believe in yourself and your ability to reach that level. Most importantly, *you must believe in the level.*

This simple lesson is what separates countless people in our world today from those who are successful. Many of the successes whom we see or whom we have read about in this book have reached their levels because they have followed a lot of the lessons discussed in this book, but most importantly they believed in themselves and their ability to use those lessons, reach their desired levels, and keep going past them.

You must believe in yourself, your mission, your goals, your abilities, and your plan. Much of this book has been devoted to giving you the skills, principles, qualities, traits, and actions needed to get you to your desired success, wealth, and fulfillment.

*While many of these things can be measured and held accountable by yourself and others working with you, believing in yourself cannot. You, and only you, know if you are doubting, and thus, cheating yourself.*

Hold yourself accountable to believing in all that you are and that you do every day. Remember: "What you focus on expands in your life."

## Concept 6: Stop Trying and Start Doing.

In order to get where you want to go, you must take action and you must *do* what is necessary to get you there. Thus far, we have covered specifically some of the things you must do to get on or move yourself further on your ten-year career path.

One other task you must commit to *do* is to eliminate the word *try* from your vocabulary.

If you think about it, we don't really "try" anything—we either do it or we don't. For example, if I told you to try to drive a car, what would you do? Would you get in, start it up, and get on the road? Well, that is great, but remember, I did not tell you to drive the car—I told you to try to drive the car. I did not actually tell you to drive it.

While this example is a little over-exaggerated, it makes the point. You cannot "try" to drive the car—you will either drive it or you won't.

Resolve to eliminate the word *try* from your vocabulary and start *doing*.

## Concept 7: Learn the Power of Leverage.

The topic of leverage is fascinating. I could probably write a whole book on it and the impact learning how to use it has had on my life.

To me, leverage means to do more with less.

What are some ways that we leverage? We leverage others' efforts to get things done. We leverage our money by having it work for us to generate more returns, more money. We leverage our minds by learning how to get better at things so we can do them faster and more efficiently. Much of this book's purpose is to give you leverage on getting onto a ten-year career path and moving rapidly faster on it. The book itself is actually a form of leverage. Instead of coming and speaking to you in person and telling you all that is in this book, I can write it once, and then it remains for you and all to see and refer back to.

Leverage is the secret of most successful businesses. They build systems that leverage people's efforts, technology, marketplaces, and so on. A real business with great systems that deliver leverage can perpetually keep growing or prosper, even if the founder is not there. Take Microsoft for instance. Bill Gates can leave, travel the world, help millions of people in poverty, and return a year later, and Microsoft is just moving along more profitable than when he left.

I use these examples to illustrate a bigger picture of leverage, a vision of some sorts, showing you how many ways that you can possibly use leverage. Your success and wealth will grow much faster if you learn to use leverage to your advantage. You can use the lessons you learn in this book to leverage knowledge to get to the next level. Leverage is a compilation of everything we have learned so far, working together.

The Internet is a wonderful example of leverage that you can use today for wealth. There are so many ways to make money on the Internet, it is truly amazing. You can sell stuff on EBay and have access to millions of customers, right now. Talk about leverage! Can you imagine if you had to go find them all on your own? Google has done the same things for search and selling things. In fact, the best part about the Internet is that, with a good idea and a few hundred or a few thousand bucks, you can access the world and possibly make as much as you do working in a job from your home today!

When I buy a rental property and receive rents, it gives me leverage because I do not have to be present to earn the money.

Smart stock and options investors are masters at using leverage to control stock positions and create exponential returns.

Ultimately, leverage gives you control over your time and freedom. Use the basic principle of leverage: doing more with less. Look for it in all aspects of your life, and put it to work as much as possible!

**Concept 8: Words Are Powerful.**

Words are powerful. Did you know that the more words you master and have control over has a direct correlation to how intelligent you are? More importantly, for those on a ten-year career path, a whole different vocabulary exists.

It is very important for you to learn this vocabulary. Words such as *ROI*, *cap rate*, *triple net*, and *rate of return* are all part of real estate vocabulary. Words such as *back month*, *expansion/contraction*, *bull/bear market*, *technical/fundamental analysis*, and *call*, *put*, *spread*, *straddle*, and *collar* are all part of stock market investing vocabulary. Every area of the ten-year career path will have a different set of words and vocabulary.

Learning the words of the path of wealth you aspire to is critical to your success. You can learn them from seeking out people who are doing what you aspire to do and shadowing them, or reading, listening to, and seeking out information that pertains to the specific subject. What is important is that you realize you need to learn the vocabulary of the ten-year career path and that your learning in this area will never stop. There is always something new or changing!

Another very important concept about words is that *the words you use transform you into who you are.* This can be confusing, so really pay attention to this:

*The words you choose to use every day can help to make you either poor or wealthy.*

The poor and the wealthy have totally different vocabularies. Along with believing in yourself and where you will go, your words and what you say must support the mission. If you want to be wealthy but are using phrases such as "I can't" or "I won't," you will never get there. Instead, why not say, "How can I …?" or "I will learn what I need to so I can …"

If your daily vocabulary is filled with statements and words that are the exact opposite of where you want to go, it will hold you back without you even knowing. It goes back to our subconscious mind and how it has been "trained" to think a certain way. The only way to change it is to be aware and catch ourselves when using words, statements, or phrases that are debilitating to our goals.

I call it "developing your inner coach." Your inner coach is the little voice in your head that, now that you are *aware*, recognizes a thought, words, statements, or phrases that are opposite of your mission and makes you think, "Wait a second—I don't want to think that" or "This will not help me get where I want to go. I will not accept it."

At the same time, the words you *write* are extremely important as well. As we have said, our mind is very powerful and has been "trained" to act a certain way, so we have to find ways to undo some of the training that is debilitating. One of the ways to do that is by paying careful attention to what we write down, especially on things like our to-do list. For example, if you are in sales and you have an appointment on your to-do list for the day, do not just write, "Appointment with XYZ Company." Instead, you should write, "Sell and gain the business of XYZ Company today."

Why the difference? Well, the reason is twofold. First, when you look at the previous statement, what are you saying to yourself? You are saying that you "will sell the client." Contrast that with the first statement: "Appointment with XYZ Company." There is a big difference between "selling and gaining business" and "just an appointment." By doing this, you are conditioning your mind to "*do* the act of selling" and not "just meet with someone." This is very helpful to retrain your subconscious toward the results that you desire. Second, if you put this on your to-do list and are looking at it throughout the day before the meeting, you keep repeating to yourself every time you look at it, "Sell and gain the business of the client, Sell and gain the business of the client." By the time you get to the appointment, your subconscious and conscious mind will believe that you will sell it, and you will.

Over the next week, really be conscious of the words you use. Take inventory of all the words, statements, or phrases you use that are debilitating to your goals. Write them down. At the same time, when your inner coach starts to recognize these words, statements, or phrases, think of new ones to replace them and write those down. Lastly, pay attention to how you write things down for yourself and do the same as above. This exercise will change your life.

## Concept 9: Build Your Network.

You have heard before that it is "not what you know, but who you know." In some respects, this is correct. If you seek out and find the right people to help you get to your desired levels, you will get there much faster. Many times, in order to "get in" with those people, the *information* you must know is critical. So I would say the statement is half right. You must have the right knowledge and information to find and gain the trust of the people who can help you on your ten-year career path.

That is why the skill of networking is so important to learn. *Notice I say that it is a skill.* You will need much of what we have discussed in this book and this chapter (people skills, stepping out of your comfort zone, leverage, the right words, asking for what you want, etc.) to find and network with people at higher levels. Believe it or not, it is much easier than people think.

If there is someone whom you would like to meet with, you can be introduced through people you have met who know them, or you can simply call them and *ask* to take them to lunch to learn more about them. People love to talk about themselves and their interests, hobbies, talents, and so on. You can use the power of leverage to meet like-minded people through the Internet on sites like LinkedIn or even Facebook. You can join entrepreneurial networking groups in your area, such as a Young Professionals group or Toastmasters. Toastmasters is a great organization if you are shy and need help with speaking in public. There are also networking organizations in all parts of the world that exist to help people make the right connections and do business. Some of these require fees to join, but many times they are minimal for the results that you get. One such organization—BNI, Business Network International—is all over the world.

Whatever your interest, there is an organization to help you either close by or probably in your community. In fact, many college campuses now have "sales fraternities," where members are solely those interested in professional sales. It is a great way to get the information you would like to learn to sell.

The point is that there are groups for whatever you desire—real estate investing, stock investing, and so on, right in your back yard. All you have to do is look.

I personally love to network and meet other like-minded people. For that reason, in the past, I have actually started my own networking groups for different topics that I am interested in. The best part is that if you create your own local group for whatever you aspire to, you can start with a few friends, ask them to bring people they know, and soon the group grows and you begin to meet people who can help you on your journey. Everyone knows others whom you do not. Why not tap into their networks?

Start today on developing your network. Write down all of the people whom you know that can help you on your journey. Take them to lunch and find out who they know; ask them to be a part of a local networking group and bring some friends. Lastly, think of ways that you can help them. It may be as simple as sharing this book or a skill you have mastered!

## Concept 10: Get an Exercise Plan and Stick to It.

Yes, that is right. If you want to have a ten-year career, you have to stay in good shape. You have to have high energy and be physically fit because it is hard work and will take its toll otherwise.

Just as we are exercising your mind with this book, you need to keep physically fit as well. You don't have to be a bodybuilder or workout fanatic, but you do need to take care of yourself. This includes eating right, getting enough sleep, and other healthy habits. The challenges on the road to great wealth, success, and fulfillment are immense, and as stated throughout the previous chapters, you have to always operate at optimum levels.

This means having a consistent workout and sleep routine, taking vitamins, and taking general good care of yourself.

Studies have shown that when you are physically fit and well rested, it can help your mind work better, give you more energy, and help you get more accomplished. I have personally been in a consistent workout routine, day in and day out, for over fifteen years. I almost never miss a workout and can say from experience that it helps to keep me fresh and at optimum levels every day.

Now, as we learned earlier in this chapter, leverage is very important. And since I am not a certified workout expert, I have *leveraged* my network and asked my good friend and nationally recognized trainer Brian Schiff to come up with a simple weekly workout that just about anyone can do, so that you can start getting in a routine. He describes it below:

### Brian Schiff's Thirty-Minute Express Home Workout

This simple exercise routine is designed for the person on the go who wants a full body workout that requires little to no equipment and can be done on the road as well. Performing this routine two to three times per week will build strength and lean muscle and keep you fit all at the same time.

*Warm-up*
- Jog in place x 60
- Squats x 30
- Jumping jacks x 30
- Arm circles forward and backward x 30
- Trunk rotation back and& forth x 30
- Arm punches forward to rowing motion x 30
- Side-to-side weight shift (straddle lunge) x 30
- Trunk side bending back and forth with arms overhead x 30
- Alternate leg-forward lunges x 30

*Circuit A*
- Push-ups x 30
- Tubing rows x 30
- Plank x 30
- Speed skater x 30

*Circuit B*
- Squat to overhead tubing shoulder press x 30
- Tubing curls x 30
- Tubing overhead press x 30
- Mountain climber x 30

*Circuit C*
- Tubing upright row x 30
- Lunges or lunge walk x 30
- Superman or swimmer x 30
- Squat jumps or jog in place x 30

*Notes:* Perform two to three cycles of each exercise in circuit A without rest. Rest one to two minutes and then perform circuits B and C in the same way. You can increase time, resistance, or the number of cycles to raise the level of difficulty. The entire workout (including warm-up) should be completed in less than thirty minutes. For more information or clarification on exercises, contact Brian Schiff at www. BrianSchiff.com.

The concepts presented in this chapter are what I have consistently seen as the most successful in all different areas or fields of practice. I think you can see, after reading them yourself, how important they can be in helping you in your ten-year career path. To start implementing them in your life, I would suggest not doing all of them at one time; just pick one, implement it for a few weeks, and then go to the next one and so on.

Remember, success is a journey and process over time. You do not have to do everything all at once. It took me almost six years to make everything in this book part of my life. It will take you time as well. Always remember that "Rome was not built in a day" and that it will take hard work and repetition of the concepts in this book to make them part of your life.

The best part is that once they are part of you, it is easy to keep them, remember them, and put them to use. *As world-famous Chicago Bears running back Walter Payton said, "It is much easier to stay in shape than to get in shape!"* You will put some hard work in with the teachings in this book to get in ten-year career shape, but once you have done it, it is so easy to keep it going and expanding. Our next chapter will help you to grow and expand even more.

"Formal education will make you a living; self-education will make you a fortune."

—*Jim Rohn*

CHAPTER 9

# BECOME A LIFELONG LEARNER

As you have seen, most of what you have learned in this book is not what you get taught in the formal schooling system. School teaches you the basics; school prepares you to have a very broad academic base of knowledge. The subjects in this book are taken from another system—that of the business, investing, and wealth worlds. This book is self-education, and the techniques will make you wealthy in many of the different areas of your life.

The most important thing that you can take from this book is not that its lessons will get you on a faster path to success, wealth, and fulfillment, but that you must continue learning, growing, and self-educating. This book only touches the surface of all that is out there for you.

So, how do you keep educating yourself? Well, there are many ways. You can read more books, go to seminars, seek out mentors, listen to audios, and always be on the lookout for new and interesting methods to study.

Since this book advocates self-education so much, I felt it pertinent to help you get started in your self-education journey. As the quote from Jim Rohn says at the beginning of the chapter, "Formal education will make you a living; self-education will make you a fortune!"

Self-education will make you more intelligent, more savvy and better prepared, help you develop and hone your skill sets, and give you a tremendous amount of other benefits.

To help you, I have taken the time to compile a list of the top books and audios in each of the major topics in this book and more to give you a starting point to grow your knowledge further. I have read each one and painstakingly dissected it, putting many of the principles to the test. The following titles are must-reads on your ten-year career path.

## Helping You to Get Your Plan and Your Map

*Rich Dad, Poor Dad* by Robert Kiyosaki. *Rich Dad, Poor Dad* is one of the most widely recognized financial books of all time. I believe that it is more than that. This book will fundamentally change the way you think about your success and wealth path and give you some insight on how to change your thoughts.

*Good To Great* by Jim Collins. While much of this book is centered on companies and not individuals, *Good to Great* can give you insight into becoming more successful. It is a five-year study of companies that made the leap from being good companies to being great companies. If you think of your ten-year career path as *you* being your own company, much of the information can be translated into helping you develop a better plan to help you reach even higher levels!

*Lead the Field* by Earl Nightingale. *Lead the Field* is a great audio pulling together many concepts to help you create your plan and put you on the path to success. Earl takes years of experience and working with successful people from all different backgrounds, all over the world, and gives you some great insight into how they got to their levels. Pay close attention to the "Acres of Diamonds" section. You never know what you have right under your nose!

*The Leadership Secrets of Colin Powell* by Oren Harrari. Why is this book in the section on helping you to get your plan and map? Because great leadership skills make it easier to develop and execute a great plan. This book is what I consider one of the best leadership books, focusing not only on how to lead and develop yourself, but how to do it with others and through all situations.

*The 21 Irrefutable Laws of Leadership* by John C. Maxwell. I consider this the top book to have in your library for leadership. The twenty-one laws are relevant to every aspect of your life, and the book itself is designed for you to take each lesson in a small chunk and then put it to work. I refer to this book often in leading my own companies.

## Harnessing the Power of Your Mind

*Think and Grow Rich* by Napoleon Hill. This book is the mind-set bible. It will teach how to think properly to get you to your highest levels of success and wealth. It should be the first book you read after this book.

*Secrets of the Millionaire Mind* by T. Harv Eker. This book changed my life because it opened my eyes to the fact that I have a choice in my path and that I can change it at any time to get me where I want to go. This book will show why and how you have come to think the way you do and then teach you how you can change it (if you want) to move you further down the road to success and wealth.

*The Power of Positive Thinking* by Norman Vincent Peale. A classic literary work, this book has changed the lives of millions and is the book Zig Ziglar credits with getting him on his path. This book will make you mentally stronger.

## Goal Setting

*Goals: Setting Them and Achieving Them on Schedule* by Zig Ziglar. As I stated earlier, I am a big fan of Zig's goal-setting program. It is simple, thorough, and easy to implement. Zig also has an audio with him and another speaker, Krish Dunham, that is excellent for setting goals as well.

*Mentored by a Millionaire, The Master Strategies of the Rich* by Steven K. Scott. I found this audio set while looking over Nightingale-Conant's audio library one day, and something told me to get it. This audio set gives one of the best programs for setting, as Steve calls them shoot-for-the-moon goals and takes you through the steps to achieve them. It covers much more, but the goal-setting exercise is fantastic.

*Goals: How to Get Everything You Want—Faster Than You Thought Possible* by Brian Tracy. This book is one of the most complete goal-setting books I have ever read. Brian Tracy has probably forgotten more about how to become successful than you or I could ever learn! He truly is amazing, and this book will help you to become successful in any way you choose.

## Becoming Financially Smart and Investing

*Cashflow Quadrant* by Robert Kiyosaki. I am a big fan of Robert because he takes complex subjects and makes them very easy to understand. In *Cashflow Quadrant*, he takes the complex subjects of money, taxes, and the rules of the business world, and not only makes them easy to understand, but helps to show you how you can use the rules to your advantage. As with *Rich Dad, Poor Dad*, this book will change the way you think about money and your success.

*Automatic Millionaire* by David Bach. I like this book because it gives a concrete plan for helping people to not only get out of debt, but save money and reach a budget surplus in their lives, and shows you how, on just a small amount of money, you can become a millionaire. This book is to complement you on getting your base with which to aggressively expand your means to your desired level.

*Rule #1* by Phil Town. Here's a question: "Do you think if you sat down with Warren Buffet (the world's wealthiest investor) for a day, you would learn some pretty valuable insight on investing?" Of course you would. Well, *Rule #1* takes it a step further. Phil Town shows how even the beginning investor can follow the process of value investing similar to Warren Buffet and get results. This is a must-read and the foundation for all of those who have an interest in investing in the stock market. The process is simple and easy to learn, and when done right, will get you great results.

*The Intelligent Investor* by Ben Graham. Benjamin Graham, mentor to Warren Buffet and some of the greatest investors of all time, wrote this book in 1949. It still remains today arguably the most-respected guide to investing. This book is where we first learned to buy a dollar for fifty cents and the other processes to become successful investors. *Rule #1* goes hand in hand with this book.

*Mastering the Trade* by John Carder. I was introduced to this book through a mentor of mine on trading credit spreads, a more-sophisticated option trade. This book is for those who aspire to be professional traders and should be worked up to. The concepts demand an established investing vocabulary and intense study.

## Time Management

*The 4 Hour Workweek* by Tim Ferris. This book changed my life because it opened my eyes even more to the world around us, taking the concepts of time management and leverage to a whole new level. Even though I have been successful at doing business on the Internet, it showed me that I had not even scratched the surface. Use this book's advice for managing your time, and you really do not need anything else besides the techniques I have taught you!

*Eat That Frog: 21 Great Ways to Stop Procrastinating and Get More Done in Less Time* by Brian Tracy. Brian does a great job in this book of expanding on some of the time management techniques that we discussed in our chapter. His simple concept of "eat that frog" is powerful and will expand your ability to get more done in less time. This book will help you become much more productive.

## Sales and Salesmanship

*The Accidental Salesperson* by Chris Lytle. While part of this book is about learning to sell, I realize that many of you do not have the word *sales* in your career path, but still realize that you need to understand selling. This book is for you. In his aptly titled book, Chris takes you on the journey from being thrown into sales to becoming a professional salesperson. I have had the opportunity to meet Chris and hear him speak about his book, and I must say that it is one of those gems of a book that only comes around every so often. It has changed many people's lives and increased their income. If you want a great foundation on sales and salesmanship, read this book first!

*The Art of Closing the Sale* by Brian Tracy. Brian is arguably the most renowned and most widely studied and read sales trainer in the world. He has been impacting sales careers and teaching people the secrets of successful salespeople for decades. This book is no exception, giving you the specific tools and tricks of the trade to be successful in sales.

*The Ten Keys to Negotiating and How to Handle Objections* by S. G. Lewis. S.G. is a friend and business partner, as well as one of the most respected sales minds that I know. As stated earlier in this book, his negotiating training is the finest I have ever seen, and his objection-handling training is even more on point. S.G.s insight and keys will not only help you to get more of what you want, but help you to make more money and expand your income. Visit our site, www. TheTenYearCareer.com, to learn more.

## Traits of Success

*Talent Is Never Enough* by John C. Maxwell. This book gives a fantastic and enlightening account of why talent alone will not get you success. John goes through numerous traits and cites some wonderful examples as to why you must have "a little bit more" than just talent.

*Winners Never Cheat* by John Huntsman. I know that I mentioned John earlier, but his book *Winners Never Cheat* is one of the greatest on being true to your values and not compromising in the face of pressure and the society we live in. In short, it will give you all you need to make sure you are doing things the right way, with integrity and honesty.

*How to Win Friends and Influence People* by Dale Carnegie. The first of its kind and still the best, this book should be read four times per year. Each and every quarter you should pull this out and read it. It will help you to deal with all people and situations, and most importantly, help make you a better person in all areas of your life. We have already talked briefly about some of the examples from this book, but all of its teachings put together will really help you make a difference.

## Internet Strategies and Ideas

*Crush It* by Gary Vaynerchuk. Have you ever heard about the guy or girl who started a blog and within just a short time was making more than they ever have in their lives, or even millions? Well, Gary is that guy! This book is a treasure. It tells the story of how Gary went from nothing to making millions, all with just a blog. The best part is that he tells you step-by-step how he did it and how you can too. It is quick, concise, and easy to understand.

*The Millionaire Messenger* by Brendon Burchard. Within days of being released, this book was a best seller. How did Brendon do it? Well, that is what the book is about. It gives you a ten-step plan for making an impact and an income with what you know. It shows you how the lessons you've learned in life and business can become your greatest asset and your greatest legacy.

## Books That Will Change the Way You Think and Your Perspective

*The Tipping Point* by Malcolm Gladwell. This book is one of the most fascinating books I have read in recent times. Why do certain things like *Sesame Street* become such huge successes? How do things travel so far by word of mouth? What is a connector or a maven, and how can they help you?

Many such questions are answered in this book, showing you new insight into the world around you.

*Pour Your Heart Into It* by Howard Schultz. This book is one of the best stories I have ever read about what it requires to take a company from an idea to reality. This story shows how, if you are committed to your goals and do not stop, you will reach them. It is almost four hundred pages long, and I read it in about a day. If you want to build your own company, this book is a cornerstone for your library!

*Blink* by Malcolm Gladwell. If you are noticing a trend, Malcolm Gladwell seems to write books that are very much outside the box. *Blink* is no exception. I love the book because it goes over our intuition and our sixth sense, hammering home how we are usually right when listening to our instincts! It shows us that the best decision makers are not necessarily those who process the most information or spend the most time thinking, but those who can filter the factors that matter most from all of the information and act accordingly.

*The Breakthrough Company* by Keith R. McFarland. How do businesses become "big" businesses? Only one tenth of one percent of businesses are persistent enough to break through to sales above $250 million a year. This book shows that it doesn't take luck to make an everyday company extraordinary. Instead, for a company to make it big, it takes a specific set of skills and strategies that can be used by anyone, from a startup to a major company. These skills can also be used by you in your life and success journey.

**Books on Economic and Business History Relevant for These Times**

It may seem odd to put some books about economics and history in a book about success, wealth, and fulfillment, but it is very true that history has a tendency to repeat itself. The more prepared you are to see the changes coming; the better and faster you can react and take advantage, especially in economic times such as those we are experiencing now. Remember, information is the new currency, and those who have the information and use it the fastest are the winners.

*The Forgotten Man* by Amity Shlaes. I like this book because it is an objective, thorough assessment of the history of the Great Depression. The attention to detail and research that went into this book is incredible. This book is very important, as it gives insight into what works and does not work during an economic downturn and gives you a chance to compare the things being done in our current economic situation to what was done in the Depression. You must read this book at this time!

*The Creature from Jeckyl Island* by Edward G. Griffin. Did you know that the Federal Reserve is not actually federal at all? Who is in charge of our money, and what decisions are they making behind the scenes? How do we take advantage of their decisions? This book reads like a story and will surprise you about how one of the most important entities in the world came to be and affects our lives. This is not taught in history class!

*The 5000 Year Leap* by W. Cleon Skousen. This is a fascinating book about the founding of the United States and the principles that the founding fathers said must be understood. It will amaze you how smart our founders were and give you insight into why their principles and the United States have brought about more progress in its short existence than was made in the previous five thousand years.

Please note that I have tried to select books in this section that are not politically charged or on one side or the other. I feel it is important for you to have the objective facts and then make up your own mind. That being said, the above books for the most part follow this rule, but do have some connotations toward a side or two. Just be independent and make up your own mind. The books will help you to understand what you can do to profit in our current situation and any situation in the years ahead.

Many other wonderful books and audios exist on just about every topic you can think of, so do not stop at the books and resources above. These are just stepping-stones. As I stated at the beginning of the chapter, you must become a lifelong learner. Some of the smartest and greatest mentors in the world are all around you! Many times you can learn from them for *free* just by going to the library, or for just a few bucks you can get their books or CDs online or at bookstores. One of the best places to go looking is on iTunes. There are many *free* audio downloads from great mentors on great topics at iTunes University, and you can also buy audios from many of the noted authors above.

How do you know which books and audios to pick? You don't, but just do what I do. Many times when I am looking for a new book or audio, I will just go to the bookstore and start scanning the books as I walk through the aisle. Just about every time, one title or subject will grab my interest, and I'll end up picking the book. Many of the books above were found in just that way. Just go to the store; your instincts will put the right book and mentor in your hands.

Keep learning and growing, and you will find, as many others have, that your path will be less than ten years!

"The way to get started is to quit talking and begin doing."

—*Walt Disney*

———

## CHAPTER 10

# TAKE ACTION!

———

Right on, Walt! In order to get started down the ten-year career path, you must take action—now! Do not hesitate or delay. If you have already started doing some of the exercises outlined in this book as you read along, great job—you are already starting down the path! If not, there is never a better time to get started. After reading this and the next chapter, you can go back to the beginning and get started down your ten-year career path to success, wealth, and fulfillment.

*I was once told that "knowledge without action is just information." I believe wholeheartedly in this statement. The one thing that holds people back from reaching their goals or dreams, when they have the right information, is that they do not act.*

Have you ever had a great idea and then seen that idea become a reality somewhere else? We all have in some way, and we always say the same thing: "I had that idea two years ago!" or "I can't believe that somebody stole my idea!" The truth is that he or she may not have thought of it before you; they may have just acted quicker.

It is not enough to just take some action. As many of the authors cited in this book say in some way or another, you must get started now and you must take *massive* action, not just a little action. Furthermore, you need to do this not just today, but every day in your life!

I have met many people who get excited and take action—for a few days. Do not be one of these people! You must take massive action toward your plan, your goals and dreams, harnessing and keeping the right mind-set, becoming financially smart, learning to sell and negotiate, managing your time, and embodying the success traits and everything else we have talked about in this book *every day*! If you do this, you will be flying down the ten-year career path. You will become more successful and have greater wealth and personal fulfillment than you ever could imagine.

If you go to www.TheTenYearCareer.com, I have placed a specific set of action steps for each chapter, along with the materials cited all throughout this book. After reading the next chapter, go back and start on each one of these steps and take *massive* action!

## Time to Step Out of Your Comfort Zone

It is time to step out of your comfort zone. As I have said a few times throughout this book, I am going to give some ideas that you can use to start increasing your success and wealth now. Again, these are just ideas and potential ways to go. You will need to research any area of interest and make sure you know what you are doing to make it work. I have put each idea below and have listed them from easiest to most challenging.

### *Finding Work*

First, if you do not have a source of income, you need to get one. For most people, that is getting a job. You already know this, but what type of job should you get? I suggest looking at the areas that you would like to eventually have your income come from and then find a business in that area to work for so that you can learn how it works. For example, if you want to own a landscaping business, go apply to landscape companies. If you want to own a restaurant, go find the closest one to the type you want to own and work there. If you want to make money in real estate, go get a job with a realtor's office.

Remember, the point is to give you *leverage* in that you are not just making income, but learning valuable skills to help you on your success and wealth path.

You will also want to use whatever opportunity you choose to network yourself.

*Do not get a job just to get a job.*

## <u>Starting a Business</u>

### Starting a Business in Direct Sales

Starting a business is an important decision. You are choosing to go out on your own, create your own success, and play in one of the hardest games in the world. But does it have to be that hard? Do you have to spend a bunch of money getting something off the ground?

The answer is "No." Not in the Information Age. There are literally millions of ways that you can make money with start-up costs less than $500.

One of the easiest ways is to find a system that is already built and plug into it. You still get all of the tax advantages of owning a business, but do not have to do all of the work and spend all of the money to create the system. The best place to look for these businesses is in direct sales or network marketing.

There are many companies in this arena, so you will need to find the ones that interest you, do your research, look at their track records, and speak to some of their current business associates. You will want to see, first, if they feel the company supports them and helps them with their business. Second, with the right amount of work, is the compensation as advertised?

Direct sales and network marketing companies are incredible opportunities for you and your growth. They not only teach you how to run your own business, but are fully invested in your development and your success. They are also excellent places to learn to sell. As with any business, to make money, you will have to work hard, but the system is already there. Also, please pay particular attention to the training programs of any that you are considering. The training and development of the company's business associates should be central to their business philosophy. If it is not, then the company most likely "churns and burns" people, and many of their associates are probably not making a lot of money or they have a high dropout rate—so stay away.

Many famous authors, businesspeople, and investors got their start in businesses like this, including people like Zig Ziglar, Brian Tracy, and many others. During college, I was fortunate to find a direct sales company. I spent the last few years of school learning from some great mentors and working on the fundamentals of selling. I then went into direct sales full-time for my first year after school. The lessons I learned were priceless. Some of the best lessons in this book were learned during that time. I highly recommend starting your first business in this way.

How do you pick a good direct sales or network marketing company, and what is the difference between the two?

First off, the difference is that direct sales really encompasses network marketing, but there are distinct differences. Direct sales is where you sell a product or service directly to a consumer or business. There is no middleman or stores where the product is sold. Only you and other associates like you can supply it. Examples of items sold directly include vacuum cleaners, knives, encyclopedias, wine, food, candles, and just about everything else that you can think of. With a direct sales company, typically, the only way to get paid is when you sell something.

Network marketing, sometimes called multilevel marketing, is different in one particular way. If you remember, one of the most important rules of the ten-year career is finding *leverage* in everything you do. It is no different in direct sales. The difference in network marketing is that you are able to bring other people into the business, teach and train them to be successful, help them get that success, and because of both of your efforts, you get paid as well.

It allows you to gain leverage in that you can build a sales team, just as in any Fortune 500 company, and get paid not only off of your efforts, but off of your team's efforts as well, just as sales managers in Fortune 500 companies do. The secret is that your team will only be as good as you are and the training they get. That is why it is so important to find a company with a good track record and a great training program. You can create a CEO-style income from this type of business.

Please be aware that many people take a negative point of view on direct sales and network marketing, as they are not "traditional" avenues of making income such as a "job" or owning a "brick and mortar" business. Just remember that the Internet has changed the world we live in, and as such, business has changed as well.

Many direct sales companies even give you your own website, so that people can order right online from you. How is that much different from Amazon? Or eBay? It is not.

Many times when people say negative things about these types of businesses, it is because they do not know anything about them or are scared that you will fail in taking one on. First, they cannot advise you if they have never done something themselves. Second, as we have talked about throughout this book, there is nothing wrong with failing! By failing we learn our biggest lessons that help us grow and achieve more. I will tell you that it is much easier to fail in starting your own business from scratch than when you plug into a successful system that has a vested interest in your success.

Some of the greatest companies in the world are direct sales companies, such as Amway, Mary Kay, Pampered Chef, and so on. If you are interested in finding accredited direct sales companies to work with, visit the Direct Selling Association's website at www.dsa.org.

One more extremely important way to leverage a direct sales business is to find a product that is a *residual* product, meaning that customers have a need to keep ordering it over and over again. Why? Well, it is nice to do good work and get paid, but it is even better to do that good work *just one time* and then continue to be paid for it again and again. Examples of products that fit this description are anything that is perishable or comes in a month's supply, such as vitamins, makeup, or wine. I still get checks today for work I did many, many years ago! Now that is leverage.

### *Starting a Business around Your Talent*

Do you have a particular talent or skill that sets you apart? If so, you can start a business around it right out of your home. For example, if you are a dog lover and have studied how to take good care of dogs, why not start a dog-walking service? All you would have to do is make up some flyers about what sets you apart, describe your services, and list your rates. Next, you can either put them at doors in neighborhoods or leave them on the counter at your local pet store. You certainly know a few people with dogs if you are a dog lover, so you can probably get your first few customers there. Presto! You have a business.

Now, why is this after the last section? Seems pretty easy, right? Well, getting the business started is easy, but you now need to be mindful of the legal and accounting worlds. In a direct sales business, all of the legal and major accounting functions are taken care of for you by the company. When you start your own business, you need to take care of this yourself, and it adds a little cost.

For example, using our dog-walking scenario above, you would probably need to contract a lawyer to draft a service agreement for your business to protect you in the case something happens to a dog while under your care. You will probably also want the lawyer to set things up in a business entity that protects you if something goes wrong. You also may need to purchase a form of insurance to protect you as well. Lastly, you will need a good accountant to help you in filing the right tax documents and managing your income for taxes, expenses, and so on.

Now, the above work might seem a little daunting, but I assure you that it is not and can be done in a very short time with a minimal charge—a few hundred bucks or so. There are also many other things to consider, such as if you will have employees, other services to offer, and on and on, but you can start a business around your talent from your kitchen table in just a few weeks and create more income for yourself. Again, it is not that hard; it just takes a little research, meeting with a few professionals, and ultimately *action*.

### Starting a Business on the Internet

Starting a business on the Internet has become my favorite place for income generation. With a little bit of work and study, almost anyone can have an Internet business in something. You can also use your talents on the Internet as well. The best parts about the Internet is the leverage of being able to sell to the whole world, the leverage of extremely low startup costs compared to traditional business, and the leverage of using search sites like Google to put you right in front of someone who is looking for your product. How cool is that?

Depending on what you want to do on the Internet, the startup cost can start at a few hundred dollars and go up from there.

There are a few ways that I have used to make money on the Internet. The first is through affiliate programs. What is an affiliate program? An affiliate program is when you sign on to an existing site to sell their products on your site. For example, if you wanted to create a website of products for animal lovers, you *do not* need to actually make or come up with the products. You could simply find a name that you like for a website, create the look of it, and then go to all of the other product sites that you like and become an "affiliate." You then put all of those products on your site and advertise your site in whichever ways you feel are the best (Google, SEO—search engine optimization, social media, giving out flyers, linking to other websites, networking through friends and family, and so on). Every time someone orders from your site, you do not have to do any work—the affiliate company fills the order, and you get paid a commission on the sales. Many online companies have programs like this, including ClickBank and Amazon.

Another way to make money is through building a website around an idea that you may have. How do you create a product? Well, there are many products that you can come up with and have made, but I believe that that is too much work. The easiest product to sell and manage on the Internet is *information.* The Internet is where information really is currency. If you have a special skill, talent, or interest, you can write an e-book and sell it or create a monthly newsletter and get a residual income monthly—or you could just start a blog about your favorite topic and sell advertising on it. There are so many ways to go—these are just a few examples—but the point is that anyone can have a business on the Internet with just the information he or she already knows. Will you make millions? I don't know. It depends on how good you get at using the ways on the Internet to sell and build a list of clients' e-mails and how good your information is, but you certainly can make money.

You will have some investigating to do on how to get things started and will probably look into buying someone else's *information* from the Internet or bookstore, but the processes are not that hard—you just need to choose the way you like the most. One of the reasons I recommend Brendon Burchard's book *The Millionaire Messenger,* Gary Vaynerchuk's book *Crush It,* and Tim Ferris's book *The 4 Hour Work Week* is because all of them have a concrete, tested process for making money online in different areas. If you are interested in making money in this way, I suggest you pick up these books and look at the Internet resources available at www.TheTenYearCareer.com.

As with the example above on starting a dog-walking business, you will need to consult a legal and accounting professional in starting your business in these areas as well.

I could go on about a bunch of other types of businesses you can start, whether it is a franchise, a service business, or others, but I believe that if the above ideas do not interest you, then you must take the time to find the ideas that do or are unique to you. Use the principles from this book on networking, finding mentors, and stepping out of your comfort zone to help you.

## *Investing in Real Estate*

Okay. This will not be a long section, but it will be important. I am not going to go into all the ways to invest in real estate. The first thing you must do, as I stated earlier, is to get at least two books on the subject that you are interested in in real estate (rental property, commercial, flipping, etc.), read them, and then go take at least one seminar on the subject before you start.

That being said, I will give you a little direction. The type of real estate investing I like to do is what I call "cash flow real estate investing." It is the way most wealthy and successful real estate investors make their money. Cash flow investing is not "flipping," or looking for the "quick buck" or "big payout." It is 1) finding a good, well-kept property in a good location, 2) buying it at a below-average price, and 3) making a steady stream of income off of it for as long as you want to keep it.

The former are my top three rules for real estate investing. What is funny is that if you decide to invest in the stock market as well, the rules are pretty much the same: find a good, well-managed company in a good niche, buy it when it is below its "real value" in the market, and manage it until you have made the income you desire. (We will cover more about the stock market in the next section.) This is essentially what Warren Buffet does and what Phil Town writes about in *Rule #1*. The nice thing is that the rules are simple, and I like things that are simple. Most importantly, they are easy to learn and put into place after practice.

D. M. Lukas

So, if you want to invest in real estate, look for cash flow. It may initially be by buying a duplex and living in one side and renting the other out, having the tenant pay most of the mortgage. Or if you are a student, maybe it is buying a house near campus and renting to your friends; or if you are a parent of a college student, buying a house for your son or daughter to live in while at school and have it paid for by rents from their friends. Who knows? You may continue to rent it after graduation. Areas around colleges or businesses that are always needed, such as electric companies, oil companies, gas companies, other utilities, and such are great because they typically are still employing people in a downturn, and in the case of colleges, you have a constant, self-refreshing marketplace each and every year to pull renters from. This is why location is so important.

What about fixing toilets at 3:00 a.m.? First off, if you have done your research properly, have found a good, well-kept property, and have had it inspected, you rarely have to deal with these issues. Second, even if you did get a call at 3:00 a.m., do you really think that you are going to get up and be the one to fix it? Of course not—you are going to call someone for the problem and have it fixed. No big deal. One thing that I suggest to people just getting started is to *network* and ask around for a good handyman in the area. You can even look at ratings on sites like Angie's List, www.angieslist.com, or at the Better Business Bureau, www.bbb.org. Interview a few handymen or services, and pick the one that is right for you. Many people use the fixing toilets excuse as a way to not have to learn to invest in real estate, because many times they are just too lazy to do it.

Real estate is a fun and exciting investment. It allows you to leverage other people's (a bank's) money. Think about it: you cannot get a $50,000 loan to trade stocks, but you can for a piece of real estate. *It is nice to pay back other people's money with essentially other people's money (your renters')!*

Real estate is one of the top ways that many people use to become extraordinarily wealthy. Investing in it definitely accelerates one's ten-year career path. You must take the time to learn and practice before investing. Robert Kiyosaki made most of his money by investing in cash flow real estate and has authored many books and programs for success in this area. You can learn more at www.richdad.com.

## *Investing in the Stock Market*

Do you remember above when I said that real estate is one of the top ways that people become extraordinarily wealthy? Well, one of the other ways is in the stock market. Many people like the stock market over real estate because they do not "have to own property" or "worry about tenants." Again, if you learn to manage property correctly, neither do you, but they have a point. If you are looking for a way to make money without owning real estate, dealing with employees, or having to go to an office, stock market investing may be for you.

Now, before you get excited and have visions of lying in a hammock on the beach with your laptop in the Caribbean making millions, I will tell you that I have had an opportunity to network with and be mentored by some incredible professional investors. These investors consistently make returns of 50 percent or more on their investments and in many cases more than 100 percent. I will tell you that these people work harder than most people in a job do. Fifteen-hour days are not uncommon for professionals who are really trading and investing.

A lot of study, prep work, risk management, money management, and information is needed to stay at their level. Now, the good news is, yes, they make a lot of money; and for many of them, they enjoy what they do so much that the fifteen hours goes by quickly and they do not even notice.

Professionals are disciplined and know that they are not going to make money on every trade; in fact, they do lose big sometimes, but they also know that they just have to win more times than they lose. Armed with that fact, they are methodical, follow rule sets, and take emotion out of the process (remember how important that is when it comes to money; in market investing, we must think logically).

Let's take a quick look at why traders have to be so disciplined and remain logical and grounded. A professional trader wakes up in the morning with her plan to purchase 1000 shares of XYZ stock at $30.00 per share, because she has done her research and knows that the company is selling below market price, has a good niche, and is well managed. Her goal is to take advantage of the pricing discrepancy in the market. She will be outlaying $30,000. Her rules tell her that she must make sure to put a stop-loss on after the stock has risen 20 percent to preserve some gains and then follow it up from there to the price of $62.00, which is what the trader believes is its actual market value.

A stop-loss is simply putting in an order to sell a stock at a certain price if it falls to that price from a position that is higher. So in this case, putting a stop on after the stock has risen 20 percent would put the order in to sell the stock at $36.00 if the price fell back down from a higher level—not a bad profit ($6000). But how long will it take the stock to reach that level, or even better, go to the $62.00 and double the trader's money? The truth is, we really do not know—the trader has some idea from the research she has done, but she cannot predict it exactly.

So what happens? Well, the stock market opens, and the trader gets the $30,000 in shares. Immediately after that, about five minutes later, the stock price drops $2.00, from $30.00 to $28.00, and the trader is losing $2000 if she sold right now. But wait … about twenty minutes later, the stock is now back up to $31.00 per share, and the trader will have made $1000 if she sold right now. The stock continues to rise—this could be a good day! It's $31.50 per share, $32.00, $33.00—the excitement is building, and it is 3:00 p.m. Only one hour to go before the market closes … But wait: some bad news just came out about the economy that particularly affects the trader's company. Immediately, the stock falls back to $29.00 per share and then to $28.00, and then the market closes. On paper, the trader has lost $2000 that day.

This roller-coaster ride happens every day for traders. How would you have handled it? Would you have panicked and sold when the stock lost $2000 of your money right out of the gate, or would you have had the patience and waited until it got to $33.00 per share, making you $3000? What would you have done when it sank quickly after the news? Do you see why the stock investing world is one for people who are very disciplined and do not let emotion get in their way?

That is why learning to evaluate companies and creating rules is so important. Even when the craziest of things happen, the rules must be followed. That is how people make money in the stock market—they learn through practice, losing money by making bad or emotional decisions, learning from them, and then vowing never to lose that way again (creating rules).

In our case above, what if I told you that the next day, that stock began its run and over the next two weeks, it made it up to $37.00 per share, the investor put her stop-loss on, and then a week later it fell back past $36.00, but the trader's stop-loss sold the stock at $36.00? In just about three weeks, the trader made $6000 off of that one trade. Not bad for three weeks.

The point is that this is being done by people all around the world every day, and on the other side, there are people all around the world losing $6000 every day. You must learn to manage risk and yourself to be a professional investor.

Now, the example above was just that, an example. Everyone has different rules, me included. On a trade that size, depending on my strategy, I might have had a stop-loss on it earlier, or I might have been selling options on it—or I might have been investing because the stock is a great company, well-managed, in a great niche, selling way below its value, has a great dividend, and was at a great price, so I was going to buy it strictly for cash flow and hold it for years.

As with real estate, you must take the time to learn about the specific ways you want to invest. If you have not heard about options before, the type of trades that I do a lot, you will need to go find two books and take a seminar. If you have never heard of a stop-loss, same thing.

Many people ask, "Gee, do I have to be a professional trader? Do I have to be in front of a computer all day watching this stuff?" The simple answer is "No." It depends on what you want to do, what type of market investing you like, and how much time you want to put into your investments. Am I a professional investor? No way! I have a long way to go, even if I decide I want to be one. But I have found a few strategies that I understand that are easy enough for me to do, and I have failed enough to know how to make them work, so I focus there. Those areas are covered calls, selling naked put options, cash flow investing, and most recently credit spreads.

Credit spreads are fascinating. The easiest way to explain them is that every month, you are "insuring" that a trading instrument will stay in a particular range. For example, if the S & P 500 is at 900, I may "sell" a spread, or "insure" that the S & P will stay between 1000 and 800; as long as the market stays in that range for the month, I get paid. This is a very simple explanation. These trades are very complicated and require disciplined rule sets and some advanced training.

Does this mean that you cannot do these? Of course not! I learned the basics from scratch in about a month and practiced for a while after that. The nice part is that once I have placed the trade, managing it only takes about fifteen minutes a day. If the market is staying in the range and not significantly moving one way or the other, there is nothing I need to do.

Notice that I said "sell" the spread above? This may be hard to understand, but I am not using my money on this trade or buying anything. I am selling risk. Someone is willing to pay me up front to take my bet that the market will stay in that range, because he thinks it will go outside that range. He pays me up front, but if I lose, I have to pay him more than he paid me. So you have to know your stuff, or you can and will lose. That is why rules are so important. It is nice that I do not use my money, except if I lose. This is a form of leverage in the market.

If you would like to learn more about this style of trading, you can visit my mentor at www.optionsmd.com. In fact, Doc Severson, my mentor and founder of Options MD, and I have recently collaborated with Todd Mitchell from Trading Concepts Inc. on a program called *Power Stock Trading Strategies*. You can find out more about it on the resources page of this book's website, www.TheTenYearCareer.com.

Also, I recently interviewed Doc about his system and created a *free* video from it. You can get it at www.TheTenYearCareer. com

Okay, so let's pull it all together. The stock market is an incredible place to make money and lose money. You need to study hard, focus on one type of trading style, become successful with that before you move onto the next one, develop a set of rules for each style, and check your emotions at the door. You have to resolve yourself to the fact that you will lose, but you will also win, and you will need to figure out the ways that allow you to win more than lose. You will need to learn how to use different investing vehicles and types of trades and how these different types of trades work, and you will have to look for your best way to leverage them.

The best place to begin are with programs from a company like Trading Concepts (www.tradingconceptsinc.com) and books like *Rule #1* by Phil Town, to get started on your fundamentals.

Lastly—and this is extremely important—*learn by paper trading*. In order to trade, you will need to open an account at a brokerage firm. You can do this online at a company like E-Trade, www.etrade.com, or my favorite, Think or Swim, www.thinkorswim.com.

*Before you start to use* your *money*, "practice" by opening a paper trade account. A paper trade account is simply trading with fake money, like Monopoly, but you can use it to get better at the style you choose before you enter with your own money.

## A Lot of Ways to Make Money and Create Wealth

As you can see, there are a lot of ways to make money and create wealth. Some are more complicated than others. As I stated at the beginning of the chapter, I am just highlighting ideas that I have used to create wealth. What matters is that you open your mind to all of the ways around you to get ahead on your ten-year career path and look for the ways that appeal to you and that interest you. That is most important. Do not work, own a business, or invest just because that is what other people do to get wealthy. Find the one or two things that really interest you and you can be passionate about. Go after them with all you've got. Be prepared to fail and to learn from it, but never quit. If you can follow those rules and what we have learned throughout this book, you will reach every goal that you aspire to, have anything you want to have, and be able to help all those around you to do the same.

*Remember, it all starts with taking action—massive action!*

*It's time for you to act.*

"Life is a gift, and it offers us the privilege, opportunity, and responsibility to give something back by becoming more."

—*Anthony Robbins*

---

## CHAPTER 11

# YOUR FINAL DUTY

---

Up until now, this book has been solely focused on giving you everything *you* need to have a ten-year career and helping *you* to reach your desired level of success, wealth, and fulfillment. It has been focused on giving you the tools, information, and processes you need to get the results you want and desire.

There is, however, one thing that is more important than everything you have read in this book so far: Once you have made it on your ten-year career path and are reaching, achieving, and getting the levels of success, wealth, and fulfillment that you aspire to, you have a duty to give back to the world around you.

If I can impress one thing upon you, it is that this is the most important lesson to take away from this book. It is great to reach your desired level of success, wealth, and fulfillment, but it is for nothing if you do not share with those around you, help them get to their desired levels, and give your talents to the causes where you feel you can help make a difference.

I am always amazed at the examples of giving that exist in our world. I find it amazing that Bill Gates has created a foundation, on which he is very focused nowadays, that is giving billions in aid to people and countries around the world. I find it even more amazing that the richest investor in the world, Warren Buffet, gave the bulk of his wealth, $37 *billion* (that's not a typo!) to the Bill Gates Foundation a few years back! What is amazing is that this is not an uncommon behavior of those who have reached their desired success, wealth, and fulfillment levels. You can find numerous examples throughout history of this type of giving. One that comes to mind is Andrew Carnegie, the early 1900s steel entrepreneur. While many of his charitable works can be seen throughout the country, I find it truly amazing that he made hundreds of millions of dollars throughout his life and at the same time gave away hundreds of millions of dollars. He gave almost exactly what he had made.

I hear a lot of people say, "But I don't have a ton of money; I'm just getting started on *my* ten-year career path. I have had a little success, but I need the money to keep growing it." Of course, I understand this; I have been there. But giving does not necessarily have to be in the form of monetary donations. It can come in many forms. It can be helping someone get on their feet by teaching them some of the principles you have learned from reading this book. It can be donating your time to help the cause that interests you. It can be as simple as taking the time to give attention to someone whom you normally would not, whether it be a child, coworker, old friend, or neighbor.

*What matters most is not* what *you give, but the* act *of giving in some way or some form.*

And you can be shy and still give. You do not have to tell anyone or put your name on things. My wife and I have given to many causes that we feel passionate about, anonymously, as we just want to help the cause.

There is another fact about giving, and it is that the more you give (because you truly and sincerely want to help), the more you will get in return. It is an odd phenomenon, but it happens. It has been called the Law of Reciprocity—that you will get what you want in direct proportion to the amount that you help others get what they want. I cannot explain why this happens—it just does—and I have been very blessed to be on both sides of the law, giving and receiving.

Whatever it is that you do in your ten-year career and whatever level you reach, please do not forget to give back. It is the most important work that you will ever do. It is your duty and your responsibility.

Thank you for reading this book, and I wish you all the best on the journey toward your desired success, wealth, and fulfillment. Remember: Change the way you think, and you can change your whole world. I know you will do great things. Get going, take action, and make it happen!

Sincerely,
D. M. Lukas

# ABOUT THE AUTHOR

Dave M. Lukas is a modern day "Renaissance Man." Recently turned 31, Dave has been able to accomplish an incredible amount in his life. Whether it is traveling to remote corners of the world, working with thought leaders and their organizations such as Brian Tracy, Tony Robbins, Zig Ziglar, and many others, speaking to Fortune 500 companies and Universities, developing his own companies, and investing in real estate and the stock market, there is little that Dave has not accomplished. He has been published in numerous publications, including Forbes online, and is known for his no-nonsense, common sense approach.

As he says, "Nobody typically succeeds alone. I am so fortunate to have had the support, mentors, and guidance that I have had in life. The Ten Year Career is a culmination of some of the best minds and best advice ever assembled and given."

He founded his first business at a very young age (5 years old!) and continued to develop successful businesses through college. Dave then took that early success to a national F500 company where he earned recognition as Rookie of the Year, Sales Consultant of the Year, Top 25 Producer (out of 1500 sales reps). He became an accomplished management professional and built numerous top performing organizations. Today, As Vice President and co-owner of Grasp Technologies, Dave and his partners have architected over 50% growth every year for each of the last 5 years.

Dave is also very involved in internet business and start-ups. He speaks to companies, organizations, and universities on the mindset of success and the everyday principles of The Ten Year Career. Through all this, he feels most at home when he is helping someone learn a new trait or skill, or reach new levels in their life. Helping others reach their true potential is a passion for him. Dave is also involved with several non-profit organizations.

Dave's hope is that The Ten Year Career will help others find their path to success and create the life of their hopes and dreams.

He lives with his wife, Jennifer, in Columbus, OH

# TEN YEAR CAREER BIBLIOGRAPHY

**Books:**

Tracy, Brian. *Eat That Frog*. San Francisco, CA. Barrett-KoehlerPublishers, Inc., 2007.

Tracy, Brian. *Goals! How to get Everything you Want Faster Than You Ever Thought Possible*. San Francisco, CA. Barrett-KoehlerPublishers, Inc., 2003. 2004

Maxwell. John. *Talent is Never Enough*. Nashville, TN. Thomas Nelson Publishers., 2007.

Kiyosaki, Robert. *Rich Dad Poor Dad*. New York, NY. Warner Books, Inc., 1997. 1998

Kiyosaki, Robert. *Cashflow Quadrant*. Paradise Valley, Az. TechPress. Inc., 1998. 1999

Aristotle. Jonathan Barnes (Editor). *The Complete Works of Aristotle I & II*. Bolligen., 1995

Waitley, Denis. *The Psychology of Winning*. Berkley. 1986

McCormack, Mark H. *What They Don't Teach You At Harvard Business School: Notes From A Street-Smart Executive*. Bantam. 1986

Bach, David. *The Automatic Millionaire: A Powerful One Step plan to Live and Finish Rich.* Crown Business. 2005

Eker, T. Harv. *Secrets of the Millionaire Mind: Mastering the Inner Game of Wealth. New York, NY.*, Harper Collins Publishers, Inc., 2005

Ziglar, Zig. *Great Quotes from Zig Ziglar.* New York, NY., ZGrammercy Books. 2004

Ferris, Timothy. *The Four Hour Workweek: Escape 9-5, Live Anywhere, and Join the New Rich.* Crowne Architype., 2009

Nobel Lectures, Peace 1971-1980, Editor-in-Charge Tore Frängsmyr, Editor Irwin Abrams, World Scientific Publishing Co., Singapore, 1997.

Carnegie, Dale. *How the Win Friends and Influence People.* New York, NY. Simon and Schuster Inc., 1936. 1964

**Web:**

United States National Debt. http://www.treasurydirect.gov/NP/BPDLogin?application=np

United States Gross Domestic Product. http://www.bea.gov/national/index.htm#gdp

Doering, Christopher. "Food Prices Could Reach 2008 Level." 24. February 2011 http://www.reuters.com/article/2011/02/24/us-usda-forum-foodprices-idUSTRE71N4TT20110224

# INDEX

information and, 202
starting a business on, 200–203
strategies and ideas, 187
Interviews, 130
IPO. *See* Initial public offering
IRA. *See* Individual retirement account

J
Jordan, Michael, 150

K
Keller, Helen, 146–48
Kiyosaki, Robert, 26, 52, 68, 180, 183, 205

L
*The Leadership Secrets of Colin Powell* (Harrari), 181
*Lead the Field* (Nightingale), 181
Leveraging, 169–70, 195, 198
Lewis, S. G., 130–33, 186
"Lexus factor," 63
LinkedIn, 52, 116
Lists, 89
Lombardi, Vince, 157
Lytle, Chris, 112, 185

M
Madoff, Bernie, 73
Manning, Peyton, 150
Mariotti, John N., 1–3
Marketing, networking and, 197–98
*Mastering the Trade* (Carder), 184
Maxwell, John C., 18, 181, 186

McCormack, Mark, 49
McFarland, Keith R., 188
*Mentored by a Millionaire, The Master Strategies of the Rich* (Scott), 182–83
"Mercedes factor," 63
Microsoft, 140–41
*The Millionaire Messenger* (Burchard), 187, 202
Mind, harnessing power of, 21–32, 182
    awareness of change and, 28–32
    example of, 25–27
    goals and, 38–39
    obstacles and, 22–23
Mitchell, Todd, 210
Money, 51
    amount of, 23
    as an idea, 27
    interest and, 82
    management of, 52
Mother Teresa, 142–44

N
Negotiating, 130–33
    baseline for, 131–32
    leveraging and, 169–70, 195, 198
Networking, 173–75, 195. *See also* Social networks
    marketing and, 197–98
Nicklaus, Jack, 150
Nightingale, Earl, 181
Nobel Peace Prize, 142

O
*Onward, How Starbucks Fought for its Life Without*

224

# Can't Remember What I Forgot

*Your Memory, Your Mind, Your Future*

## Sue Halpern

THREE RIVERS PRESS

NEW YORK

*The names and identifying characteristics of certain people mentioned in the book have been changed in order to protect their privacy.*

Published in the United States by Three Rivers Press, an imprint of the Crown Publishing Group, a division of Random House, Inc., New York.
www.crownpublishing.com

THREE RIVERS PRESS and the Tugboat design are registered trademarks of Random House, Inc.

Originally published in hardcover in the United States by Harmony Books, an imprint of the Crown Publishing Group, a division of Random House, Inc., New York, in 2008.

Library of Congress Cataloging-in-Publication Data

Halpern, Sue.
    Can't remember what I forgot: your memory, your mind, your future /
Sue Halpern.—1st ed.
        p. cm.
    1. Memory disorders—Popular works.   2. Alzheimer's disease—Popular
works.   3. Memory.   I. Title.
RC394.M46H35 2008
616.85'23—dc22                                          2007033895

ISBN 978-0-307-40788-7

*Design by Lauren Dong*

First Paperback Edition

For Barbara Epstein

*no forgetski*

# Contents

# Author's Note

ON THE CANTED CEILING above my desk is a map of the brain. It shows the frontal lobe and temporal lobe and parietal lobe and occipital lobe as if they were places to visit—Rome, Milan, Trieste, San Remo. The map, of course, is dumb. It says nothing about what goes on in those places: that deep in the middle of the temporal lobe, which itself is deep in the middle of the brain, there is a tiny, cashew-shaped region called the hippocampus that is essential to forming new memories, or that the prefrontal cortex, which sits behind the eyebrows, is vital to foresight and being polite and paying attention, or that the occipital lobe, which brings up the rear of the brain, is central to sight itself.

I look at that map sometimes and think about how it is my own brain apprehending it, and that to do so, it is traveling express. And then my mind, declaring its independence from my brain, begins to wander among the events of the day, past and future, and plans for summer vacation, and concern for a friend who is sick and the dog in the yard, but never getting so far afield that it doesn't heed its own call back.

Near the map, tacked to the wall, is a picture of the brain that is doing all of that and all of this—this writing, thinking, typing, seeing—my brain, in bright colors, which was taken a few years ago in California. When I look at that picture I am not only seeing it, but recalling that day, or aspects of it, so much has gone out with the tide. I took notes on that trip, and carried a digital recorder, and have read and reread those notes over the years, and listened to the conversations, so I remember that day better than most, and what I remember comes with a certain confidence, but even so it is fuzzy. I cannot say, for instance, what kind of rental car I drove, or what book I was reading later that afternoon when I went to the beach, or which beach, specifically, it was.

We rely on memory not only to remember, but to walk and dream and talk and smell and plan and fear and love and think and learn and more and more and more. Memory is how we know the world— that is a tree, this is a sentence—and know ourselves—I like chocolate ice cream, I am a singer—and know ourselves in the world. Amnesiacs make the case well: it is not, simply, that they don't remember their name or where they live, it is that absent memory, they are strangers to themselves. The English philosopher John Locke believed that we came into the world with our mind a blank slate, a "tabula rasa," ready for the pen of experience to inscribe. It's a perfect metaphor (even if it's not exactly true), because it works to describe what it's like to gain knowledge, and what it's like to lose your mind. Stroke by uneven stroke, the eraser plies the board.

My father, before he died at the age of seventy-seven, had begun to know this intimately, though never to the extent that the board was wiped so clean that he approached Locke's natal state. He knew, and he talked about it—about how frustrating it was to read the newspaper and then have to read it again, or to stare at a can opener, not knowing what it was for, or to pick up the phone to call a friend, whose funeral he'd attended two years earlier.

While it might have been natural for me to worry that my father's fate someday would be my own, I didn't, really. The doctor said he didn't have Alzheimer's disease, and since Alzheimer's disease tends to run in families, I figured I was safe. This was not one of those calculate-your-odds kind of conclusions. It wasn't a calculation at all. At best it was a passing thought. Call it denial, call it repression, or maybe arrogance, I just figured that if he didn't have AD, what was it to me?

But later, after he was gone, and all that was left were my memories, some photos, and the key-chain recorder my mother made him carry like a pair of military dog tags at the end in case he got lost, into which he spoke his name, his phone number, and his street address in the flattest of voices, I began to wonder. What if the doctor had been wrong? Almost everyone I knew had a parent or an in-law or a favorite aunt or a colleague or a neighbor or a grandfather or a friend or a friend of a friend who had Alzheimer's, as if the standard six degrees of separation had been universally abridged to one or two. But another question bothered me more: what if the doctor had been right? What I mean is: what if my father hadn't been sick?

This was not a wishful fantasy about what my father's last years would have been like if, when going to the basement to sort the recycling, he didn't lose track of which items went in which bin and stood there, paralyzed by confusion, for half an hour, or if he hadn't thought he'd filed his income tax when he hadn't. He knew who his children were. He remained interested in politics. He had never needed to activate the key-chain recorder. The question, rather, was a kind of private, one-person, one-vote referendum on sickness and health: if he wasn't sick, what was going on?

Since it is the nature of questions to beget more questions before they yield answers, I soon stopped thinking about my father, specifically, or about myself, even when I wondered why, for instance, the memory of a forty-four-year-old was generally better than the memory of a seventy-seven-year-old (or was it?), and why the memory of a twenty-six-year-old was better than both. The answer to this was not as obvious as it might appear. If age were the culprit, what, precisely, was it stealing?

In the popular literature I kept coming across references to the brain that made it sound like a muscle. "Use it or lose it" was the standard dogma. I read countless self-help books that promised to help their readers "use it," and compiled a stack of newspaper articles that touted crossword puzzles and sudokus as the mental equivalents of jogging and strength-training, and the more of these I looked at, the more curious it all seemed to me: I understood that these activities were supposed to be good for you because, apparently, they built mental muscle, but why was that? Was there a physiological response to crossword puzzles, something that happened to the body by doing them, and just whom did they help? Anyone of any age? People with mild memory problems? The worried well? People who were sick? And if they were beneficial for people who were sick as well as people who were not, was that because the same thing was going wrong in the healthy brains that had already gone awry in pathological ones?

The questions piled up in my notebook, a sign, perhaps, that I was using my brain, but to what end? Books evolve idiosyncratically, their single law of natural selection being, it seems, that they choose you. I began calling up neuroscientists and spending time with doctors and sometimes their patients. They were in New York, New Haven, San Francisco, Minnesota, Massachusetts, Chicago, Los Angeles, and Irvine. They were in England and the Dominican Republic and Canada and Italy and Iceland. To friends or acquaintances who, upon hearing what I was doing, told me their particular memory complaint or expressed a more generalized worry, I could tell them how many smart and committed people were out there looking for genes and molecules, developing drugs and vaccines, searching out cures and therapies in plants and minerals already at hand. These bench scientists and clinicians were making headway. Moore's law—the one about the speed of microprocessors doubling every eighteen months—didn't quite apply, but there was progress being made and I was seeing it. (I was also seeing rogues and patent medicine salesmen, but doesn't every court have its jesters?)

The other thing I kept running into was lots of exclamations. A week couldn't go by, it seemed, without an announcement of a breakthrough drug, a breakthrough gene, a breakthrough gene mutation, a breakthrough cognitive therapy, a breakthrough food, a breakthrough herb—so many breakthroughs that it seemed as though whatever wall there had been between us and the dark should have come down already, letting us bask in the sunshine of the eternal mind cure. But hey, not so fast.

Before a drug can come to market, before a therapy can be designed, and (more often than not) before a body can be healed, you have to know where the problem lies. In medicine that knowledge is often found at the cellular or molecular or genetic level, somewhere in the mix of proteins of which we are made. To get through the hyperbole and hype and promises and platitudes that now attend to most public discussions about memory (which almost always, these days, seem to be about memory impairment), I had to find out what the molecular biologists and cell biologists and biochemists and geneticists knew. This meant spending time in brain-scanning suites and chemistry labs and mice nurseries and hospitals and pharmaceutical companies, and attending scientific meetings, and reading research papers with unintelligible titles. Because there are now many ways to look at the brain, I also made sure mine was examined using each of them, in honor of one of the first scientists of memory, Hermann Ebbinghaus, who made it a point to experiment upon himself. Still, as a neuroscientist at Yale pointed out to me, "you can't tell much from an N of 1."

In our own lives, by definition, we are always Ns of 1, which is one reason why the prospect of getting sick can be so scary, and why being sick is scarier still, especially if either of those conditions entails the loss of self. (Can there be an N of −1?) If we're lucky, of course, our Ns connect—directly, contiguously, through each other—which is how families and communities are formed. It is also how, in science, evidence mounts and findings are made and then confirmed.

In the years that I was writing this book, crucial findings about memory loss and Alzheimer's and normal memory and medicines and cognitive therapy were made and confirmed, and even where they were not, the ball was pushed farther up the pitch. From my seat the view has been outstanding, and from what I have seen there are many reasons to cheer.

*Ripton, Vermont*
*November 2007*

# Can't Remember
# What I Forgot

*Chapter One*

# Anxious

IT WAS ONE OF THOSE SHADOWLESS, late November days in New York, where the city is drained of color and fitful gusts of wind hopscotch litter along the gutter, where pedestrians draw up their shoulders and walk eyes to the sidewalk, aiming to get inside. Dr. Scott Small, in a dark green shirt and darker green tie—no coat—hastened down 168th Street in upper Manhattan and pushed through the glass doors of Columbia University's Neurological Institute. He went past the bank of elevators, turned right, and moved toward another set of doors, these with the sign LUCY G. MOSES CENTER FOR MEMORY AND BEHAVIORAL DISORDERS written on them. Inside, in a practiced movement, he picked up a stack of file folders and a white jacket with his name embroidered on the pocket and stepped into a windowless room that was artificially bright and professionally drear, its walls unadorned except for a blood pressure cuff hanging in the back above an examining table and a black-and-white photograph of Central Park in a different season.

"Welcome to my office," he said a little ironically, since we had just left his office, a sunny aerie on the eighteenth floor of the old Presbyterian Hospital building, where he was telling me about his work tracking down molecules in the brain that control memory. Like this room, that one was spare, too, but for effect. A table for a desk, a matched pair of chrome chairs that looked like they'd been ordered from a museum catalog, piles of CDs, a pointed absence of books. Between long views of the East River, Small had hung enormous, brooding abstracts painted by his wife, Alexis England-Small, who once sang backup for Stevie Wonder. On an adjacent wall was a blackboard—the old kind, before they became green. Small shuttled between that office, where he did his research, and this place, where he saw patients one afternoon a week, a kind of joint-custody arrangement of his dual vocations, doctor and scientist.

The patients, who were mostly in their sixties and seventies and eighties, were assigned to him either because they had made an appointment to be seen at the clinic and it was his day to be there, or because they had heard about the young neurologist from a relative, or a neighbor, or a friend of a friend; New York was small that way—people gossiped about doctors. Still others had done their homework, looking up the names of the clinic doctors on the Internet and scanning their publications, trying to find the one who might be the most sympathetic, or the smartest, or the best trained. If it was Small they chose, it was because they had read of his breakthrough invention, a way to scan the brain at high resolution, or because he had been the chief neurological resident at Columbia University Medical Center, or because, at forty-four, he had recently been awarded a prestigious McKnight Fellowship. Or maybe they just liked his face, which was open and familiar, like they might know him already, although Small, the son of a Holocaust survivor, had grown up in Israel, where he served in an elite commando unit in the Israeli army during the Lebanon war.

A SEVENTY-THREE-YEAR-OLD woman was Small's first patient of the day. Her son, whose idea this visit was, guided her in and helped her into a chair. She was wearing blue slacks and a pink-and-white-striped man-tailored shirt and had a white scarf around her neck and pearl earrings. She was smiling broadly. Small and the woman's son talked for a while. The son, a Brooklyn cop, was carrying a folder with his mother's previous MRI films, plus her medical records, plus a list of all the conditions that might explain his mother's profound lethargy, none of which were Alzheimer's disease.

"I'm going to say three words to you," the doctor said to the woman, who continued to smile, "and I want you to repeat them back to me. Penny, apple, table." This, I knew from spending time in the Memory Disorders Clinic, was the most basic test for dementia, part of the standard Mini–Mental State Exam. The woman was having none of it. She said not a word. "Mom," the cop pleaded, "do what the doctor says." "Penny, apple, table," Small repeated. The woman looked over at her son, the expansive smile lifting up the corners of her deeply blue eyes. "Mom, say 'penny, apple, table,'" her son urged. Though it was November, though he was wearing a short-sleeved shirt, he had begun to sweat. "It's hard for her to talk," he said, giving up.

Small pushed a piece of paper and a pencil across the desk to the woman. "See these three figures on this sheet," he said. "I want you to draw them on this other sheet." She cocked her head and grinned, like he'd said something funny. Her son, though, looked grim. He had one hand inside the other and was rubbing them back and forth as if he were washing.

"Pick up the pencil, Mom," he said in his best cop voice, and roused, perhaps, by its authority, she did. "The doctor would like you to make copies of these figures," he told her, his voice becoming gentle again, his tone solicitous. She wrapped her fingers around the pencil and scratched a few lines on the paper before pushing the pencil and paper back across the desk. Even from where I was sitting I could tell that what she had sketched was not a cube or a house or a three-dimensional abstract of intersecting squares and polyhedrons. Halfway across the room and I could see that what she had drawn was the glyph of disease.

Minutes later the doctor spoke the words. "Alzheimer's disease," he said. By then the woman was snoozing quietly in her chair and the doctor was telling her son, and because love is invested with hope, he protested, naming other conditions, listing various syndromes, enumerating different possibilities. Small listened, nodded, and then repeated the diagnosis. He was unequivocal. He asked the cop if he understood. Because I could not bear to look at the son, I looked at his mother who, even in sleep, had a smile on her face, and fixed on the steady in and out of her breathing. Breath for breath, I synchronized to her. It was a way of not thinking. Still, the thoughts came anyway: This is the person we are afraid we will be. This is the one we are afraid we are already, unwittingly, becoming.

HERE ARE some numbers: Eighty-three percent of us are worried about not being able to remember one another's names. Sixty percent are concerned about our tendency to misplace the car keys. Fifty-seven percent of us are disturbed that we can't recall phone numbers a few minutes after we've heard them.

Lots of people—most people—have a memory that leaks and dissociates. When researchers from the University of Maastricht in the Netherlands queried four thousand people, one in two people over sixty-five said they were forgetful. While that may not be surprising, the researchers also found that one in three people between twenty-five and thirty-five reported memory problems, too.

Invariably, though, the younger folks attributed their lapses to stress, while the older ones thought that they were caused by disease.

We are anxious, and our anxiety has a name: Alzheimer's disease. According to a survey conducted in 2002 for the Alzheimer's Association, 95 percent of respondents—*essentially everyone*—said that they considered Alzheimer's disease to be a serious problem, and well over half—64 percent—of those between the ages of thirty-five and forty-nine, the baby boomers, my peers, noted that they were worried about getting AD themselves. Similarly, when the MetLife Foundation in 2006 asked respondents which disease they most feared getting, cancer was first and Alzheimer's disease second. But for respondents over fifty-five, those answers flipped and it was Alzheimer's that was dreaded most. As the poet and naturalist Diane Ackerman observes in *An Alchemy of Mind*, "Most everyone I know frets about memory loss, and in what's become a mass phobia, worries whether each slip foretells the reign of Alzheimer's disease."

To some extent, this mass phobia is fed by well-intended public service journalism, which is making an industry out of articles touting possible cures, impending breakthroughs, and tips for preventing the disease in the first place. Just a glance at *Time* magazine's "Can You Prevent Alzheimer's Disease," and *Newsweek*'s "The Quest for Memory Drugs," and the *AARP Bulletin*'s "Ten Ways to Get Your Memory in Shape" rouses dormant queries: Do I need a drug to boost my memory? Am I the one who is going to lose my mind? Are my memory losses significant? Are they irrevocable?

Add to the stack of magazines the exponential number of health-oriented newsletters being published by reputable medical schools, who have discovered gold in the veins of our anxiety. Not long ago, in the course of a few weeks, I received a copy of the University of California at Berkeley's *Wellness Letter*, which featured its "Best Bets for Preventing Alzheimer's Disease"; a brochure from the Harvard Medical School called *Preserving and Boosting Your Memory*; an ad from the Mount Sinai Medical School in New York for its new publication, *Healthy Aging*, that began: "Are you constantly misplacing your car keys, forgetting people's names, failing to come up with the right word in conversation"; and a solicitation to subscribe to the Johns Hopkins quarterly *Memory Bulletin*, which I did.

And then there are the products like Focus Factor and Memory Support and Memory Max and NeuroPower and Alert! that promise to massage the brain until it's supple and dexterous, and herbal supplements with names like phosphatidylserine ("to reverse age-related cognitive decline") and acetyl-1-carnitine ("to boost neurotransmitters"), and vinpocetine ("derived from the periwinkle plant")—names that you could not spell even when your brain was tip-top. (But when was that?) Peak Brain Performance, an amalgam of, well, it's not clear what, since its "revolutionary formula [containing] a powerful blend of natural ingredients that have been researched for decades" is called Procera AVH, which, as far as I can tell, is also a revolutionary—which is to say made-up—term, was developed by the same person who invented the mood ring and the Thighmaster, two products that defined their zeitgeist as this one defines ours.

We are worried and we are scared. We are worried enough and scared enough to spend nearly $200 on the Nintendo Brain Age, a portable gaming device reconfigured for the growing gray market, and for a light-sound machine called MindSpa that is supposed to "entrain" your brain to its pulses of white light and industrial noises, so you can focus better, faster, more clearly. ("One of the subtests I used to study the effects of MindSpa was for memory and the scores jumped significantly," Ruth Olmstead, a psychologist who helped develop the machine and uses it in her practice with kids and, increasingly, adults with attention issues, told me after I'd spent about forty minutes a day for a month lying in the dark with my eyes shut behind the machine's light-emitting "glasses," listening to what sounded like jackhammers and subway trains, wondering not if my memory was improving, but if I was going to have an epileptic seizure, which I'd read could happen. I'm not sure if my memory improved or not—I wasn't conducting a controlled clinical trial—but I did notice that my Ping-Pong game got better. I could hit shots in all the corners and anticipate volleys before the ball landed.)

We temper our fears by joking about them—all those little asides about "senior moments" and "it must be early Alzheimer's." We're not really serious—or maybe just a little. But when some television doctor mentions that Alzheimer's disease might be prevented by taking a daily dose of ibuprofen, or eliminating deodorant made with aluminum, or drinking black tea, a lot of us start swallowing Motrin, and toss out the Speed Stick, and brew pots of Earl Grey. Take me as your case in point the morning I came across a list of home remedies touted on a website called FatFreeKitchen.com as memory boosters. Eating seven to eight almonds a day and drinking one teaspoon of honey mixed with one teaspoon of cinnamon, it counseled, will benefit one's cognitive health. And though I knew, rationally, that a couple of nuts and a little honey laced with less than a gram of cinnamon wasn't going to do much, if anything, for me, I headed down to the kitchen to make a cup of tea—ginkgo biloba tea, for good measure—in which I infused the cinnamon and honey. While it was brewing I munched on a handful of almonds. I mean, why not? Eating a dozen almonds may just be my generation's version of Pascal's wager.

The simple statistical truth, though, is that most of us will not get Alzheimer's disease. Many of us will, but most of us won't because, in large measure, AD is a disease of the very old, and most of us will not live to see eighty-five, when half of that cohort is expected to be experiencing diagnosable symptoms, or ninety, when that percentage moves up a few notches. Those numbers—50 percent, 60 percent—are measures of the disease prevalence, or the number of existing cases, as opposed to incidence, or the number of new cases. Prevalence is what we, as a nation, as members of the human community, should be worried about, because as the population ages, and people live longer and longer, Alzheimer's will mutate into a public health emergency, with an estimated 16 million Americans, 16.5 million Europeans and residents of the United Kingdom, and 62.8 million Asians with the disease by 2050.

In contrast to prevalence, incidence is what we, as individuals, will need to reckon with, for it lays out the rough odds of any of us joining the haves or staying among the Alzheimer-free have-nots. Incidence figures are tricky, but from all accounts it appears that starting at age sixty-five, you have about a 10 percent chance of developing AD—which is to say that you have a 90 percent chance of not getting it, which are not bad odds.

Still, it doesn't appease us. We hear numbers like 106 million—how many people, worldwide, who are expected to be suffering from Alzheimer's by 2050—that 5 percent of the American population already has AD, and that every 72 seconds someone develops the disease, and are unsettled. We read in the fact sheet distributed by the Alzheimer's Disease Research Program of the American Health Association that "common symptoms include: disturbances in memory, attention, and orientation, changes in personality, language difficulties, and impairments in gait and movement," and are deeply concerned. Even this statistic, from a Danish study, that among people with severe memory problems, only 43 percent actually had Alzheimer's disease, fails to impress. Why? Because even if you consider 43 percent to be a relatively small number, you've got to be wondering about that other 57 percent: what's going on with them?

"Let me show you something," Scott Small said to me the first time we met, that day in late November. We were sitting in his eighteenth-floor office, and he jumped up and grabbed a piece of chalk and began to draw an upward-sloping line on the blackboard. Then he drew a downward-sloping line. One line represented age, the other memory function. "What do you see?" he asked when he was done. "As age goes up, memory declines," he answered. "Is that pathological? Is that a disease? Memory decline occurs in everyone. It doesn't matter where you start from. That is not a known fact. I would say that people do not know that. But by and large, if we talk about normal aging, the reason why we can call it normal is because it happens to everyone, inexorably."

Small is one of the few scientists who study normal memory decline, though the field seems to be growing. As Dr. Mony de Leon, across town at the Center for Brain Health at New York University, put it, "Normal is the new frontier."

You might have expected the order of study to have progressed the way our health typically progresses, from that place where everything is basically okay, to that place where things have gone to hell—from good knees to joint pain, say, from red hair to white. But normal is hard to pin down—it's elusive—where with disease, at least, there tends to be something to look at, like a tumor or clogged arteries. In the case of Alzheimer's that something—those somethings—has been thought to be clusters of a protein called beta-amyloid distributed throughout the brain, twinned with neurofibrillary tangles found inside the brain cells. The amyloid plaques look like wads of chewing gum; the neurofibrillary tangles bear a likeness to strands of hair. Together, they colonize the brain of an Alzheimer's patient.

Until quite recently, plaques and tangles could only be seen after death, at autopsy, when the brain could be opened, sectioned, stained, and observed under a microscope. But new techniques being developed and studied at the University of Pittsburgh and at UCLA are enabling doctors, for the first time, to see plaques and tangles in a living brain, and to figure out if they really are the perpetrators of disease. Soon they may be able to see them in their earliest stages, as they are forming, before the brain begins to fail. In the meantime, doctors will continue to diagnose AD as they have since the 1960s, when they first realized that what they had been calling "senile dementia" in older patients was actually the same pathology described in 1906 by the German physician Alois Alzheimer, whose patient was much younger. (Until the 1960s, Alzheimer's disease was thought to be a rare illness that struck people in their forties and fifties.) They will give them a battery of neurological and psychological tests, prod their reflexes, look into their eyes, watch them walk a straight line. And they will take a picture of the brain using a magnetic resonance scanning machine.

There are two basic kinds of MRI scans: structural ones use a high-powered magnet to reveal the architecture of the brain, and functional ones train those magnets on blood flow to show which parts of the brain are most active, especially during a task like remembering a list of words. An fMRI takes advantage of the fact that nerve cells carry oxygen, and oxygen can be detected by the magnet in the MRI machine; the more active a particular brain area, the more oxygen it will need, the brighter—or "hotter"—that spot on the fMRI. The fMRI picks up the gradations in cerebral blood flow, even when the brain is at rest. It was fMRI that researchers at Yale employed to show how dyslexic children use different parts of their brain to process language than do typical readers. It was fMRI that allowed researchers to show that the brains of Democrats are emotionally different from the brains of Republicans. (From an Associated Press story about the experiment: "[W]hen voters were shown a Bush ad that included images of the Sept. 11 attacks, the amygdala region of the brain—which lights up for most of us when we see snakes—illuminated more for Democrats than Republicans. The researchers' conclusion: At a subconscious level, Republicans were apparently not as bothered by what Democrats found alarming.") It was also fMRI that was generating a whole new way for companies to reach consumers—actually, to reach *inside* consumers to identify their preferences—and a new field, called neuromarketing. DaimlerChrysler had already used it to assess how people felt, say, about the Mercedes-Benz B Class or the Jeep Wrangler. (It turned out, for instance, that the human brain had evolved so that a particular region "lit up" when a brand name was encountered.) And researchers at Cal Tech, working with film executives, were using fMRI to see how we reacted to movie trailers.

For doctors aiming to diagnose a case of Alzheimer's, MRI scans are helpful because they use them to rule out conditions like stroke and head injury, conditions that themselves may damage memory. MRIs are also useful because they allow a clinician to determine brain volume and the size of specific areas within it, like the hippocampus, that are known to control memory. At NYU they were finding that people who eventually developed Alzheimer's disease started out with smaller hippocampi, which continued to get smaller over time. It was such a consistent finding that it was beginning to appear that it had predictive value. There was also clinical significance in measuring the whole brain, which could be done by looking at the ratio of liquid to solid—cerebral spinal fluid (CSF) to gray matter.

All brains sit in a protective bath of CSF and have four fluid-filled cavities in them called ventricles that serve, among other things, as the brain's sewage treatment plant, carrying away toxic waste. Cerebral spinal fluid shows up nicely on an MRI. Seen from above, healthy ventricles look like kidney-shaped swimming pools. But the ventricles in an Alzheimer's brain are different. They are wetter, more substantial. And the corona of CSF circling the Alzheimer's brain is more like the sky itself. That is because Alzheimer's brains atrophy. They shrink. And when they do, fluid takes up the space that once held personality, words, time, and space.

I WAS thinking about what Shakespeare called the "ventricles of memory," but might have, had he known better, called the "ventricles of forgetting"—one afternoon in midsummer as I made my way from the New York University Medical Center in midtown Manhattan to Corinthian Diagnostic Radiology three blocks north on First Avenue, where I was scheduled to have a routine structural brain scan. NYU has a number of MRI machines in the hospital, but the one Mony de Leon liked to use was in a private radiology clinic tucked inconspicuously into an upscale Murray Hill apartment building. De Leon, the director of the Center for Brain Health, and, in 1979, the first person to measure and show, incontrovertibly, atrophy in an Alzheimer's brain, was in the midst of a study, funded by the National Institutes of Health, looking for signs that might predict Alzheimer's or a condition known as mild cognitive impairment (MCI) that itself was often predictive of AD, long before a person was even aware of a problem. He was looking for markers in the blood and in spinal fluid, as well as measuring the way a brain metabolizes glucose—its fuel—and also assessing responses on a six-hour battery of psychological and neurological exams. In addition to having an optional spinal tap and a radioactive PET (positron-emission tomography) scan and taking two days of paper-and-pencil exams, the three hundred volunteer subjects had to have a routine physical and a structural MRI. I was one of them. The only criteria for participating were being older than twenty, having a high school education, and not suffering from obvious dementia.

So I was making my way up First Avenue in order to lie inside a giant magnet to get my head examined, and as I walked a question nagged at me: Was I truly, for the purposes of this study, a healthy volunteer? How would I, or could I, know? Reflexively—anxiously— I began to generate a random interrogatory: Did I know where my keys were? (Yes, in my pocket, where I was uneasily toying with them.) Could I recite my Visa card number? (Yes.) Did I know my husband's social security number? (Yes.) The birthdays of all my dogs since childhood? (Yes.) Could I name all of my elementary school teachers? (Yes.) I could recall that Dr. de Leon was wearing a brown sport coat, but could I say what color tie he'd had on? (No, not unless I looked at my notes, which would be cheating.) But wasn't the whole thing cheating? Wasn't asking my own brain to come up with questions to measure if it was healthy or not like seeing the answer key before taking the test? Wouldn't I automatically, unconsciously, ask my brain questions I knew it could already answer? I mean, I wasn't asking myself to recite the lyrics to "Yellow Submarine," to name my high school homeroom teachers, or to state the mileage of my last oil change, none of which I could do. Clearly, I was a crummy judge of my own brain health. For months, as a kind of thought experiment, I had been keeping track of my memory lapses when they occurred, writing them down in a journal, trying to get a picture of my brain from the outside in. "Trying hard to remember a character in Maupin's *Tales of the City*," I had written the week before. "I can see him clearly and can list many pertinent details about him. I even know his name starts with 'Beau. . . .' I keep trying out all the obvious Beau . . . names—Beaumont, Beauman, Beaucoupe—but none sounds right. Sometimes my memory feels like what a Magic 8 Ball looks like as the answer floats obscurely under the hazy scrim of blue water." Was *this* normal? I headed into the building to find out.

Corinthian Diagnostic Radiology, which appeared to occupy the building's entire second story, was deserted. On the one hand, this was encouraging to me—not a lot of glioblastomas and transient ischemic attacks today, it seemed. On the other hand, it was unsettling, and a little creepy. Then a woman in a lab coat emerged from a side room with a glass window, found some papers for me to sign about privacy and liability, and asked me to hand over all the metal I might be wearing, any bit of which could depolarize the magnet. She asked me to witness her putting it all in the office safe—though without my glasses, which with their metal screws required relinquishing, too, watching was out of the question. I followed her into a room filled by a loud and constant *lub-dub*, the heartbeat of the large beige machine straight ahead, into which I was soon to be inserted. She handed me a pair of foam plugs to go inside my ears, and then a pair of sound mufflers to go over them, the kind used by people who work on airport tarmacs or shoot rifles. Even so, the *lub-dub* invaded. The woman gestured for me to lie down in the curved bed of plastic that would soon be slid, with me on it, into the magnet. A technician secured my head with a strap. Any movement, he warned me, could blur the image.

"Ready," he said.

I was about to nod, but, for good practice, restrained myself.

"Sure," I said, and he pushed a button, and the cradle moved me slowly, headfirst, into a tunnel that extended to my shirt cuffs. In some MRI machines, the technicians tape a picture of a beach in Hawaii or a triptych of the Rockies to calm people down, but not here. Here they were dealing with New Yorkers. What was the point?

"Okay," the technician said, "we are going to do a training scan, just to get you used to it. It will last thirty-six seconds. Try to keep still. Ready?" And then a startlingly loud, percussive, Brian Eno–ish sound was broadcast inches from my head, and just as suddenly it passed.

"Good," the tech said. "We're going to start. You feel okay? You know not to move, right? There will be three scans. The first will be nine and a half minutes long. The second scan will be six and a half minutes long. And the third one will be four and a half minutes. Remember, don't move. Do you have any questions?"

"What's with all the half minutes?" I wanted to ask, but didn't.

"Are you ready?" he said. The sound started up again, and this time it really did resemble "Music for Airports," but with the volume at eleven. Still, it was mildly hypnotic. The almost ten minutes flew by, and without segue we were in the second sequence, which had a whole other timbre and pitch, something like a person leaning on a door buzzer, demanding to be let in. Sometimes it sounded like a word, and the word I kept on hearing was "Duarte, Duarte, Duarte," all three syllables, fast and loud, like someone was shouting. Even so, I fell asleep and didn't wake up until the voice calling for Duarte called it quits and the register changed, and the quality of sound, too, and it was like someone picking a guitar while holding down the strings so you didn't get the tune, just the sound of the pick on the strings. Then, out of nowhere, as I was anticipating more tuneless picking, there was a kind of response to its call, an antiphonal response of a single note played very fast on what I imagined to be the open D string of a bass guitar. It was all in eights. First eight beats of the muted picked string, then eight beats of the manic D, back and forth, back and forth, for nearly five minutes.

And then it was over. The machine ejected me and the technician came over and unstrapped my head, and I sat up, disoriented and chilled, the heartbeat of the MRI now restored to prominence in the room. I was handed back my glasses, and when I put them on, I could see a distinguished-looking older man, with salt-and-pepper hair and a trim mustache, wearing a tan tweed jacket and brown pants, sitting on the other side of the scanning room, looking at a picture of a brain on a computer screen. My brain as it happened, he told me, introducing himself as the radiologist, Dr. St. Louis.

We stood there for a few minutes, he with his back to me, fiddling with the resolution, me trying to get a glimpse of my brain over his shoulder, but not wanting to, feeling vulnerable and exposed. I thought: This man knows more about me than I do. This man can see into my future. The open book that I like to think of as my life not only had its final chapter written, but this fellow knew what words were written there. I wasn't sure I wanted to know what they were.

"Here's your cerebellum," Dr. St. Louis said, pointing to a tree-like structure hanging off the bottom. "It's what controls balance and coordination. This is your brain stem." He gestured toward a column sloping vertically under the cerebellum. "It's what keeps you breathing without you having to think about breathing." I nodded, but to tell the truth, I wasn't really looking, not at that screen, which showed my brain in profile. The one in which I was interested was the view from the top, which showed the ventricles and the girdle of spinal fluid between my skull and brain. I wanted to look at it and I wanted to say something casually definitive to the doctor, like "The vents look okay, don't they?" But that seemed too presumptuous and I couldn't. I stole a quick look. The ventricles didn't seem bloated, but what did I know?

The doctor went back to adjusting the images, and I continued to stand there, dumbly, hoping he'd say something conclusive and positive about what he was seeing, but he didn't. "I'm going to read the film and send my report over to NYU later," Dr. St. Louis said. I understood that it would be months before I knew what the MRI really "said," and that he was dismissing me, but I didn't want to leave until I had some kind of assurance, something more than me telling me that I was okay. Then, after a while, he casually let out, as much to himself as to me, "There's no white matter disease," which was enough.

For researchers trying to figure out why a certain number of apparently normal people begin to slide down the slope of forgetting, compromised white matter was a recent finding. At the Maastricht University Brain and Behavior Institute in the Netherlands, Dr. Jelle Jolles and his colleagues had a hunch that the memory problems experienced by people who didn't have Alzheimer's disease were caused by subtle structural changes in the brain, probably in the white matter, so they scanned a thousand healthy volunteers, all over sixty, and also gave them a series of memory and other cognitive tests, and it turned out that the participants who exhibited memory problems also had subtly damaged white matter.

Jolles's results dovetailed with findings reported by Ian Deary of the University of Edinburgh. Once Deary and his collaborators at the University of Aberdeen found out that on June 1, 1932, every eleven-year-old schoolchild in Scotland sat for the Scottish Mental Survey, a comprehensive intelligence test, 87,498 children in all, they set out to track down, sixty-seven years after the fact, as many of those children as they could. Born in 1921, they were then seventy-eight. Deary and his colleagues found five hundred of them, and from these recruited eighty-two to participate in a follow-up study, which involved cognitive tests similar to the ones they had taken at age eleven, as well as spending an hour or so inside a machine that had not even been conceived in 1932, getting a magnetic resonance image of their brain. What the researchers found was that white matter abnormalities "are common, even in people with no dementia or other neurocognitive disorders." Nonetheless, what they also found was that the people who had lesions of the white matter, which showed up like bright stars on the MRI, did worse on the cognitive tests than people who didn't. As Deary put it: "If Mary tested better than Billy at age 11, they didn't necessarily test the same way at 78—because of white matter lesions."

*No white matter disease*, Dr. St. Louis said, and I was released, even though white matter disease was not in my repertoire of fears, though it should have been, and not because of Doctors Deary and Jolles, but because of another doctor, a surgeon, my uncle. *White matter disease.* As soon as Dr. St. Louis said those words a little movie began to roll in my mind, me at ten, walking through the main terminal of the Miami International Airport at the end of a visit with my cousins. My parents and their mother are walking ahead. I am trailing behind. Between us is my uncle, the surgeon, strapped upright in his motorized wheelchair, breathing through a plastic tube. He was trying to get his wife's attention, but she was too far ahead, too engrossed in conversation with people her own height, and he had no more voice. His voice had been reduced to a whisper, and only I, because I was closer to the ground, could hear him. And it seemed so remarkably sad and pathetic that he was un-able to do this simple thing that I didn't help him. I thought that would be worse, that I would humiliate him. He called "Ruth," and it didn't carry, and I kept on walking, pretending that I, too, hadn't heard. He was about twelve years into the multiple sclerosis that had been diagnosed when he was in medical school, and about twelve years from death. The progressive demyelination of the white matter in his brain—the cables through which brain cells communicate—had taken away his ability to breathe without assistance, walk, or hold his head up. Eventually it would disconnect his brain from his arms and his hands and his fingers. He would no longer be able to swallow. But right then he couldn't raise his voice, and it took me a while to understand that I was wrong about his pride. He just wanted to talk to his wife. So I finally called out and he thanked me.

That was my understanding of white matter disease—that you got left behind. That you had no voice. And I worried about it. At ten and eleven, throughout high school, into college, it was in the back of my mind: *this could happen*. And then I got past the age he had been when he lost his balance, and then the age when he could no longer walk, and eventually I stopped thinking about it, and that day at the airport (and my guilt) faded, too. Not all at once, but gradually, like a puddle evaporating.

Back out on First Avenue again, I stood and watched as people moved by me, on foot, on bikes, in taxis, talking on phones, talking to each other, talking to themselves, listening to music. There was a sweet innocence to it. The future was a promise, and memory a habit of mind.


That memory of my uncle, the movie trailer that played in my head, prompted by the three words *white matter disease*, was the kind of recollection that people who study the subject call declarative memory. Scientists tend to categorize. If you were to ask a neuroscientist, for instance, to define memory, she would likely ask you which kind of memory you had in mind. This would be true, too, if you queried a cognitive psychologist, though the categories wouldn't necessarily be the same. There is memory for facts and events and people and ideas, which is sometimes called *declarative memory*, or *explicit memory*, or *memory with record*. There is memory for doing, muscle memory, the kind of memory that lets you drive a car or ride a bike or use a spoon, which is sometimes called *implicit memory*, or *memory without record,* or *nondeclarative memory.* The neuroscientists and psychologists also sometimes refer to *episodic memory,* a kind of explicit memory, when they are talking about recalling personal experiences, like what you ate for breakfast or wore to the prom; and *semantic memory,* another kind of explicit (or declarative) memory, the memory for facts and concepts—who wrote the Gettysburg Address, say, or the structure of a sonnet; and *procedural memory,* which is a kind of nondeclarative (or implicit) memory, the unconscious memory that lets us learn new skills and hang on to old ones; and *working memory,* which is the capacity to hold information in your head and manipulate it, like a phone number or what the teacher just said or how to get to the airport, which is yet another kind of explicit memory.

Working memory is also a kind of *short-term memory,* which itself suggests a whole other way of talking about memory—by chronology, by time. So the scientists refer to *sensory memory* and *short-term memory* and *long-term memory,* each type distinguished by how long it remains available to you. Sensory memory, the briefest, is what happens when you first perceive something and take it in. A car driving by, for instance, or the flames of a fire, or the first three bars of Bach's Mass in B Minor. You see the car. You feel the heat. You hear the music. Your senses are engaged, and the information moves into short-term memory, where it may stay for seconds or even minutes. Unless the synaptic connections that make up that memory are reinforced through a series of biochemical signals in the brain, a few minutes later you won't remember if the passing van was silver or blue, you won't remember that you had been listening to Bach. Long-term memory, in other words, describes those memories that stick, that stay with you over days and years and sometimes decades, like the memory of that day in Miami.

All these distinctions, all these different kinds of memory, are not purely academic. They have clinical value, too, since different kinds of memory have been linked to particular parts of the brain— procedural memory to the cerebellum, for instance, and working memory to, though not exclusively, the prefrontal cortex. If the hippocampus, the small cashew-shaped region of the brain that is responsible for short-term memory, gets damaged, as it does in Alzheimer's disease, the ability to remember what has just been encountered will be impaired. Which is why an AD patient may ask the same question numerous times, or eat a second lunch. Parsing memory enables doctors to diagnose disease or to give the all-clear.

Still, when most people think about memory, they conceive of it as a single thing, an entity that is nearly embodied. "My memory," they say, as they would "my foot" or "my hair." And just like a foot or like hair, it can be lost. Until we forget, even, how to breathe, we survive the loss, for the most part, at least in body. Meanwhile, the people around us say "She's not herself," which suggests that memory is more than our ability to remember, that it's more than the bits of information we've socked away. We are made of memories. Memories, for sure, of what we've seen and what we've heard and what we've felt and where we've been. Memories of what we've learned. (All learning is a memory.) Memory constitutes personality; it both holds and defines our *selves*. (Of course we are worried.)

ARISTOTLE, ONE of the first philosophers to contemplate the meaning of memory, believed that it required a lapse of time. "To remember the future is not possible . . . ," he wrote, "nor is there memory of the present, but only sense-perception. . . . Memory relates to the past. No one would say that he remembers the present." But what of genetic memory, memory that we come into the world with, memory derived from our collective evolutionary experience? Similarly, there is only a future because we can project ourselves into it. How else but by memory do we have expectations?

We expect people to be who we know them to be—that is, who we remember them to be; it is how we take stock. Your friend, your mother, your wife, your partner, whose rhythms and cadences and passions and strengths are known to you, begins to speak slowly and grows disaffected. (Or maybe this is you. You are the apathetic one. You're the one who is getting lost.) You are concerned. This is when you begin to say that someone is not herself. We even say this about ourselves. But how can that be? Philosophers enjoy this kind of conundrum: how can you be anything but yourself? The obvious, rational answer to the question—that you can't—may be driving our anxiety about AD. As Aristotle points out, there is only now—the past is a re-creation, the future a representation. You are only yourself now. And what if that self is one who can't remember itself? What if the person you had been is only a memory—episodic, declarative, explicit—held by others?

Where is the line between past and present, between before and after, between "she's not herself" and this is who she is now? Though it's unanswerable, I thought I caught a glimpse one day in Scott Small's office at Columbia's Neurological Institute when a couple came in for a follow-up visit in order to monitor the patient, whom Small had diagnosed six months earlier as being in the early stages of Alzheimer's disease. But which one of them was sick? Scott hadn't had time to tell me, and at first, when the two of them came in, tanned and smiling, she dressed in smart, brown-and-black tweed slacks and a black turtleneck that looked to be cashmere, and he in charcoal gray trousers and a light blue sweater under his navy blazer, I couldn't tell. They both seemed fine to me—fit and attractive.

Then the woman made a passing reference to the photograph of Central Park on the office wall, and her husband grimaced, and I realized that it was him, that he was the one with Alzheimer's.

"How was Florida?" Scott Small asked warmly. "You look good," he said. "When did you get back?" The woman glanced at the man, who shrugged.

"A few days ago," he said, an answer that was sufficiently vague for me to take as more evidence of his debility.

"How was the golf?" Small asked.

The woman frowned. "I'm playing the nine-hole course now," she said. "The arthritis. What do you think of Bextra? Can't I take that?"

The doctor laughed. "Where did you hear about Bextra?" he asked.

"TV," she replied.

"I spend a lot of my time dealing with the effects of pharmaceutical company advertising," he said to no one in particular. And then, instead of answering her directly, he looked at his watch and stood up. "Sharon," he said, using her first name for the first time, "let's address this later. Right now I'd like to talk to Randall by himself."

Sharon made a little face and uttered a few words of protest, which I took to mean that she didn't want to leave Randall alone with the doctor, but Small had opened the door—what choice did she have?—and she retreated obediently.

"So," he said, when the door was closed again. "How has it really been? How is she? How are you?" And the man, Randall, bowed his head and put his thumb over one tear duct and his forefinger over the other, but it was of no use: the tears came anyway. "Awful," he said after a while—and I still didn't know. And then he began to name the things that had been lost to the confusion and agitation and incontinence—the easy companionship, the dinners with friends, the games of golf and bridge—and as he spoke I understood, finally, that it was his wife who was sick. I had missed it because her neat appearance and apparent clarity did not fit with my assumptions about memory loss. She had seemed so normal, so above average, even.

Randall was complaining about his wife's driving, which he thought was dangerous, but she had recently passed a driving test, so there was little he could do. Small invited her back into the room, and they talked about the driving, but only for a minute, because Sharon was adamant, and petulant, and had the sanction of the state.

"I'd like you to walk a straight line," Dr. Small asked her, drawing an imaginary one on the floor, from the examining table to the middle of the room. Sharon stood up and took a few uneven steps and turned around.

"These new shoes they're making today . . . ," she joked.

A joke—especially a joke at your own expense—requires self-awareness. A joke meant that even if your left foot had inched out and was resting precariously on a rock in the middle of a rushing stream, your right foot was still anchoring you to the bank where you started. We call that bank normal. We say that bank is safe. Even if it's eroding.

*Chapter Two*

# Certainty

EROSION HAPPENS UNDERFOOT, or the winds are scouring, the rain comes down. There are grooves in the stairs that appear over time—we see them being made, but it doesn't register. Epistemologists want to know how we know what we know; intuition is not the same as perception. Science, meanwhile, offers all kinds of assurance—certainties—about the physical world, a world that can be measured and weighed, that conforms to laws and properties. Is it any wonder that science inspires belief, so that we look to it for truth and comfort, and place our trust in it, failing to see that like religion, science is a story, and like all stories it can be plot-driven or character-driven, moved along by heroes and villains, people like the elfin, balding man standing at the podium in the Boston Radisson meeting room, Dr. Daniel Amen, psychiatrist, *New York Times* bestselling author, health columnist ("Heads Up!") for *Men's Journal,* and, depending on whom you were asking, savior or charlatan. He was projecting images of brains onto a screen— vibrant, unwrinkled brains that looked like someone had taken mottled knobs of blue, pink, and yellow Play-Doh and given them a quick squeeze.

"My blessing and my curse is to make things simple," he was saying. "Some of my colleagues get angry because they say I make things too simple." In the back of the room was a table piled high with a smattering of Amen's prodigious oeuvre, the books *Change Your Brain, Change Your Life* and *Firestorms in the Brain*, and his most recent, written with Dr. William Rodman Shankle, *Preventing Alzheimer's: Ways to Help, Prevent, Delay, Detect, and Even Halt Alzheimer's Disease and Other Forms of Memory Loss*. It was an audacious subtitle—no one had yet successfully prevented Alzheimer's disease, let alone halted it, but Amen was a provocateur who clearly liked attention, even negative attention. For years he had been selling people on the idea that he could use a brain imaging method called SPECT (single photon emission computed tomography) to diagnose psychiatric disorders, learning disabilities, and dementias like Alzheimer's. He made a compelling argument, too—that brain scans were to him as X-rays were to an orthopedist or EKGs were to a cardiologist, and the brain was the only organ most doctors were content to treat blindly. But not him. He claimed to have done something like twenty-three thousand SPECT scans over thirteen years—more than anyone else on the planet—and that over that time he had observed consistent patterns that correlated with various illnesses. He said he could look at one person's scan and not only diagnose attention deficit disorder, for instance, but know which medicine to prescribe, based on which areas of the brain needed to be sparked, and which needed to be calmed. As he wrote in a column for *Newsweek* in 2001, his methods (though "yet to win broad acceptance") were so precise that he was able to distinguish six unique kinds of attention deficit disorders, each of which required a different, highly specific intervention. The failure of other practitioners to treat ADD successfully, he suggested, was due to their reliance on outdated methods.

In academic circles Amen's work was largely dismissed. Little of it had ever been accepted for publication in peer-reviewed journals—the gold standard of scientific credibility—because Dr. Amen did not follow standard research protocols and his evidence was often subjective. (A reprint article of his that he was handing out at the seminar, from the well-respected journal *Primary Psychiatry*, was actually a paid supplement that came with the disclaimer: "Funding for this textbook has been provided by The Amen Clinic For Behavioral Medicine.") So far the consensus among neurologists and neuroscientists was that scanning technology wasn't yet able to be used to diagnose individual cases. In their opinion, Amen was offering patients something that didn't really exist. "SPECT is an experimental procedure that may eventually teach us a great deal about how the brain functions in health and disease, but it is premature to use it for diagnosis and for guidance in treatment," fumed a squib on a website called Confessions of a Quackbuster that investigated medical scams and fraud, written by a retired family practice physician and former air force flight surgeon from Washington named Harriet Hall. And, she went on, "SPECT is an invasive procedure requiring injection of a radioactive material, with additional radiation exposure from the scanner. The findings have not been validated as useful in diagnosis, and as far as I can see, all [Amen] is accomplishing is using a 'picture' to help reinforce what we already know—that the brain is the organ that determines behavior and psychology. He claims to be able to direct therapy based on scan results, and there is no research to support that claim, only anecdotal evidence and testimonials. It is unconscionable to charge patients thousands of dollars for an unproven technique and to give them the impression that it can accomplish more than it really can."

Hall's opinion was seconded by Amy F. T. Arnsten, a professor of neurobiology at Yale, who looked at some of Amen's images and was disturbed. "He does SPECT scans and he says he can tell what's wrong with you based on your pattern. It's total nonsense. He's measuring blood flow. But this isn't something you can just throw in there and do. There are sophisticated measures. There are pitfalls. You don't need to put someone through a radioactive procedure. That's what the patient interview is for."

Still, the fact was that using brain scans to diagnose dementias and psychiatric illness was not out of the realm of possibility—someday. As Randy Buckner, a cutting-edge brain-imaging researcher and professor of neuroscience at Harvard, saw it, "With a lot of these psychiatric diseases, we're going to start to learn about ways of seeing these networks and how they behave, optimally or not. We are going to be able to scan people and say if they're depressed or not, but probably more relevant is if there are multiple ways of looking at these diseases so you'll have different ways of treating them. We might come to understand how different forms of depression are, once we can see them." Which is what Daniel Amen claimed he was doing already.

"You want to know what gets me into the most hot water?" Amen asked the audience, about seventy health care professionals—social workers, psychologists, rehab counselors, physicians—who had paid $225 each to attend his all-day seminar, "From ADD to Alzheimer's: Healing and Nurturing the Brain Throughout the Lifespan." "Most people think we have some level of free will," he continued. "But it's not true. That's why brain images are kept out of court. Most psychiatric illnesses are not single or simple disorders. Giving someone a diagnosis of depression is like giving someone a diagnosis of chest pain. It's a symptom. If imaging really worked, then why don't the smart people at Harvard, the NIH, and UCLA get it? Because when they see scans they said they didn't see one thing. They are research oriented. When I look at scans, I am just seeing people."

I guessed he was kidding about free will. I mean, there we all were, sitting in neat rows, sipping expensive coffee, jotting down the occasional note. We'd chosen to be there, even those who were motivated by the seven continuing medical education credits coming their way if they chose to claim them at the end of the day. Indeed, the only one of us whose free will seemed to be compromised was Dr. Amen himself. This was the twentieth time in two months that he had given this same talk, and from Boston he was going on to Washington, New York, Dallas, St. Louis, and Atlanta, a Cook's tour of windowless hotel conference rooms.

Still, it seemed fresh. Amen was impassioned, enthusiastic, and a little whiny, which made him seem all the more genuine. His own kids had attention deficits, he shared with us, but different kinds that required different medications. He himself, he confessed, had never felt more vulnerable than when he'd had his first brain scan. Among the other intriguing and mostly unsubstantiated things he said: "Scans help with compliance—people want to see that they have a physical problem"; "Bulimics are three times more likely to have ADD than anorexics"; "Girls with untreated ADD account for half of teen pregnancies"; "Chronic fatigue syndrome is a brain infection"; "People who don't finish school are at a higher risk for Alzheimer's disease—thirty-five percent of ADD kids don't finish school."

"Look at these two brains," the doctor said, projecting two images side by side that looked nearly identical—blue, with dark planetary craters scattered throughout. "This one on the right is the brain of someone with advanced Alzheimer's, and this one is the brain of an alcoholic. There is basically no difference. They are blue because they are 'cold.' There is very little activity." Amen let that sink in. "The brain is involved in everything you do. The kind of person you are has to do with how your brain works."

The way my brain was working was by entertaining three very

different notions at once. One, that Daniel Amen was a brilliant entrepreneur who had figured out how to get anxious people to part readily with many thousands of dollars in exchange for the opportunity to peer into their own brain. (And do it with almost no time-consuming paperwork on his end, since diagnostic brain scanning using the SPECT method was not covered by insurance.) Two, that he was definitely selling snake oil—even though in his talk, the only oil he actually mentioned was a mercury-free, omega-3-rich fish oil, whose distributor just happened to be in the audience, which he recommended taking at a dose of one tablespoon a day, along with a supplement called SAM-e (S-adenosylmethionine), plus ginkgo biloba, plus coenzyme Q-10, plus a multivitamin. He said he was taking all of these, along with a prophylactic dose of the Alzheimer's medicine Aricept, though there was no clinical evidence that Aricept was beneficial to people without the disease. ("I travel with a tackle box full of this stuff," he said.) Three, that maybe Dr. Amen was onto something vital and new, and that as with others who had attempted to overthrow conventional wisdom, his insights were deeply threatening to the medical establishment, which was why it was so critical of him.

"This is the cingulate gyrus," Dr. Amen said, projecting a new slide onto the screen and pointing to a spot smack in the middle of the brain. "It is heavily involved in memory. It first goes low in Alzheimer's disease, and it's a way to distinguish AD from other dementias. SPECT can detect dementia five to seven years before the onset of symptoms."

As ungrounded as I knew this claim to be—no research group anywhere in the world had found scanning alone to be predictive—it relieved, if only briefly, the cognitive dissonance I had been experiencing. For the first time all day I knew one thing, and one thing only: I wanted a SPECT scan of my brain.

~

You might be thinking that this was nutty—or, at least, not a rational desire based on all the known facts—and if you are, I will remind you that something like twenty thousand people, from the ages of 10 to 101 according to Dr. Amen, had gone before me. (Or maybe it was ten thousand, if they'd each had two scans. The exact number is not important.) Like me, I suspect, they were motivated by the chance to claim the artifact Amen would produce—the SPECT scan itself—to study it like a rune, to find in it explanations for the inexplicable, for the untoward, for the quirks and mysteries of a single life. I was in my forties, just on the verge of fretting about the significance of misplaced car keys and unremembered conversations, and here was someone who said he could tell me that five or six or seven years hence I would not be in some doctor's office listening to a diagnosis of Alzheimer's disease. The dangled lure of certainty caught me, even though I knew it looked too shiny to be real.

But if I was a sucker, I was only partially a sucker, because even though I wanted a SPECT scan, I didn't want to pay for it. At the break, right after Dr. Amen exhorted us to get something healthy to put into our bodies because he didn't want our blood sugar to drop in the afternoon when he had a lot of important information to impart, I asked him about becoming one of his lab rats. (I had seen on his website that he was looking for healthy brains to scan to add to his library of images.) Which is how I came to be seated on a bench overlooking the Pacific at Inspiration Point in Newport Beach, California, five months later, talking to a middle-aged man named Martin who "worked in plastics" and was carrying a book about the Kabbalah and, in his own laid-back way, was possibly trying to save me. He wanted to know what I was doing in California, so I told him I was going to have my brain scanned the next day, which

seemed to me to have something in common with his affinity for
Jewish mysticism, which was, he said, "about the energy." Wrong.
"You need to ask that doctor for the numbers, for the statistics to
prove his methods are effective," he said, clearly disturbed that I
was going to allow myself, *on faith*, to be injected with radioactive
poison. "You need to be more skeptical," he warned me.

It was good advice, but I was already committed. ("It's less radiation than I got flying across the country," I told Martin, repeating
the "fact" that I had been told when I asked about the dangers of
getting scanned, a fact that I also took on faith.) The next morning
I found my way to the Amen Clinic, a ground-floor storefront office
in a suburban office park, and sat down to wait my turn. There were
two video monitors going, each with Dr. Amen on the screen, and
a display case with the doctor's books, audiotapes, instructional
posters, and DVDs for sale. There were nine people in the waiting
room already—a well-heeled mother (Coach bag, expensive hair-
cut) and her grumpy teenage son, each playing games on their cell
phones; an African American boy in a Jamaica shirt leaning sleep-
ily against his mom; a young Latino boy reading an oversize library
book; a blond teenage girl in a Cal sweatshirt and jeans flipping
through a copy of *Lucky*; two women who didn't appear to know
each other; and a slender little girl of about seven with dark circles
under her eyes who was rhythmically banging her sneakers on the tile
floor. Whoever wasn't reading was watching Dr. Amen on the screen
talk in dulcet tones about the neurological dangers of youthful drinking. He could have been Mr. Rogers.

The actual, embodied Dr. Amen, it turned out, was out of town.
A wan young woman who looked like no one had ever told her she
worked ten minutes from the beach let me know as she sat me down
for my final screening, which consisted of word list recalls, and animal analogies, and something called the SKID test, where I had to

answer questions like "Do you feel like you've committed a crime?" and "Have you ever felt like life is not worth living?" Unlike the yes or no Minnesota Multiphasic Personality Inventory, which she gave me to fill out at my leisure over the next two days—#279, yes or no, "I drink an unusually large amount of water every day"; #474, yes or no, "I have to urinate no more than others"; #293, yes or no, "Someone has been trying to influence my mind"; #470, yes or no, "Sexual things disgust me"—there definitely seemed to be right and wrong answers on the SKID. I proceeded cautiously, not wanting to have come this far only to be disqualified on account of my bathroom habits or hydration proclivities.

"No one in your family has been diagnosed with Alzheimer's, right?" the young woman, whose name was Jill, asked. Though it was not intended to be so, this was a trick question for me. Not having a family history of Alzheimer's was one of Dr. Amen's criteria for getting scanned, and I was asked this during the initial telephone screening a few months earlier. Then, as now, I said no, but it was complicated. "My father had some kind of dementia before he died," I told Jill, "but his doctor said it wasn't Alzheimer's. My father had high blood pressure and had had at least two strokes, and his doctor said that he assumed the memory problems had to do with the fact that he had vascular problems."

There, I had said it. I had confessed to a crime I felt I had committed. The truth was that my father's doctor didn't really know. My father refused to have an MRI, and there was no autopsy, so the diagnosis of vascular dementia was really just a best guess.

"Okay," Jill said. "We're all set. I'll bring you over to Mike."

Mike was, he said, a Yale-hospital-educated nuclear medicine technician. He was the one who would be injecting the radioactive dye, Ceretec, into a catheter he was inserting in a vein in my right forearm. Ceretec, he explained, took a few minutes from the time it entered my bloodstream to migrate to my brain. Once it was there, it essentially stopped time, fixing the pattern of oxygen then in my brain. The SPECT machine would be taking a picture of what had been going on in my cerebrum when the dye first settled there.

What had been going on outside my brain was that I was sitting in a darkened room in front of a monochrome computer monitor, attempting to hit the space bar as soon as a letter—K or L or S, but not X—flashed on the screen. If an X appeared, Mike explained, I was to do nothing. The letters came at random intervals. This was the Conners' Continuous Performance Test, typically used to assess attention deficits. P would appear, and I had to press the space bar, then M, then X, then X, then B. As I tried to concentrate, Mike walked in and out of the room. The door to the scanning room was ajar, and I could see a pair of shoes sticking out of the SPECT machine. I missed a few letters looking at those shoes, wondering if they were Merrell's or knockoffs, then banged the space bar on X. C appeared on the screen, then M. The letters floated away. I wondered if having the door open, and the conversations drifting in, and Mike walking in and out were all on purpose, to measure my distractibility, which I then realized was severe. When they look at my scan, they are going to see that I have ADD, I thought as another M shot across the screen—bang!—and then a C—bang! I wonder what Ritalin will be like? I thought.

AROUND THE same time that I was sitting in front of that computer in the Amen Clinic's Newport Beach office, 421 miles north, in Berkeley, a neurobiologist named Adam Gazzaley was running his own scanning experiment using fMRI to see how attention affects memory as people age. Anecdotally, at least, it was well known that as people get older, their attention starts to flicker. It was also well known that the prefrontal cortex, the very part of our brain that distinguishes humans from other species, because it is the area that controls planning, organization, abstraction, and forethought, and is the same part that allows us to focus and concentrate, starts to diminish in size well before middle age. It also begins to use the brain's fuel, glucose, less efficiently and becomes sluggish, while also losing about half the amount of the neurotransmitter dopamine it once had, which slows down the time it takes to respond to stimuli.

Gazzaley recruited two groups of subjects, one between the ages of nineteen and thirty, the other between sixty and seventy-seven, and scanned their brains while they were looking at pictures of human faces and then when they were viewing landscapes, so he could map out where, exactly, in each of their brains, they were taking in these images. That was part one. In part two, he put the volunteers back in the scanner, told them that he was going to show them four pictures—two of faces, two of scenery—and that he wanted them to focus only on the faces. When the younger volunteers did this, they showed increased activity in the part of the brain that dealt with facial recognition and decreased activity in the part that considered landscapes. Not so the older participants. Their filtering mechanism seemed to be broken. When they looked at the faces, they couldn't shut out the scenery. They couldn't focus on just one thing. "These data suggest that older individuals are able to focus on pertinent information, but are overwhelmed by interference from failing to ignore distracting information, resulting in memory impairment," Dr. Gazzaley and his collaborators wrote in an article in *Nature Neuroscience*. Inattention, which seems to come at the same time as the hair grays and skin wrinkles, interferes with memory, though not universally. Six out of the sixteen older volunteers in Gazzaley's study showed patterns of attention similar to those of their younger counterparts. Inattention wasn't inevitable, but it was common.

"With normal aging we get ADHD, but it's attention deficit/ hypoactivity—not hyperactivity. You get this weakness with the prefrontal cortex," Dr. Amy Arnsten, the petite, deceptively easy-going middle-aged dynamo who ran her own neurobiology lab at Yale Medical School, told me one day when we were chatting about her success in rousing idling monkey and rat brains with a medication called guanfacine, which appeared to amplify the circuits of the prefrontal cortex (PFC). It had already been tested on children with ADHD, as well as on people with traumatic brain injuries, post-traumatic stress, and schizophrenia, and in each case it seemed to revitalize their working memory. Once the dosage had been worked out, it would be tested on people with normal, age-related memory problems, and Arnsten expected good results as well. "What I've been doing for about twenty years is figuring out what the prefrontal cortex needs, chemically, to function well, and what makes it dysfunction. My main motivation for that is that PFC dysfunctions occur in just about every neuropsychiatric disorder there is, and also with normal aging, quite early, even in middle age. We can test for that, and when we do we can see that as we get older we are much more susceptible to distractions, interference from outside sources, from our own thoughts, from previous memories.

"Drugs like Ritalin and Adderall increase the release of the neurotransmitters dopamine and norepinephrine in your brain, but with normal aging you lose about half of your dopamine cells over your lifetime. As long as you give drugs that are kicking the horse, they become progressively less receptive. The way these drugs work doesn't help."

So, no Ritalin for me. And anyhow, according to Chris Hanks, the friendly research director of the Amen Clinic, who vaguely resembled the actor Tom Hanks (tall, good head of hair, wearing a collared shirt, jeans, and sandals with socks), and who was sitting in for Dr. Amen and reading my SPECT scan, my cortex looked "fabulous." To me, however, it mainly looked . . . hot pink, which meant that I was, according to the clinic's explanatory handout, probably not having trouble with impulsivity and planning.

A SPECT scan, unlike an MRI, does not show the constituent parts of the brain but, rather, a kind of global view. My brain looked pretty much like the ones in the clinic's brochure, *Why SPECT? What Brain SPECT Imaging Can Tell Clinicians and Patients That Cannot Be Obtained Elsewhere.* It was relatively smooth, though on one picture there was a distinct hole in my head, right at the crown, that looked like it had been bored by a bullet. In my marginal notes on that scan I wrote "wasn't operating in the top 45%," the meaning of which, unfortunately, my cerulean blue temporal medial lobes now no longer offer any assistance in recalling. All I remember was that it was distressing to see the hole there, and I was relieved when Chris Hanks pulled out a second image, this one with the hole mostly erased, and told me not to worry, it had been nothing, just computer "noise."

Hanks pointed out that my medial lobes (which sit on either side of the head, near the ears, and include the hippocampus and the amygdala, all of which are crucial to memory) were "really nice" looking, and observed that there was "symmetric profusion in the cerebellum. We like to see that the cerebellum is the hottest part. It controls gross motor skills and muscles and is also linked to your prefrontal cortex. The left cerebellum is linked to the right prefrontal cortex and vice versa. When the cerebellum isn't working right, neither is your prefrontal cortex. I'd expect your thalamus to be hot, because it gets hotter with age. It also tends to be hotter if you have depression, and gets cold when you are concentrating. You've got a couple of hot spots on the right side. It probably means you were listening to music in your head."

This seemed impossible. How could he know that the whole time I was lying in the SPECT machine, with its hydra-headed camera rotating not four inches in front of my face, I was "listening" to music—that is, I was running through a playlist of show tunes and Bach's Brandenburg highlights and Rolling Stones melodies to pass the time. I was doing the same thing right after my second Ceretec injection, when Mike came into the room, gave me a shot of the dye, and instructed me to sit still for the next fifteen or so minutes in advance of my resting scan. It was well known that doing something—playing soccer, for instance—was represented in the same part of the brain as thinking about doing that thing. For all intents and purposes, listening to *Eroica* in Carnegie Hall was the same as remembering the concert or hearing it internally, through your neural iPod. And somehow, remarkably, this was picked up by the SPECT. Either that, or nearly everyone has a sound track for their boredom, which Hanks, who was trained as a statistician, not a neuroscientist, already knew. "This may seem like phrenology," he said to me, and it did.


"THAT'S RIDICULOUS," Dr. Christopher van Dyck said when I mentioned that the Amen Clinic SPECT scan had been able to "see" me singing to myself. Van Dyck was an associate professor of psychiatry at Yale and the director of the Alzheimer's Disease Research Unit there. A few years back he was on a panel reviewing Amen's work and was not impressed. "Look, if you want to see what music looks like in the brain, you'd first get a group of people and scan them in two conditions—singing or listening to music, and not doing that, and you'd quite likely see the same areas light up. You don't do an *N* of 1 and say you see the place where music resides."

So what about my beautiful prefrontal cortex and my good-looking temporal medial lobes? "Unless there are gross abnormalities," Professor van Dyck said dismissively, "someone reading your SPECT scan should tell you that it looks 'grossly unremarkable.' Right now using PET scanning to distinguish Alzheimer's disease from non–Alzheimer's disease is in its infancy. It might become a diagnostic tool someday."

WE THINK we want to know what the future will bring. How else to explain the undying affection for Nostradamus, tarot cards, Ouija boards, the popularity of pay-by-the-minute telephone psychics, the prevalence of horoscopes in newspapers and magazines. "Will I get the promotion?" "Will I get pregnant?" "Is this true love?" we ask, as if these might be scripted a priori, and the screenplay embargoed but out there, and ultimately knowable. We want a copy because we believe we can edit it, which is to say that we also believe that our lives, our fates, are malleable.

Medicine trades on this belief, too. The doctor says your cholesterol level is "through the roof," and if you don't do something about it you'll be a candidate for a bed in the coronary care unit. Your fate is to have a heart attack, but you cheat it by choosing instead to go running every day and never eating another strip of bacon and by taking statins.

Knowledge is a kind of currency; it lets us, some of the time, buy our way out of (the otherwise) inevitable. Why else submit to the perceived indignity, say, of a colonoscopy?

But if knowledge can't be spent, is it worthless? Apparently, most of us think so. Years ago, before the discovery of the gene that causes Huntington's chorea, a neurologically devastating disease that wipes out memory and causes inexorable writhing, researchers did a series of surveys of people who were at risk for the disease, asking them if they'd be interested in being tested if a predictive test were available. Most said they would. About a decade later, after the gene had been found, and such a test had been developed, only 15 percent of those who were eligible actually chose to be tested. "What was the value in knowing when there was nothing that could be done?" people asked. The disease was incurable. The researchers called this point of view "protective ignorance." It seems to hold for Alzheimer's disease, too.

In 2004, the same year I visited the Amen Clinic seeking the certainty of a negative diagnosis, researchers in Israel set out to examine if the notion of protective ignorance held for the population at large, not just for those whose family history put them at risk of disease. They posed the following question to a group of random people: "Disease X is a terminal illness that typically appears between the ages of 35 and 50. The disease causes brain degeneration, and hence progressive deterioration of physical and mental abilities over a period of 10–20 years, until death. The frequency of disease X in the population is 1 in 10,000. The disease is caused by a genetic defect and can be detected before the onset of symptoms by taking a blood sample. Individuals found to be carriers of the gene have a 100% chance of developing the disease. Those found not to be carriers of the defective gene will not develop the disease. There is no known treatment that can effectively prevent or cure the disease." Not surprising, perhaps, more than half of those surveyed said they would not want to know their disease status. Even less surprising were their reasons: "There's nothing I could do, so why should I find out about it?" "I cannot control my fate." According to the researchers, "Only the treatment factor had an effect on respondents' willingness to be tested. . . . The availability of treatment increased greatly individuals' interest in being tested. . . . The concept of protective ignorance—a 'veil of uncertainty' about the outcome— seems an adaptive approach vis-à-vis outcomes that are threatening and uncontrollable at the same time." Thus, the researchers concluded, "Abundance of evidence both from informal observation and experimental studies shows—what almost needs no proof— namely, that people both seek and highly appreciate certainty."

Jennifer Williamson, a serious young woman with long, dark hair and a professionally unreadable face, knew this better than most of us. A genetic counselor at Columbia University, where she was a colleague of the neurologist Scott Small, Williamson frequently had to deliver bad news that was made worse by the fact that the diseases for which her clients were being tested—Huntington's or frontal-temporal dementia or Alzheimer's—were incurable.

"Let's say someone comes in and they are healthy and young, but there is a strong family history, so genetic testing is warranted," she said the day I went to see her in her cramped office on the nineteenth floor of the old Presbyterian Hospital. "What does it mean for that person to get this information? We're talking about someone's family experience with a disease for which there is no cure. My job is to help them prepare for the potential impact and to make sure that the support they may need is in place and that they've thought through about what a diagnosis means for them.

"It's pretty much next to impossible to know how this information will affect someone psychologically. It's very hard for me. You wonder why we are doing this before we have something medically to offer. It's a gift for those who find out that they don't have the disease. And for some people, the burden of not knowing is worse than the burden of knowing. They need to know because they can know."


IT WOULD be too cruel to devise a test to predict the inevitability of Alzheimer's disease (or Huntington's or Parkinson's or ALS), if it were an end in itself and not a first step to a cure. All over the United States, and in Europe, Asia, and the antipodes, there was an informal race on, not only to find an accurate predictive test, but one that could detect the disease early, before words and where-withal had gone missing. At the University of California at Irvine, Dr. Rod Shankle, Daniel Amen's writing partner on *Preventing Alzheimer's,* was finding that the standard ten-word recall test that I had been given before my SPECT scan, and which doctors rou-tinely pull out of their diagnostic tool kit when making a first pass at diagnosis, was in fact a pretty accurate way to tell who was going to have trouble down the line and who was not. In a (peer-reviewed) paper published in *Proceedings of the National Academy of Sciences* (*PNAS*), he and colleagues at UCI showed that the word test was able to discriminate, almost without fail, between people who were normal and those who had mild cognitive impairment. Because people with MCI often segued to full-blown cognitive impairment, the word test could be said to be, if not predictive, then a useful early warning signal.

"When you do the word-recall test in a normal person, the number of words they remember keeps on increasing because they are encoding the words in their brain," Dr. Shankle explained one day, when I called to find out if it was true that he was transplanting a part of the stomach, called the omentum, to the brain to stimulate the growth of new neurons. Though he wouldn't confirm or deny—omentum surgery was not only controversial, it had cost a couple of surgeons their jobs at other medical centers—Shankle was eager to talk about the efficacy of the ten-word recall test. "Then you introduce a delay and there's some decay, but the person who is normal still remembers most of the words. A person who has Alzheimer's disease, however, may get many of the words, but he fails to benefit from repetition, because with AD the problem is with the ability— the inability—to recall information. You can see this early on. It makes sense to do an annual screening after the age of fifty, otherwise you're just waiting for symptoms to arise."

But what if you can see into the brain even earlier, before words start to slip away? Recognizing that a brain impaired by Alzheimer's loses its ability to perceive and discriminate certain smells, researchers had been working on a simple scratch-and-sniff test, and the results were promising. Strawberry, smoke, soap, menthol, clove, pineapple, natural gas, lilac, lemon, and leather—these were the odors put under the noses of a group of people with MCI every six months, and a group of normal controls once a year. While those in the normal group had no trouble identifying lilacs or smoke or leather, those in the MCI group often did, and those who misidentified two or more smells were nearly five times as likely to go on to develop Alzheimer's disease.

Still, it was already well known that a certain number of people with MCI went on to develop Alzheimer's disease. A more potent test would be to find the people who will go from normal to MCI. At the University of Maastricht in the Netherlands, researchers tried to piece together data from one of the most comprehensive longitudinal surveys of cognitive health in the world, the Maastricht Aging Study. When they did that, they discovered that healthy people with no memory complaints who had difficulty identifying certain smells—cinnamon, spearmint, oregano, and aniseed among them—had more memory loss over the subsequent six years than those who were able to identify the smells without fail. Scientists at Columbia were using that finding to develop a simple scratch-and-sniff test for AD.

"HERE, PUT this on your head," Albert "Skip" Rizzo said, handing me something that looked like a pair of safety glasses attached to a gray plastic visor. I slid it on and colored rows of cubes appeared in three dimensions. I turned toward Rizzo, and as I did, I was looking at the blocks from the side, as if I'd taken a few steps to the right. "That's the tracking device," Rizzo said, sensing my disorientation. "It adjusts for pitch and roll and yaw. It moves with your head. You get the illusion you're actually in the environment when you wear the headset." We were standing in the midst of circuit boards and rows of old PCs in the annex to Professor Rizzo's virtual reality lab in the engineering department at the University of Southern California in Los Angeles. Rizzo, though I could not at that moment see him, was wearing distressed jeans and a white Harley-Davidson turtleneck—he rides a classic Harley 1200, which, he pointed out, was, despite its reputation, "not a girls' bike." There was a garnet stud in one ear, barely visible under his longish, wavy hair—black, with a touch of gray—and when he spoke, his voice was surprisingly graveled, as if he were channeling Johnny Cash, whose square-jawed face also resembled his. Years ago, not long after he got a doctorate in clinical psychology from the State University of New York at Binghamton, Rizzo took a job in New Jersey as a cognitive rehabilitation therapist, working with people who had suffered traumatic brain injuries. "A lot of young males are in that population," he said. "The high-risk takers. The drunk drivers. Gang members— all of that. With that population it was sometimes hard to motivate them to do the standard paper-and-pencil drill and practice routines.

Cognitive rehabilitation is just the same as motor rehab, you have to start real simple and build it up, but these guys didn't want to do it. Then, in the early 1990s, Game Boys came on the scene, and it seemed to me that all my male clients, at every break, at every meal, they had become Tetris warlords. It showed me that they were motivated to do game tasks, and that they got better at them the more they did them. Then, by chance, someone gave me a copy of SimCity for Christmas. It's a game where you build virtual cities. It's the ultimate executive function task—you're constantly having to make decisions and monitor multiple streams of information. I brought it in and clients who wouldn't do anything were suddenly spending three and four hours a day building cities and working collaboratively, and at that point it hit me that there could be a link between cognitive rehabilitation and virtual reality. I eventually left my job and took a postdoc at the Alzheimer's Disease Research Center at USC. I pounded on doors, holding this set of blocks, and said, 'We can build this in VR, where the blocks can be manipulated.' I started to do that, and test it on older folks at the Alzheimer's center. When the postdoc was over I moved to the school of engineering and started working with engineers and computer scientists and just started building this stuff like crazy. The blocks you are looking at—they're primitive. They are twentieth-century technology."

Even though we were already halfway through the first decade of the twenty-first, I was having trouble stacking the blocks to replicate the figure presented on the screen in front of me. Women often did, Rizzo said, but with training they tended to get as good as men. Getting better through practice is the obvious goal of exploiting virtual reality for cognitive rehabilitation, but Rizzo had taken VR steps further, employing it both as a therapeutic tool—in collaboration with the Department of the Navy, he was using it to treat veterans of the Iraq War who were suffering from post-traumatic stress disorder—and as a diagnostic device to measure and identify early memory deficits.

Rizzo had been working with Hollywood producers and military brass at USC's Institute for Creative Technologies to develop the PTSD protocol. Funded by the government, the production values were top-notch. In scenes that simulated Fallujah and Kirkuk, bursts of machine-gun rounds were intermittently punctuated by blasts from improvised explosive devices (IEDs)—homemade bombs that came out of nowhere, destroying vehicles and lives. (In the VR environment, however, the clinician was the one setting off the IEDs.) Humvees careered around corners or inched along the road to the Baghdad airport. The sun beat down. Soldiers looked warily through rifle scopes or joked around and then boom, the scene was a mass of body parts and warped steel and cries from fallen comrades and the stench of war—of diesel fumes mixed with perspiration mixed with the homely smells emanating from the Iraqi kitchens nearby, delivered by a perverse "aromatherapy" system. The idea was to bring the traumatized soldiers back to their worst nightmares again and again—the digitized version of Pavlovian habituation—and it was working. The military was even beginning to use it in the field, before soldiers had become veterans, and before the sounds and smells of war had to be manufactured.

"I'm trying to steal ideas for rehab from the military," Rizzo said, leading me to another room and another bank of computers. He handed me a visor that slipped over my skull like a camper's headlamp and rested in front of my eyes, displaying what seemed to be an animated office filled with a bunch of typical office accoutrements—a desk, a calendar, a pencil sharpener, photographs—and about the same number that were clearly out of place there: a stop sign, a basketball, a dog, and a guitar among them. Rizzo had designed the room and its sixteen objects to assess memory problems.

"We tested this on twenty subjects who had had severe traumatic brain injuries. We asked them to scan the environment. Then the experimenter moved a hand into the room and pointed out all the different objects, naming them. 'That's a dog. That's a pencil sharpener. Those are flowers. That's a stop sign.' What we found was that sixteen of the twenty subjects could remember all sixteen objects within three tries. That's amazing. Then we gave them a sixteen-word recall test, and they all sucked. Every one of them. If they had only been given that test, we would have said that they had severe memory problems. They did have problems, but by putting them in this environment, we were able to find layers of preserved memory for visual objects that would be lost in a standard test."

Rizzo must have pushed a button, because all of a sudden, all the objects disappeared from the room. The office was virtually empty. "Okay," he said. "I want you to tell me what was in the room, and put it back where it was."

I pointed to the desk. "There was a pencil sharpener here, and a dog over here, and a basketball on the shelf—"

"There's a whole career's worth of research just in this one environment," Rizzo said as I stumbled through it, trying to remember if the stop sign had been propped against the left wall or the right, and if there were books on the bookshelf, or if I was making that up.

"There are so many ways of looking at visual memory," Rizzo went on. "What's valuable about this is that it may have more functional relevance in terms of predicting real-world performance than, say, a word-list test. How does being able to remember a sixteen-word list relate to being able to remember a doctor's appointment or where you left your glasses or if you turned off the stove?"

Encouraged by his success using VR to assess memory dysfunction and to uncover memory reserves that might otherwise have been unknown, Rizzo was now using VR to diagnose Alzheimer's disease in its earliest manifestations. He had designed a VR amphitheater that could hold a couple hundred virtual people, if it hadn't been largely vacant. I entered from the back mezzanine, looking down to the stage. My task was to find my way to seat 257—there were numbers on the seat backs. It was fairly straightforward, no problem.

"What we do next," Rizzo told me, "is blindfold you and put you in a wheelchair and bring you to a different entrance. We take off the blindfold and tell you to find your way back to your seat."

He didn't really blindfold me or bring out a wheelchair, but as I looked out through the visor, I was at stage right, looking up at the terrace of seats. Because the numbers were on the seat backs, this time there were no obvious visual giveaways. I was just supposed to remember. I gazed back up to the door where I had first entered the auditorium, hoping to work down from there to seat 257, but all the seats looked alike. It occurred to me that the only way I could possibly find my way back to my seat was to use the stage as my point of reference, so I tried to remember where my seat was in relation to the center of the stage, wishing I had thought to do that when I first found my way to seat 257. I knew basically where I wanted to go, so I headed up that way, then wandered up and down the aisles like a person in a supermarket parking lot who has "lost" her car.

"The goal of this task is to spot Alzheimer's at its earliest point, even just to know that it's beginning. In traditional AD assessment, the cardinal symptom is difficulty in naming—you know, name as many words you can think of that begin with the letter S, think of all the ones that begin with L, name as many animals as you can, that sort of thing. That's where you see the best predictor of

Alzheimer's," Rizzo said. "But in the real world, in everyday life, if someone can't remember a word they don't really notice it, or they say they are having a senior moment and laugh it off. The theory behind this VR test is that the impairment may show up in a less overcompensated way, by memory for learning and space."

I picked my way back to seat 257, or what I thought was 257. I didn't ask. My cortex may have been fabulous, my brain might have been grossly regular, I might have been able to distinguish the scent of lilacs on a spring breeze, but at that moment protective ignorance was in play and I didn't really want to know if I had or—more likely—hadn't made it.

Chapter Three

# Diagnosis

THE HUMAN BRAIN has been described as having the consistency of tofu, of soft butter, of being like a three-pound Brie. It is often compared to a computer, though that's a misguided analogy, since the brain does not operate through digital logic. Seen sliced, from the side—the sagittal view—the brain looks remarkably like a boxing glove. The thumb is the brain's temporal lobe, the region that controls hearing, visual perception, emotion, short-term memory. The leading edge of the fist is the frontal lobe, home to the prefrontal cortex, which is also crucial to memory, to organization, to abstraction, to thinking ahead. The parietal lobe sits catercorner to both the temporal and frontal lobes; it contains the structures that mediate spatial perception and sensations. Behind it sits the occipital lobe, the seat of vision—actual and recalled—in the brain.

It's a simple, if deceptive, map. If the lobes were states, or the countries of Europe, you wouldn't assume they were discrete or cut off or isolated behind impassable borders. And they are not: despite their regional specificity, like the states of America or Europe, there's a great deal of commerce between them. Parts of the temporal lobe do business with parts of the frontal lobe, the parietal lobe depends on the occipital lobe, the occipital lobe sends messages to the temporal lobe. A long branching arm called an axon is sent from a neuron in one region to hook up with a neuron in another region, which it's able to do because the other neuron sends out a connector called a dendrite to greet it. Still, axon and dendrite don't quite meet, and the gap between them, the synapse, has to be spanned by a remarkably ephemeral bit of infrastructure, a chemical called a neurotransmitter, which allows one side to communicate with the other. Serotonin, the chemical enhanced by antidepressants like Zoloft and Prozac, is a neurotransmitter. So are acetylcholine, which is augmented by the Alzheimer's drug Aricept, and dopamine, without which, Parkinson's, and norepinephrine, and glutamate. No thought or action happens without the intervention of a neurotransmitter.

"This is not rocket science," Scott Small liked to say, especially when he was explaining some particularly wily concept, like the biology of intercellular transportation, and while the brain's 100 billion neurons were often compared to the Milky Way's 100 billion stars, as if this were a measure of the comparable complexity of neuroscience and astrophysics, Small had a point. Brain science is not rocket science—it's not even *like* rocket science. It's more like dendrology, which is a subject for foresters. (It's no coincidence that the branches that extend a neuron are called dendrites.) A single neuron—just one of the billion—may have a few or a few hundred or possibly a few thousand synaptic connections, which makes your three-pound Brie home to the most extensive root system in the universe.

"Why do we need a brain? Why do we need all the different areas of the brain?" Randy Buckner asked one day when he was showing me around Harvard's unprecedented 7-tesla, 32-coil MRI scanner, a machine of such power that it caused the person in the machine to see flashing lights when he blinked his eyes. "I find the answer to that in the work of Eric Knudsen at Stanford. He studies, actually, a very simple thing: how can a barn owl launch off the ledge over there, swoop down, and pick up a mouse on the floor over there. What it has to do is to localize the mouse from hearing. And the really interesting thing about hearing and localization is that unlike vision, where the light tells you where the thing is, sound doesn't do that. It's not given to you from the environment. You actually have to compute it. And it's not an easy computation. You have to use several different things to make the computation. And the thing that we use to do that—and humans are not great at it, we're good at it—we use the loudness differences between our two ears. We use the timing difference—it hits this ear faster than that ear. But that's the key thing—they can't be computed together. So one part of the brain computes loudness differences, and one part computes timing differences, and the reason why you need a brain is to put them together."

Our brains are also expert mapmakers, cartographers of the known and anticipated world. One area makes maps relative to landmarks, and another makes them relative to the body in space, instantly superimposing one upon the other. (The late neurobiologist Patricia Goldman-Rakic found that there are cells that fire to keep in mind 90 degrees that turn off at 235, and others that turn on for 0 to 90.) This is why you don't overreach when you pick up your cup of coffee in the morning, and why you can find your way home from work—or get back to seat 257 in Skip Rizzo's virtual concert hall. Your senses report to your hippocampus and your hippocampus decides what to send along to other parts of the brain for storage. The map of the moment is constantly being made.

~~

"ONE OF the best ways to determine the function of brain struc-tures is to damage them and then observe the results," an article from the American Psychological Association's journal, *Monitor on Psychology*, reported cheerily. And it was true. The reason why so much was known about how a small ridge at the bottom of the brain, one on the left, the other on the right—the hippocampus—controls short-term memory was that in 1946 a nine-year-old boy fell off his bicycle. After the accident the boy began to experience unremitting seizures, seizures so severe that when he was sixteen, with no prospect for a decent life, his doctor removed a part of his temporal lobe, including his hippocampus, hoping to eliminate the tissue that he believed was causing the young man's body to con-vulse uncontrollably. It was a radical move, but the doctor was right—the operation cured the young man of his seizure disorder. But it turned out that without a hippocampus, the young man was no longer able to make new memories. He could find his way to his childhood home, but not to the house where he lived after the op-eration. He greeted his doctors each day as if they had never before met. Over the years, when he looked in the mirror, he saw a stranger too old to be himself; his self-image had been fixed in his brain in the days and weeks leading up to the operation.

In some ways, the boy who fell off his bike is not unlike a person with Alzheimer's disease—both are locked out of the present. This is not surprising, since the hippocampus malfunctions early on in AD, and imaging studies have shown that people with Alzheimer's typically have smaller than average hippocampi. Meanwhile, as the hippocampus is shrinking—due most likely to a loss of synapses, not from the death of cells—the pathway between it and the prefrontal cortex, the prime site for working memory, also begins to degrade. Signals peter out and fade away, and questions take their place: Do I know you? Who are you? Who am I?

"The hippocampus changes with aging, late in life," Randy Buckner explained, "but it's relatively stable in volume till about sixty. People with Alzheimer's disease, though—they slide off the cliff."

Buckner and I were watching two colleagues of his scan a bottle of water as we were talking. The bottle was meant to simulate a head, so they could get a bearing on where a body would be located in the scanner. On the four computer monitors in the console room, the water bottle looked surprisingly human—two ears, a flat forehead, a mouth, eyes.

"We're trying to push imaging to its limits," Buckner said. "We need to push in all directions. Motivated by the neuroscience questions, we need engineers and physicists, people to push the computational procedures forward, and these skill sets tend not to exist in the same people. I, myself, have always been focused on memory, and on the contributions made by the prefrontal cortex and the hippocampus to memory.

"Last night I was in that scanner as a subject in probably the most sophisticated study to date that looks at the hippocampus. Because it has thirty-two coils around the head, it's able to get an extremely high resolution. I was in there for hours and hours. The magnet is so powerful it leaves a metallic taste in your mouth."

BEFORE THERE were scanners there were pencils. And paper. And a series of tests created by psychologists to assess memory, cognition, and behavior. The tests were like a camera with multiple lenses, able to focus on specific deficiencies—problems following directions, for example, or a subpar working memory—as well as providing a wider, panoramic view. Psychologists and neurologists still use paper-and-pencil tests diagnostically. They're a lot cheaper than MRIs, portable, and generally considered to be pretty reliable.

"We not only look at, say, memory, but different aspects of memory. Verbal, retention over time, abstract reasoning. We don't look at global IQ but a profile of performance across the subtests," Dr. Yaakov Stern explained the day I caught up to him after he had given grand rounds at Columbia's Neurological Institute on the subject of why some people live long lives without a hint of dementia.

A tall, loose-limbed, clinical psychologist in his late fifties who happened, also, to be an Orthodox Jew with a long history of Alzheimer's disease in his family, Stern had developed neuropsych tests at Columbia for the past quarter century. (Now they were paired with imaging studies.) "We've learned over time which functions seem to be affected earlier [in terms of disease]. In AD, it's not just memory. Memory problems are almost always there, but there are other things that are almost always there early as well. Naming. Certain visual-spatial functions like putting blocks together to make a design. Even in people with mild AD, it looks different. It's just 'not normal.' But it's that border zone, between normal and not, that's the problem.

"An even harder issue is early detection. There are studies where there's more than ten years of neuropsych data, where some people go on to develop AD and some don't. We can look back and see very subtle differences—in memory, in reasoning, in naming—but too subtle to use for diagnosis.

"There's one test I like. It's a paired association test—one thing belongs to another thing, across space. It looks at both memory and spatial memory. The reason it's interesting is because in animals that's what the hippocampus is really for—for spatial memory. In mouse labs, the tests are always about, do the mice remember where to go."

We were, at that moment, walking past the building where mouse memory was tested, up on the twelfth floor, a place where I had spent some time. There was a large white plastic tub in the testing room—a deep kiddie pool minus Nemo or the Little Mermaid adorning the sides—filled with opaque white water, in which a small plastic platform was submerged. Because mice are not fond of getting wet, the platform was there as a kind of sanctuary. If the mice found it, they could get out of the water. Getting out of the water was its own reward—no need for cheese bits. But how do you find something that can't be seen, and was, therefore, unknown? Only by chance—and chance does not lend itself to scientific rigor. Instead, the mice were placed on the platform for twenty seconds, so they knew it was there. Then they were taken off and released somewhere else in the pool and given a minute to find their way back. If the mouse did, it could stay there for twenty seconds. If it didn't, it was plucked from the water by its tail and placed on the platform for twenty seconds. The mice were given three tries. All the while, a camera suspended from the ceiling was recording their adventures.

The other things suspended from the ceiling were a blow-up dinosaur, an inflatable cheetah, and a yellow playground ball. They were the only visual referents (except for the investigator) in the room. The only way a mouse might remember where, in its white world, the platform lay, was to recall, say, where the platform was in relation to the flying cheetah. That was what Yaakov Stern (and Skip Rizzo at USC) meant by spatial memory, and it was why the Morris water maze was a useful way to test mice for memory impairments. Mice with healthy brains remembered that there was a platform and where it was. Mice whose hippocampi had been removed or damaged could not. It was that straightforward.

"My feeling is that the best tool we have for diagnosing AD is still neuropsych," Yaakov Stern said, as we were about to part. "It is sensitive to early changes. But the point of transition where someone starts to develop problems—it's hard to make a fast rule about any one person that they are going to develop AD, or is it just a normal, age-related problem?"

So WHAT would neuropsych reveal about me? It was ten in the morning, a few months after that conversation with Yaakov Stern, and I was sitting at the edge of my chair in a cramped, interior office at NYU's Center for Brain Health, about to begin the first half of six hours of testing. Neuropsych, I had decided, was the SAT for grown-ups—there was no way to study (so they said), and the outcome could determine the rest of your life. A brain scan was one thing—it was an immutable, physical fact—but a written exam was something else. You could do badly. You could clutch. You could publicly demonstrate your intellectual "insufficiencies." Neuropsych felt like a referendum on me, on my essence, on my capacities and limitations, on the progress of my inevitable decline, more than a real-time picture of my resting brain ever could be.

The tests began with basic orientation—did I know the date, the season, the address where we were, the time—and progressed to word pairs—two words twinned in unlikely combinations, like "dog-spatula" and "table-nostril"—so that hearing one wouldn't automatically cue the other as, say, "dog-house" or "table-chair" might. By the second go-round, though, I was able to invent little stories (the dog licked the spatula, her nostril resting on the table as she slept) to jog my imagination. The stories weren't actually narratives, they were more like verbal pictures, so when the tester, Schantel Williams, a stylish young African American woman who was not

allowed to be overly friendly, said "dog," I saw a furry creature standing by a dishwasher, eagerly scouring a greasy spatula.

"Everyone has strategies for remembering," Williams's boss, Dr.
Susan De Santi, the psychologist running the clinical trial, had told
me on an earlier visit. "Making lists, repeating a phone number out
loud—it's just that they're not always aware of the strategy, it's not
always conscious."

To remember long lists of individual words, I adopted the "loci"
strategy of Simonides, an ancient Greek poet, which I had read
about in *The Memory Pack: Everything You Need to Supercharge Your
Memory and Master Your Life*, by Andi Bell, a British fellow who was
identified on the book jacket as the "world no. 1 memorizer." Under
Simonides' sway, I had, earlier in the morning, visualized a room in
my house and found places in that room where I would "deposit"
any words I would be asked to recall. Each pillow in the bedroom,
the night tables, the bookshelves, the closet, the windowsill, the
dog's bed, her water bowl—twelve spots in all. "Clock," Williams
said, and in my mind I put a clock on my pillow. "Elephant," she
said, and an elephant was on my husband's pillow. When it came
time to recite the list, I did a mental tour, counterclockwise, around
the bedroom. How could I fail to remember the word *elephant*,
when one was sitting on my husband's side of the bed?

Most of the time, we expect that we will remember more than
we typically do. The call came at seven, just when I was flipping the
pancakes—I'll never forget. The bride wore an off-white gown, off
the shoulder—I'm certain. I'm pretty sure his eyes were green. Details fade and leave an aura. We *feel* that the call came before breakfast. We can say where we were sitting when the phone rang, and
how, minutes before, our only worry was if there would be enough
maple syrup. But more often than not, our memory is less proficient
than our imagination.

A number of years ago, two weeks after a meeting of the Cambridge Psychological Society, those who had attended were asked to write down everything they could remember about the meeting. These were graduate students and clinicians for the most part, people without known memory complaints. According to the psychologist Elizabeth Loftus, when the attendees' recollections were matched with a recording of the meeting, "the comparisons were striking. The average number of specific points recalled by any individual was barely more than eight percent of the total recorded. Furthermore, almost half of the remembered points were substantially incorrect. Events were recorded that had never taken place at all. Happenings were remembered that had taken place on some other occasion and were incorrectly recalled as having occurred at this particular discussion."

In another experiment, researchers asked a random group of people to describe a copper penny with as much specificity as possible, and though pennies are common, even ubiquitous, almost no one was able to say much about it at all, beyond its color and the visage of Abraham Lincoln on one side. (But what was on the other?)

Most information—conversations, observations, sights, smells, tastes—never register with our memory system. We wake up and smell the coffee, and then we get on with our day. Something else tugs on our attention like an impatient child, or we're half listening because the radio is on and the announcer is about to mention last night's baseball score, or we are worried about the budget that is due the next day, or how to pay off our credit card debt. But it doesn't have to be as obvious as that. We don't remember most things because we can't. We're simply not built like the Russian journalist Solomon Veniaminovich Shereshevskii, the man who could not forget a thing, and whose life was not any richer for it. Most of the time, forgetting is a virtue.

⁓

I WAS having no trouble forgetting the details of the story Schantel
was telling me. It had something to do with an airplane crashing
into a bowling alley. I was supposed to listen carefully, and then repeat the story, verbatim, back to her. "Anything else?" she'd prompt,
which was just about the same thing as telling me I was leaving
things out. But I knew that already.

She moved on, pushing a tattered, spiral-bound book in my direction. "I'm going to show you three pictures," she said. "You can
look at them for thirty seconds. Then I'm going to show you nine
pictures. I want you to pick out the three that you've seen before."
She looked at her watch. "Ready," she said, and flipped over the
first set of images. Whatever I had been expecting—landscapes,
cityscapes, pictures of birds or flowers—this was not it. This was
Mondrian before he knew about paint. Black, white, and gray, they
were not pictures at all, but intricate, linear, geometric puzzles, rectangles within squares within rectangles within rectangles. I looked
at them, lost, unable to invent a single strategy for remembering a
single image, let alone three. "Time," Schantel called, and flipped
the page. Now there were nine indistinguishable pictures, and my
only strategy was to punt. I pointed to three of them, randomly, relying on chance and my subconscious. Maybe it had seen something
my shallower self had not.

"We all have strengths and weaknesses," Susan De Santi observed later, when I had finished the first three hours of testing and
was sitting in her office, restored to the more comfortable role of
being the questioner, not the respondent.

"I'm really visual," said De Santi, whose open face and persistent enthusiasm for her subject, twinned with a voice that hinted

strongly of the city, were invariably reassuring. "Give me a map and I'm fine. Give me written directions and I'll get lost."

The Mondrian test, I learned later, was designed to look at a kind of processing called figural memory—memory for exclusively visual information, information that cannot be remembered by translating it into words. In this it was quite different from another visual memory test I was given, where Schantel showed me an abstract shape paired with a color that my brain automatically processed verbally. (Blue lariat, I told myself, looking at something that looked vaguely like a cow-catching round of rope. Yellow foot. Red bat wing.) Purely verbal memory, meanwhile, was being poked and prodded in numerous ways, starting with the word pairs and the paragraphs I had to hear and then recall, both immediately and after a significant delay.

"Delayed recall is particularly sensitive to ferreting out decline, and so is verbatim recall," Dr. De Santi told me months after I had taken the tests, when I was questioning the rationale for having what seemed to be a lot of redundancy in them, like being asked to remember four different one-paragraph stories, two of them word for word, the other two as accurately as possible. "When we ask people to remember a story verbatim, it tests more of their capacity to *really* remember, and people who are just beginning to have problems stand out. Remember, we are looking at healthy people. If the tests we give them are too easy, they won't be able to discriminate those who may be getting sick from those who aren't." Already, De Santi told me, the NYU team had had to adjust the tests because they were too easy for their research volunteers, who consistently outperformed the norms. "Only four percent of the people who have ever walked through our doors have less than twelve years of education," she said, "and that includes older people, minorities, immigrants, women. We had to open a satellite office in another neighborhood to recruit people who are less educated."

The norms were also adjusted to account for the educational backgrounds of the volunteers, as well as age. Younger volunteers were expected to do better than older ones. People who completed college were expected to do better than those who had not, though they were expected to do less well than their peers who had attended graduate school. My results would be measured against norms for forty-five- to fifty-five-year-olds who had had more than sixteen years of education. When I was in my twenties, I spent a few years at Oxford University reading nineteenth-century novels and making desultory stabs at a dissertation in the field of political theory. Did that really give me a cognitive advantage over my college classmates who had spent those two years in the Peace Corps or at Merrill Lynch or building houses? How could anyone know?

BACK IN the testing room, Schantel had been replaced by a graduate student who wouldn't tell me how many words she was going to ask me to remember. This was disconcerting—if there was overflow, where would I put them? I quickly imagined two additional spots in my bedroom where they could go, but at the expense of not really hearing the first three words, which caused my heart to beat so hard I heard it in my ears and two more words to elude my comprehension.

Stress affects memory. Under duress, the body produces a hormone, cortisol, that breaks open a dam of neurotransmitters and other chemicals in the brain; like any flood, it overwhelms things downstream, causing serious damage. People with chronically high levels of cortisol have smaller hippocampi. The torrent of cortisol also staves the prefrontal cortex. "The prefrontal cortex is like the stomach. When you're under stress, your stomach turns off," explained Yale professor Amy Arnsten, who was an expert on the effect of stress on the brain. "The PFC gets overwhelmed by a kind of chemical called catecholamines and the cells can't connect with each other. We become these reflexive, instead of reflective, creatures.

"There you are. You haven't studied enough for a test, and you're reading a question and you can't remember anything, and go blank. That's due to the disconnecting of PFC circuits. Just relax and it will go away."

"Blanket, horse, deceit, toothbrush, lavender, cough, dolphin," I said, taking a mental tour around my bedroom. "Toaster. Blink. Guppy . . ." Arnsten was right, the bumper sticker on my neighbor's car that said "Breathe" was right, and soon it was time to name all the items found in an office that I could think of that began with the letter *P* in ninety seconds. "Pencil, pen, paper clip, protractor—if you worked in that kind of office—pencil sharpener, paper, paper shredder, pad," I said quickly, as if I were on a game show. "Palm Pilot, phone, photos, planners, potted plants." I paused. Did I know any other *P* office items? Random words beginning with *P* came to mind: pastel, pear, pumpkin. I tried to get my brain back in gear. Pemmican? No. "Pedal!" I shouted eagerly. "You know, if you do dictation," I explained. I dug deeper—and hit rock. This was not good. "How much more time do I have?" I asked. The tester said she couldn't say. "Polish! Phone book! Posters! Partitions!" (Where had that come from? I wondered.) "Pointers!" Some neuroscientists think this kind of fluency test is most revealing of an underlying problem. I knew that, so I ransacked my brain, searching for more words, frantically, indiscriminately, like a robber who is worried that the home owners will be back any minute. But it was of no use; all the *P* items were locked away in the safe.

The strange thing about stress is that you might expect it to help you remember more, not less, to act as a magnifier, serve as a funnel, to poke a peephole in an otherwise solid wall. What is post-traumatic stress disorder but a vivid memory, born of real and horrific circumstances, that will not go away? Nonetheless, it turned out that neither intensity nor even personal experience guaranteed accuracy. Consider the case of an Australian forensics expert named Donald Thomson who was a guest, along with an assistant commissioner of police, on a television show devoted to exploring the unreliability of eyewitness accounts. Not long afterward he was summoned to a police precinct, put in a lineup, and identified by a woman as the man who had raped her. Though he had an incontrovertible alibi—he was on national television at the time of the attack and seen by hundreds of thousands of viewers—he was charged with the crime on the basis of her unwavering eyewitness testimony. It was only later, when an investigator discovered that the woman's television had been on during the assault, that it became clear that in the midst of her trauma, the woman had conflated Thomson's face with that of the rapist.

Or take the cases of about five hundred soldiers at Fort Bragg, who had just finished a terrifying mock prisoner-of-war interrogation as part of their psychological warfare training. The interviews had lasted half an hour and were brutal. As soon as they were over, the soldiers were asked to pick out their interrogators from a lineup or identify them in a photographic face book—and many of them could not. Some were so far off the mark that they got the gender of their tormentor wrong.

"Even under the best circumstances, for a highly stressful event, we found that at least one in three people is wrong," reported Andy Morgan, the Yale researcher who led the study. "And if you don't have a picture from the scene of the crime, it's probably no better than a coin toss. [These were] special operations personnel and maybe pilots and Marines, so not real timid, anxious people. They were very confident in their responses to the test, but their confidence had no relationship whatsoever to accuracy."

Psychologists also study a phenomenon called "flashbulb memory," a moment in time when an outsized news story like the events of September 11, 2001, or the assassinations of John Kennedy or Martin Luther King Jr., is so encompassing and emotionally laden that it merges with an individual's personal history. Something happens, something big enough to grab our collective attention, to make us stop in our tracks, so that when we retell it, later, the narrative often begins, "I was on my way to [fill in the blank] when I heard that an airplane crashed into the World Trade Center." The story goes on, blending historical and personal details that, together, provide a certain authority because, in a sense, you were there, and eyewitness testimony is often privileged. It's called "flashbulb memory" because, at the moment of discovery, it's as if a camera flash goes off, briefly illuminating the scene, with you in it, and fixing it (rather like Ceretec in the brain) for all time. Ulric Neisser, a professor at Cornell and Emory who has written extensively about flashbulb memory, can recall precisely where he was and what he was doing when he learned that the Japanese had bombed Pearl Harbor: he was at home, listening to a baseball game. He remembers it vividly. The only problem is that it could not have happened. Pearl Harbor was bombed in December, a month when baseball is not played in America.

It turns out that flashbulb memory is no more reliable than eyewitness (or earwitness) accounts. The day after the space shuttle *Challenger* exploded, Professor Neisser asked 106 people to fill out questionnaires detailing where they had been and what they were doing and what they knew about the disaster. Not only were their memories of the event largely inaccurate the first time around (though their confidence about their accuracy was high), three years later, when they were asked to answer the same set of questions, there were significant discrepancies between what they (thought they) knew then, and what (they thought) they knew now.

Memory, it turns out, is an expert storyteller. If there is a context, it fills in the blanks. If there are characters, it fleshes them out. If there is no plot, it suggests one. This is because human memory does not record in real time; it is not an archive; it functions neither as hard disk nor flash drive. Memories reside in the brain in chemical traces. The traces can fade—why your college roommate's brother's name feels just out of reach—and they can be augmented, the layering of experience and observation, which can lead to a more secure memory, though not necessarily a more accurate one, as memories merge. Even without specific memory complaints, even without a pathology like Alzheimer's or mild cognitive impairment, human memory is less reliable than we remember it to be.

THOUGH I cannot say that the last three hours of neuropsychological testing flew by, they did pass unremarkably. After a while the tests got redundant—more stories to repeat verbatim, more "unreadable" (to me) images to sort out, more time trials requiring me to pile on words beginning with the consonant du jour. I was asked to draw, to do simple math, to define a long list of words, to repeat strings of numbers forward and backward.

Every so often there was something challenging, like a fourteen-item shopping list to remember, which I was asked to recall ten minutes later, after I'd completed a simple logic exercise on the computer (which may have been intentionally distracting, to woo my brain into forgetting the broccoli and peanut butter) and then to recall again, a half hour after that, when I was asked not only to repeat the list but to speak it in alphabetical order. (This time I did manage to forget the broccoli.) Mental manipulation like that is a test of working memory, and it was mildly reassuring that after so much virtual prodding and poking, mine still was.

When I had repeated my last verbatim paragraph and listened to my final list of words, Susan De Santi invited me back to the center's control and command center—a room full of computers and people hunched over them—to look at my brain. Not the black-and-white structural MRI I last saw over the shoulder of Dr. St. Louis, and not the mottled neon-mass-with-the-hole-in-the-head SPECT that I took home from the Amen Clinic, the scans Susan had were a different set that had been taken with positron-emission tomography (PET) at the Brookhaven National Lab, a sprawling government research facility in Upton, Long Island. Known primarily for its work on high-energy physics, for its massive particle accelerators, for its multiple Nobel Prize winners, for the discovery of the charmed baryon (a three-quark particle), and even, in some quarters, for the invention of the first video game, Brookhaven was no less distinguished for its medical research, particularly medical research that could be advanced by the application of high-energy physics. It was at Brookhaven that scientists figured out how to harness certain kinds of X-rays to diagnose heart disease and to radiate certain kinds of otherwise untreatable brain tumors. It was here, too, where L-dopa to treat Parkinson's disease was discovered, here where doctors were sorting out the role of neurotransmitters on the alcoholic brain, and here where they were tracking down sources of infection. Over in Building 906, an undistinguished, one-story boxy brick structure, one of many dozens of similar utilitarian bungalows that gave the place the feel of a minimum-security prison, researchers were conducting a variety of brain studies using PET. Like SPECT, PET assessed glucose metabolism in the brain. It could show if a brain was underactive or healthy, and which parts were drawing down the most energy. Unlike SPECT, though, PET imaging occurred in real time; pictures were taken as the radioactive dye snaked through the veins and infiltrated the brain.

The radioactive isotope that would soon be traveling through my body was being made right there, at Brookhaven, though in a different building, and would be arriving soon. Phone calls were placed, announcing that the isotope was being mixed, and that it was on its way, and that it was in the house—and it was like the excitement that builds in advance of a visiting celebrity, or on death row right before the lethal injection. This image was not completely fanciful on my part. Years before, I had spent some time in the death house at the Louisiana State Penitentiary where the gurney in the execution theater didn't look all that different from the long plastic slab I was stretched out on at Brookhaven, though the one at Brookhaven didn't have leg restraints. But my arms were strapped down, and there was an intravenous line attached to my right arm, where the isotope would enter, and a deeply painful arterial line plugged into my left wrist, where blood would be drawn and tested every few seconds, and I was immobilized from the neck up in a foam helmet that had been made from a mold of my head. Also, right before I gave up my glasses and watch and wedding ring and shoes and went into the scanning room, I was given a take-out menu and asked what I would like to eat.

"I don't want you to think about anything," Susan De Santi said to me after my head had been secured in the helmet and the radioisotope was minutes from entering my bloodstream. De Santi was speaking through a microphone—she was in another room, one with a lot of computer monitors, looking down at me through a window.

"How do you think about nothing?" I asked. It seemed an impossible, almost philosophical task—not that I could ponder it.

"Just don't lie there and do math problems," she said. "It will skew the reading."

"I would say that there is absolutely no chance I am going to lie here and do math," I said.

"Or recite poems," she added. "Don't do that. What we're looking for is an overall picture of how your brain uses glucose, which is its fuel. If you concentrate on a particular task, the brain region involved in that task will demand more glucose, which will show up on the scan."

It is difficult not to think of anything. I lay there, arms splayed, watching the assembly line of vials moving in and out of position to catch samples of arterial blood, jerking away from that observation, noticing the halo of light around the recessed bulbs overhead, pulling away from that, wondering about the Red Sox—did they stand a chance this season, and how was Pedro Martinez doing over at the Mets, and remembering the 1986 World Series. . . . My thoughts were like pinballs caroming off the bumpers every time they verged on getting serious or complicated or involved. Though I was lying down, with a warming blanket over me, and my wrists were resting on heating pads, it was enervating and nerve-racking: what if I was thinking about too much of nothing?

Then it was over. My wrists were untaped and the IV lines removed, and my head was released from its case. Pressure bandages were applied to my arms, I was given back my glasses, shoes, ring, and watch, and escorted to an alcove with a Barcalounger and a VCR and a box full of old movies—*Butch Cassidy and the Sundance Kid* and *Sleepless in Seattle*, that sort of thing. My lunch was on a tray table, but I didn't really want it. "You need to drink a lot of liquids," a nurse said, coming over to check on me. "The more you drink, the quicker you will get rid of the radioactivity. Just make sure that after you use the bathroom you wash your hands really well."

So I was hot, radioactive, and would be for the better part of the next twenty-four hours. "Please don't use the front door when you leave, either," she cautioned. "You'll set off all the alarms."

"THIS IS Yee Li," Dr. De Santi said, introducing me to a slight young man in a button-down shirt and jeans who was in the process of calling up the images of my brain that had been made that day in Brookhaven. And there it was, in living color, mostly green, yellow, and orange.

"The colors show the glucose metabolism," Yee Li explained. "The brighter the color, the higher the metabolism, the more glucose being used, which is good. When someone is sick, there is a lot less activity, and it's less colorful."

"This is basically what a healthy brain should look like," Susan De Santi added, "but you have to understand that a diagnosis is not made from one modality. That's why we look at the MRI, the PET, the neuropsych, the medical exam, and do a clinical interview. The thing is, some people who have healthy brains in terms of their PET and MRI scans do really well on the neuropsych tests, but some of them don't. I look for patterns. If people are going to have trouble, they are going to have trouble in more than one area. But sometimes people have a lot of stress or anxiety and they are not really impaired, but it's hard to tell. Performance anxiety is a real factor. Sometimes people get so anxious that we're going to find something, they almost make us find something, because they just can't perform.

"Would we tell someone if we found a problem? When we send them their report, we might say something like 'Your cognitive performance is consistent with MCI.' We've done that, yes. But you know, not everyone who gets MCI goes on to get Alzheimer's, and not everyone who gets diagnosed with MCI is really impaired." De Santi called up a series of graphs on her computer that showed people with MCI at two different points in time, the first when they were initially diagnosed, the other two years later.

"As you can see," De Santi said, "some of them continued to have mild cognitive impairment, and some of them went on to develop Alzheimer's disease, but some actually went back to being normal. I wanted to find out if there was any way to distinguish the ones who went back to normal, and the first thing I found was that they were younger and more educated than the group as a whole. But here's the other thing," she said, her voice growing quiet and conspiratorial. "People think that MCI is only about memory, and in fact, only those who converted to AD had significant declines in memory. But we also found that it's not memory alone. It's memory problems combined with problems in some other cognitive domain, like fluency or spatial reasoning. Seventy-one percent of those who had memory problems and some other problem ended up getting sick with AD, but only eight percent of people who had only memory problems got sick. That's significant. For people who went back to normal, the significant thing was that they had no attention deficits. Attention, not memory, was really the key." For these folks, at least, the prefrontal cortex turned out to be the gatekeeper.

I left Susan De Santi's office wondering about my own prefrontal cortex. For what it was worth, I knew from the pictures that it was grossly regular, but how meaningful was that? The test results would be more telling, I decided, walking across Thirty-fourth Street, east to west. It was a brisk day in winter, but sunny. Valentine's

Day decorations were in all the drugstore windows. I couldn't say what, exactly, among displays of red velvet hearts filled with chocolate and pyramids of Secret deodorant, jogged my consciousness, but all of a sudden I had cause to question both prefrontal cortex and hippocampus and whatever other part of my brain had conspired to let me leave my tape recorder and notebook back at the Center for Brain Health. Chagrined and embarrassed—here was empirical evidence of my faulty memory as glaring as any errors that might show up on a list-learning test—I turned into the wind coming off the East River and headed back to NYU.

Still, almost as soon as I was finished with the neuropsychological tests, I forgot about them. The experience, of course, did not slip away, but the details did. By the time I was back at Thirty-fourth Street and Third Avenue they had begun to fray at the edges, or what I assumed were the edges, and an hour later, a day later, a week later, I remembered less—that there were many word-list tests, for example, but not how many, and certainly not the words themselves. That I had had trouble with the abstract visual battery, though I couldn't say with any specificity what those images looked like. (Nor could I then.) Life itself, which comes to us through our senses, which is encompassing, which ebbs and flows, is like the tide washing over the water's edge, eroding and rearranging it, rasping channels, filling them in. This is how memory is undermined, but also how it is formed. Biologically it's a matter of chemicals and electrical impulses that bridge synapses and then reinforce them—or not.

IN 1957, when the first papers about H.M., the boy who had fallen off his bike and had been subsequently relieved of his hippocampus, were published by Brenda Milner, a Canadian psychologist, a young physician and bench researcher named Eric Kandel, then working at the National Institutes of Health, read in them a suggestion of where to begin his own research: in the hippocampus, looking for cells that store specific memories. Milner had discovered the where. Kandel was searching for the how. In collaboration with Alden Spencer, another young NIH researcher, Kandel began examining hippocampal neurons, trying to understand how they stored memories. Twelve months into their pursuit, Kandel and Spencer made a seminal observation: that "the cellular mechanisms of learning and memory reside not in the special properties of the neuron itself, but in the connections it receives and makes with other cells in the neuronal circuit to which it belongs." Those connections were reinforced when either neurotransmitters or an electrical charge jumped the gap between neurons, binding them. The better the connection, the more secure the circuit, the stronger the memory.

Kandel turned to the giant marine snail, *Aplysia*, an animal that first entered recorded history in the work of Pliny the Elder, to puzzle out how this happened. With a mere 20,000 neurons (as opposed to our 100 billion) clustered together in groups called ganglia, some of which were visible to the naked eye, the sea snail was an ideal reductionist laboratory in which Kandel could carry on research. Taking a cue from Pavlov's work on behavioral responses to stimuli, he decided to look at how an individual brain cell would change in response to particular patterns of electrical pulses. One kind of pulse simulated habituation—as when a dog, upon hearing a bell ring again and again, learns that it is harmless. Another replicated sensitization, the opposite of habituation—as when the dog is given a shock to its paw and pulls it away. The third possibility, classical conditioning, involved the pairing of a neutral and an averse stimulus—as when the shock is administered at the same time as the bell is rung, and the dog comes to associate the sound of a bell with a shock to his paw and recoils upon hearing it, even in the absence of the shock.

I had seen something like this in the mouse behavior lab at Columbia, where there was a glass cage, inside a Formica cabinet, at which a video camera, attached to a computer, was pointed. The cage had a floor of polished metal rods that looked like the rack of an oven before it left the showroom—which wasn't a completely random association on my part, since the rods were hooked up to an electric current. Mice would enter the cage, look around, explore, check out the view. Then a bell would ring, after which the floor was electrified for twenty seconds, causing the mouse enough discomfort that it would freeze in its tracks. On subsequent visits to the chamber, the bell would sound, and if the mouse remembered the earlier sequence of events, it would freeze even though the switch had not been toggled and the floor did not throw spikes of electricity up through the mouse's feet. The images of the mouse, arrested by fear, taken by the camera, were fed to the computer, which had an algorithm that determined just how afraid of the bell that mouse had become. Fear, in this case, was a stand-in for memory.

REDUCTIONISM ENDED up serving Eric Kandel well. (It also inspired a host of other neuroscientists to look for clues about human cognition in animals with very simple nervous systems.) Sifting through the two thousand neurons that made up a single *Aplysia* ganglion—a ganglion being a cluster of nerve cells—he and his collaborators made the novel observation that the strength of synaptic connections, rather than being fixed and constant, is augmented or weakened by experience; habituation weakens the connection and sensitization enhances it. Plasticity—the capacity to change—is built into the molecular architecture of the synapse. In other words, who we are, our essence, is mutable by learning. Kandel began to make an inventory of *Aplysia*'s different behaviors, looking for one that he could manipulate in an effort to see, firsthand, the synaptic effect of learning. He ended up choosing the snail's most basic response, its gill-withdrawal reflex: touch its body near the gill—its breathing mechanism—and *Aplysia* quickly and defensively retracted its gill. Touch its body near the gill numerous times, though, and it stopped withdrawing the gill; the snail had gotten habituated to being stroked, which it no longer perceived to be threatening. Shock it with an electrical pulse, however—Pavlov's sensitization—and it quickly and emphatically pulled back again.

Kandel and his colleagues also found that to establish long-term memory in *Aplysia*—to make the learning stick—it was best to train the snail slowly, over several days, rather than intensely, at once. Touching it forty times in a row, for instance, caused the snail to become habituated for a single day. When those forty touches were spread out over ten days, however, the snail stayed habituated—it didn't withdraw its gill—for an entire week. So how did that happen? How did that short-term memory become a long-term memory? What was going on in the snail's brain cells?

It had taken Kandel fifteen years to be in the position to answer those questions. He knew from his research that long-term memory was not simply enhanced short-term memory, that not only did the synaptic changes in long-term memory last longer, but the number of synapses changed in response to stimuli. (The number went down in habituation and up in sensitization.) Kandel and his group had a hunch—that the release of one neurotransmitter, serotonin, augmented a second neurotransmitter, glutamate, causing a kind of biochemical domino effect in the cell. In a paper published in 1971 in the *Journal of Neurophysiology*, laying out their theory, they further speculated that a molecule called cyclic AMP was causing the cells to retain those changes.

Kandel and his associates did not come across cyclic AMP by chance—it was already known to amplify the biochemical signaling in fat and muscle cells. They surmised that it might be doing something similar in the brain as well. Already, in 1968, a researcher at the University of Washington had shown how that amplification worked: cyclic AMP activated an enzyme called protein kinase A, which in turn acted like a switch, turning some proteins on and some proteins off. In the case of *Aplysia*, Kandel found that a shock to its tail not only released the neurotransmitter serotonin, but that serotonin then stimulated the production of cyclic AMP. Later, when a postdoctoral student in Kandel's lab injected cyclic AMP directly into *Aplysia*'s sensory cells, not only did the amount of glutamate increase, but the synapse between the sensory neuron (the neuron registering the shock) and the motor neuron (the one that signaled the gill to retract) was noticeably stronger. Here, at last, were "the first links in the chain leading to memory storage," Kandel recalled. Twenty-four years later, that work won him the Nobel Prize.

My NEUROPSYCH exams continued to fade. I had no reason to forget them—research out of Stanford had recently shown that people are able to will themselves to forget—but no reason to recall them, either, and trigger the cyclic AMP that would bind the experience more securely. Smell is often a lazy conjurer, inadvertently eliciting memories that otherwise seemed lost, because odor is most resistant to forgetting—odor memory can remain intact for a year, while images start to fade almost as soon as they're seen—but there was no smell attached to those hours in the testing room to seduce my hippocampus into bringing them back. Days went by, then weeks, then a month, and when the thin envelope with the Center for Brain Health return address arrived in the mail, I was at a loss, for a moment or two, about what it was. And then it was like a stampede, though the memories were not of the tests themselves, but of the way they had made me feel—anxious, worried, exposed.

It was a short letter, but I skipped right to the summary paragraph at the end. My physical exam was fine. My heart beat at 51 bpm. My neuropysch was fine. "Overall," the letter said, "your neurological and neuropsychological evaluation was within normal limits. There are no indications that your [sic] are suffering from a memory disorder such as Alzheimer's disease, or that you are at risk for this condition in the future."

So I was normal.

Chapter Four

# Normal

So I was "NORMAL," but what did that mean? That I performed on a par with my peers, that I was average, that there was no obvious evidence of disease? Being normal, of course, was no insurance against getting sick. It was no guarantee that my body wasn't already ganging up on my brain, or that my brain was not plotting against itself. Researchers still did not know when a disease like Alzheimer's began. Was it twenty years before there was actual evidence? Was it fifty? Or was disease, as the Harvard neuroscientist Randy Buckner said, an inevitable artifact of staying alive longer than evolution had planned?

"The big question is, how do we disentangle what may be just a normal developmental course in the modern human condition, where we live well beyond our reproductive fitness?" he mused one day, after observing changes in his own, thirty-five-year-old brain. "Maybe a lot of changes we see in advanced aging are because we have a preprogrammed, normal developmental course that's now being expressed well beyond what evolutionary pressures have been placed on it. And then there may be changes that are pathological and disease-related, some of which may come from normal brain events, but now are so detrimental they cause clinical impairments and therefore we label them as disease. Maybe some of the changes in advanced aging are good."

Talk to people like Randy Buckner or Mony de Leon at the Center for Brain Health at NYU ("Humans have a series of clocks in their bodies, all ticking, and we don't know the mechanisms or how they work") and whatever solace you might have taken from the declaration of "normal" quickly went away. They did not even have to say it: normal now didn't guarantee normal in six months, let alone normal in two years, when I was scheduled to repeat the battery of neuropsychological tests, have another structural MRI, another PET. That was the point of longitudinal studies. Even then, no one would know if normal would be a temporary condition or if it would endure.

In the month of March, just weeks after scoring normal, I put the butter away in the microwave, could not remember if the word *occurred* had two *r*'s or one—both ways looked strange—and forgot to pay the phone bill. These things did not happen at once—it wasn't that I was having a bad day or was sleep deprived. (Sleep deprivation is a known memory disrupter, which is why the United States military is spending massive amounts of money on sleep research, with some of that money going to Yaakov Stern and Scott Small at Columbia. One morning I went down to the scanning room in the Presbyterian Hospital basement where a twenty-six-year-old volunteer, who had been awake for a couple of days, was lying in the scanner having his brain analyzed as he performed some basic memory tests. The problem was that soon after he lay down in the machine, he fell asleep, and the experiment had to be called off.) Memory glitches like the ones I had noted in my journal were part of being normal. Indeed, there were probably many others that I had either forgotten or forgotten to write down. Part of being normal is not being a reliable self-reporter. Another part, especially if you are, say, fifty, is forgetting to pay the phone bill now and again. The tendency to forget explains why automatic bill-paying services have become so popular: memory can be jobbed out.

One reason normal has become synonymous with forgetful, at least in the harried, driven, overworked, wired cultures of affluence and aspiration, has to do with the simple mathematics of overcommitment: if the average digit span is seven, then most people have too many things to hold in their heads at once—meetings and phone calls that need to be returned and doctor's appointments to keep and birthdays and medications to take, and not just one's own, but one's kids', and partners', and parents', and friends'.

Add to ordinary human limitations the physiological effects of normal aging—the shrinking, slowing prefrontal cortex, the diminution of neurotransmitters circulating in the brain, the weakening synaptic bonds, the death of synapses, all of which was normal, too. Still, there was some good news. According to the authors of the Johns Hopkins white paper on memory, "studies repeatedly show that older people who do poorly on timed tests actually do as well or better than their college-age counterparts when they are permitted to work at their own pace." The machinery was slow, but it worked. It was dial-up, not broadband, but it was still connected.

Not all kinds of memory were susceptible to aging, either. Personal history survived intact well into old age. So, too, emotional memory. Implicit memory—the motor skills that most of us take for granted, for instance—also held. Moreover, in high-functioning older adults, there seemed to be some kind of compensatory mechanism at work, where the brain began to draw on its own resources, recruiting parts of the brain that, when younger, were idle. If cognition as one gets older is a dimming hallway, then the brain is not only photosensitive, it is able to throw a few switches to put out more light. It does this, for instance, by relying on both sides of the brain for tasks that, earlier, had taken only one. According to researchers at Duke University, led by a neuroscientist with the wonderfully eponymous name of Roberto Cabeza, older adults who performed as well as younger ones tended "to enlist the otherwise underused left half of the prefrontal cortex of their brain in order to maintain performance." It was like what happened when a skinny little kid used both hands to pick up a suitcase that an average adult could carry in one; however many hands it took, the bag still got moved. Now, of course, most travelers roll their suitcases, which is not only a compensatory strategy, but a technological one. Similarly, the discussion that followed the Duke finding was, in part, about whether there were technologies—which is to say, drugs—to induce bilateralism in those elderly adults who didn't default to it.

Not everyone who looked at the images, though, interpreted what they saw as compensation. Elkhonon Goldberg, for one, a Russian émigré neuropsychologist who had studied in Moscow under A. R. Luria, whose book *The Mind of a Mnemonist,* about the Russian journalist who could never forget anything, is a classic of the psychological literature. Now a clinician in private practice in New York, who modestly described himself as a "peripatetic gadfly" who freelanced research with collaborators in Australia, Japan, and Germany, Goldberg believed that bilateralism was something altogether different. He believed that it was a physical manifestation of wisdom.

It was snowing hard in New York the day I went to visit Dr. Goldberg, a physically imposing man with a slightly opaque Russian accent laminated to perfectly inflected English. All of his patients had canceled, so we settled in, he at his desk, me beside it, and I thought we were alone, till he called out a command for coffee, and a young man with a thicker accent than his, who had been quietly on call in the next room, jumped up, grabbed an umbrella, and rushed out the door. Goldberg was telling me about his early years, his interest in the brain as a high school student in the 1960s, and studying with Luria, who only wished to advance Goldberg's career when he urged him to join the Communist Party. Goldberg resisted and, secretly harboring a desire to escape from the Soviet Union, dropped out of school shortly before defending his doctoral dissertation, deliberately broke off his relationship with Luria, and moved to the hinterlands to become . . . no one. A smart Jew with a doctorate from Moscow University, Goldberg reasoned, would never be allowed to emigrate. But a menial worker with few prospects—who would care? He moved back home to Riga and took a job as a hospital orderly, moving cadavers. It was just the ticket that he needed, ultimately, to get out of the country.

Though I had read all of this before, in Goldberg's book, *The Executive Brain*, it was more urgent hearing it in his own voice. He had just finished a new manuscript, he told me, that was going to be called *The Wisdom Paradox*. It, too, was about the frontal lobes but, he hinted, radical, heterodox: it took on a central question of philosophy—what is wisdom—and answered it with images from modern psychology—PET scans and MRIs. Wisdom, Goldberg told me, was not some ephemeral notion. It was not even especially philosophical. Rather, it was a biological process. It could be seen on film.

"How do younger adults differ from older adults?" Goldberg asked rhetorically. "Over the last decade, this question was asked in a number of functional neuroimaging studies using PET and fMRI. . . . The findings showed an ongoing progression of the right-to-left shift of the 'center of cognitive gravity' throughout the life span." The significance, Goldberg argued, was this: the right side of the brain is where we encounter new and novel situations—it is where we struggle to understand; it is the hemisphere of youth and inexperience. But then we get it. The light goes on. That's the left side, making the connections, the left side, where the patterns of experience eventually come to reside. Pattern recognition, a left-hemisphere attribute, allows us to chance upon the world with a measure of omniscience—call it wisdom—because what we are encountering is already in us. It is not that the right side of the brain is abandoned for the left, but that with age the left side is more fully engaged. Or, simply, it is more full.

THE BODY makes do with the resources at hand. But if we have to rely on compensatory strategies—that is, if compensatory strategies are indeed normal—are we really okay? The answer was given to me one day when I was sitting in on the monthly neurology autopsy meeting at Columbia, and the doctors were discussing a patient whose brain showed evidence of plaques and tangles, but who had been lucid and independent up to the end. Maybe, the doctors surmised, she would have gone on to exhibit the emotional and intellectual effects of Alzheimer's, but while she was alive she was never given that diagnosis. Reality trumped pathology until she was dead.

"There have been a number of findings that show various changes in the brain that are observed in all individuals as they age," Harvard's Randy Buckner pointed out to me. "That shouldn't be surprising, given the other ways in which our bodies react to getting older—hair-color changes, thinning hair"—he paused and touched his scalp, which was beginning to show through what had been a thatch of wavy brown hair—"muscle tone lessens. Everyone agrees there is volume loss in the brain as we age. What's surprising is how early it begins. Look at ten-year-olds versus eighteen-year-olds and there is already a volume loss. Our idea is that there are a number of normal changes in brain function that may still actually have subtle cognitive changes associated with them, and there are distinct changes such as you see in AD that not everyone experiences that represent aberrant processes.

"One way to see that is that you can take younger people with early-stage Alzheimer's and compare them to much older adults who don't have the disease. You can directly oppose the effects of aging with those of disease. And what you can see if you do that is certain changes in the frontal cortex will track with age and are not accelerated by having AD. By contrast, there are changes that you see that are related to AD and will be much more prominent in younger individuals with the disease that look like they are disease related. We can see effects of aging on the hippocampus and we can see additional, additive effects of Alzheimer's disease. Our findings are consistent with what Scott Small is finding. His findings are motivating us to look at different subregions of the hippocampus."


SCOTT SMALL picked up a piece of chalk and drew what looked like a bicycle chain on his blackboard. Then he drew another loop, this one vertical, and then a third. It was December 2004, and he was trying to explain his most recent finding. Small was being generous. Not only with his time, but with his assumption that if I did not understand what he was saying, it was because he was a crummy teacher, not that I was a bad student. But I was getting this. It wasn't hard, at least schematically. The hippocampus is essentially a circuit, Scott was saying, and it is not unlike the electrical circuits that bring power to our houses, where a break anywhere in the system takes the whole thing down. Scott's hunch was that it mattered where the break occurred, even if the end result—that the lights went out—was the same no matter where it had happened. His hunch—and now his latest finding—was that a different part of the hippocampus was broken in Alzheimer's disease than it was in normal aging.

"The hippocampus is implicated for everyone," Scott said, looking at me to make sure I was following him. "We know independently that AD targets the hippocampus. There are two conflicting views on this: One camp says, look, Alzheimer's is a disease of old age. It has a long incubation period, so maybe everyone with age-related hippocampal dysfunction has early AD; if they live long enough, they will get AD.

"The other view says that this can't be. Not everyone who ages ends up developing Alzheimer's disease. Look at our mammalian cousins. They all develop age-related hippocampal dysfunction, yet they don't develop AD."

One of the goals of Small's lab was to try to resolve that debate. Since Scott approached the hippocampus as a circuit, and the hippocampus was made up of different nodes, and each one had a distinct molecular profile, he predicted that if Alzheimer's disease and age-related memory loss were separate processes, then each should blight a different node.

At first, there was no way to see it—the scanning machine just wasn't sharp enough. Like a pair of glasses that hadn't been adjusted to account for an astigmatism, it could take in the landscape but failed to distinguish sky from sea. Small knew that it could be years before the technology caught up with his need for it. He also knew that he didn't have years, and neither did his patients. So he did the only reasonable thing—he did it himself. Scott Small invented a new way to see structure and function using MRI. And when he did, sea parted from sky, and he was able to peer deeply into the space in between.

"What we found is that in humans, monkeys, and rats, normal

aging targets a node called the dentate gyrus. The dentate gyrus is the most impaired, but a different node, the entorhinal cortex, is relatively spared. But in Alzheimer's disease it's almost the exact reverse. It's the entorhinal cortex that's vulnerable."

Small paused, and then, in case I might have missed what he said the first time, in case I missed how significant and novel and revolutionary this finding was, said it again:

"We have these two areas, and the dentate gyrus is, relatively speaking, the most vulnerable to aging, and the entorhinal cortex is relatively spared. In AD it's the entorhinal cortex that's relatively most vulnerable, though, because a person who has Alzheimer's is also aging, the dentate gyrus may be vulnerable, too."

TWO YEARS had passed since that conversation. Scott Small and I had become friends, checking in every so often to find out how the other was doing. I'd stop by his office when I was in New York, and he'd bring me up to date about the progress in his lab, and the new pug puppy at home, and the sheep and donkeys he and his wife kept at their small farm upstate. He'd tell me about a meeting at NIH or the Society for Neuroscience, and usually mention that he may have offended some senior scientists there by his insistence that he was right and they were not, but the fact was, every time I'd go anywhere—to UCLA or Harvard or UCI or to the NIH itself—the conversation almost always found its way to Scott Small and the work he was doing, and how he was pushing the field along. Sometimes this made sense to me, like when Randy Buckner mentioned Small's work, or when Molly Wagster, a program director at the National Institute on Aging, included Small in her very short list of researchers doing cutting-edge work on normal cognitive aging. But sometimes it would come out of the blue, like the time I'd spent two days in meetings run by Greg Petsko, a physical chemistry professor at Brandeis, meetings that had nothing at all to do with science— we were interviewing prospective fellowship students. I hadn't known Professor Petsko before the meetings, and when they were over I asked about his work, and he began to talk about making yeast models to test different hypotheses of disease, a discourse that led, eventually, to some of the most exciting work of his, with a young neuroscientist at Columbia, who was "the real deal," who of course was Scott Small.

"I'm such an Israeli," Small would say, which was shorthand for his being direct and impolitic, though if he was, I didn't see it. In meetings with his staff, a virtual United Nations of men and women, some still undergraduates, most with advanced degrees, he was un-failingly gracious. People vied to work in his lab. (I was there one day when a woman from Tokyo showed up, hoping to join Small's staff. She had a doctorate in engineering, and had made a fortune in Japan developing plasma television screens, but now she was tired of that and wanted to do something that mattered. She had read about Small's imaging work on the Internet and had come to New York at her own expense because she wanted to be a part of it.)

Invariably when I visited, Small would end up in front of his blackboard, chalk in hand, explaining concepts, drawing diagrams, as I wrote down his words. They had become less foreign—he could say *dentate gyrus* and I knew what he meant, or *transporter molecule*, or *gene expression*. Elkhonon Goldberg would say that I was wiser, and on his terms I was: I had asked Scott to repeat his story so many times that it was no longer new, even as it advanced. I recognized its pattern, as when he began his update by saying "I got into a fight with one of the grandfathers of this kind of re-search. It almost got ugly, because it almost got personal. But then everyone thanked us, because there is nothing like a good fight to clarify things."

The kind of research to which Small was referring might be called complex, though it was based on a simple, and seemingly obvious, calculus: complex problems must have complex answers. Small, however, didn't buy it.

"Every level of brain science is a network," he said, standing at the board, moving the chalk emphatically through the air and looking right at me, as if I might be a potential adversary. "Networks are defined as multiple variables that are interconnected. At every level of analysis, from the gross anatomical level down to the molecular level, the different regions interact. In many ways, the evolution of brain science has worked its way down the levels of analysis. So two hundred years ago we were looking at gross anatomy, fifty years ago we were looking at cells, and now we are looking at molecules. At every level of analysis there has been this gut feeling that the solution to the problem can't be driven by a single variable. Take language. Two hundred years ago the greatest debates in the field were that language was diffusely distributed throughout the brain and not driven by a singular variable, right? To be able to speak, you need your whole brain, ultimately. But that's different from saying that if I lesioned area forty-four it's going to be different than if I lesion area two. Does this mean that's where language resides? Not necessarily. Does memory reside in the hippocampus? No. But that's what's driving the network.

"When you get down to the molecular level, the same argument occurred. No way a disease as complex as Huntington's can be accounted for by a single molecule. No way the social-sexual behavior of prairie voles can be accounted for by a single molecule. No way a single molecule can account for memory. We just believe that these complex phenomena can't be solved by univariate drivers. But they can. There is a mutation in the gene called *huntingtin* that causes this complex behavior. There is a molecule called CREB that is fundamental to learning new memories. There's a molecule, the oxytocin receptor, that's responsible for a male prairie vole's monogamy and sociability. Again, does that account for everything? No. But it is clearly my bias that there are univariate solutions to a complex phenomenon like cognitive aging." Small paused to make sure I was getting this. And I did get it. I had heard it before. Because science, ultimately, is a narrative, an account that makes sense of the physical world, I knew he'd take no offense when I nodded yes, and said, a little skeptically, "It's a compelling story."

Small nodded briefly and went on. Clearly, the story wasn't over. "In the dentate gyrus we have found a molecular pathway to account for cognitive aging. We found this in brain tissue, in brains that had no Alzheimer's disease. Cognitive aging occurs in the dentate gyrus, not the entorhinal cortex. That's the special pattern. The temporal pattern is that it declines across the life span. We looked at the molecular profile of the dentate gyrus and the entorhinal cortex, and we found a molecule in the dentate gyrus, RBAP48, that is down when there are memory problems. We just got a grant to develop a knockout mouse with that molecule removed. We'll know in about a year."

To AN outsider, especially, time moved slowly in science. Whatever eureka moments there were were typically preceded by moments that drip-dripped till they overflowed days to months to years. In *The Structure of Scientific Revolutions*, Thomas Kuhn argues that science goes about its business, secured by its conventions, until—boom!—it is undone by an idea, a finding, a theory so incendiary that nothing is left of the old way. "Novelty emerges only with difficulty,

manifested by resistance, against a background provided by expecta-
tion," he wrote. Still, the revolutions of science, explosive in their
impact, came after the slow burn of a long fuse. Scott Small had this
renegade idea—that the giant, complex thing called normal memory
decline could be accounted for by a single molecule—and it was taking years to prove. It would be big news, revolutionary even, when
that happened, but right now, and for the foreseeable future, the
center—the dominant paradigm—was holding.

At times, listening to Small hold forth, hearing him lead off one
of his periodic updates with the words "things are going very well,"
I worried that I was in the thrall of a gifted salesman, a guy who
could sell a car without an engine. He was so confident, and his
confidence so filled the room, there was little room for doubt. Most
of the time, therefore, I was buying what he was selling, engine or
not. And the fact was, evidence had begun to mount that Small *was*
onto something, that his hunch was right. A collaborator of his at
the University of Arizona found not only that Small's molecule,
RBAP48, declined in the dentate gyrus of rats as they aged, but that
the rats that expressed the molecule the least had the worst memories. The collaborator, Carol Barnes, the past president of the Society for Neuroscience, had recently moved on with this research to
monkeys. Correlation studies were not definitive proof, the way
mouse models would be, but they were pretty good nonetheless.
With Barnes's results, things were going very well indeed.

And there was something else. Small not only believed that the
source of normal memory loss was the dentate gyrus, he was convinced that it could be molecularly distinguished from Alzheimer's
disease, which, he argued, originated in the entorhinal cortex. Only
in Alzheimer's patients, in other words, was the entorhinal cortex
dysfunctional.

"Right now there is no gold standard that defines what

Alzheimer's is," Scott said during one of our catch-up sessions. "There are different criteria, but none are categorical. It's a numbers game. It's not like when you have sickle-shaped cells in your blood, which means that you definitively have sickle-cell anemia. For Alzheimer's disease there is a board that meets every so often and decides what the criteria are—and it keeps on changing. Right now there are the Reagan criteria, which were decided in 1996. Before that there were the Khachaturian criteria. It's a nightmare.

"If it were up to me, I would reclassify how we define AD. I'd stop talking about plaques and tangles and do it by cell biology. My rule would be: anyone who has entorhinal dysfunction has AD. That's playing the game with a different set of criteria. If, through my work, I can show that anyone with entorhinal dysfunction has Alzheimer's disease, I win. If I can predict that five years from now someone with entorhinal dysfunction will be as demented as a doorknob, then entorhinal dysfunction will be the diagnostic gold standard."

It occurred to me, transcribing Small's words, that they might come across as arrogant and insensitive, but that is not the way I heard them. To me, rather, they were two parts frustration at the old and inconclusive method of defining Alzheimer's, and one part hope that there might soon be a better way. If there was arrogance, it was the necessary antidote to the winnowing fear that, having staked hundreds of thousands of dollars, and years of his life and years of others', on being right, he was wrong.

SOMETIME AFTER this conversation with Scott Small, I was in California, visiting Dr. Susan Bookheimer, a neuropsychologist at UCLA's Brain Mapping Center and a professor in the Department of Psychiatry there, a friendly, vivacious woman in her mid-forties, with flowing, Goldie Hawnish hair and a tendency to talk and type quickly, often at the same time, punching up relevant papers and video clips to illustrate her point. In the 1990s, Bookheimer was best known for using imaging to map the brains of dyslexics before and after treatment, showing how the dyslexic brain processes the sounds of letters and words, as well as for her studies of autistic emotions. While she continued to do that work, Bookheimer had turned her attention, and her imaging expertise, to Alzheimer's, hunting for a way to see the disease so early that in its development the body itself hardly had an inkling it was there. Which is why she had begun to unfold the hippocampus. Not really—not physically, which would be impossible—but virtually, using MRI and math.

"What we do is take the brain apart and measure its cortical thickness," she explained, stopping to field a call about her son's after-school plans—"If you want to see your son again, call this number," a big sign on her whiteboard said—then redirecting a graduate student, who was standing in the doorway, looking for guidance. Actually, to be perfectly accurate, what Bookheimer said was, "What we'll do is take your brain apart and measure its cortical thickness," since I was scheduled for both a structural and a functional scan the next day. After that, they'd unfold my hippocampus mathematically, looking closely at its anatomical composition.

The human hippocampus, it turns out, has six layers, one atop the other, like sedimentary rock. By unfolding it, Bookheimer was able to measure each one, and this is where her work had begun inadvertently to lend credence to Scott Small's: the second and fourth layers of the entorhinal cortex of people who carried what was then the only known risk factor gene for Alzheimer's disease, a gene called APOE4, were significantly thinner than those for people who did not. These were people who, in every other way, were normal.

"What matters from a clinical perspective is that the brain is changing much earlier than we thought it was for people known to be at risk for Alzheimer's disease," Bookheimer told me. "This may be a fifty-year process. And the neuronal loss seems to be sequential. It starts in the entorhinal cortex and since the neurons there project into the next area, the neurons in those areas will die because they have no connections. It's a long process that will spread and spread." As she said this I imagined a long line of dominoes falling one after the other till they were scattered on the floor, but even so, I knew it was an inadequate image. What Bookheimer was describing was more like a guy with a gun, mowing down a crowd of innocent bystanders.

THE DAY after I met Susan Bookheimer, I returned to the UCLA Medical Center and made my way to the Brain Mapping Center, a freestanding building at the edge of the grassy campus that was dwarfed by the hospital behind it. Apparently people—it was unclear which people—had been finding the center's leatherish sofas a little too comfy, because there were signs posted explaining that this was not a lounge, that the sofas were not for sleeping, and that serious research was going on in the building. Two high school lacrosse players, girls in blue and white uniforms, wandered in while I was sitting there, paused on the sofas for a few minutes to talk about the next day's history test while instant-messaging their boyfriends, then moved on, leaving me alone in a building where I could hear people walking on the floors above me, their footfalls funneling down the open central staircase preceded by their shadows. Here was Plato's new cave.

Someone came to get me eventually, and she led me into the anteroom of the scanning suite and we went through the usual ritual: I handed over my wedding ring, watch, and glasses. She locked them up. She asked me if I had any metal in my body. I said I did not. I signed the consent forms. She asked me if I understood them. Of course I did. I removed my shoes but kept on my socks. I was a compliant subject. I knew the drill.

Only this time, it was a little different. After I handed over my glasses, I was given a pair of goggles, which, when I slipped them on, seemed to drop a video screen in front of my eyes. *Winged Migration*, the French documentary about bird flight, was playing in theater one.

"How is it?" the woman in the control room asked through a microphone that broadcast directly into my ears. "Can you see it?"

"I've already seen it," I said.

"But can you see it all right? We have to adjust the clarity now. Once you're in the machine, it will be too late." The movie stopped abruptly and I was looking at an alias of her computer desktop. Then some words were projected onto the screen, and I worked to adjust my eyes, it was all so big, a billboard of random words. By then I'd slipped into the machine, entombed in plastic. It reminded me of those sensory deprivation tanks people used to pay money to float in years ago, where the top would close over you, and you'd lie on top of a bed of warm salted water in the dark, for some reason that I could not remember, if I ever knew. I wasn't floating, and it wasn't warm, and it was quiet only in the way repetitive sounds whiten noise, but with my eyes tricked into seeing what wasn't really there, and the backbeat of the machine filling the space between me and it, and my body stilled by straps and by will, my senses were confused and dulled. I was like a blind person reading a face with gloves on.

"We're about to begin the cognitive stress test," a voice said directly into my head. The screen went white. My heart began to beat fast, lobbing itself against my chest wall as if it were claustrophobic and seeking a way out. From my perspective, the stress test had begun the moment I surrendered the central hippocampal function—to sort and send sensory data to other parts of the brain—to the woman who took my glasses.

A cognitive stress test is not unlike a cardiac stress test. In the case of a person with, say, chest pain, but no obvious signs of heart disease, a physician will have her walk, then run, on a treadmill, until the heart is pumping to capacity, and problems that might have been hidden are forced into the open. With a cognitive stress test, the brain is to take in new information, encode it, and retrieve it, while the MRI is taking pictures that show which parts of the brain are being activated, which parts are working harder than normal. Asking subjects to remember words that are in some way linked—doctor/nurse, for example, or tree/branch—is a much easier task than asking them to remember random pairs, like doctor/tree and shoelace/squid. The pairs that were being projected on the screen in front of my eyes were of the shoelace/squid variety, fourteen in all, and then another fourteen. When it came time to retrieve them, only one member of the pair was projected. I had to conjure the other.

And the odd thing was, it wasn't hard. If the words had been pictures, my brain would have been straining, like an underpowered engine creeping up a 12 percent grade. But words were no problem. I was flying up that hill. I could have been deluded—the machine would eventually tell—but lying there, recalling random word pairs and watching snippets of *Winged Migration* between tasks, as the testers primed the computer for the next exercise, my brain was not panting. But was that meaningful? What Bookheimer and her colleagues were finding was that for some people—typically, those who carried the *APOE4* Alzheimer's risk-factor gene—there was more

activity in certain subregions of the brain than there was for everyone else. On paper-and-pencil exams, those people tested normal.
Their brains, though, under stress, looked anything but normal.

"You've got a long hippocampus," the tester allowed when the
stress test was over, pointing to the parenthesis in the middle of the
image of my head on her computer monitor. Was this good? Bad?
Irrelevant? "We'll probably have it unfolded in a few months," she
said when I asked.

MOST OF us are constantly seeking reassurance that our bodies are
not failing, an interior monologue that allows a certain amount of
fudging and denial. It took months before I would call Susan De
Santi at NYU to ask her to "unpack" the diagnosis of "normal," and
once I did I realized I'd been hauling that diagnosis around in the
back of my mind like a padlocked old trunk whose key I only
vaguely wanted to find.

"You have to remember that even with a healthy brain, some
people do really well on these tests and some people don't," she
began in her soothing, almost conspiratorial, way. "Sometimes people are so nervous that we are going to find something so they can't
perform and they do really badly and it really does look like they
have a serious problem." I knew she was not talking about me—I,
after all, was normal—but still.

If someone were going to make a paint-by-numbers portrait of
me based on my neuropsychological scores, where blue is higher
than the mean, green is the mean, and yellow is below it, it would
be a portrait primarily in blue. On almost every test where there was
a list of words to remember, or a story to retell, I performed comparable to my peers the first time around, and better than they, after a
delay. This was promising, De Santi suggested, because the ability to

keep things in mind is compromised by both aging and Alzheimer's disease. So is verbal fluency. "What is this?" Schantel Williams would ask, pointing to a picture of a high-heeled shoe, or a pumpkin, or a baseball bat, objects so common it seemed impossible not to obtain, as I did, the deep blue of a perfect score. But naming, it turns out, is eroded by AD. "Language," Susan De Santi said, "is one of the big-ticket items."

It made sense that I'd do well on tests of verbal fluency—after all, I work with words. But that logic is flawed. If you are sick, it doesn't matter what you do or who you are. Painters lose their sense of perspective, three dimensions fold into one, and writers lose their words. So maybe it was hubris, being verbally confident.

In the other domains, like attention and visual recall, I was less sure of myself. When Williams or De Santi asked if I had any cognitive complaints, whether I had begun to notice changes in memory or perception, I sometimes mentioned that I now concentrated less well than I had earlier, an observation so vague as to be nondescriptive. In my journal I noted that I had less tolerance for picking through the purple loosestrife of academic science, with its arcane language and stunted prose, but maybe that was a sign, instead, of good sense, an example of Elkhonon Goldberg's notion of wisdom. And there was more and more going on around me—a teenage daughter, a husband who traveled, commitments to one thing and another—which meant that the volume was turned way up. Of course it was difficult to concentrate. On the other hand, wasn't one of the debilities of getting older the incapacity to block out distractions? (So I was normal!)

"Do you remember the test where we gave you progressively longer runs of numbers, like 2548575648576?" De Santi asked me. "On that test you did a little worse than the mean when we asked you to remember them going forward, but you did better than most people going backward. We said 37659875 and you had to say 57895673. You actually remembered more numbers going backward than you did going forward. Going backward is much harder. You'd think that if you could do very well going backward, you could do even better going forward. I've seen this before. Because it's harder, you snap to attention. When you have to, you can really pay attention."

For a moment, hearing this, I was appeased. I could really concentrate! When it mattered, I could turn on the high beams! But then I thought of Susan Bookheimer in California, unfolding all those hippocampi, and seeing how hard some people's brains were working to be normal, and how those were the people, years down the line, who were expected to run into trouble. (No one knew for sure. The hypothesis needed more time to be proved or tossed out.) Maybe I was one of them. Thinking on this, I hardly heard De Santi when she said that in all the tests of visual memory—the one where I had to draw a ridiculously abstract figure from memory, and the gray-scale Mondrian test, where I had to pick out three indistinguishable geometric patterns from a page of nine indistinguishable geometric patterns—on whose downslope I'd resided all my life, I had, inexplicably, done better than my peers.

I MUST have been having a good day. Seven months later at UCLA, where I spent a couple of hours doing neuropsychological tests before getting my brain unfolded, on a test of "visual function," when I was flashed, briefly, a complex geometric figure and then asked to copy it, angle for angle, from memory, I performed so significantly worse than my peers that I was given a grade of "impaired." It was no different when I had to draw a complex figure after a delay. I was impaired.

*Impaired* is not a word you want to hear when a doctor is assessing your capacities. Impaired implies pathology—no, it virtually shouts it. But here's the thing: it could motivate you. It's not a neutral word. You could hear it and it could lead you to jump at the chance of participating in a clinical trial, whereas the words *below the mean* might only beckon you there. It could convince you to agree to take Aricept or Celebrex—medicines with side effects, both of which were being offered to healthy UCLA volunteers—even though you are, by all standard measures, normal, even with your "impairments."

"Everyone is a mix of average, high average, superior, and impaired," the tester, Dr. Karen Miller, explained. "Almost no one is consistently average on everything. You're going to see variability. And remember, you came into the testing room saying that you had no visual memory. This is just who you are."

People tend to know their capacities innately. They tend to gravitate toward their strengths. Call it cognitive entropy. Looking at my test scores, which were consistently at the mean or higher on verbal tasks, you might say "Well, of course, she's a writer." But it may be more accurate to flip that "of course" 180 degrees and conclude that I'm a writer because I did not have the mental architecture to become, say, a neurosurgeon or a graphic artist or an engineer. We are defined as much by our limitations as we are by our strengths. One day when I was sitting in Susan De Santi's office at New York University and she was showing me brain scans of people with mild cognitive impairment, she told me about a man she had seen recently whose scores were so low on visual tasks that she was concerned that he was on the cusp of getting sick. But then he happened to mention a lifelong learning disability that interfered with his capacity to take in visual information. For him, normal was never being able to see the way others could see. For him, normal was impaired.

These days, people like to talk about "take-home messages," as if most of what we have to say to each other should be left behind. Listening to De Santi talk about that man, I realized that her take-home message was that there are two kinds of normal. There is normal for everyone, which is a measurable aggregate, and normal for you, which is sui generis, and that normal for you may look very different from normal for everyone. Individuals always deviate from the mean, and how any person does so is a crucial piece of self-knowledge. At Columbia I often heard about a professor with an astronomically high IQ who consistently scored well above the mean on his neuropsych tests, but who just as consistently complained that his memory was failing. It took years, but he eventually succumbed to Alzheimer's disease. He knew he had it long before there was any way to measure it. Similarly, I was impaired and I was normal, and they were precisely the same thing.

## Chapter Five

# Inheritance

THE FIRST THINGS WE INHERIT from our parents are our chromosomes, and the second are our genes, which bestow their own legacy: green eyes, say, or bad eyes, or brown hair, or curly hair, or dark skin, or acne, or cystic fibrosis, or flat feet, or some kinds of intelligence, or, possibly, Alzheimer's disease.

There are two kinds of AD. The first, known as early-onset Alzheimer's, tends to strike between the ages of thirty and fifty and is very rare, occurring in less than 5 percent of cases, and there is the much more common late-onset disease, which tends to afflict people who are sixty-five and older. About half the cases of early-onset Alzheimer's are genetic and follow the simple, deterministic law of Mendelian inheritance: if you are born with the mutated gene, you get the disease. Late-onset Alzheimer's is thought to be genetic, too, but in a much more messy way: rather than being caused by a single gene, it appears to be the result of a passel of genes that, individually or together, are believed to increase one's risk of dementia. APOE4, the gene on chromosome 19 that Susan Bookheimer believed to be connected to the thinning entorhinal cortex in her unfolding experiments, was one of those risk-factor

genes. In fact, it was the only risk-factor gene that had been conclu-
sively identified and confirmed. But that was about to change.

It was early May 2005. Two white SUVs left the parking garage
at the Gran Almirante Hotel and Casino in Santiago, the Dominican Republic's second city, just as the gamblers and prostitutes were
calling it a night, and headed half an hour north, to the town of
Navarette. The lead vehicle was driven by Dr. Angel Piriz, a thirty-
seven-year-old Cuban doctor who lived in New York. Beside him
was Rosarina Estevez, a recent graduate of medical school in Santiago. Both were working as research physicians at Columbia University under the supervision of Richard Mayeux, who was Scott Small's
boss, too. For nearly twenty years, Mayeux, a neurologist, an epi-
demiologist, and a co-director of the Taub Institute for Research on
Alzheimer's Disease and the Aging Brain, had been compiling what
had become the most comprehensive genetic library of families
with Alzheimer's disease in the world. The family members were either residents of the largely Dominican neighborhood of Washington Heights where Columbia University Medical Center was
located or, like the family the Columbia researchers were hoping to
see, from the Dominican Republic itself.

Navarette wasn't much of a town—a strip of concrete shops on
either side of the road, and street vendors selling pineapples and
mangoes and goat meat so fresh that the goats were still tethered to
the stall—and the family didn't have much of an address. "It's called
Ginger Alley," said Vinny Santana, the driver of the second vehicle, as he turned sharply into a narrow dirt track patrolled by chick-
ens. Piriz, who had briefly gotten lost, pulled in behind Santana, and
without much conversation, he and Estevez assembled their medical
kits. Meanwhile, Santana, who was in charge of the fieldwork,
gathered the notebooks and questionnaires they would need to ad-
minister the neuropsychological tests that, along with the medical

exam, were crucial for determining who would be diagnosed with Alzheimer's disease, and who would be said, so far, to be exempt.

"This is a branch of the original family we saw here last year," explained Santana, a soft-spoken Dominican American whose face was often knotted with worry. (Were the directions good? Would the subjects be home? Would they still be willing to volunteer? Would the data be useful? Would they get enough of it? Would the blood spoil? Would it make it through customs? And what about the Yankees?) He directed Estevez to interview an elderly couple who lived across the way, then headed down the alley with Piriz, past houses made of concrete and tin, cutting through someone's dim, fly-infested kitchen to a narrower alley and a warren of corrugated houses, asking for a man named Vargas. "The proband—which means the first person in the family we saw—who was in her late sixties, died in February," Santana said. "She's confirmed with the disease. In her generation a couple of cousins and siblings have AD. One of her children has it, and a couple are borderline. There's some first-cousin intermarriage. These people we're seeing today are her cousins. If we can find them."

As they went they attracted little boy after little boy, a whole parade of them, who eventually led the researchers to a spare, three-room dwelling: Vargas's house. Vargas, a gaunt eighty-three-year-old, tanned from a life growing bananas and tending fields of rice, was in bed lying bare-chested in blue shorts on top of yellow smiley face sheets, surrounded by two of his five wives, four of his fourteen children, two of his daughters' daughters, a great-granddaughter, a brother, two cousins, the sister of one of his wives, and an indeterminate number of children who might have been related to the assortment of adults. He wasn't saying much. A few months before he had been diagnosed with pancreatic cancer and wasn't expected to outlive the year. Even so, he had consented to Santana's request to participate in the study.

Although Vinny Santana was meeting the man in the bed for the first time, he had known about Vargas for about a year. In his notes from his interview with the proband the spring before, there was a reminder to identify and track down all her cousins and their siblings, in order to map out how they were related. Constructing accurate genealogies—what Vinny Santana did—was fundamental to figuring out how a disease traveled among kin—what Richard Mayeux did.

"I STARTED off thinking Alzheimer's was not a genetic disease," Mayeux told me the first time I visited him in his surprisingly neat office, one floor up from Scott Small's in the old Presbyterian Hospital. (The office of a man who is rarely at his desk.) "I thought it was environmental, associated with aging. But the accumulating data convinced me, seeing that this disease tracks in families. It doesn't always follow a pattern, but it does track in families, so that if you have family members with the disease you have a much higher risk of getting it, and siblings with the disease give you an even higher risk. The evidence was very hard to counter."

Mayeux selected a bound volume the size of *Webster's Third* dictionary from a set of nearly identical bound volumes that took up most of a wall and began flipping through the pages as he spoke. It was an encyclopedia of the family trees of people in his study that showed who was related to whom and which ones had the disease, who was disease free, and who was living in the border town between lucidity and dementia.

"What we wanted to do was find a population where we thought the rates were higher, because the thing about genetics is that if you try to identify people who carry the gene, you are looking for unusual people. It's not like epidemiology, where you try to get random samples of random people. Genetics is just the opposite. You want a biased population. You want families where there is more of the disease because you have a better chance of figuring out what the gene is.

"That's how we stumbled into this study of people in the Dominican Republic. We noticed when we were doing a general population study of elderly people who live around the hospital that Dominicans had about three times the rate of Alzheimer's disease compared to the whites and blacks in the community. So you have to ask yourself why that would be. Then it starts to explain itself that at least in the DR, Dominicans tend to marry other Dominicans, and you don't have different populations moving in there. You have a smaller genetic pool, and first cousins marrying first cousins, so the gene pool tends to stay enriched. Here's one," Mayeux said, pointing to a page in the book. "These two people are twins. Look at how many people who are related to them are affected and how many are beginning to experience symptoms."

Mayeux, who was raised in Louisiana, has a nasal drawl and a deceptive air of someone with time on his hands. He was fifty-nine years old, with a full head of brown hair going slowly to gray and an unlined face, and looked so young that his colleagues joked that he was a graduate of the Dick Clark School of Aging. He was constantly in motion, typically late, and driven: in addition to his role at Taub, he was the director of Columbia's Sergievsky Center, which conducted epidemiological research on neurological diseases; a professor of neurology, psychiatry, and epidemiology; a practicing physician at Columbia's Memory and Behavioral Disorders Center; and the coordinator of a nationwide effort to collect, sort, and make available to researchers genetic material from families with late-onset Alzheimer's disease. (The project was initiated in 2002 by the National Institute of Aging, which also funded the bulk of Mayeux's research.)

Since getting his medical degree at the University of Oklahoma in 1972, Mayeux had studied diseases of the central nervous system: epilepsy, Parkinson's, Huntington's, Alzheimer's. He also oversaw a staff of 185 neurologists, geneticists, psychologists, epidemiologists, data-entry clerks, cell biologists, biochemists, genetic counselors, and animal modelers spread over five floors of the hospital building, as well as the clinic at Columbia's Neurological Institute. Under his direction they were pursuing the medical version of "big science," drawing on a dozen separate disciplines, each with a distinct vocabulary, methodology, and way of seeing. Many of the team members—like Scott Small or like Dr. Joe Lee, who sifted through the thirty thousand genes that make up the human genome looking for a genetic quirk that could explain the colonization of the brain by sticky plaques and neurofibrillary tangles—took the conventional academic route of medical degrees and doctorates. But a surprising number never intended to chase what Mayeux calls "the great white whale of neuroscience." There was a former Wall Street accountant who deconstructed MRI data and a German particle physicist who developed diagnostic imaging algorithms. There was Angel Piriz, the Cuban doctor, who spent three years working for a Manhattan construction company until he found the Columbia job on the Internet. And there was Vinny Santana, who was a twenty-year-old security guard in the Presbyterian Hospital emergency room when he was offered extra hours to escort Mayeux's field researchers to interviews in Washington Heights, his home neighborhood. Eventually Santana became one of those researchers himself, expert in administering and scoring complex neuropsychological tests, and then the research coordinator, and, at thirty-five, a coauthor on four of Mayeux's scientific papers.

The neuropsychological tests that Santana and the other field researchers were carrying to Ginger Alley were developed by the psychologist Yaakov Stern, who had worked with Richard Mayeux for twenty-five years. To determine who in the Dominican population had the disease—as opposed to who would develop the disease—Stern and his colleagues had come up with a mathematical formula that gave them a score that they had found to be clinically reliable.

"What day of the week is it?" Santana was asking Vargas. "What is the date? What year? Where are we? Can you count backward from twenty? Can you name the months of the year in reverse order? I am going to tell you a name and address and I want you to repeat what I've said: Juan Perez, Avenida Duarte cuatro y dos, Samana." This was the warm-up, and Vargas was doing okay. He knew he was in the bedroom, not the kitchen; he knew the year; he knew it was summer, though technically it was spring.

Santana leaned in close. "I'm going to read you a list of twelve words, and when I'm done I want you to repeat them back to me. *Juego*," he began. "*Lava*." Vargas fingered the religious medal he wore around his neck and looked lost. "I can't remember," he said, pointing to his head. In the algorithm developed by Yaakov Stern, the cut score on this test is twenty-five: if someone, given the opportunity to repeat any of these twelve words six times, for a top score of seventy-two, can't get to twenty-five, he can be considered for "case status." When the test was over, Vargas's score was fifteen.

In the next room, Angel Piriz was going through the same routine with one of Vargas's wives, a short seventy-year-old woman in a faded housedress and worn flip-flops, who was eyeing him warily. "Do you ever find yourself getting lost?" Piriz asked. "Hell no," she said. He took her blood pressure, looked into her eyes, tested her reflexes. Then he put on green latex gloves, took out a syringe, and prepared to draw her blood.

NOT FAR from the Columbia University Medical Center, in the basement of the New York Brain Bank, there was a room with industrial freezers containing 28,544 samples of blood plasma. In 1988, when Mayeux inaugurated what is known as the WHICAP study, a sweeping epidemiological investigation of the health and habits of twenty-five hundred elderly residents of Washington Heights, he instructed the researchers to collect blood in addition to recording demographic and medical data. The field of Alzheimer's genetics was in its infancy and putting blood on ice was either capricious or prescient, depending on who was paying the bill. It had only been four years since scientists at the University of California, San Diego, succeeded in isolating amyloid, the key constituent of the plaques that accumulate in an Alzheimer's brain, and two years since they discovered that amyloid was a peptide—a protein fragment that came in different lengths. The researchers called the peptide "beta-amyloid" and proposed that a genetic mutation causing its overproduction would be found somewhere along chromosome 21, the chromosome that goes awry and appears in triplicate in Down syndrome. The amyloid they had sequenced had come from Down patients, and by middle age most people with Down syndrome experience Alzheimer's-like symptoms, so it seemed logical that chromosome 21 would be implicated.

And that is where, in 1991, geneticists at the University of London found the first Alzheimer's gene. It was called APP, an acronym that stood for amyloid precursor protein, and was associated, in mutated forms, with early-onset Alzheimer's. An APP mutation caused the overproduction of beta-amyloid in the brain; without exception, a person who carried the mutation developed Alzheimer's disease. The gene gave scientists a way to begin to understand what was happening in an Alzheimer's brain and a rudimentary hypothesis: Alzheimer's disease was caused by clumps of beta-amyloid that strangled neurons and synapses. If, before, scientists were looking into a black hole of disease, they were now peering into a tunnel, and they believed they knew, with some confidence, how a small number of people tumbled through its entrance.

"When it was first discovered, we thought that APP was *the* Alzheimer's gene," recalled Mayeux. But the math didn't work: of the millions of cases of Alzheimer's disease, the APP mutation occurred in less than two hundred of them.

The search for additional Alzheimer's genes took off during the 1990s, and by mid-decade three more had been found and confirmed. Two, called presenilin, caused early-onset Alzheimer's. Like APP, they interfered with amyloid production—though differently, by cleaving the amyloid protein—which gave further credence to the idea that too much amyloid precipitated dementia. Still, the presenilin genes weren't *it*, either, for they were carried by only a few hundred families worldwide.

The fourth Alzheimer gene, *APOE*, though, was different. It wasn't Mendelian and deterministic, it didn't cause early-onset Alzheimer's, and it wasn't rare: we all carry it. A common variant of this gene is *APOE4*; it significantly increases the risk of getting AD, but it doesn't cause it. Many who have the *APOE4* gene never get Alzheimer's disease, while many people who don't carry it do, and still, more than a decade after its discovery, no one could say why that was.

IN THE lectures Mayeux gave to people who were unfamiliar with the simplest facts of genetics—that genes, which code for proteins, are made from a sequence of chemicals called bases, and if any one base is out of sequence the protein may be dysfunctional—he often ended up talking about cops and robbers.

"Our colleagues at the Genome Center in the United States tell us that there may be three billion base pairs in the entire genome and that there are one hundred twenty million base pairs in each of the chromosomes, and about two thousand to two hundred thousand base pairs in a gene, and what we are doing is looking for a single base pair that is different or out of sequence," he told a group of sixty Dominican professors and students at the Universidad Tecnológica de Santiago, the day after his field researchers completed nine more interviews in the northern coastal city of Puerto Plata and four more that morning in Jicomé.

"So we're looking for that one base pair, which is like having the police know that someone has committed a crime somewhere, but they don't know where, and they have to start looking for him all over the universe," Mayeux went on. "That's basically where we are. The goal of genetic family studies is to try to get down to the earth, and then into the neighborhood, and eventually to find the culprit."

If mutations are the bad guys, and scientists are the good guys, then since the discovery of presenilin and *APOE4*, the good guys had made something like a hundred false arrests. In peer-reviewed paper after paper, research teams all over the world claimed to have identified about one hundred unique genes that influenced or in some way triggered late-onset Alzheimer's disease, but not one of those genes had been able to be replicated consistently by other researchers, if at all.

There was one simple reason why no one had found a new Alzheimer's gene in more than a decade, and another reason that was less simple, and they both came down to the same thing: statistics. Risk-factor genes, the genes that will explain common, late-onset AD, are inherently elusive because carrying them does not automatically result in disease. More challenging, there may be a lot of risk genes, each with a potentially minute effect. Risk genes, in other words, are quiet, and it will take a very sensitive microphone to hear them. In the case of Alzheimer's, that microphone was a large family study like Mayeux's, with reams of information over time about each individual's health issues, eating habits, work, and leisure pursuits, as well as genealogies that show the genetic path of AD. The big numbers picked up on small effects, and the detailed histories parsed the sample. Mayeux's thick books of pedigrees and database of DNA allowed researchers to define a person's genotype—what genes she carried—as well as a phenotype—what traits she embodied—and then to subdivide the phenotype according to which traits very specifically correlated with the kind of dementia that characterized Alzheimer's disease. On the nineteenth floor of the old Columbia Presbyterian Hospital, the crucial distinction was coming down to a person's performance on certain memory tests, and the researchers were seeing a pattern in performance and disease that they hoped would show up in the genes.

"Age of onset is a wimpy phenotype," Mayeux said to no one in particular at one of the team's weekly genetics meetings. "Memory is better."

"Delayed recognition is the most sensitive test we have for AD," Joe Lee, the geneticist, told him. "That and another test that I can't recall. I may be a subject for this study soon myself."

"We all may be," said Mayeux, laughing. It was a measure of the prevalence of Alzheimer's disease that the seven people sitting around the table had a mother, a father, an aunt, a grandmother, and a grandfather with AD. (Vinny Santana realized his grandmother had the disease on one of his research trips to the Dominican Republic, when he knocked on her door to deliver groceries, put the first bag on her kitchen table, went out to the car for a second bag, found the door locked on his return, knocked, and was greeted by his grandmother—who had no recollection how the groceries had arrived in her house, or that he himself had put them there—as if he had been gone for months, not minutes. In Alzheimer's disease, short-term memory loss is the most obvious phenotype.)

A few months after that genetics meeting, a number of the same researchers who had been there, plus Yaakov Stern and the research physicians Angel Piriz and Rosarina Estevez, were gathered in Mayeux's office when Santana rolled in a cart piled three feet high with the two hundred interviews that the field researchers had completed in the weeks since their last diagnostic case conference. In the stack were the files of first-time participants from the Dominican Republic and follow-up examinations of subjects who had been seen on previous visits, as well as of their relatives in Washington Heights. The day before the meeting, which was about three weeks after their long day in Ginger Alley, Santana, Estevez, and Piriz had finally interviewed Vargas's sixty-year-old niece in her apartment a few blocks down Broadway from the hospital that offered the same view of the Hudson River and the bend of Manhattan that they would have been seeing from Mayeux's office if their heads hadn't been bowed over the case files like students cramming for an exam. Despite being diabetic and overweight, the niece had no memory complaints and no signs of impairment, even though diabetes itself is a risk factor for Alzheimer's. Her case was one of the ones on the day's docket.

Santana, who was a college dropout when he started working for Mayeux and was about to complete an MBA, dealt out score sheets—officially called "clinical core diagnosis"—that looked surprisingly like an IRS 1040 short form, with various sections and schedules and subtotals, all leading to a bottom line: did the participant have Alzheimer's disease or not? To get there they had to rule out Parkinson's disease, prion disease, alcohol dementia, dementia with Lewy bodies, frontotemporal dementia, and anything else that might mimic the symptoms of AD. They had exactly an hour for the meeting because this was Mayeux's last day at Columbia for three months—though that last day turned out to be fungible—before he started a "mini sabbatical" at Rockefeller University, where he was going to study genetics.

"We'll just get through as many as we get through, and then get the data to Joe Lee so he can put it into the computer," Mayeux said, pulling a dozen folders off the cart. "Here's someone you saw," he said, waving a folder at Rosarina Estevez, who was sitting next to him. "What was his blood pressure?" He looked at her intently, not letting on that he was pulling her leg—in fourteen days in the Dominican Republic the researchers had examined ninety-eight people, and there was no way that Estevez could possibly remember, nearly a month later, any individual's vital signs. She looked a little stricken. As the newest member of the team, Estevez had not yet grown accustomed to Mayeux's ability to tease, compliment, and assert his authority all in the same sentence. "One seventy-five over ninety," she shot back. Mayeux looked stunned. "That's amazing. How did you do that? Did you know, or did you guess?" But there was no time for an answer. "Okay, what else do we know about this guy?" he asked.

Accurately diagnosing a subject was crucial to looking for genes, and the design of Mayeux's field studies, with their repeat visits every eighteen months, increased the odds that they would get it right. According to the University of Toronto geneticist Peter St. George–Hyslop, who used Mayeux's Dominican cell lines in his discovery of the first presenilin gene, "the way most studies are done is that a person is seen once and diagnosed as either having Alzheimer's disease or not having Alzheimer's disease, and then not seen again. In the Washington Heights and Dominican studies, people are followed up again and again. There may be some individuals on the borderline when they were first seen, but when they were followed up later they had developed a clear case of Alzheimer's, so you can be quite certain about the diagnosis. Conversely, there are people who are seen the first time who are normal, and if you follow them for years and they are still normal there is a much greater chance that they are really normal controls and not just presymptomatic carriers."

To refine their diagnostic powers, the Columbia group convened an autopsy meeting once a month to see how close their assessment of a person while alive was to the incontrovertible pathological truth. The meetings were run by Dr. Lawrence Honig, another Taub associate, in the institute's airless conference room, often to standing-room crowds. The neurologists, pathologists, and psychologists typically sat around a long seminar table that dominated the room, with everyone else squeezing in around them. Honig would present a patient's history and tentative diagnosis, then project slides of the brain, first whole, then in slices, stained in red and blue to show its dominant features. Then the doctors would decide, based on the one crucial piece of evidence they had been missing, if they had been right.

A week after the August autopsy meeting, I stopped by Larry Honig's paper-logged office at the opposite end of the nineteenth floor from Richard Mayeux's, and he showed me the slides of a woman whose case had been discussed that day, a case that illustrated how difficult it could be, even with years of data, to get a diagnosis absolutely right. Honig, though in his late forties and balding, had the boyish affect of someone who had always been the smartest kid in the class, and he started out by walking me briskly through an abridged version of the woman's medical history: a clerical worker with a year of college, she had been first seen in 1992 at the age of sixty-eight. At the time she was besieged by numerous ailments—cirrhosis, gallstones, pulmonary disease, carpal tunnel, and facial palsy among them—and, in addition, was a former smoker and recovered alcoholic. In later years she was found to carry the *APOE4* gene, and an MRI showed some brain atrophy. She had done well on all her tests, though, the medical ones and the neuropsychological ones, and not just that first year, but at every interval until 2000, when there was a decline in some of her memory scores. Two years later there was a further decline in memory, and a spirited discussion among the clinicians whether or not to move the woman from the nonaffected category to a diagnosis of early Alzheimer's. The neurologists, led by Honig, were pretty sure, based on the fact that the woman's test scores had been stable for over a decade, that her recent memory problems were the result of her multiple physical ailments. The neuropsychologists were sticking to their algorithms. Unable to agree, they left the diagnosis unchanged, waiting to see what would show up the next time around. But there was no next time. By late 2004, when the woman was scheduled to be seen again, she was dying of congestive heart failure.

Honig called up a couple of slides of the woman's brain on his computer monitor. To my untrained eye the brain seemed pretty normal—there was nothing in the slices that looked like measles, which is how plaques show up when they've been stained, nor did the woman's brain appear especially shrunken, as Alzheimer's brains tend to be.

"We couldn't even find a single plaque." Honig beamed. "There were no signs of AD. So I can crow that I was right. But we're not always right, so we have to be modest."

NEUROLOGISTS HAVE spent the past hundred years waiting for pathologists to prove them right, since 1906, when Alois Alzheimer

autopsied the brain of a fifty-six-year-old woman who had been ex-
hibiting the kinds of behavior that most of us now would reflexively
call Alzheimer's disease and found it riddled with something that
looked like discarded wads of gum (plaques) and matted strands of
hair (tangles). Still, pathologists had waited almost as long to find
out if the plaques and tangles were actually meaningful—if they
caused disease or were just an artifact of some other biological process. What were they to make of the people who died with all the
pathological evidence of Alzheimer's but were not demented? And
how to account for the presence of both plaques *and* tangles? Were
the plaques, which are made of beta-amyloid, more important
agents of disease than the tangles, which are composed of a protein
called tau, or were the tangles the prime suspect, or were the two
accomplices in fleecing memory? These questions consumed researchers for decades, often contentiously, and still do to an extent.
But what Professor Rudy Tanzi of Harvard has called the debate between the "Baptists and the Tauists"—those who believed in the su-
premacy of beta-amyloid and those who favored tau tangles as the
primum mobile of forgetting—was becoming more civil all the time;
the Tauists were getting more research money, which in science was
a show of respect, and no one was disputing the central role of beta-
amyloid in making an Alzheimer's brain, especially a soluble form of
beta-amyloid called abeta 42, though what the plaques were doing
in that brain could still rouse a heated discussion. Oddly, the geneticists, who, as the scientific literature shows, have never shied
away from a fight, were the inadvertent arbiter of these rows, for the
answers were coming not from the examination of slices of gross tissue but from investigations at the molecular level, from the interrogation of genes.

    "So much of the work that we've done, going forward, is asking
'How do these genes cause disease?' 'What are the biological path-

ways involved?' 'What goes wrong?'" observed Tanzi, who has been at the forefront of the search for Alzheimer genes from the start and shares credit for discovering presenilin. "What goes wrong is that you produce too much abeta 42.

"What was controversial was whether the plaques, where abeta 42 eventually makes its home, are the cause of Alzheimer's disease. And the answer is probably not." Plaques are a problem because they cause inflammation, which can make things worse, but more recent data were suggesting that the real damage was in the way the peptide—long before it had formed into plaques—interfered with the synapses.

"The main place where abeta 42 does its work is in the synapse," Tanzi explained. "So every minute of the day an Alzheimer's patient is producing abeta 42, for one reason or another, and it's accumulating in the brain, and where it's accumulating is in the synapse. Way, way before the plaques form you get tiny little aggregates of abeta 42. The peptides stick together and they get into the synapse and they disrupt the most basic synaptic function for learning and memory. For all we know, plaques may be a beneficial attempt by the brain to sequester abeta away so you don't have it in synapses anymore. It's the newly made abeta 42 that is relentlessly attacking the synapses and probably this is why an Alzheimer's patient has trouble remembering what happened five minutes ago. When you impair the synapse, when you cause it to not function properly, eventually it starts to break down. And eventually it goes away."

This point, exactly, was illustrated in a short article published in the fall of 2004 in the journal *Nature Neuroscience*, about mice. Mice don't get Alzheimer's disease unless they are genetically altered to develop plaques and tangles, which these mice were. The title of the paper, "Fibrillar Amyloid Deposition Leads to Local Synaptic Abnormalities and Breakages of Neuronal Branches," was not exactly sensational, but the accompanying photographs—images of real mice brains in real time—were vivid, and chilling. In the pictures, dendrites and axons, the parts of a neuron that carry information to and from a cell, highlighted in a radiant shade of green, start out as long, robust, motile tentacles. Then they encounter the amyloid, which shows up as tomato-red clumps, and something creepy happens. The tentacles break apart. They wither. They disappear.

ONE OF the authors of that paper, Karen Duff, was also the "author" of one of the original transgenic Alzheimer's mice. Duff was a young British molecular neuroscientist who developed the first mouse model of the presenilin mutation when she was a postdoctoral fellow in London. Duff continued to make mouse models of neurodegenerative diseases at the Nathan Kline Institute in Orangeburg, New York, though she was being wooed by Mayeux to move to Columbia, which she eventually did. NKI is about half an hour north of Manhattan, on the grounds of the Rockland Psychiatric Center, a state-run facility for the mentally ill. It, too, looked institutional, in a scrubbed, white-walled sort of way. Duff's office, though, was cheerier, with a bobble-head doll of James Watson on the desk, a cuckoo clock on the wall, and a stuffed mouse toy perched on a bookshelf. The real mice were across the hall, in clear plastic cages that looked like neonatal incubators, where Duff, who had recently received a $7.5 million grant to work on tangle diseases, was raising multiple generations of mice made to come down with something like Lou Gehrig's disease.

To model a human disease in a mouse Duff had to microinject select bits of human DNA into a mouse egg with a tiny needle. ("You're going from the outside to the inside and sometimes the eggs burst.") The introduced DNA integrated with the mouse DNA and was passed along to offspring. The first mouse born with this engineered DNA was called the founder mouse. Breeding the founders produced the actual "models"—real, live mice—which were then used to observe the progression of a disease or to test therapeutic interventions. With the Lou Gehrig's mice, Duff was doing both.

"When I was in school I wanted to study physics, but I couldn't do the math," Duff said as she picked up a paraplegic mouse and gently stroked its back. "Then, when I was sixteen I went to a lecture about genes and learned that you could change one thing in two million and have an effect on the whole organism and I said 'That's it.' I wanted to make that one change and see what it did, what pathways were involved, and then go on to treat it. My postdoc was making transgenic mice. Making mice is very hard. You have to be very specific with what you've done. If I have a demented mouse that can't get around a water maze, I have to know that that is because I changed one gene.

"I'm happy with mice. I think mice are a lot harder to work with than flies or worms, and they are more accurate. They're more like humans." She ran her finger along the sick mouse's spine, then laid it back into its cage.

Though Duff had shifted her focus from making mice that mimicked human disease processes to making mice that allowed her to test drugs and therapies that had the potential to reverse or limit the progression of those diseases, she still supplied her old established mouse models to other researchers, including Mayeux's group at Columbia. Mayeux, too, was one of the few researchers for whom Duff was still willing to create a whole new mouse model—once he had a whole new Alzheimer's gene to give her.

"It's a symbiotic relationship," Duff explained. "The geneticists want their findings to be more than a gene on a piece of paper. They want to look at its functionality, want to see it really does cause disease by putting it into animals. Richard needs me to put the genes in the animals, and I need someone like him to give me the genes to put into my animal models to see what they do. It's a multipart process. Finding the gene is just the first bit."

As tricky as finding this first bit had been, by the summer of 2004, six years into the Dominican genetics study, the Columbia team, working in collaboration with Peter St. George–Hyslop in Toronto and Dr. Lindsay Farrar at Boston University, had a hunch about where a rogue risk-factor gene resided. Having hunted through the entire genome searching for places where shared patterns of DNA showed up in people with Alzheimer's disease, having pored over thousands upon thousands of genes, some four spreadsheets long, they began scrutinizing a number of genes that had appeared in their random-association studies.

It was standard work for Joe Lee, the Columbia group's lead geneticist, and he began examining chunks of DNA, looking for variations in the genetic code that were segregating with the disease. Each block—what the scientists call a haplotype—was like a sentence in a paragraph from a chapter of a book. By comparing the length of that particular sentence in every copy of the book, the researchers could see in which copies the sentence was the same, and in which it was messed up—maybe there was a misspelling, maybe a missing word. And if the copies of the book with the misconstructed sentence were possessed by people with AD, maybe, just maybe, there was a connection between those two things. The scientists would examine the sentence more closely, looking for the precise character, the one extra consonant, the repeated verb—something—in that particular sentence that was consistent in the copies owned by the people who were sick.

While the Toronto group, led by Peter St. George–Hyslop, examined the DNA of a few hundred people of European descent, and the BU team, led by Lindsay Farrar, looked at the genetics of sibling pairs—one with the disease, one without it—Lee focused on the thousands of samples gathered from the Dominican Republic and Washington Heights studies. By sheer size alone, Mayeux's genetic library, with its branching trees of large, extended families that often spanned two or more generations, offered Lee great power to see which haplotypes were segregating with the disease. But the design and scope of the complementary Columbia studies, WHICAP in New York and the family genetics survey in the DR, also gave Lee another advantage: where the large families from the Dominican Republic enabled him to more easily find segregating haplotypes, the large numbers of Dominicans in the Washington Heights study allowed him to see if those same chunks also showed up more generally in all the Hispanics enrolled in the Washington Heights study.

Meanwhile, as Lee and the researchers in Toronto and Boston systematically moved along the chromosomes, a funny thing happened: they began to converge on the same gene. It was as if, having read the same book cover to cover, the teams had each come to focus on a single sentence. Yet the exact place in the gene where something went wrong was different for different populations. There seemed to be at least three ways that the gene in question could go wrong.

The lead scientists were growing more convinced that the gene upon which they had converged was one of the undiscovered late-onset risk-factor genes. The association was strong, and not just in one sample population, but five, and not in one racial group, but three, scattered around the globe. Each researcher had replicated the work of the others, and in their line of work replication was rare. By nature, the three admitted to being skeptics, but as the evidence mounted, their ability to explain it away deserted them.

"The 'aha!' moment happens to different people at different times and sometimes it never really happens," St. George–Hyslop said. "We are aware of little bits of data as they come out that say 'yes, it's real,' but not very strongly, so what you get is not really a eureka moment, but something that is incremental. It starts out as 'uh-huh, but it's probably a fluke,' to 'maybe it's not a fluke,' to 'this could be real, let me see what I can do to make it go away,' to 'well, it seems pretty robust but there are still problems,' to 'we've taken this as far as we can and we concede that there are many things to be done on this story, but before we do too much more it needs to be put in the hands of some other people, with totally different data sets and totally different ways of analyzing things and see if they get the same results.'"

ON THE morning I first visited the neurology mouse lab at Columbia, a lab technician was taping a breathing mask over the snout of an inert black mouse, dosing it with anesthetic gas. Once the mouse was knocked out, it was wrapped in plastic and laid on a tiny bed that fit into a long tube, and its head was strapped in place. The mouse did not stir. Then the technician inserted the tube into a machine that looked like a storage tank on a dairy farm but was actually a relatively petite magnetic resonance scanner made specifically to look inside the bodies of small animals. He turned to his computer. On the screen were images of the mouse's brain, its beating heart. The mouse looked peaceful in there, unperturbed by the percussive, hydraulic noises issuing from the machine, noises that overwhelmed the room.

The mouse nursery, where this mouse was raised and lived, was one flight up. There were white mice, black mice, wild mice, sick mice, genetically designed mice, and, though I did not know it then, a mouse that would, many months later, support the finding that the particular gene on which Mayeux and his collaborators were closing in influenced the development of late-onset Alzheimer's disease. The mouse was transgenic, the descendant, many generations re-moved, of a founder mouse bred fourteen years earlier. Mouse mod-els are expensive to produce, and this one had been perpetuated for many years with the idea that someone in the future might find its particular collection of disabilities, including memory deficits, to be of use.

That someone was Scott Small. Using his newly developed, super-high-resolution functional magnetic resonance imaging pro-cess to peer into specific regions of the brain at work, Small had been able to see that within the hippocampus of Alzheimer's pa-tients, it was the entorhinal cortex that was impaired, while in peo-ple who were not sick, just forgetful, the dentate gyrus was the site of calamity. Then, pairing these high-resolution fMRI images with a gene-sifting technique called microarray, Small examined every single cell in the entorhinal cortex to see which ones were con-tributing to disease. And there, serendipitously, he had come across "Mayeux's" gene, which turned out to be part of something called the retromer complex. That discovery suggested a whole new way to explain what was going on in the brains of people with AD.

To explain it to me, Small was standing in front of his black-board, trying to illustrate how the retromer complex worked, and how it contributed to disease. The picture he was drawing had a big circle with four smaller circles inside of it, and a Lego-like multi-decker bus next to it.

"God solved the problem of having different kinds of molecules that didn't like each other by compartmentalizing the cells," Small said. "The garbage disposal is separate from the refrigerator. You have a cell, which is the big circle in this picture, and you have different compartments called organelles, which are the small circles. Once there is separation, you need a way to take something from the refrigerator to the garbage disposal." He pointed to the multi-decker bus. "That's what the trafficking molecules do. They act like a shuttle bus."

Small drew the outline of another cell. This time he put only two organelles inside of it, one on the right, which he labeled with the word *endosome*, and one on the left, the *golgi*. Between the two organelles he drew a square. Then he added what looked like a bicycle seat to the middle of the square, and on the seat he put a small shopping bag. The square was the retromer, Small explained, the bike seat was the retromer receptor, and in the shopping bag was the retromer cargo. "The retromer complex has only been known about in mammals since 2000," he said, putting the finishing touches on his drawing. "It's called a complex because it's made up of a number of different molecules, not just one." He tapped the Lego bus in the first drawing to make his point. Each of its many levels was a different molecule.

One of those molecules, it turned out, was the very gene that showed up so convincingly in the data of Mayeux and his collaborators. Until it appeared in his own unrelated microarray analysis of the cells of Alzheimer's brains about a year before that, Small had never heard of it. (Now Small holds U.S. Patent 60-518,250, filed November 7, 2003, "Retromer-based Assays for Treating Alzheimer's Disease.")

"So how does this tie into Alzheimer's disease?" he said. "If there is retromer dysfunction, the cargo can't be removed. It builds up. We believe the cargo is the amyloid precursor protein, APP—which would account for there being too much amyloid in the brain. If our model is right, we've uncovered something completely novel that contributes to late-onset Alzheimer's. All the other findings were genes that might have affected AD, but they were not actually primary to the disease process. What we've found is primary to the disease process. We've shown it in a petri dish—when we turn down the retromer gene the level of beta-amyloid goes up—and now we're working with the mouse, and the results look very promising. I can't say more than that right now."

FOR MONTHS the name of the promising new gene was written on the whiteboard near the door in Richard Mayeux's office, but I had no idea that the word I was seeing was the gene we were talking about, since no one would utter its name in my presence. There was some concern that if I knew it I might inadvertently tip off another research group, which could claim the finding as theirs. In science there is only one winner, Karen Duff had said in the spring, describing how, during the race to make the first presenilin mouse, she was afraid to spare the time to get her broken arm set, for fear that she would lose too much ground to her competitors. And then there were the cautionary words of Scott Small when he finished explaining the retromer complex: "If tomorrow someone publishes the whole story I just told you," he said, "I can cry till I'm blue in the face but they will have published first." It was only at the end of the summer, when I was sitting with Mayeux in a small cabin on a lake in the Adirondacks where he was vacationing with his wife, relaxing by taking forty- and fifty-mile bike rides, that he said the name—it was *sorLA*—and I realized that it had been in front of me for half the year.

There was also a matter of protocol. As real as a finding might seem in a lab, it had to debut in a peer-reviewed scientific journal before it was accepted as real science. Announcing it first in the popular press could queer that. For the longest time I didn't want to know the name of the gene, did not want to possess the ability to compromise Mayeux's work and the work of his collaborators. And the name seemed beside the point, anyway. Names of genes are really only descriptive to scientists. By then, too, I had come to understand and appreciate the gene not for what it was called but for what it might do—for how it might add to the amyloid story, and how it could give researchers a new way to treat Alzheimer's. Scientists had already launched clinical trials on vaccines and immunizations that aimed to mobilize antibodies against amyloid plaques. At an earlier stage of development, a number of geneticists—Karen Duff and Rudy Tanzi among them—had been working on drugs that exploited the molecular pathways described by the original, early-onset Alzheimer's genes. These therapies were meant to intervene long before plaques formed.

"Any way of getting at a molecule—whether it's from microarray, or looking at genes, or God whispering in your ear to look at a particular protein—when you can pinpoint the primary molecular defect, you're more likely to develop effective treatments," Small explained. "That's Pharmacology 101."

Small, in his own lab and also in collaboration with researchers at Brandeis University and the University of Wisconsin, had already begun to look for a biochemical way to take advantage of his microarray and mouse findings in order to regulate the buildup of amyloid. Together the scientists had developed a screening assay to test potential compounds and expected to be able to turn over to chemical engineers a handful of potential drugs in a couple of years; the engineers would modify the drugs' structure to make them more amenable to entering the brain. From there, the compounds would be tested in mice, and two or three years after that, if all went well, human trials would begin.

"HERE'S THE thing," Richard Mayeux said one day when we were talking about possible treatments for memory loss and if there were ways to prevent AD. "Right now you don't know what the hell to do. You don't know whether you should take vitamins, whether you should take ibuprofen, and if you do if you'll get a stroke, whether you should take estrogen, and if that will give you a stroke. People tell you to use your brain, to use your body, and those are all well and good, but you don't know if it's a lifetime of doing those things, you don't know if it's starting to do crosswords when you're ninety. If we can solve some of these genetic puzzles, we'll know how to treat the disease."

When he said this it had been three years since he, St. George–Hyslop, and Farrar had begun their active collaboration, and despite their successes—the statistically significant association of the same gene in five independent Alzheimer populations and the functional studies that showed that when the gene was knocked out of a cell more beta-amyloid was produced—Mayeux remained circumspect. There was still more work to be done: having found the gene they now had to find the mutation, and they had to show how the mutation influenced the course of the disease. It might be another few months of hard labor at the very least before they could be sure.

"Let's say this is a real finding," he said, avoiding the presumption of a declarative sentence. "You can bet there will be a ton of work on how this particular gene fits into the big picture. It's really a jigsaw puzzle with five hundred pieces. You can look at it and see some of the key pieces and you can tell that there is a brain on a brown background, but you can't figure out where all the other pieces go. But then you get one piece in there that fits and it helps you get a whole section together.

"We think we got a piece—it may be more—but you don't know till you nail it. What I feel best about is that the collections I'm making are going to be around for a while. Collecting these Dominican families, putting the data together, having them very well characterized, having the cell lines—if it's not us who finds the gene, then someone will find the genetic variant eventually and that will help.

"It's a lot like the movie *The Maltese Falcon*. You look for, you look for, you look for, and you find something—and then you realize it's not the right thing, and by that evening you're booked on another ship to begin the next search. If this fizzles out, we'll be on that boat."

But it didn't fizzle out. On January 15, 2007, seventeen months after that conversation, a headline in the *New York Times* declared "Study Detects a Gene Linked to Alzheimer's." The gene was *sorLA*, the finding of Mayeux and his collaborators. It made its formal entrance into the scientific canon in *Nature Genetics* the next day.

## Chapter Six

# The Five-Year Plan

FIVE YEARS. When I asked almost any scientist with a memory drug in development, that was the answer to the obvious and most pressing question: when would it be available? It was so reflexive, so predictable, that Scott Small had a name for it: "the five-year plan." It didn't matter if I had asked in 1995 or 2005. It didn't matter if I queried the same researcher month by month or year after year—the answer was always the same, as if time and distance were fixed. So it was unusual, even exhilarating, to be admitted into the closely guarded laboratories of Sention, a memory-drug start-up company in Providence, Rhode Island, where the researchers were said (by the venture capitalists, who should know) to have two years left to go, three at most, before their breakthrough drug, C105, would be ready for the market.

Housed in an out-of-the-way industrial park on a spit of land that elbowed its way toward the ocean, Sention's public relations office kept a low profile. It had issued only two press releases, each announcing a new round of financing, not a promising experimental drug. Sention's scientists had published no paper relating to the drug. They had given no talks. When I showed up in the winter of

2002, not a single word had been written about the company in the popular press. The "Decade of the Brain"—Presidential Proclamation 6158 of 1990—had passed without a nod in its direction. I was the first writer allowed through the door, and then only after signing a wad of nondisclosure statements that bound me to Sention's code of silence, and only because I was friends with one of the money guys, which in that world was like being a money guy myself.

"I think we're past the cusp," Leon Cooper, one of Sention's principals, told me as soon as I'd cleared security. Though I couldn't see him—the receptionist had handed me a phone with Professor Cooper on the other end, as she might have a cup of coffee—I knew from a picture I'd found on the Internet that Leon Cooper, who held the 1972 Nobel Prize for Physics, was in his seventies with a parenthesis of white hair around a long face. "We're way ahead of the competition. What does that mean? I hope it will mean that we've got a multimillion-dollar company." Cooper paused, and then, as if realizing he'd forgotten something, added, "And that it will help people, too.

"We intend to be the premier company in this field," he continued. "We have an enormously powerful scientific team, combined with a hardheaded understanding of how you bring a drug to market."

Money tends to chase winners, and in this case the winner was not only Cooper and his Nobel Prize but memory impairment itself. Sention's inaugural press release, the one announcing its first $13 million of venture financing, noted that memory problems afflicted 80 percent of people over the age of thirty. The implication was clear: capture even a fraction of that market, and you'd have yourself the next Viagra, only more and better.

Cooper, the Thomas J. Watson Sr. Professor of Science at

Brown University and an expert on the creation of artificial neural networks, had been joined at the Sention table—quite literally—with two other Brown University neuroscientists, Mark Bear and Mel Epstein. "Leon and I were having lunch one day and we were talking about the fact that there were no good treatments for memory loss," Epstein said later. "Leon said that the timing was right, and that there had been some discoveries at the university in Mark Bear's lab that could be the basis for a company. We got a group together, and we'd meet every week for half a day discussing what was known about memory and known about existing drugs, and that's how we came up with C105."

Those meetings took place in the late 1990s. In November 2001, the company envisioned by Cooper and Epstein, based on Bear's development of C105, submitted a new drug application to the Food and Drug Administration, and by April had begun testing the compound in a small number of subjects in England. Phase 1 trials test for safety, and within weeks C105 was deemed safe enough to go on to phase 2, which tests for efficacy. Where phase 2 is off Broadway, phase 3 is the Big White Way—the same script but a larger stage and a bigger audience. Phase 3 trials routinely involve thousands of subjects at multiple testing sites and typically take years to run and analyze. In the case of Sention's C105, though, it looked like the drug was going straight from tryouts to a Tony: "We expect the FDA to approve our new drug application by 2005," Sention's clinical director said when Dr. Epstein took me around to see her. "That's a very speedy timeline."

When she said this, it was shortly after my father had died, and as is common when someone just misses out on the thing that could have made a difference, I thought of him. About a year before his death, when the ground fog of mental confusion socked him in most days and left him sitting in a chair at the kitchen table from breakfast till lunch staring at a single page of the New York Times, his doctor prescribed the Alzheimer's drug Aricept to see if it might lift. Giving my father an Alzheimer's drug was not the same as giving him an Alzheimer's diagnosis; the doctor simply had a hunch that the medicine, which amplifies the connections between synapses by boosting the neurotransmitter acetylcholine, might be helpful to someone who seemed to be suffering from vascular dementia—the kind of dementia caused by "hardening" of the arteries in the brain and by stroke. Within days of taking the medicine my father reported a clarity he hadn't experienced in a long time, a sharpening of his thoughts, in which subject and object were twinned again. His mood lifted, too. "I don't go down to the basement with the recycling and stand there for an hour wondering what I'm supposed to be doing," he said. The simple tasks of living had become simple again. He even remembered to take his medicines.

Aricept—generic name donepezil—was one of about a dozen drugs and supplements my father, at seventy-five, with two strokes limning his brain, an arrhythmic heart, prostate cancer, and high blood pressure, was taking. There were medicines that had to be taken in the morning, medicines that had to be taken at night, medicines that needed food, medicines that had to be taken on an empty stomach. It was kitchen chemistry, his failing body a brittle beaker, and no one—not the cardiologist, not the general practitioner, not the oncologist, not the neurologist, not the pharmacist, and especially not my father—knew how one drug interacted with another.

Three weeks after adding Aricept to the mix, my father's heart began to beat irregularly, and he was asked to decide between mental fuzziness or heart attack. He gave up the pills and began to wander through the basement again, calling to my mother over and over, asking her what he was doing there.

NOT LONG after my father died—muddled, and of a heart attack anyway—the Food and Drug Administration approved a new drug for the treatment of moderate to severe Alzheimer's. Marketed as Namenda, generic name memantine, it, too, amplified the function of a neurotransmitter in the brain, though in its case the neurotransmitter was glutamate, not acetylcholine. Glutamate, which is essential for learning and memory, controls the amount of calcium that flows into a nerve cell, creating the right chemical environment for memories to be stored. Too much glutamate leads to too much calcium which leads to cell death which leads to memory holes. Memantine staves the flood of glutamate, slowing calcium's corrosive effects on the brain.

Two medications, and neither a miracle cure, even for someone like my father. Had he been able to continue with the Aricept, it is likely that within a year it would have stopped working anyhow. He would have been aware at first the drug was weakening, and then he would have been unaware, and then less than that. Adding memantine might have helped, though people taking memantine scored only marginally better on memory tests than those taking a placebo. The two drugs seemed to work better when taken together, which was why, once memantine was available, the two were often prescribed in tandem. Even so, the effects were modest. Nothing like what I was hearing at Sention about the benefits of C105. And C105 was said to be able to help anyone who needed a memory boost—not just people who were clinically ill with a fatal neurodegenerative disease. It was fast acting. It was expected to have few side effects. It was an honest-to-God gold mine of a wonder drug.

~~

SENTION'S C105 was able to jump the drug-development queue, it turned out, not because it was revolutionary but because it was not. Its literature was extensive, its effects well documented. The groundwork had been laid for decades. The FDA was primed. C105, it turned out, was a derivative of a drug that, on the street, and in dorm rooms, and at truck stops, was known as speed.

As almost any college student, or pilot, or shift worker, will tell you, amphetamine—speed—increases alertness. It stimulates the central nervous system and accelerates the messages going from brain to body. Like donepezil and memantine, amphetamine augments neurotransmitters—in its case dopamine and norepinephrine. People who swallow amphetamines typically do better on standard memory tests than people who do not. They do better on other kinds of tests, too, hence the brisk off-label sales of Ritalin and Adderall, which are amphetamine derivatives, on college and high school campuses. This is not simply anecdotal. Researchers in Germany, looking to find out if amphetamines might help stroke patients recover language skills, tested them on forty healthy college students from Münster and found that the group taking amphetamines learned faster, were more motivated, and outperformed the placebo group. Researchers looking to see if amphetamines might help schizophrenics improve cognitive functioning—specifically, visual-spatial working memory—found that they did. But speed had nasty side effects, like addiction and, paradoxically, memory loss. It was hardly an attractive candidate as a revolutionary memory enhancer for a start-up company hoping to at-tract millions of dollars of venture capital. That's where the "enor-mously powerful scientific team" came in.

"Since you can give the standard form of amphetamine— d-amphetamine—to people for memory complaints, we wondered if there might be another form of it that might work, but without the addictive side effect," Mel Epstein explained. "Certain molecules have mirror images of themselves called isomers—think of them as left and right versions—where all the atoms are the same, they're just arranged in the opposite order. Sometimes the one on the left has the same overall effect as the one on the right, but with fewer side effects. That's what C105 is. It's the left-hand version of amphetamine."

Epstein mentioned a popular antidepressant, Celexa, one of whose side effects, excessive weight gain, had caused many patients to stop taking it. Its developer had recently come out with its left-hand version, called Lexapro, which was said to have the same therapeutic value as the original without triggering a craving for Krispy Kremes and French fries. Even in 2002, just months after it went on sale, Lexapro's success seemed assured, and was, to the folks at Sention, inspirational. They seemed to realize, before anyone else, that sales on the left-hand would far outstrip sales on the right—which it did by leaps and bounds, catapulting over the original formulation by 1,000 percent in just four years. The Sention team was counting on something similar happening to their hot prospect. As long as it wasn't addictive, they reasoned, C105 had a shot.

To find out, Sention had to determine if the reconfigured amphetamine was less, more, or similarly addictive as the original. The company hired Virginia Commonwealth University to run a clinical trial among students who used amphetamines recreationally. Some were given l-amphetamine, some were given d-amphetamine, some were given a placebo. Then they were asked if they'd rather have the drug they had taken or 60 cents. The drug or $1.20. The drug or $2.40. Embedded in those questions was another: When did a subject cross over from wanting the drug to wanting the money? "With d-amphetamine, they always want the drug," the Sention clinical director said. "With l-amphetamine they'd rather have the money. Now we're going to have to test it on hard-core addicts."

I don't know if this ever happened. In 2005, when I called the company to find out when it would be receiving FDA approval for C105, I got one of those "this line has been disconnected" phone messages. It turned out that some months before the office had been shuttered and the powerful team had disbanded.

"I'm afraid I don't know how this research turned out, since Sention went under rather suddenly. I assume their data was not exciting enough to entice new venture capital or a large pharma sale," the chief investigator into C105, Dr. Paul Mallory, wrote to me, when I finally tracked him down. I tracked down the drug, too. As of 2006 it had been sold to yet another biotech start-up, this one called Cognition Pharmaceuticals, which was testing it as an aid for people with multiple sclerosis. Meanwhile, Randall Carpenter, the former Sention CEO, and four other Sention alumni—though not, I noticed, Leon Cooper—had founded a company called Seaside Therapeutics. Seaside, I read on its website, was taking on autism with financing from "a venture philanthropist motivated in seeing a treatment for autism on the market, not on getting a big return on his investment." Carpenter and his associates were out of the memory business altogether. "We shot for the moon and missed," he told the press.

AROUND THE same time that Sention, led by its Nobel laureate, was pursuing the amphetamine isomer as a therapy, if not a cure, for cognitive deficiencies, a New Jersey company called Memory Pharmaceuticals was being guided by its own Nobel winner, Eric Kandel, to develop a different kind of memory drug. Unlike the Brown team, which identified a need—memory enhancement—and a market— the millions of people over the age of thirty—and then sought an existing compound that could be safely adapted to that use and those people, Memory Pharmaceuticals was working off the molecular discoveries that had earned Kandel his Nobel Prize in the first place. The market was the same. The stakes were the same. The goal was the same. (An article in the February 2002 issue of *Forbes* magazine deemed memory drugs "Viagra for the Brain," for both their therapeutic and their financial benefits.) There the similarities ended. Memory Pharmaceuticals' flagship memory drugs, MEM 1414 and MEM 1917, were in fact novel and innovative compounds. Nobody—not exam-cramming students, not fatigued fighter pilots, not long-haul truckers—had seen anything like them before.

In the 1990s, it seemed that every neuroscientist with a bright idea and a couple of postdocs at hand also had a start-up company. Status was no longer measured solely in Vineyard Haven square footage or by Lexus, Porsche, or Mercedes, but in VC dollars and big pharma partnerships, to say nothing of mouse patents and gene patents and virus patents and patents on entire lines of cells. If there was a patent on the field of neuroscience itself, though, it would belong to Eric Kandel, whose career both predated the discipline and defined it.

A graduate of Harvard and the New York University School of Medicine at midcentury, Kandel had been intent on becoming a psychiatrist in order to find out where in the brain the ego, id, and superego resided. When one of his advisers, Harry Grundfest, suggested that to really understand the mind one had to study the brain "one cell at a time," Kandel took up the gambit. The timing was fortuitous. Brenda Milner's studies of H.M., the young man whose hippocampus had been excised, along with his short-term memory, were just being published, which led Kandel to the hippocampus, which led him to the question of what made memories "stick," which led him to the giant marine snail *Aplysia,* which led him to cyclic AMP, which led him to the Nobel Prize.

From cyclic AMP, Kandel proceeded to study the genes that throw the switch on long-term memory formation, and through working with those genes, he became interested in making genetically altered mouse models of memory dysfunction to study diseases like Alzheimer's and schizophrenia. In 1996, looking to exploit his cyclic AMP findings to treat cognitive and psychiatric disorders, Kandel and some colleagues founded Memory Pharmaceuticals. It was the obvious next step, and if anyone seemed poised to find a blockbuster drug, it was Eric Kandel.

In 2005, the Swiss pharmaceutical giant Roche suddenly—and mysteriously—pulled out of its partnership with Memory Pharmaceuticals to develop MEM 1414 and MEM 1917, the two cyclic AMP drugs. Though Roche offered no explanation for its retreat, a 2003 article in the journal *Neuron* offered a clue. It suggested the limits of relying on reductionist science when making the leap from describing molecular pathways to manipulating them. According to Amy Arnsten of Yale, one of the authors of the *Neuron* article, relying on a simple animal like *Aplysia,* which has no hippocampus and prefrontal cortex, provided only a partial view of what's going on with cyclic AMP in the brain. Arnsten, who worked with mice, rats, and primates, whose brains more accurately resembled ours, found that the same compounds that boosted cyclic AMP in their hippocampus had devastating effects on their prefrontal cortex.

The problems with MEM 1414 and MEM 1917, more than the lowered expectations for C105, begin to suggest the difficulty of developing drugs to enhance or repair memory. Almost every drug in development fails. Of five thousand compounds, only five make it through the $500 million gauntlet of preclinical testing to human testing, and of these five, only one, typically, gets the approval of the FDA. Even if the odds were greater with a Leon Cooper or an Eric Kandel on board, they were still lousy, and because these were drugs for the brain, which is guarded by a protective shield called the blood-brain barrier that makes it difficult for targeted molecules, such as drugs, to pass through, they were lousier still.

LIKE MOST things, memory drugs—at least the idea of memory-enhancing drugs—were faddish, with different concepts slipping in and out of fashion. In February 2002, when *Forbes* put Memory Pharmaceuticals on its cover, smart money was betting on drugs that manipulated cyclic AMP. Not long before, though, another drug therapy, conceived on an even more fantastic premise—that the amyloid plaques that swamp an Alzheimer's brain could be eradicated like milfoil in a freshwater lake—was the rage, sending its developer's stock soaring and its principals into a contagious swoon. "We're really on the threshold of a new age. I think we're coming very close to the goal line now," Ivan Lieberburg, the head of research and development for the company, Elan Pharmaceuticals, told the journalist David Shenk in 1999, at the biannual "Molecular Mechanisms in Alzheimer's Disease" conference.

The Elan idea, conceived by a scientist named Dale Schenk (no relation to David Shenk), was based on a novel, and many thought "simplistic," idea: if plaques were what was causing an Alzheimer's brain to fail, why not vaccinate against them? Since the main component of plaque is the amyloid protein, Schenk reasoned that injecting patients with a small amount of it might produce enough antibodies to tag and remove the beta-amyloid in the brain, in the same way that injecting a small amount of a weakened live virus, for example, polio, stimulates the immune system to make antibodies to that virus. Schenk further reasoned that since the brain's natural defense system, the blood-brain barrier, was not perfect, and a small number of unwanted particles were always crossing the threshold, injecting beta-amyloid into the bloodstream would result, eventually, in a certain number of beta-amyloid antibodies entering the brain.

In 2000, not long after he baldly hinted that the game was almost over, Ivan Lieberburg went public with the news that Dale Schenk's hunch had been right. Beta-amyloid antibodies had successfully removed plaques in mice. These were no ordinary mice, since ordinary mice do not develop plaques or tangles. These were transgenic mice, altered to develop something like Alzheimer's. What Schenk's experiments showed was that after vaccination those plaques were flushed like ducks from a blind. They were there one minute, and then they weren't.

Dale Schenk and others were able to replicate these results with guinea pigs, rabbits, and monkeys. Further confirmation came from researchers at the University of South Florida. Their mice not only got better, they apparently got "smarter." Rid of plaques, they were able to negotiate mazes that had stumped them before. "They were normal now, apparently," David Shenk wrote in his book, *The Forgetting*. "For these humanized mice, at least, Alzheimer's disease was now preventable."

When Elan Pharmaceuticals announced the preliminary success of the Alzheimer's vaccine, it was, understandably, very big news. The wire services picked it up and sent it around the world; CNN, the BBC, and *Time*, among others, followed suit. Their reports noted not only that the Elan experiments had shown success in the animal models, but that in further trials the beta-amyloid vaccine had proved safe for humans. This did not mean it worked, only that the vaccine was safe enough to test it further to determine its efficacy. AN-1792 had made it through phase 1, and was being sent off, with great fanfare, to phase 2.

If the story of AN-1792 were a movie, it should end there, at the pinnacle of great promise. But in science, as in life, the cameras keep rolling, and what might have been the end of the story recedes to the middle, pulling triumph out of view. When the world next heard from Elan Pharmaceuticals about what was being called the Alzheimer's vaccine, in January 2002—a month before the *Forbes* piece touting Eric Kandel's breakthrough memory drug—it was without fanfare, quietly, on its website. Inexplicably, without warning, four people participating in the phase 2 trials had developed encephalitis, a life-threatening brain inflammation. No one could say why. A month later, eleven more participants out of about three hundred were similarly stricken. "We never saw a hint of this," Ivan Lieberburg told a reporter for the *Washington Post*. "It came as a total shock to Elan." In March of that year, the company permanently halted its trials of AN-1792.

Because this wasn't a movie, the story didn't end there, either, in tragedy. Even where there was brain inflammation, the vaccine seemed to be doing what Schenk thought it would do, which was to clear the brain of amyloid. Elan researchers continued to monitor patients who had taken part in the aborted trial and found that not only had they developed amyloid antibodies, but they were declining a bit less precipitously than Alzheimer's patients who didn't have the antibodies. The scientists went back to the lab, too, looking for a safer way to get the antibodies into the patient, a way that wouldn't trigger encephalitis. Four years later, the Elan vaccine was back: the antibodies were carried directly into the bloodstream in a process known as passive immunization, which did not require the patient's body to manufacture its own. By the summer of 2006, phase 1 trials were done, and Alzheimer's research centers all over the United States were recruiting Alzheimer's patients to take part in a series of phase 2 tests. This is exactly where the company had been in 2001, when Ivan Lieberburg, who in the ensuing years had become the company's chief medical officer, had been so enthusiastic, so sure. This time, if anyone was looking ahead, they weren't saying so out loud.


"I DIDN'T sleep last night," Gary Lynch said as he did a slow 360-degree turn in an ergonomic office chair, making one pass by the second-floor interior glass wall of the conference room of the University of California at Irvine's neuroscience building conference room before settling back at the table and putting his booted feet on a nearby chair. He shrugged himself out of a brown Diesel jacket, his shaggy fringe of grayish hair ticktocking like a pendulum across the back collar of a pink and lime green seersucker shirt tucked neatly into a worn pair of jeans. He was smiling in a cheeky, rebellious, adolescent kind of way—a sixty-something bad boy of science with no shortage of ego or drug patents that could, he was saying, change the course of history. Not just Lynch's personal history, not just the history of science, but human history, the history of our species and, oh, maybe the planet's, too. And I might not have believed any of it, except that Lynch was one scientist who Harry Tracy, the editor of a $300-a-year insider's newsletter called *NeuroInvestment*, thought was close, really close. Closer than Leon Cooper at Sention ever had the chance to be. Closer than Eric Kandel.

Lynch's patents, which he held jointly with UCI and his company, Cortex Pharmaceuticals, were for a class of drugs called ampakines that increased the excitatory activity of the neurotransmitter glutamate in the brain.

"It's a little hard to believe this," Lynch said, "but there is nothing like an ampakine. How does it turn out that you can have a drug that works for ADHD, MCI, sleep deprivation, schizophrenia—and if it doesn't work for that you can always use it for shoe polish? There's simply no analog. About ninety percent of the synapses in your brain aren't being treated pharmacologically. The entire pharmacological community has been working on about five to ten percent of your synapses. The other ninety percent they left to me. The big gun, all the communication you have in your brain, is mediated by one kind of excitatory synapse. They left that to me. Why? Because they like me. Despite the rumors."

Lynch stood up, took my notebook and pen, sat down again, and started to draw what looked like the side view of a brain.

"Everyone was convinced that because the glutamate system is everywhere, that if you take a drug, you're going to turn off the spinal cord or the brain. Honestly, that argument holds for all the neurotransmitters they're working on, but it didn't bother them then." He sketched a brain stem and cerebellum that looked like an aerial view of an elephant head, only smaller.

"Science offers constraints on what you can think. Science is the system that brings people in contact with the real world. Which they don't spend too much time in, it turns out, intellectually. Here's the real world and here's science"—only he kept working on his drawing of the brain, adding a cortex and ventricles. "Science is just as faddy, bitchy, and backstabby as everything else.

"There was a huge fad called 'block the AMPA receptor.' So all the drug houses were building agonists. I came along and said I was going to build a positive modulator. They said I was crazy, that it would cause brain damage. It was known that brain damage is caused by glutamate receptors. Have a stroke and the brain floods with glutamate, so it must be glutamate receptors causing the damage. Apparently everyone knew that but me. That's why I had the field to myself, and that's why we were able to get the patent."

The drawing, when it was finished, had what looked like a lot of arrows coming out of the brain stem, shooting directly into the parietal lobe, though it was a little hard to tell. It was a little shaky, with what looked like random initials—DA, NE, SHT, and ACL scattered about. Gary Lynch—to whom it made perfectly good and rational sense—said it was a representation of the seminal idea of a nineteenth-century English neurologist named John Hughlings Jackson, the idea that gave him his own seminal idea about ampakines.

"Here's the brain," Lynch said, tapping his drawing. "Down here you have serotonin, dopamine, acetylcholine—all the neurotransmitters—projecting into the forebrain and all over the place. They're called monoamines. The monoamines go to the cortex and back and the cortex regulates them. The more cortex, the more regulation. My guess was that if you enhance the cortex, you enhance the monoamines. How do you enhance cortical functioning? You take an ampakine." He leaned back in the ergonomic chair till it looked like it would snap. He had a satisfied look on his face, as if he'd just thought of this idea for the first time, though in fact he'd been working on ampakines, through his company Cortex, for six years. At that moment, "the military has a whole bunch of soldiers locked up in a barn somewhere in Ohio," he said, testing the Cortex ampakine for sleep deprivation. The drug had already been tested on monkeys who had been awake for days. According to Lynch, they did "just as well as if they had slept," on a battery of memory, intelligence, and motor skills tests. "Not only did they go back to normal, the balance of their brain activity went back to normal. The whole balance shifted back to normal. I don't think there is anyone out there who knows the story who doesn't think this drug is going to work."

Just who the drug was going to work for was up for grabs—anyone, it seemed. Cortex Pharmaceuticals had just finished a phase 2 study on adults with attention deficit disorder using ampakines, with no adverse effects. Ampakines were also being developed as a treatment for Alzheimer's, mild cognitive impairment, fragile X syndrome, Parkinson's, autism, traumatic brain injury, spinal cord injury, narcolepsy, and stroke. If that wasn't enough, Lynch also saw in it the potential to help anyone—everyone. People with normal memory loss, for sure, but those without it, too.

"What is a thought?" Lynch mused. "It's a transient neural network. How big can you make that neural network? We're going to give you a drug that increases communication and therefore increases the size of the network. What is intelligence, what is thought? It's the interaction of cortical neurons. It enhances the signal from one neuron to the next. Why shouldn't the ampakine let you have bigger thoughts? No one can know what happens to people when we expand their capacity. We are boldly going where no humans have gone before. We're talking about pharmacologically building another species."

As he talked, Lynch spun around in the chair like a top, pausing now and again to look me in the eye, to make sure that I was with him. Which I wasn't, really. I mean I understood what he was saying, but I couldn't quite believe it. Or didn't want to believe it. And as if anticipating my objection—the obvious ethical one—he started to sing. "Once the rockets go up, who cares where they come down, that's not my department, says Wernher von Braun."

Okay, he was sleep deprived. And he was spending a lot of time in Big Pharma boardrooms, pitching the ampakine story, hoping to find a well-endowed company with which to partner. But still. Did ampakine work for mania, too?

Not long after I said good-bye to Gary Lynch, the FDA put a clinical hold on CX717, one of Cortex Pharmaceuticals' ampakines, after looking over preliminary data from one of its animal studies. Later I read that all those soldiers who had been holed up in the barn in Ohio had been simulating night-shift workers who were only able to get a few hours of sleep a day. Some were given 1,000 milligrams of CX717, and some a placebo, and when it was all said and done, one group was not distinguishable from the other: cognitively they were the same. I also read that another Cortex ampakine—CX516—being tested in people with mild cognitive impairment had also fizzled out. There were some bright points, though: in that same MCI study, people with the most serious memory impairments who were given the ampakine tested significantly better than those who were given a sugar pill. And back in the lab, Gary Lynch and Dr. Christine Gall were able to reverse age-related cognitive decline in old rats. After ingesting the ampakines, the old rats were just as smart as they used to be.

"Take a middle-aged rat, give it a shot of ampakine, and guess what, the deterioration is gone!" Lynch had told me, after commandeering my notebook again and drawing an $x$ and $y$ axis—one for age, the other for memory—that made a decisive downward slope. "Ampakines increase BDNF. BDNF is what we like to call 'big-deal neurotrophic factor.'"

In fact, BDNF is brain-derived neurotrophic factor, a protein that, among other things, encourages the growth of new neurons and the survival of existing ones. If Lynch and Gall were right, and ampakines increased BDNF in people, ampakines would turn out to be a big-deal factor in many of our lives. But not yet.

"By the time you get to old age there are so many things wrong with you that I don't think you're going to fix them all," Lynch said. "I like to look at the things when everything is nice and normal. It's a cleaner background against which to find a biological deficit.

Which I intend to fix. It's too late for me! You ought to write that down: what an altruistic character!"

LESS THAN a hundred miles down Highway 1 from Irvine, at TorreyPines Therapeutics, Rudy Tanzi's boutique drug company, a promising AD drug that was well into phase 3 trials had recently failed, though there were three others, each at least ten years behind it, that were getting hopes up. The therapies being pursued there, some based on genetics, others working along what had become the more established neurotransmitter route, suggested that the reason the answer to the question "When will there be a workable memory drug?" was always "in five years" was not simply that the incremental process of drug discovery was fundamentally slow, but because the biological process of encoding and storing and retrieving memories was not located in a single place in the brain. If memory is not one thing, if it resides throughout the brain, it is by design a moving target. Researchers were hoping to fix memory by manipulating genes, by manipulating neurotransmitters, by manipulating molecules, by manipulating cells. Some were attempting to redirect the slide of normal memory loss. Others were working on a known pathology. But even there, no one knew for sure how it worked. The amyloid hypothesis, though well established, had not been proved to be causal. Even if a gang of antibodies could bully amyloid plaques out of a living Alzheimer's brain, what did it mean? Analyzing the data from the first Elan trial of AN-1792, researchers could only show the mildest improvement in memory, even where the plaques had been chased away.

Since clearing plaques could turn out to be only a palliative or a stopgap or ultimately ineffectual—if plaques were the artifact, not the fact—researchers were also trying to develop therapies that would prevent the body from producing beta-amyloid in the first place. They knew that it was produced when two different enzymes (beta secretase and gamma secretase) moved through the bloodstream like drawknives, slicing a protein called APP into smaller, stickier pieces, which clump together and gum up the brain. If they could only dull the knife, they reasoned, they could reduce or prevent APP from being hacked. The problem was that beta-amyloid and the two secretases were found throughout the body. Taking them out of one region ran the risk of compromising others.

Bristol-Myers Squibb, the first drug company to pursue a secretase inhibitor, gave it up in 2001 because of unwanted side effects (though it didn't say publicly what they were). In 2006, another big pharmaceutical company, Eli Lilly, began testing its own gamma secretase inhibitor, LY450139, with limited success. It was going to be tricky. In mice, at least, high doses of gamma secretase inhibitors were toxic. They compromised the immune system.

The yin to the yang of novel drug development was drug appropriation—the old-medicine-in-new-vials method of therapy, where existing drugs aimed at other ailments were redirected to a different target. For a while, anti-inflammatory drugs like ibuprofen were thought to curb Alzheimer's, and then it was cholesterol-lowering statins, then nicotine, and then it was estrogen, though none had yet proved to have a statistically significant effect. At New York University, researchers looking into the connection between diabetes and dementia were hoping that they could rev up the metabolism of the brain by changing how sugar finds its way there.

"If you give Alzheimer's patients some glucose, their memory gets a little better," NYU's Mony de Leon mentioned one day. "Why should that be? Because there is something broken. My fantasy is that the technology we need is going to come from diabetes.

Not from insulin. Insulin is not going to do the job. It's going to come from drugs that improve glucose transportation."

Transportation, though of an altogether different sort, was also on Scott Small's mind as he tried to sort out the puzzle of the retromer complex, and how to take that solution to the next level, the only level that truthfully really mattered to most of us, the one where it morphed into a cure or a preventative or a palliative, the one that was going to be there when we needed it. Knowing how the retromer worked was good—it was intellectually satisfying, it was cool, even. But it would be better, more satisfying, and cooler, if discovering it and knowing how it worked meant that at least the kind of dementia it triggered was not in our future.

"As you know, because I've said this before, Pharmacology 101 says that if you locate the molecular defect, then you are much more likely to develop effective treatments," Scott Small pointed out one evening when we were at dinner and I was asking, again, the dreaded "when" questions: when would there be a drug that impeded normal memory loss, when would there be a cure for Alzheimer's. "That's a truism. Look at the drugs we have. They came out of faulty logic. Acetylcholine is not a primary defect in Alzheimer's. You're blowing the smoke out of the fire when what you want to do is put out the fire.

"The retromer is a trafficking complex. It helps move molecules from region A to region B. When you turn down the particular retromer molecule we found, you prevent the retrieval of its cargo. So you have a backlog of cargo. And what we're finding is that one of the molecular building blocks that make beta-amyloid is the cargo of this trafficking molecule. If that's true, it immediately solves the question of how you can have an increase in abeta production without any abnormality in the building blocks. It's because you have faulty distribution."

As Scott talked, I began to think about the garbage barges not far away, hauling commercial waste across the Hudson River, and what would happen if the sanitation workers had a work slowdown. The barges would continue moving trash around, but a lot of it would be the same trash. And it would begin to rot and putrefy, and bacteria and parasites would colonize, and rats and mosquitoes would become carriers, and that would be that. Scott's molecule was the sanitation workers on a work slowdown. The problem was not only that there was no mayor to deploy the National Guard and no union with which to negotiate, but that there was no drug to restore the status quo, and there wouldn't be for a long time.

"Here's one way to think of drug development if you're talking about Alzheimer's," Scott said, invoking a river metaphor of his own. "You can develop drugs that affect abeta processing upstream, or you can make drugs that affect the toxicity of abeta. Drugs being developed out of the discovery of the original, early-onset mutations are upstream. Aricept, on the other hand, is downstream. Acetylcholine is downstream from the primary neurotoxin. Elan's vaccine works on the problem downstream, too. It basically says 'Okay, fine, whatever molecular defect is causing the production of abeta, we're not going to try to affect that, but what we're going to do is try to clear it out.' It's like taking Lipitor for high cholesterol.

"There are many drugs that work in a dish or in an animal and fail when they get translated to humans, not because of lack of efficacy but because of unacceptable side effects. And the reason for that is most diseases are regionally selective and most drugs are systemic, and so you get collateral damage. So, can you develop a smart drug? Can you impose regional specificity? One way would be if, in fact, the retromer is expressed only in the hippocampus, then even if a drug got into the whole body it would only hit a single target. But the retromer is actually expressed throughout the body.

"In the future we may be able to impose specificity for a drug by using clever molecular manipulations. It's fairly sci-fi at this point."

For Scott Small, the univariate guy, the one who believed it was not necessary for complex problems to have complex solutions, upstream was the only way to go. Anything else—for him—was beside the point. Calling it sci-fi was not capitulation but, rather, a way to bypass the five-year clock. Doing a molecular end run around Alzheimer's was in the future, Scott was saying, though maybe not in my future, or even his. Same for fixing the broken circuit in the dentate gyrus in order to alleviate "normal" memory loss. Even so, he was not unconflicted. Patients came to see him, concerned that they could not remember the names of their clients, or the title of a book they'd read a month before, or its crucial plot points, worried that they were getting sick. "Most of the time they're fine, and I say, 'Good news, it's just normal aging,' to which they almost all invariably ask me to give them a drug to stop it. I say, 'No, it's not a disease.' But who am I to say that? It's not straightforward. The distinction between normal and diseased tends to blur with these slow neurodegenerative diseases." Scott sounded a little anguished, but there was a smile on his face. "I was a philosophy major in college," he said. "I like to think about this stuff."

## Chapter Seven

# Gone to Mars

ONE DAY, WAITING FOR Scott Small to get off the phone, I noticed a large cardboard box, the size a computer might come in, on the floor near his desk. The top flaps of the box were bent back like an open door, beckoning. Inside was a trove of sweet things: 3 Musketeers and sacks of Tropical Skittles and Dove bars and Mars bars and peanut M&M's and peanut butter M&M's and almond M&M's and crispy M&M's and Starbursts and Combos and I could go on.

Scott put his hand over the receiver. "Take some. Please," he said, but I didn't even know where to begin. "The Mars people sent it."

Why was Mars, a privately held snack-food company based in New Jersey, sending Scott Small, an associate professor of neurology at Columbia, enough sugary treats to stock a couple of vending machines? It was a mystery cloaked in an enigma inside a candy wrapper.

"I can't tell you," Scott said when I asked. "Trade secrets. I think I could get into trouble if I told you. You should definitely take some of these," he said, pointing to a vertical foot of Milky Ways.

"You're a neuroscientist," I pointed out. "Aren't you supposed to be working with Merck or Pfizer?"

"I've told you," Scott said, sounding mildly peeved, "I don't do work for drug companies. If I worked for a drug company, do you think I'd be here talking to you? They wouldn't let me."

"You mean like Mars won't let you talk to me?"

"Exactly," Scott said, smiling, as if he had proved something. He pushed the box closer to me.

I nudged it back in his direction with my foot. It was like tug-of-war without the rope.

"So Mars is interested in memory research," I tried.

"Yes," he said.

"Why?" I asked, though as soon as I had, the answer was obvious: Mars was interested in memory for the same reason a pharmaceutical company would be—market share, money. At the supermarket, the "functional" candies—sweets that promised to improve my concentration, enhance circulation, promote healthy gums, and aid in weight loss—were stocked on the same shelves as herbal supplements that could make me sharper, brighter, smarter, quicker. We tend to assume that the products in the health food section of the supermarket are inherently healthful and benign— certainly we want them to be—forgetting, or choosing to forget, that that is exactly where the thirty-eight people who died from taking the herbal supplement L-tryptophan and the 155 who died from dieting with ma huang (ephedra) found them. How were they to know? These were "herbal" supplements, which is to say "natural," which is to say safe.

Lately, the sheer number of vitamins, herbs, and foods being sold as memory aids had spawned a whole other industry: warning off unsuspecting consumers. The editors of the University of California at Berkeley's *Wellness Letter*, after chasing down claim after claim about the supposed cognitive benefits of scores of vitamins, herbs, spices, foods, and supplements and never quite catching them up, finally published a stand-alone reference guide, a *PDR* to this corner of the nootropic universe. For anyone hoping for less exegesis and more straight-up advice, which is to say people like you (probably) and me (definitely), forget it. The evidence about the efficacy of most of these things, both anecdotal and scientific, was contradictory at best and confusing at worst. There was no bottom line here, no arbiter to tell you, once and for all, if walnuts, tofu, red wine, black tea, green tea, vitamin E, fish oil, chocolate, folic acid, almonds, or ginkgo, to name just a few potential agents of hope, or Snickers and Twix, judging from the box from Mars, were going to save you from yourself.

The Mars work, as much as Small would allow, was part of a collaboration with Fred "Rusty" Gage of the Salk Institute in La Jolla, California. Gage, who was in his late fifties, was by far the most popular neuroscientist in the world, if popularity was measured by the number of times his research papers had been cited by other scientists in their research papers—104 times per paper—which was a lot more than anyone else's. In the late 1990s Gage had turned neuroscience on its head, upending the conventional and long-held belief that we are born with a fixed number of brain cells which diminishes as we age. The assumption was that this loss of neurons was why, as people got older, their memory faltered.

"The genesis of new cells, including neurons, in the adult human brain has not yet been demonstrated," Gage and his collaborators wrote in what has become a seminal piece in the journal *Nature Medicine* in 1998. "This study was undertaken to investigate whether neurogenesis occurs in the adult human brain. . . . [W]e demonstrate that new neurons . . . are generated from dividing progenitor cells in the dentate gyrus of adult humans. Our results further indicate that the human hippocampus retains its ability to generate neurons throughout life."

Since then, Gage, a professor in the Laboratory of Genetics at Salk, had been working out the implications of the finding. Did new neurons matter—did they *do* anything, were they value added? How did they form? Why did neurogenesis occur in the hippocampus, the gatekeeper of memory, and nowhere else in the brain (except the olfactory bulb)? How did neurogenesis work in a healthy brain, and was it compensatory in a sick brain? If it was compensatory, and if it could be induced, was it a way to fix a brain that had been impaired, where neurons had died off? Apparently, in addition to his work at the Salk Institute, where he had recently identified how new neurons made their way into mature neural networks, Gage was engaged in top-secret brain research at one of the most guarded candy companies in the world.

"So all this candy has to do with neurogenesis?" I ventured.

"Do you know what GRAS compounds are?" Small asked, and proceeded to tell me: GRAS compounds are anything that exists in the world that the U.S. Food and Drug Administration has deemed "generally regarded as safe." When the Food Additive Amendment to the Food, Drug, and Cosmetic Act was passed in the late 1950s, certain food ingredients that were commonly used were exempted from having to undergo the testing and approval process typically required for food additives. Instead, they were labeled as GRAS—as long as they were used the way they had always been used. Ginger, licorice, cinnamon, and basil, for example, were all GRAS compounds.

As Small spoke, I began to understand what he was getting at. GRAS compounds did not have to be tested with the same rigor as medicine. Nor did they have to go through the lengthy and expensive approval process required of a new drug. If a GRAS compound that caused new neurons to grow could be found, and if the growth of new neurons could stanch the memory loss that typically comes as we age, whoever found the compound would be able to work on it in virtual secrecy, without government interference, synthesize and patent it, bring it to market quickly, and make a tremendous amount of money. Imagine, Scott Small suggested, if the fountain of cognitive youth turned out to be a standard salad bar item?

Which is why, many weeks later, I was driving across the George Washington Bridge into New Jersey, driving past Newark and then Parsippany, the gauzy industrial skyline giving way to the architectural drone of indistinguishable suburban tracts, and these finally segueing to a long corridor of trees interrupted by the occasional reservoir or lake, as I put fifty-two miles between me and Manhattan, the same fifty-two that were between Manhattan and Mars, Mars being located in the leafy township of Hackettstown, New Jersey. It had taken about three months for the company sentinels to agree to let me visit; as a privately held company Mars was, if nothing else, deeply, and suspiciously, private. But after a number of back-and-forths about my intentions, and a promise that I would not be carrying a camera, a meeting was arranged between me and Harold Schmitz, the chief science officer of the company, though in fact it was between me, Harold Schmitz, and a pleasant public relations minder, who was sitting in on the meeting, presumably to keep him on point and me off it.

The Mars headquarters, where they made M&M's, the company's "spokescandy," was an island edifice of poured concrete surrounded by acres of asphalt parking lot, on what passed for a country road in New Jersey. Twelve hundred "associates" punched the clock there, almost all of them working in vast, wall-less rooms, not a cubicle or partition between them, which was the corporate equivalent of either an open classroom or the dayroom at a minimum-security prison. On the ground floor, the desks offered a clear view of the fully functional bodega-sized model of a standard convenience store set up behind plate glass at the front of the room. Inside the store the shelves were stocked with Mint Milanos and Hostess Twinkies and Planter's Peanuts and Fritos and Dr Pepper and Coke and Tampax and Crest, with a freezer full of fudge ripple and butter pecan ice cream and a magazine rack with a complete complement of tabloids and slick magazines, as well as *Star Wars* tie-in Milky Ways and bags of Snickers' "poppables," so the people at the desks could see how their products looked against the competition.

The laboratories, where over seventy Mars researchers were working to understand the chemical properties of various foods, were in a different wing of the building, this one stocked with an impressive array of electron microscopes and spectrometers, each one of which probably cost many hundreds of thousands of peanut M&M's. Harold Schmitz, boyish with a curtain of blond Dutch-boy bangs hanging just above a pair of stylish wire glasses, wearing black jeans, sneakers, and a blue shirt open at the collar, was waiting for us back there—though oddly, not another soul was present. The workstations had been cleared out.

"Most of our interest is directed toward foods we already make," Schmitz said before I could start in on my list of questions, all of which were aimed at getting him to reveal exactly which salad bar ingredient caused neurogenesis. I had already ruled out tofu, first because I had just come across a study of elderly Japanese men living in Hawaii where "poor cognitive test performance, enlargement of ventricles and low brain weight were each significantly and independently associated with higher midlife tofu consumption," and was betting on walnuts (high in omega-3 fatty acids and known to lower cholesterol), onions (which had been proved to lower blood glucose levels), and bell peppers (chock-full of vitamins C and A and $B_6$), with tomatoes ahead of them all.

Lycopene, the chemical that puts the red in tomatoes (and the pink in grapefruit), is a phytonutrient with a long list of well-documented health benefits. According to a tomato fact sheet posted on Tomatofest.com, "The Tomato Lover's Paradise," citing research by Professor Edward Giovannucci of the Harvard School of Public Health, as well as by scientists at Technion in Israel and the University of Illinois at Chicago, lycopene can reduce the risk of prostate cancer by 21 to 43 percent, guard against cervical tumors and age-related macular degeneration, inhibit heart disease, prevent clogged arteries, and raise a man's sperm count. If it could do all these things, I reasoned, why couldn't it encourage the growth of new brain cells as well?

"Lycopene!" I blurted out when Harold Schmitz turned his back for a moment to show me the elegant high-performance liquid chromatography machines the Mars biochemists used to analyze compounds. "Wouldn't you say that lycopene has some real health benefits?"

Schmitz turned and looked at me. He had been talking about the company's fifteen-year search for the molecular properties of chocolate; I was talking about tomatoes.

"There is some circumstantial evidence that lycopene may help with prostate cancer. Very circumstantial," Schmitz said, taking up my gambit. (This was before a 2007 study of 28,000 men found no correlation between lycopene and prostate cancer prevention.) "It's definitely an interesting story, but the real contribution to public health is irrelevant because there is no good science. Here at Mars we're attempting to understand a huge array of natural chemicals in nature. We're interested in how the chemicals in food influence how ingredients taste and in their nutritional value. Our interest in taste and flavor issues led us to try to understand the chemistry of cocoa, which led us to understand what those chemicals were doing in terms of nutrition, which is why, for the past fifteen years, we have been studying the properties of flavanols. The scientists here are able to measure which flavanols are in each food, and to measure them in a test tube, and to see if they can make a difference for human health."

Schmitz, who received a doctorate in food science from North Carolina State University in 1993, had spent all of his career at Mars, much of it working out the cocoa story. To understand the story, you had to master a confusing, Russian-nesting-doll vocabulary: flavanol, flavanoid, flavone, flavonones, flavan-3-ols, isoflavones. A flavanol, which is what cocoa is, belongs to a class of plants called polyphenol flavanoids, which are well distributed in nature, relatively nontoxic, and therefore widely incorporated into the human diet. Flavanoids, which can be found in tea, red wine, walnuts, onions, and berries, have health benefits even more remarkable and demonstrable than lycopene's: they have been shown to be anti-inflammatory, antiallergenic, antimicrobial, and anticancerous. In the case of cocoa, in particular, according to Harold Schmitz, it can improve blood flow in the brain and kidneys, and relax the blood vessels leading to and from the heart.

"The story is not about chocolate or cocoa, really," he said. "It's about flavanols. The food industry has been trying to eliminate them from most foods because they are associated with bitterness and grayness in some foods. It's frustrating with dark chocolate. People hear the message that dark chocolate is good for their health, so they go out and buy chocolate with a sixty or seventy percent cocoa content. But the cocoa content doesn't matter if the cocoa hasn't been grown and processed in the right way." Not surprisingly, Schmitz said, only Mars, with its intense effort to measure the specific molecular structure of each cocoa molecule—"it's like finding the key to a lock"—really got this. "Nutrition is an obfuscated area of science," he said.

"Food is a complex chemical matrix. The monetary reward for attempting to understand it is a lot harder to justify than in the pharmaceutical industry. We can do it because we are privately held and don't have Wall Street breathing down our necks."

This was a good story, too, one about how the little guy—or at least the solitary, go-it-alone maverick guy—motivated by the desire to unlock one of the great mysteries of the world, a mystery that, once solved, had the chance of improving individual lives as well as world health more generally, won out over the greedy, crass money handlers. I would have believed it whole hog, too, had I not, in preparation for my trip to Mars, read an article from the *New York Times Magazine* by Jon Gertner, who had talked with Harold Schmitz a year earlier. It was in Gertner's article that I learned that the family-held Mars company, one of the three or four biggest corporations in the United States, "has no obligation to shareholders and no need to justify its larks. Indeed, the company's longstanding and intense culture of privacy has made it corporate America's supreme enigma." When Gertner visited, there had been no scientists in the lab either.

Though Mars had been pursuing and promoting the health benefits of its products for years—including a misguided effort in the 1990s that championed chocolate for dental health—its research into the molecular structure of cocoa was motivated by something altogether less wishful, a fungal infection in the 1990s that threatened to wipe out the Brazilian cocoa crop. It was then that Mars scientists began studying the chemical composition of the cocoa bean, hoping that once they understood it, they could replicate it in the lab, which might ultimately protect the company from the vagaries of pests and weather. After about five years it was seeming doubtful.

At the same time, though, Schmitz had begun to hear about the health benefits of red wine and green tea, both of them flavanols, like cocoa, and wondered if the flavanols in cocoa might be similarly advantageous. In addition to his own efforts to determine if cocoa flavanols might stimulate the body to produce nitric oxide, which would then relax and open the cell lining of blood cells, causing better circulation, Schmitz was seeking out academic scientists who, with the financial backing of Mars, would also investigate the health benefits of the bean. One of these scientists was Norman Hollenberg, a professor at Harvard Medical School and the former editor of the *New England Journal of Medicine*.

Hollenberg was interested in the genetics of hypertension, and one day he came across an article written by a U.S. Army doctor in the 1940s, stationed in the Panama Canal Zone, about a group of native people from the San Blas Islands, the Kuna Indians, who had remarkably low blood pressure that did not rise even as they aged. Wondering if the Kuna might have the very gene he was looking for, Hollenberg went off to the San Blas Islands, and indeed, it was true, the Kuna, young and old, were free of hypertension. But an odd thing happened when the Kuna moved off the island: their blood pressure began to rise like everyone else's. If their low pressure wasn't genetic, could it be environmental? While he was on the island, Hollenberg noticed that the people there drank large quantities of a native cocoa. On the mainland, however, the Kuna drank commercially processed cocoa. He wondered if that could be the difference. It was. Back in Cambridge, examining the Kuna cocoa bean, he found it rich in something that the processed cocoa lacked: flavanoids. In a paper written by Hollenberg and Dr. Naomi Fisher of Boston's Brigham and Women's Hospital, published in the *Journal of Hypertension* from research funded by Mars, the Kuna cocoa pod was found to have 4,000 milligrams of flavanol per 100 grams, while commercially processed cocoa had less than 5 percent of that.

Other studies, many of them also funded by Mars, showed similar cardiovascular effects from flavanol-rich cocoa or chocolate. In one, researchers in Germany and the United States found that people with "poor vascular responsiveness" who were given specially formulated, high-flavanol cocoa showed increased blood flow due to the relaxation of their blood vessels. So did healthy volunteers. And in a study where participants were fed an average American diet or were lucky enough to have that diet supplemented with flavanol-intense chocolate bars, "[a]fter four weeks, participants who consumed a diet supplemented with flavanol-rich cocoa and chocolate experienced a number of favorable heart-health benefits including a decrease in LDL or 'bad' cholesterol oxidation, an increase in HDL or 'good' cholesterol, and an increase in total antioxidant capacity in the blood."

Rust is the kind of oxidation most of us are familiar with, or so we think. Our bodies, though, are walking oxidation factories, their cells under constant assault from a class of molecules called free radicals that are normal and natural constituents of us all. Free radicals are the molecular equivalent of people who can't bear to be alone. Their unpaired electron needs a mate to become stable, and it is not picky. Lipids, proteins, DNA—any molecule will do. The problem is, this random coupling can have a devastating, sometimes fatal, effect on the unlucky mate. This is oxidation. The human body produces antioxidants to neutralize free radicals, and vitamins, like C and E, as well as certain nutrients found in food are also able to disarm more, but it's never enough. The brain, which uses about 20 percent of the body's metabolic oxygen, is especially vulnerable, for it is unable to supply enough antioxidants to fend off all the free radicals produced in the process. Oxidative stress has been linked to premature aging, to heart disease, and to dementia. Not only does it cause the death of neurons, it creates a feedback loop of infinite destruction, where oxidation encourages the production of beta-amyloid and beta-amyloid leads to oxidative stress. Unless, it seems, you ingest certain polyphenol flavanoids. In a study of rat brains engineered to have amyloid plaques, those exposed to the flavanoids in green tea appeared to acquire some kind of protection. The same researchers, Rémi Quirion and Stéphane Bastianetto at Montreal's Douglas Hospital Research Center, also found that exposure to red wine actually cleared the brain of plaques.

I read about the first study in a magazine called *Healthcare Quarterly* and the second in the journal *Neurobiology of Aging,* and because the claims they made seemed so stunning to me, so profound, I called one of the authors, Stéphane Bastianetto, to make sure I understood what I was reading. Dr. Bastianetto himself had been spurred to this research by seeing study after study suggesting that people who drink red wine in moderation, as well as people who regularly consume fruits and vegetables, had lower rates of neurodegenerative disease. "We wanted to see which element is responsible for this," he explained. "The common element is polyphenol. Polyphenols are able to block amyloid toxicity. They work upstream to block the accumulation of amyloid plaques, and downstream to clear them. If you clear plaques in mice, you can reverse some of the damage. The results with Alzheimer's patients will give us the answer in humans."

Doctors Bastianetto and Quirion, however, did not work with humans—not in the aggregate, anyway. They worked with cells. This was an important distinction, and one that was easily elided when scientific findings were reported, and especially when they were reported to a public that was eager for good news and happy endings and cures. But what happened to individual cells in the lab did not necessarily correspond to what happened to individual cells in the body. Red wine and green tea in a petri dish cleared amyloid. Whether anyone would be able to take that finding and translate it into a viable research protocol for everyday folk remained to be seen. (Which polyphenol? Grown where? Processed how? And if the alcohol in red wine is somehow complementary to the polyphenol itself, would that preclude it from being synthesized into a pill, a patch, a nasal spray?)

"Right now we can't say that if you drink a couple of cups of green tea starting at age forty that you won't get Alzheimer's disease," Dr. Bastianetto told me. "It's all a matter of probability. What we can say is that if you put together all the factors that we know to be beneficial, like drinking red wine and green tea, it will reduce *the risk* of a neurodegenerative disease like AD, at least indirectly, by reducing the risk of cardiovascular disease, since cardiovascular disease is a risk factor for AD. Should you drink green tea or red wine? Should you eat more fruit? This, of course, is up to you. You should use your common sense. Let me say, though, that after our first study was published, my brother called up to say that he now drinks a few cups of tea every day."

Just as green (and black) tea, grapes, and cocoa beans are polyphenol flavanoids, so too is the extract made from the leaves of the ginkgo tree, ginkgo biloba. Ginkgo, which has a long history in Chinese medicine as an aphrodisiac as well as a cognitive enhancer, tops the list of ingredients of almost every over-the-counter memory compound on the pharmacy shelf. If, like me, you are skeptical about ginkgo by the company it keeps there, remember that it's also keeping company with the flavanoids, which should count for something, and apparently does, since the United States government, among other grant-making bodies, has dropped a lot of money in the ginkgo cup, funding legitimate scholarly research to determine if it boosts memory or has any measurable medicinal value at all. But even under the auspices of the National Institutes of Health and the National Institute on Aging, the studies have been inconclusive and inconsistent, one to the next, which may have had as much to do with the study designs or the soils in which the trees grew or how the extract was prepared, as it did with the actual answer to the original question: was it effective? (Which was a more formal way of asking: should I be taking it?) A cautious person might look at the evidence and conclude that the prudent thing would be to take ginkgo, just in case the studies that demonstrated increased blood flow and better performance on tests of verbal memory, as well as Stéphane Bastianetto's finding that ginkgo extract cleared beta-amyloid from hippocampal cells—in a dish—turned out to be the salient ones, and the large, double-blind study reported in the *Journal of the American Medical Association* not long after Bastianetto's work was published, which demonstrated that ginkgo had no measurable effect on memory and learning, turned out to be wrong.

If ginkgo biloba—or, for that matter, Kuna cocoa, Merlot, or jasmine tea—were a medicine and not either a food product or a supplement, it would be taken under the supervision of a physician. She would determine the dose, consider the side effects, determine if there are any countervailing medical problems that could compromise its effectiveness or, in turn, compromise the patient's health. This is what Dr. Joyce Lashof, the former dean of the School of Public Health at the University of California at Berkeley, was getting at when she testified on September 10, 2001, at the U.S. Senate Special Committee on Aging hearing on "Swindlers, Hucksters and Snake Oil Salesmen: The Hype and Hope of Marketing Anti-Aging Products to Seniors":

"One of the likely outcomes of aging is a slowing down of the renal and hepatic systems, which means that drugs of any kind, whether prescription or botanical, are not cleared as quickly through the kidneys and not metabolized as efficiently by the liver. This makes the elderly more susceptible to the effects and side effects of any drugs. Because older people typically take many forms of medication for chronic conditions, the likelihood of adverse interaction is also greatly heightened. Some of the most common dietary supplements have known adverse effects in the presence of certain conditions, many of which are common in the elderly. One example of this is ginkgo biloba which is heavily marketed to improve memory and has a potent inhibitory effect on the platelet activating factor. This could lead to excessive bleeding and is especially troublesome for anybody already taking blood thinning medications or aspirin."

Lashof urged people—particularly those on modest and fixed incomes—who were inclined to spend their money on products like ginkgo (close to $3 *billion* in 2005 in the United States alone) to save it for the inevitable rainy days of illness and debility, when they might need the services of a doctor, who might have to write a scrip for a legitimate and, though she did not say it, costly medication.

Herbal "remedies," too, were produced with no regulatory agency overseeing how they were made or if the concentration of the active ingredients listed on the label were consistent with the concentration of the active ingredients in the bottle, and typically, it seems, they were not. According to an article in the October 2003 *Archives of Internal Medicine*, of a survey of popular herbal supplements purchased at twenty stores in the Minneapolis area—echinacea, Saint-John's-wort, ginkgo biloba, garlic, saw palmetto, ginseng, goldenseal, aloe, Siberian ginseng, and valerian—fewer than half of 880 products were consistent with the recommended ingredients and dosage. In an earlier piece in the Dallas city magazine, *D*, where many of the same popular supplements were tested in an established pharmaceutical laboratory, one in three products did not contain the amount of the herb stated on the bottle.

Moreover, because of a loophole in the Dietary Supplement Health and Education Act of 1994, manufacturers, while not able to make health claims without FDA approval, could make claims like "Peak Brain Performance has been designed to support the natural chemistry of your brain and increase the blood flow, nutrients, neurotransmitters and energy required for better learning and recall," or "The herbal formula Alert! has ingredients that help increase the level of neurotransmitters, particularly acetylcholine, and improve blood flow to the brain, thereby increasing its oxygen and nutrient supply, which will aid brain function and memory," because the law allowed them to make claims about how the supplement would affect the structure or function of the body. The label couldn't say the supplement mitigated dementia, for instance, but it could say that it helped improve memory function. Go figure. In a talk to the Good Housekeeping Institute a few years after the 1994 act was passed, David Kessler, then dean of the Yale Medical School and a former FDA commissioner, recalled: "I remember talking to the [congressional] staff at the time. I said, well, what about a claim that says 'improves memory'? Is that a disease claim or is that a structure or function claim? You could predict—and many did argue back in 1994—what would happen if you open up the opportunity to make structure or function claims. . . . I was talking to someone in the industry recently. I asked 'How do you decide what goes on the label? How do you decide what claims to make?' The answer was striking. . . . 'You know how we decide what to put on the label? We do focus groups.' . . . [I said] 'For the last fifty years effectiveness meant something very important in food and drug parlance. Effectiveness meant—at least to me—that there'd be the scientific evidence to demonstrate that something worked.' The person said to me: 'Effectiveness is measured whenever something moves off the shelves.'"

~~

A FEW years ago I had an idea for a magazine piece: I'd go to the pharmacy and root around the shelves devoted to memory enhancement, select what looked like the most promising products based on their manufacturers' claims, and give them a try. So I went to the pharmacy and found myself overwhelmed: did I want a complement of B vitamins, did I want Focus Factor, what about ginkgo, what about ginseng, what about a ginkgo-ginseng combo, what about phosphatidylserine, how about a bottle of acetyl-l-carnitine or colloidal gold? And it occurred to me, standing there, that there was no way to do it right. I could only take one supplement at a time. It might take weeks for one supplement to take effect, and weeks for it to be cleared. The experiment could take years. How could I come up with an objective measure of effectiveness? Any pencil-and-paper test I took or any online brain exercises would become overly familiar before too long. And what would happen to my body, to my brain? I had, not long before, read an article that attempted to explain that a toddler's dietary pickiness—no yucky green foods—was evolution's way of keeping a newly mobile child out of harm's way, but it seemed to me that people would pretty much swallow anything, given the mildest encouragement. Then I came across an old FDA website detailing the harm that had befallen those who had blindly ingested supplements, thinking that because they were "natural"—which is to say, found in nature—they were safe, that included blindness, brain damage, paralysis, and death. I abandoned the experiment, though for a while I was fairly religious about taking the multivitamins I had purchased that day.

Multivitamins tend to contain the B vitamins, as well as folic acid and vitamin E, and while, again, the health claims were still murky, taking one a day seemed harmless, if expensive. My own motivation came in the form of a paper I'd come across by two researchers at Queen's University in Ontario about homocysteine, which is an amino acid found in the blood. (Amino acids, you will remember from high school biology, are the building blocks of proteins.) For the body to produce the right amount of homocysteine, it needs the B vitamins and folic acid. Without these, homocysteine levels rise, and when that happened, the authors observed, there appeared to be a concomitant increase in dementia and brain atrophy. Although they pointed out that "there is no proof at present that treatment with B vitamins will reverse cognitive deterioration or dementia, even though it may return homocysteine levels to normal." Taking a multivitamin seemed like an easy thing to do while someone worked that out.

The multivitamin also contained a hefty dose of vitamin E, whose antioxidant properties were well known, as was its tendency to thin the blood (which was why it was dangerous in large doses). Whether it enhanced memory, however, was yet another medical mystery waiting to be solved. A large population-based study of a diverse group of people in Chicago suggested that people whose diets were rich in vitamin E were less likely to develop Alzheimer's disease. But population studies were notoriously unreliable—more social science than science—and anyhow, the subtext of the finding was that synthetic vitamin E, vitamin E from a bottle, had no capacity to forestall dementia. Another study, of people already suffering from mild cognitive impairment, showed no relief from vitamin E at all.

The vitamin E story would seem to be over, except for this: the researchers might have been studying the wrong people. When scientists at the University of Pennsylvania dosed young mice who had been genetically engineered to develop amyloid plaques with vitamin E, the young mice developed half as many plaques as older mice, for whom the vitamin E made no difference. "My prediction was that the early phase would work, so it was quite exciting to have that confirmed," said the researcher, Domenico Pratico. "But I had predicted that also in the late phases it would have done something significant. That it didn't was for me quite surprising." What he learned from this, he said, was that "if you start to take [vitamin E] too late, it's just a waste of time and money."

BUT CHOCOLATE? How could chocolate ever be a waste of time and money? The more I sat in the presence of Harold Schmitz, the more I began to see chocolate—or, at least, specially processed, high-flavanol chocolate—with his Wonka-ish enthusiasm. I accepted that flavanoids were good for the heart. I accepted that what was good for the heart was good for the brain. I accepted that it was a GRAS compound. "Dietary supplements can be abused," he told me right before I was walked back through the room with no walls, past the model convenience store with a copy of O, *the Oprah Magazine,* in the window touting the "Comforts of Sex." "In a food product there might be days when you go overboard, and you might get tired of the taste, but it fills your stomach. And cocoa has been consumed for so many millions of years. There is no doubt about its safety." It seemed not in keeping with the spirit of things to bring up cocoa's regular dance partners, sugar and fat, and what they brought to the party, so I didn't. "We are reinventing cocoa into a great-tasting health product," he said. The nice PR minder handed me sample boxes of Mars' new "heart healthy" super-flavanol dark chocolate and some heart-healthy chocolate almonds, the latter providing a double dose of heart health, since almonds were known to lower cholesterol.

"How much of this should I be eating a day?" I asked. "Does it matter?" She said it was up to me. This seemed the weak link in the chain that joined food as sustenance to food as remedy: how much I took in was my choice, which made it seem that if a pack of eight chocolate-covered almonds delivered a straight-on antioxidant punch, then maybe four packs, or eight, would be better. And if not better, not bad. About four months later, though, long after every nut and every heart-healthy chocolate bar I'd been given that day had been consumed, I learned that the FDA was having a little bit of trouble with this as well. In a letter to the Mars, Incorporated's parent company, Masterfoods, on May 31, 2006, it noted that due to their saturated fat content, Cocoa Via products were misbranded because their labels made heart-health claims. "[Cocoa Via bars] do not promote a healthy heart when consumed daily as recommended on the product label, even though the products also contain ingredients, such as plant sterol esters, that have been shown to lower LDL cholesterol when consumed as part of a low fat, low cholesterol diet," the agency wrote. "As a matter of fact, the regulation authorizing a health claim for plant sterol/stanol esters and reduced risk of heart disease includes the requirement that the food bearing the claim be low in saturated fat (1 g or less of saturated fat per reference amount and not more than 15% of calories from saturated fatty acid.)" (Cocoa Via's were in the neighborhood of 30 percent.) The FDA also pointed out that the claim on the Cocoa Via Original Chocolate Bars and Blueberry & Almond Chocolate Bars that they could lower cholesterol levels made the products drugs, not foods. Clearly, the folks at Mars needed some guidance from Ray and Terry.

But what about neurogenesis? What about Scott Small and his top-secret work for Harold Schmitz? What about Rusty Gage and his? As soon as I had turned in my visitor's badge and was trekking across the asphalt parking barrens, eager to break into the generous sampler of milk chocolate and peanut butter spokescandy I'd been given as I exited the building, which was talking to me a lot louder than the box of Cocoa Via balanced on top of it, I realized I'd been schmoozed. Harold Schmitz had given nothing away. The only thing I knew for sure was that it wasn't going to be tomatoes. Tomatoes were not going to save us.

BUT BLUEBERRIES — blueberries were a whole different kettle of phytochemicals. If you talked with Jim Joseph long enough, as I did one day, sitting in his sliver of an office at the Jean Mayer School of Nutrition at Tufts University, where the United States Department of Agriculture has a few floors of laboratories, you'd soon think that they were the perfect phytochemical, the quintessential polyphenol, the most potent flavonoid. That was because, in addition to their antioxidant properties, blueberries did what few foods did: they promoted neurogenesis. That's right: if you eat blueberries, you'll grow new neurons in your brain. If you're a rat.

Jim Joseph, I'd been told by Harold Schmitz, was a "character." When I arrived at his office a few days after visiting Mars, I found him sitting under a giant mimosa tree, listening to the radio, muttering about how the singer Harry Belafonte had been "down cavorting with that Chávez guy in Venezuela who wants to be the dictator of South America." A gnomish man with a beard who breezed through his lab in black zip-up Nikes, Joseph didn't have much good to say about government—ours or anyone else's—even though the U.S. government issued his paycheck.

Joseph, who trained as a neuroscientist, not a nutritionist, ended up as the world's leading blueberry researcher by chance. A fellow scientist, Ron Prior, bought a house in his neighborhood and the two began to ride together to work. They got to talking about a test that had been recently developed by another colleague that identified which chemicals were good free-radical scavengers—that is, which ones sucked them up and put them out of commission.

"Ron [the neighbor] said, 'I think we should test fruits and vegetables.' I said, 'Pick the most powerful ones and I'll put them in my aging tests.' He had a lab next to my office and after a while it looked like a salad bar. Our first paper [about the antioxidant power of blueberries] came out in 1998. The big one came out in 1999. Nothing I ever did took off like this. When the Tampa newspaper did an article on our findings, the next day you couldn't find blueberries in the supermarket because all these old people glommed them up. Basically we turned around an entire industry. Before, people stuck blueberries in muffins, but nobody thought to eat them as a health food. That's the most interesting part for me because I'm a hard-nosed neuroscientist. I could care less about being published in a nutrition journal. I think nutrition journals spend too much time telling you about some micronutrient you don't have but you need. It's pretty dumb. People don't eat like that."

Joseph folded his arms across his chest and leaned back in his desk chair, which, in turn, leaned into his bookshelves, which were adorned with tall bottles in which red and yellow peppers floated in baths of olive oil, as well as with multiple copies of his book, *The Color Code: A Revolutionary Plan for Optimum Health*. It was an unusual volume—two parts diet book (recipes included) to one part guide to the biochemistry of edible plants—whose main point seemed to be that we should jettison the food pyramid and eat instead by color, because colored foods have healing properties in the very pigments that give them their hue.

While Joseph had good things to say about any number of naturally colored fruits and vegetables, like corn and beets and pink grapefruit and strawberries, and advocated eating around the color wheel every day, he was especially partial to blueberries and not only because Wyman's, one of the country's largest blueberry companies, paid some of his bills. Blueberries seemed to zap free radicals and reverse aging. Blueberries seemed to have anti-inflammatory properties, too. Blueberries enhanced cognition. Blueberries—and this was the kicker—appeared to cause new neurons to grow in rat brains. Joseph launched himself out of the chair and into the hall, beckoning me to follow. A few doors down was his lab, which looked like a lot of other labs—microscopes, balances, pipettes, stains, and graduate students working with small rodents—except for an area way in the back. It looked more homely, with blenders and spatulas and ice cube trays nesting on a shelf. This was the kitchen where Joseph and his crew concocted blueberry rat chow.

"First we grind the blueberries up," Joseph explained. "Then we put the ground blueberries into a centrifuge and separate the liquid, which we pour into ice cube trays and freeze. Once they're frozen, we throw the cubes into an ice crusher. Then that's freeze-dried. It takes about a week and a half, and then it becomes a powder. We send the powder to the rat food company and they superimpose it into the standard rat food. These rats eat better than most Americans."

In one of his rat studies, Joseph and his associates developed a series of motor skills tests that they called the Rat Olympics. Rats had to walk rat-sized balance beams and stay upright during a log-rolling competition. Those raised on the blueberry diet did significantly better than those who were not, leading Joseph to conclude that "amazingly, blueberries were actually able to reverse motor deficits in these aging animals." And four years after Joseph's attention-grabbing 1999 study, the group published findings that were equally astonishing: when genetically altered Alzheimer's mice were put on the blueberry diet, though they still developed plaques and tangles, they did not experience memory loss.

"Old neurons and those in individuals with Alzheimer's disease are like old married couples. They don't talk to each other," Joseph said. Blueberries "make them communicate like young lovers again. For the first time it may be possible to overcome genetic predispositions to Alzheimer's disease through diet."

Of course, we all want to believe it will be so easy: eat a handful of blueberries (or blueberries and strawberries and avocados and carrots) and we'll be saved. It's probably not going to be so simple, though the health benefits of a diet rich in fruits and vegetables is well known and the reasons why, uncovered by people like Jim Joseph, were getting clearer all the time. In the case of blueberries, it had to do with a kind of flavonoid called anthocyanins, which put the blue in the berry and protected young fruit from harmful UV rays. There were three hundred anthocyanins in nature, seventy of which are found in fruit, and forty of which are in blueberries.

"When we fed our rats the blueberry diet, the more anthocyanins that they ingested, the better they performed on memory tests," Joseph was saying as we walked over to the industrial freezer, where cubes of blueberry extract were in the process of freezing. "We know that it's getting into the brain, but we think it's not acting like a traditional antioxidant. So if it's not doing that, what is it doing? We think it has to do with signals. We think that rather than scavenging or sucking up free radicals like an antioxidant, it may be changing the signaling parameters of the body's oxidative stressors."

Joseph also believed, and had evidence from rat brains to back it up, that the blueberry diet spurred the growth of new neurons, and that rats with new neurons did better on memory tests.

So what does that mean for me and you? Should we be eating a pint of blueberries a day, or a gross? And despite our (genetic) similarity to rats, will it matter? "We've worked a little on this," Joseph said. "We gave folks in their sixties blueberries and it was in their bloodstream in an hour. The ones who had a cup of blueberries had a three percent increase in speed on their psychomotor tests, but the ones who had two cups had a six percent rise."

I started to do the math—seven cups of blueberries and they'd fly off the charts—and by the time I'd figured it out (clearly this computation would have gone faster if I'd had a couple of cups of berries myself), Joseph was explaining another experiment he'd done, this one on behalf of NASA, which was looking for ways to protect astronauts from heavy solar radiation in space, since radiation (like its milder cousin sunburn) was a source of oxidative stress, which was itself a cause of rapid aging. (Which was why people who had spent a lifetime in the sun tended to look older than people who had not.) The rats were fed the blueberry diet for eight weeks and then radiated. While the control group went on to develop tumors, the rate of tumor growth in the blueberry rats was "way down." Clearly, Joseph and his team were onto something, though he was quick to remark, at least in his book, that the finer points for humans were still to be worked out.

"I want to try to keep this within the realm of what people actually eat," Joseph said as he walked me to the lab door. "People ask, 'What's the active ingredient?' but I don't really care what it is. I want them to eat the food, not the ingredient. If you purify, purify, purify, and get down to where there's only one or two things in it, I don't think it's going to work very well. We have data along these lines."

It wasn't just his data, either. It was the data of vitamin E researchers who found that the E that comes in a bottle is less effective than the E that comes in an avocado, and the data of scientists at Baylor University who showed that mice fed a diet that was superhigh in beta-carotene actually got skin cancer at increased rates, probably because the beta-carotene wasn't mitigated by the range of vitamins and antioxidants and flavonoids and polyphenols that would be present in a normal, more diverse diet. It was the data of Steven Schwartz, at Ohio State, who demonstrated that the chemistry and nutritional value of colored food was influenced by the foods that were eaten with it. Those red and yellow peppers on Jim Joseph's shelf were swimming in oil for good reason. Their pigments dissolved "preferentially" in fat. Without it, the human body can only absorb a fraction of their color value. Bring on the salad dressing.

"I don't have a problem with supplements," Joseph said as he put me on the elevator. "I take supplements. But supplements shouldn't be a substitute for a good diet. Look, it costs a lot to eat right, but in the long run, it costs a lot more if you don't."

I WAS thinking about Jim Joseph and his bags of blueberry rat chow the day I met Carl Cotman in Irvine, California. Cotman works with dogs. At a secure kennel outside of Albuquerque, New Mexico, is a colony of aging beagles who have been Cotman's research associates for the better part of twelve years. "Most of the dogs are in better shape than we are," Cotman explained. "They have their own vet. Anything happens to them, they're right in the doctor's office—they don't have to wait. Don't have to fill out any forms."

Cotman, like Jim Joseph, was interested in the relationship of nutrition to memory, and among other things, he had been looking into the effect of a diet rich in antioxidants on the memory of his dog pack. Dogs, of course, even older dogs, can learn new tricks, it just takes them a while—maybe years. But the other thing about old dogs was that they actually developed dementia. Not Alzheimer's— they don't get plaques and tangles—but measurable memory loss, and disorientation, a tanglelike pathology, and a significant buildup of amyloid. In one of Cotman's studies of eight- and nine-year-old pups, he gave one group what he called an "enriched" environment: more toys, more playtime, and a kennel mate, while a second group got an enriched diet, and still a third got both. Then, over the next three years, they and a control group were put through training to distinguish one object from another. (If this sounds easy, try putting a teddy bear, a marrow bone, slippers, and a glove in front of your dog and command her to, say, bring you the slippers. Expect to have cold feet.)

"What I was most excited about, which blew me away, was that the animals couldn't do the task when they started the study—and none of the dogs in any of the groups could do it at the end of the first year. But by the end of year three, the combined group could actually do the task and the controls still couldn't. These were all dogs who were showing age-related memory loss and this regimen brought it back again," Cotman said. "Then we looked at the brain tissue, and one of the things that came out was that the mitochondria in the diet group were making less free radicals. There was less oxidative stress. You can now buy the food at pet stores. I tried a pellet—it needed something."

The kibble to which Cotman was referring was sold commercially as Canine b/d. In its advertising, the company that made it, Hill's, showed a bar graph from one of Cotman's clinical trials that demonstrated that older dogs on Canine b/d made more than 50 percent fewer errors than older dogs who were fed regular dog food. (On the chart, the older b/d dogs looked more like young dogs.) They were "61 percent more enthusiastic" when greeting family members.

Before you rush out to buy a bag of Canine b/d—for yourself—rest assured that another of Cotman's collaborators, Dr. Bruce Ames of UC Berkeley, has a more palatable option. Ames, a biochemist who gained notoriety a few years back for his politically and in all other ways incorrect opinion that polluted air and water posed marginal cancer risks because "99.9% of the toxic chemicals people are exposed to come from natural sources," had more recently turned his attention to the toxic effect of mitochondrial decay on the body, especially the brain. Not surprising for a fellow who believed that "[t]he main distinguishing characteristic between fellow and the lower animals is the desire to take pills," Ames was a partner in a company that made Juvenon, a patented supplement. Juvenon was made from "normal mitochondrial metabolites that have been shown in laboratory experiments to help maintain mitochondrial function as cells age by maintaining the membrane potential, promoting metabolism and cell function, enhancing anti-oxidative protection, and promoting cellular health." Say what?

Here's the thing: the free-radical theory of aging, which said that the body deteriorated over time from the oxidation caused by scavenging free radicals, made sense to describe not only wrinkles and slower reflexes and memory problems but death itself. So did the mitochondrial decay theory, which had to do with the slowing down of basic metabolic functions. Both had been implicated in memory loss. But so far the evidence that any of these regimens could forestall or reverse memory loss in people was scant. There had been no large-scale, double-blind, controlled clinical trials of blueberries or cocoa or the active ingredients in Juvenon. Another supplement, DHA omega-3 oil made from algae by a company called Martek and marketed as Neuromins, was in the process of fairly rigorous testing, and looked promising. Omega-3 fatty acids grease the paths of communication in the brain, and Martek's, because they came from a plant, not from fish, which carried the taint of mercury and other heavy metals, seemed to be a better way to deliver them. Still, it was not clear if the very best way to get omega-3s was, as Jim Joseph counseled, to eat right in the first place.

"A lot of things are proving to be good for your health," Dr. Steven Ferris, the director of the New York University Alzheimer's Disease Center and a consultant to a number of pharmaceutical and supplement companies (including, at one time, Juvenon), told me. "There's the blueberry story. There's the fish oil story. A lot of things in the diet that seem to be good for your health also seem to be good for your brain. But I can't tell you to go out and get it in pill form. There's very little evidence that any of this works in pill form. And there's nothing that has been proven so far in an FDA-regulated quality sense to improve memory in normal brain aging. In the end, the proof will be in the human pudding, and it hasn't been made yet."

## Chapter Eight

# Signal to Noise

THE PUDDING MIGHT NOT have been made, but I still wanted to know which GRAS compound might be in it. Scott Small wouldn't say, and after a while I gave up asking him, so I looked at my notes as a cryptographer might, trying to prize out clues, and trolled the Internet, and despite repeated failure couldn't seem to let it go. "You can get it at the health food store," Small had said. "It doesn't even need FDA approval." I looked in the pharmacy. I looked in the food co-op. I studied health and wellness catalogs. It is one of the endearing qualities of our species, how much faith we have in our brains. If one measure of consciousness is the brain's capacity to observe itself—a capacity that is not only lost to dementia but whose loss defines it—then giving one's own brain a problem to solve, and then observing its progress (or not), should be an exercise in good mental health—only it didn't feel that way.

Then, one day, while searching the Internet, I came across a patent application that had been filed by Dr. Fred Gage and a colleague in 2004 called "Method for Increasing Cognitive Function and Neurogenesis." It didn't resolve the initial mystery, but it did advance the plot. Rusty Gage had obviously come up with something—some invention, something novel and potentially lucrative—that caused new neurons not only to grow but to prosper and benefit the brain in measurable ways. Otherwise, why take out a patent? (Another way of asking this might be: otherwise, why pay a patent attorney?)

Patent applications are surprisingly fugal. There is a subject—in this case the "method for increasing cognitive function and neurogenesis"—that is stated and then reiterated again and again, both broadly and in its particulars, in the application's claims and in its descriptions of the invention. "We claim," Gage's application began, "(1) A method for improving cognitive performance in a mammal comprising administering [sic] to a physically active mammal an effective amount of one or more flavonoids, thereby improving cognitive performance of said mammal." Said mammal, according to claim 9, was "a human" that was, according to claim 2, "undergoing a physical exercise routine." Even so, said human, according to claim 11, was "afflicted with a condition of the central nervous system," which included (but was not limited to), according to claim 12, "Alzheimer's Disease, Parkinson's Disease, dementia and sleep deprivation."

The sleep deprivation reference, I figured, was a nod to DARPA, the Defense Advanced Research Projects Agency, the arm of the U.S. Department of Defense that had been funding both Rusty Gage's and Scott Small's neurogenesis work, as well as Gary Lynch's ampakines. Still, it seemed in much too serious medical company, until I read deeper, into the section called "Detailed Description of the Invention," where it became clear that the invention was hardly limited to fixing central nervous system conditions but, rather, was applicable to *any* condition associated with an impairment in cognitive performance. These included aging and hysteria accompanied by confusion, age-induced memory impairment, attention deficit disorder and attention deficit hyperactivity disorder, as well as "subjects that suffer no chronic deficits." Clearly, we were all in this together.

What was the "invention" here that was being patented for the prospective benefit of anyone who had ever stayed up too late or gotten older? Was it a machine? A new drug? Was it something that, in the absence of its discovery, would not otherwise exist in this world? Well, no. Not exactly. Gage's "invention" was a correlation. It followed from the discovery that flavanols such as green tea and blueberries and some kinds of cocoa, plus aerobic exercise, spurred neurogenesis, and that ibuprofen plus exercise seemed to, too. Exercise, obviously, could not be patented, nor could flavanols found in food, and ibuprofen, once a patented medicine, had entered the public domain, but what happened between them, apparently, could be treated as a discovery and as property (since that, essentially, is what a patent is—the designation of a time-limited property right). It was as if God, having made woman, and woman, having made man, man took out a patent on their union.

If it seemed a stretch, that is because it was a stretch—though no more elastic than patents on gene sequences or stem cells. Since 1980, when the Supreme Court, in *Diamond v. Chakrabarty*, opened the door to patents on genetically modified oil-eating bacteria, and then when the Human Genome Project, which has inspired over 3 million gene-related patent applications so far, blew the door off its hinges, the centuries-old injunction against patenting nature drifted away like a birthday balloon. According to the justices, writing in *Chakrabarty*, patenting the bacteria was "not to suggest that Section 101 [of the United States Patent Code, which reads: "Whoever invents or discovers any new and useful process, machine, manufacture, or composition of matter, or any new and useful improvement thereof, may obtain a patent thereof, subject to the conditions and requirements of this title"] has no limits or that

it embraces every discovery. The laws of nature, physical phenomena, and abstract ideas have been held not patentable. Thus, a new
mineral discovered in the earth or a new plant found in the wild is
not patentable subject matter. Likewise, Einstein could not patent
his celebrated law that $E = mc^2$, nor could Newton have patented
the law of gravity."

Maybe. That was then, and this is now, and in this now it was
possible to patent the correlation between eating a particular kind
of food and engaging in a nonspecific amount of aerobic exercise, as
long as exercise was cast as the method of delivery. Instead of "take
two aspirins and call me in the morning," it was "work out for two
hours on the treadmill, drink a couple of cups of green tea (in the
morning, in the afternoon, at night—it didn't seem to matter—or
eat a bowl of berries, ditto on the didn't matter), and call me after
you've grown some new brain cells."

The inclusion of ibuprofen in this scenario was especially curious and seemed to point to the real cause of neurogenesis in the
adult brain. Back in the 1990s, ibuprofen, a nonsteroidal anti-
inflammatory drug that became a common remedy for toothaches
and sore muscles and creaky knees, was touted as a possible cure for
Alzheimer's disease. The thinking on the subject was so simple that
it was elegant: ibuprofen was an anti-inflammatory agent, the beta-
amyloid that builds up in an Alzheimer's brain caused an inflammatory response, so taking ibuprofen would eliminate the inflammation.
If it worked for the knees, why not the brain? All the epidemiological evidence seemed to bear out the hypothesis, too: in twenty separate studies, people who regularly took ibuprofen were significantly
less likely to develop Alzheimer's. Even better, the basic science
looked good. When Gregory Cole, a researcher at UCLA, put
ibuprofen in the food of genetically modified (and no doubt
patented) mice that had been engineered to develop plaques and

tangles, they had less inflammation, less amyloid, and fewer plaques than the animals that did not eat the ibuprofen.

Sounds compelling, was compelling, and the press, along with a public anxiously awaiting good news in the dementia department, was happy to repeat it. "We've shown that a drug that's available, that's been in use for thirty or forty years, and [for which] we know the side-effect profiles, can reduce both the inflammatory response to amyloid and the amyloid itself," said Dr. Cole in a widely reported quote that just happened to show up, more often than not, without the caveat that this was about mice, not men. With men and women it has been a different story. So far, no double-blind, controlled clinical trial has been able to replicate in people what Dr. Cole and his colleagues saw with their genetically altered mice. Not one.

Still, the ibuprofen cure story persisted. It persisted in the public's imagination and in the imagination of scientists, and it persisted in U.S. Patent 20050004046, though differently. The patent was not suggesting ibuprofen as an Alzheimer's cure or preventative, but as a means to growing new brain cells. The thing was that unlike flavanols or, for that matter, Prozac and Paxil and all the other drugs for depression that seem to act on the neurotransmitter serotonin, that were known to cause neurogenesis in rodents, ibuprofen did not. So if the brain of a person who, say, was taking ibuprofen every day while taking a daily spinning class grew new neurons, might it be that it was the spinning, not the medication, that was the real agent of change?

"I've GOT a mouse that ran three hundred kilometers last month," Scott Small mentioned one spring day when I stopped by his office after visiting the medical center gym with a colleague of his, Dr. Richard Sloan. It was midday and the gym was empty, but Sloan

was able to show me where a group of out-of-shape hospital employees could be found in the off-hours, working out on their own version of the hamster wheel, and where, when they were done
charging up virtual staircases and cresting make-believe hills, they
entered their exercise data into a computer that was connected to
Sloan's a block away. Both Small's marathon mouse and Sloan's re-
luctant gym rats were part of a larger experiment, based on Rusty
Gage's work in La Jolla, that aimed to find out whether or not aerobic exercise alone caused neurogenesis, and if so, whether, after
growing new brain cells, memory improved. So far, Scott Small told
me, the evidence in mice was compelling. He was betting the same
would be true for people, too.

"Our work with the mice is going well," he said. "We've done it
three times, and we're now able to predict how much neurogenesis
each mouse will have. No one else can really do this. We're looking
at cerebral blood volume. CBV. Wherever you have more cells you
have more blood vessels.

"Still, a correlation is not causation. What we can say for the
first time is that we can take a living subject, a mouse in this case,
and I can tell you whether that animal is going to have more or less
neurogenesis based on how much it has exercised. We're replicating
this again with mice and then we'll see what we see in humans."

A year later, this is what they saw: not only did the CBV profile
of Sloan's human exercisers mirror that of Small's mice, with the
ones who exercised more having greater blood flow and more neurogenesis, but the people who exercised more and who had, therefore, more new neurons in their brains did better on a slew of
memory tests. And the ones who exercised the most did the best. In
other words, *exercise alone appeared to improve cognition.* This was
big—bigger than the conventional wisdom, which said that what
was good for your heart was good for your brain, which was true, to

a point. In this case, though, what was good for your heart was *even better* for your brain, and Scott Small had the results—in people, not in rats or mice or a petri dish—to prove it.

There was anecdotal and epidemiological evidence, too. In a study of "previously sedentary" older folks by Arthur Kramer at the University of Illinois and others at Israel's Bar-Ilan University, those who engaged in aerobic exercise did better, cognitively, than those who stretched and toned and never got their heart rates pumping; Kramer's subsequent imaging research showed that aerobic exercise "increased brain volume in regions associated with age-related decline in both structure and cognition." Meanwhile, researchers from the Karolinska Institute in Stockholm, who had been following more than fifteen hundred people over thirty-five years, found a significantly lower rate of dementia, including Alzheimer's, in those who exercised. And then there were the walking studies. In one, of over two thousand elderly men living in Hawaii, those who walked two miles or more a day were half as likely to develop dementia as those who walked a quarter mile or less. In another, of nearly twenty thousand nurses, those who walked only an hour and a half a week scored significantly higher on tests of memory and cognition than those who didn't exercise. And it wasn't because they were strolling to the salad bar and back, piling on the GRAS compounds.

So why weren't athletes, as a class, the smartest people on the planet? Why hadn't Tour de France winner Lance Armstrong solved unified field theory or tennis great Maria Sharapova the mysteries of neurogenesis? The answer, it turned out, had to do with the law of diminishing returns. Rather than proceeding in a linear fashion, biology tended to behave like horseshoes looked—in the shape of an inverted U. Functions rose to a peak, and then they slid down the other side. Not enough neurogenesis was a bad thing, but a lot was not, conversely, a good thing. The right amount was somewhere in the vicinity of the bend at the top. "If things were linear, then more and more would be better," Scott Small explained. "But this is never the case. There is a window of goodness, but it's very difficult to know where it is."

Still, in Scott Small's world, a world where there was the possibility of a single simple solution to a persistent complex problem—a possibility that many of us, whether we're conscious of it or not, share—the results from all the exercise studies held out a particular kind of hope, not just because they pointed to the best way yet of staving off age-related memory problems, but because they suggested that hope itself was not misguided. Exercise was not a cure, certainly—it didn't eliminate plaques and tangles, it didn't reverse cell death in sick brains, it didn't stop the toxic production of amyloid—but it did appear to improve memory anyway, and not only because of neurogenesis, and not only because of the cardiovascular benefits of putting more oxygen in your lungs or blood through your heart. In addition to these, exercise also increased the amount of the chemical BDNF (brain-derived neurotrophic factor) circulating in the brain, and it was BDNF that stimulated the birth of new brain cells, and then helped them grow and differentiate and connect and become active. BDNF also enhanced neural plasticity, which was to say that it enabled the brain to prosper. In diseases like Alzheimer's, depression, Parkinson's, and dementia more generally, BDNF levels were low. In people who exercised, BDNF levels rose. You do the math.


It was a soft spring morning in San Francisco, though that wasn't completely obvious down in the crafts room in the basement of The Heritage, a venerable brick manse at the corner of Laguna and Bay with a storied history that began during the gold rush, of taking in waifs and women-in-need. Now The Heritage was a "life care" facility, where people came to enjoy the end of their days, though with its cozy, wood-paneled library and a grand piano dominating the foyer, the place seemed more like a dorm in the quad at Smith.

And then there were the classes. The tai chi and quilting and yoga and pottery and photography, and the one I was sitting in on, the brain-fitness class, which was so popular that there were two sections and a waiting list. All over the country, at YMCAs and community centers and adult ed, cognitive training was the new decoupage. In New York I'd visited a one-on-one session in the psychologist Elkhonon Goldberg's office, where a fellow in his forties who wanted to "stay sharp" was coached through a series of mental stretching exercises adapted from a rehabilitation regimen originally designed for stroke victims and people with traumatic brain injuries. There was nothing particularly wrong with him, he said, but he was now single, after years of marriage, and he was hopeful that a tuned-up memory would give him an edge in the dating game. (Later on, when we were riding together on the subway, and his hour of elaborate connect-the-dots drills had given him more clarity, he suggested that his marriage might have failed because he had had "attention" issues. I didn't pursue.)

I had also talked at length with Dr. Cynthia Green, the psychologist who had designed and taught one of the first memory-enhancement programs in the United States, at Mount Sinai Hospital in Manhattan. Interest in her seminars was burgeoning; the hospital had become a sideline to the work she now did in corporate boardrooms and hotel conference centers. "I took the program out of the hospital because I saw that it was an effective tool for all ages," she explained, noting that in the past week she had worked with a group of real estate brokers in New Jersey ("doing well as a real estate broker requires a really good memory") and at a major New York City bank, where most of the 189 participants were in their twenties. Dr. Green, the author of *The Total Memory Workout: Eight Easy Steps to Maximum Memory Fitness,* was also teaching online, as part of Barnes and Noble University, where she was attracting students from as far afield as Malaysia and the Maldives and Kansas and Tennessee, to name a few of the places where the nearly seven hundred students in one four-week session were from. And when I was in Southern California, getting my brain scanned at the Amen Clinic, the TV news aired a segment about a gym in Costa Mesa that was offering mental fitness along with step classes and kickboxing.

What was happening in the basement of The Heritage, though, was different, and not only because no one was wearing Lycra or working on their cross-strike. It was different because the Posit Science Brain Fitness program the class was following was, right then, being evaluated by researchers at the Mayo Clinic and USC in a multisite, double-blind clinical trial with five hundred participants. Whether it worked or not would, pretty soon, cease being a matter of conjecture or anecdote, though its creator, Dr. Michael Merzenich, the coinventor of the cochlear implant and the Francis A. Sooy Professor of Integrative Neuroscience at the University of California, San Francisco, *and* the developer of a systematic computer-based program for children with language-based learning disabilities, was already certain of its value. In neuroscience circles, and in the concentric waves that emanate from them, Dr. Merzenich was something of a legend, for it was his experiments in the eighties and nineties that demonstrated that neural plasticity—the capacity for the brain to change and grow in response to learning—was real and could be observed physically, tangibly. In his most famous experiment, Merzenich trained monkeys to reach for their food with their middle three fingers until, eventually, it became second nature. Meanwhile, the area of their brains that controlled those fingers, and especially the fingertips, had grown considerably larger. There were before and after pictures, and they offered clear proof that the brain was a work in progress.

"I had never heard of brain plasticity until a few weeks ago when I started this course," said Zoe Brown, a fuzzy-haired artist with yellow and red paint on her hands, who was on the cusp of eighty and had lived at The Heritage for four years. "I thought the brain grew in our heads like a cauliflower, and then it stopped growing." She paused and the other students in the class, seventy-nine-year-old Gloria Learned, eighty-four-year-old Ralph Morse, and eighty-eight-year-old Elmer George, all laughed. Neural plasticity had not been in their vocabularies, either. Zoe couldn't be sure, but she thought the training was working, and though the anecdote that she offered as evidence—that after years of being afraid to drive to the art store to buy supplies, she had ventured out in her car the previous week— was nothing more than the shortest of short stories, one thing about it was quite telling: though she wasn't saying so directly, Zoe Brown was reporting that her spatial reasoning had improved—or, at least, her spatial confidence had been restored, if only a little bit.

When brains age, and when they begin to show the effects of Alzheimer's disease, spatial disorientation is one of the first signs of impairment. Mental maps fade; muscle memory becomes unreliable; one street looks like another—or like no other. A commuter, for instance, a man like my father, who had gotten in his car and driven to the train station nearly every day of his working life, a ride that took fifteen minutes and had three right-hand turns and one left, starts losing his way, ends up on the wrong side of town or in another town, or drives aimlessly, looking for the landmark that will be a beacon, except that it's not. That's why Skip Rizzo, the virtual reality designer at USC, was developing his computer-generated

auditorium exercise as a diagnostic tool. What Zoe Brown's anecdote suggested was that when she was done with brain training, she
might have an easier time of it finding her way back to a seat in
Rizzo's fake theater.

"I HAD a memory once," Gloria Learned volunteered. More laugh-
ter, but nervous. A stylish woman with a gold omega necklace
around her neck and white hair perfectly coiffed—there was a
beauty shop on-site—wearing an elegant black blouse and pat-
terned skirt, Learned used to be an interior designer, and it showed.
"I've had some small strokes," she continued. "Parts of my brain are
just gone. I'll have something I want to do and keep forgetting to do
it. I had a jacket that had a loose piece of fabric in the corner and I
couldn't seem to remember to fix it. Each time I'd take it out to
wear I'd tell myself to remember to repair it, but I never did. One
day I thought, I'll go and fix that jacket, so I went to the closet,
pulled it out, and it was fixed, and I thought, Oh, I fixed it and just
forgot. That was the good news. Then I turned around and the needle and the thimble were right there. In other words, I had just done
it." She paused, even though we all knew the punch line. "I had just
done it," she said again, "and I had no memory of it at all."

Four weeks into the eight-week brain-fitness class and it was unclear to Gloria if it was making a difference, though, as Ralph Morse
pointed out, she did remember that whole episode. But Learned had
something else to say: "Being here at The Heritage, surrounded by
all these people who are full of life and vibrant and fun and suddenly they don't remember who they are. So you have that. And
you know you are headed in that direction."

But not if Elmer George could help it. The oldest member of
the class, George, who spent a career as a furniture upholsterer and

now found himself living among a number of women whose wing-backs and settees he'd draped in toile and damask, was the class coach. He was their go-to guy, answering software questions and adjusting headphones and offering kind words and encouragement. "Most of these ladies had never used a PC before," he confided, "but they all like to cook, so I wrote out the instructions for using the computer as if it was a recipe. They liked that."

Elmer sat me in front of a computer and gave me a pair of high-fidelity, noise-canceling earphones, the kind an audiophile might wear. I put them on and he fiddled with the volume control and with the computer mouse, and then told me to listen for the tones that would soon be broadcast through the headphones. The tones came— one two—in quick succession, and then were gone, like comets before they grew their tails. "Click the mouse," Elmer said. I looked at him dumbly. Apparently I had not spent enough time perusing *The Joy of Cooking* because I wasn't getting what I was supposed to be doing. Elmer removed my headphones and took the mouse. "There are two buttons on the mouse," he explained patiently. "One on the left and one on the right. When you hear a high tone, press the one on the left. When you hear a low tone, press the one on the right."

We started again. The tones zipped by, low, high. High, low. When I pressed the mouse correctly a bell rang. When I didn't, there was an admonishing "thunk."

Mostly, though, I was hearing bells and feeling pretty good about myself. Then Elmer upped the ante, ratcheting the program to its highest level, then standing there with his arms folded over his green knit blazer and company tie (he had cut out the logo of Posit Science and taped it on), his amusement mirroring something opposite on my face. There were still tones, but they came lickety-split and were less than momentary. Maybe somebody's brain could distinguish them, but not mine.

"Have you heard about the baby and the spoon?" Elmer said when I told him that, neural plasticity be damned, I didn't think I'd ever be able to get to level five, try as I might. "A baby picks up a spoon and tries to put it in his mouth and misses and the peas go all over the place. He keeps on trying, and he misses less and less and eventually he doesn't miss at all. That's because of brain plasticity," he said. "It's about training. It gets easier."

In fact, I had heard about the baby and the spoon. I had read about it in the "Companion Guide" to the Brain Fitness program published by Posit Science, the company that put neural plasticity on a plastic disk.

"To understand how the brain changes as you learn a new skill, think of your brain as a map of the country," I read. "As an infant, your brain 'map' was limited to superhighways. You could travel between the largest places in the simplest of ways, but all of the smaller cities and towns, the sites of interest and the thousands of alternative paths (the 'scenic routes') between any two large destinations were inaccessible. . . . When you passed into adulthood, it became possible to take many routes to get to thousands of interesting new places. The highways and roads came into sharp focus, and you were the undisputed master of your own personal road map. Your brain 'map' has a very special quality. At any point in life, you can revise it through learning. Your ability to convert a country lane into a superhighway (or a superhighway into a country lane) is one of the most remarkable facts of your brain's plasticity.

"Think of a simple skill, such as learning how to use a spoon. The brain needs to interpret specific kinds of information about the feel of the spoon on the surfaces of the hand that must grasp it.

"The brain changes required to master the art of using a spoon are accomplished through the alterations in the strengths of connections between nerve cells in the brain. *These changes are massive.*

Even for this simple skill, hundreds of millions or billions of synapses are altered. The sum of all these changes *is* the skill."

When I caught up with Michael Merzenich himself—Dr. Mike to the residents of The Heritage—he also brought up the spoon. By then the neural pathway of that image had been riven in my brain pretty deeply, and it was not what I wanted to talk about. What I wanted to know from Dr. Mike, a pleasantly abrasive sixty-three-year-old who looked like he might qualify for one of Scott Small's exercise studies, was whether or not I should spend $35 a year to subscribe to the *New York Times* daily crossword puzzle online. "Do you like to do crossword puzzles?" he asked, but not because he was expecting me to answer. "If you like to do crossword puzzles, you should do crossword puzzles."

"Yes," I insisted, "but are they good for you? And if they are good for you, why are they good for you? Are they better than, I don't know, reading a book or playing with the dog?"

Merzenich, whose rumpled white short-sleeved cotton shirt seemed emblematic of the sleepless, dot-com-start-up energy that suffused the fifth floor of 114 Sansome Street, a high-rise office building not far from San Francisco's Chinatown, where a cadre of young computer scientists buzzed around each other's monitors and psychologists sat in with focus groups and Posit Science customer service representatives fielded calls from befuddled elders and shipping clerks boxed up software, cocked his head and took my measure. He had clearly talked to a lot of writers in his time, and I got the distinct sense that he was trying to figure out if my relentless questions about the *New York Times* crossword puzzle were some kind of tic. I leaned forward, perching at the edge of a bouncy leather office chair, waiting. Someone looking through the window, if there had been a window, probably would not see the scene for the tableau that it was: oracle and seeker in the moments before the answer to what had become one of the more persistent questions of our age, the one about whether doing the crossword puzzle was going to save us. But, as it turned out, he wasn't going to tell me right away.

"Old brains are noisy," he said. "I can demonstrate this. Take a person who is over sixty-five and look at them receiving a list of words—just a list, no content. Everyone makes errors. Now compress that information, and make it come in faster and faster. It's not understandable. A twenty-five-year-old under the same conditions hears everything. It's amazing we remember anything as we get older. The whole system is degraded. When you see it that way, you see that doing crossword puzzles doesn't have a lot of neurological power."

Merzenich smiled—a little slyly, I thought—and pushed the question back at me. "You know what crossword puzzles are *really* good for?" he asked, as if he was posing a riddle.

I shook my head.

"Doing crosswords are really good for . . . doing crosswords," he pronounced. "Do the puzzle every day and you'll get pretty good at it. But does that come up very often in your day-to-day life? Look, learning tricks is always a good thing. But it doesn't address the problem. The real problem is that your brain is crappy.

"Not your brain, specifically," he said. "But brains in general. Especially as people get older.

"Look, doing the puzzle, or brushing your teeth with your left hand if you're a righty, does exercise certain things, and they do have some benefits." He proceeded to point out that every time you got a right answer (on anything) you also got a little ping of dopamine coursing through your brain, and every time you had to focus, the neurotransmitter acetylcholine was released. "Acetylcholine and dopamine are really crucial for maintaining the memory learning and memory vivification sides of the brain," Merzenich said. "But do they improve memory?" It was a question he didn't even think warranted an answer.

"Nobody told the brain about memory. The brain, in all of its operations, in order to do anything, is remembering. I can't go anywhere or do anything or even move without it. But nobody told the brain about it."

The oracle of plasticity had spoken. My $35 puzzle subscription wasn't a waste. If I kept doing the puzzle, chances were that I'd get better—at doing the puzzle. But it wasn't especially protective, and it wasn't therapeutic, especially not in the ways that Merzenich believed the listening exercises he had developed were protective and therapeutic, and the visual exercises he was working on would be. It was like pitching. Curt Schilling, the Red Sox ace, could go to the gym and lift weights and build muscle and get stronger, but if he hoped to throw more strikes, he'd have to work on mechanics—his stance, his windup, the angle of delivery. Mike Merzenich's point was that there were a number of very specific things that go wrong with the sensory systems of the brain, and if those could be strengthened, the messages getting into the brain would be easier to remember because they would be clearer right off the bat. The results of the clinical trial were not in yet, but Merzenich was betting that hearing better would "take ten years off" an aging brain. Zoe Brown would be driving to Mono Lake for the weekend and Gloria Learned could take the string off her finger because she'd never forget to darn her clothes.

It was compelling—who, except maybe a ten-year-old, wouldn't want their brain to be a decade younger?—but though Dr. Merzenich sent me home with my own copy of the Posit program, and though I accepted his analysis of the limited value of crossword puzzles and sudokus, which extended to his criticisms of online brain gym sites that aimed to train you to expand your ability to hold large random numbers in your head, and ones that tested your visual memory by flashing more and more random shapes on the screen, I couldn't bring myself to go through its paces more than a few times before I put it on the shelf next to the MindSpa light-sound machine. I was already exercising for an hour each day to grow new neurons. The Posit program demanded another hour, which might have put a hand to the back of those new neurons and pushed them along. The neurons I did have, though, resisted. They fought back. They wanted to be reading nineteenth-century English novels and watching dumb romantic comedies and sleeping under a pile of quilts and sending salivating impulses to the food centers of my brain as I flipped through the pages of *Gourmet*. And they withstood the cognitive dissonance of an affection for Dr. Gary Small's fourteen-day *Memory Prescription* quickie while simultaneously understanding, and even embracing, Dr. Merzenich's disdain: "You've got to do it a lot longer than fourteen days—hey, how about the rest of your life!"

Truth be told, even Gary Small (who is not related to Scott Small) did not believe fourteen days was adequate. "Basically, the two-week program just tells you what to do every day for half an hour each day. It's got memory training and physical conditioning and stress reduction and eating right. The idea was to throw in the kitchen sink and see if we can have an effect. People are recognizing that they can keep their brains fit, but how motivated they are, and how much they're willing to do, is not clear. Most people want something that is going to work now. They want a pill. I came up with a two-week program because I thought there was a chance that people would actually stick with it for that long. Can these things really make a difference? It's still an interesting, emerging field."

For someone who made a good part of his living selling the public on the cognitive benefits of eating a hearty breakfast and making time to chill out, all the while earning a certain amount of enmity from his academic peers for figuring out how to cash in on the obvious, Small was surprisingly candid about the limitations of the kitchen sink approach—though he was convinced (or, at least, he was convincing) that it worked. "I try to give people a positive message because I think there are things that they can do," he told me one day when we were chatting in one of his offices at UCLA. "I don't want to mislead them. But they can be proactive and take control of the areas they can take control of and have a better life."

A slight man with a soothing manner, Small stood up and rooted through a pile of papers until he extracted a brain scan, which he handed to me. "This is a picture of a forty-six-year-old woman whose verbal memory scores were average for a forty-six-year-old before she did our fourteen-day program," he said. "She did the program and her verbal scores increased significantly. Two hundred percent. So she was average for a twenty-five-year-old! The diet was not going to improve her memory. So it was probably feeling empowered by all this healthy living, plus the memory training."

It seemed unfriendly to suggest that the woman had improved because she had trained for the test, and rude to doubt out loud that simply feeling empowered by healthy living was enough to overcome a shrinking prefrontal cortex and a mental motor that was running on half a tank of dopamine, so I didn't. Small was a man of goodwill who, when he wasn't preaching his feel-good sermons to a congregation whose members wanted to believe not simply that they could be saved, but that it would be easy and fun, too, was directing some crucial, cutting-edge research into the diagnostic capacities of brain scanning.

"People in the first part of life spend a good part of every day acquiring new information and new abilities, and then they spend most of the rest of life pissing it all away. It's not the natural human condition. Life was never anything but a struggle, never anything but serious," Mike Merzenich said when I asked him if the brain could get sharper following Dr. Small's regimen for two weeks. It was his way of saying no. But neuroscientists, like many scientists, like many of us, are territorial and competitive. Dr. Mike was months away from finishing his own pop-neuropsych book, and he had his own approach to brain building that he was selling for hundreds of dollars and a business to support, which he was not averse to promoting at conferences on "neurotech investing." There was money to be made and anxieties to exploit. There was also science to be done. And there was the nagging question of whom to trust, of who wasn't scamming whom.

Scientific belief is meant to start in darkness, suffused with doubt. The null hypothesis. Peer review. Replication. All this so fools and false gods are not suffered, gladly or otherwise. But scientific narrative is different. It has plot demands. It trades on our emotions. A 200 percent improvement in just fourteen days is a good story, and look, here are some brain scans to illustrate it (no matter that you don't know what you are seeing)! What Mike Merzenich was getting at—at least, what I wanted him to be getting at—was that there were no quick fixes, not in a bottle and not on a disk and not online and not in a book. There were tricks that helped people remember, there were strategies, but none were therapeutic. There were crossword puzzles and book club meetings and volunteering at the Humane Society, and he thought that these, too, because they were mentally stimulating, were good, but not therapeutic either— but maybe that was because they didn't fit in his story about turning down the volume in a noisy brain, not because they weren't therapeutically viable.

The question was, how to separate noise from signal in the messages sent out by people like Gary Small or Michael Merzenich or Daniel Amen or Gary Lynch of Cortex Pharmaceuticals or Scott Small or Richard Mayeux or Harold Schmitz from Mars. Until there was irrefutable clinical evidence, the answer would not be forthcoming.

"What is going on in your brain when you do a crossword puzzle as opposed to, say, reading a book?" I had asked Gary Small the first time we talked, which was on the phone, not long after I reviewed his first bestseller, *The Memory Bible*. He couldn't say. Years later, sitting face-to-face, I put the question to him again, only this time I was also interested in understanding the neural benefits of ballroom dancing. Researchers at Albert Einstein College of Medicine in New York who followed nearly five hundred people for twenty-one years found that of all possible leisure activities, ballroom dancing was the best bet for avoiding dementia—it appeared to reduce the risk by 76 percent.

Maybe it had to do with the cardiovascular benefits of dancing, Gary Small said. Maybe it had to do with the spatial demands of ballroom. Or maybe it was that ballroom dancing was self-selecting, and that people who were going to get Alzheimer's disease were already finding it too challenging. Maybe ballroom dancing was, in its own way, diagnostic.

The real value of the Albert Einstein study was not its dramatic statistic about ballroom dancing, but its reinforcement of the message that at least in a general way keeping mentally active was a good idea. (Solving crossword puzzles, meanwhile, was found to be one of the least "protective" pastimes—which is to say that the people in the study who did crosswords were just about as likely to develop Alzheimer's and other dementias as people who did not go out of their way to be mentally stimulated.) This came as no surprise to Yaakov Stern, Scott Small's colleague at Columbia, who had come up with the idea that the real reason some people were less likely to lose their memory than others was that they had more reserves to draw on. If the brain were a highway system, people with more roads and spurs and bridges and tunnels—think metropolitan New York—would do better in a crisis than those whose mental map resembled the rural routes of North Dakota. A sinkhole on a Dakota road would cause traffic to back up and come to a halt. A bridge closing in Queens would also cause traffic to back up, and to slow, and possibly to stop, but soon enough people would find alternate routes and traffic would pick up again.

The good news was that there were many ways to lay down those multiple pathways. The better news, according to Stern, was that they could go down later in life as well as earlier. In his studies of thousands of volunteers in northern Manhattan, Stern had found a positive correlation between the number of years of education and steering clear of dementia. But he also found that people who went to lectures and took walks and had demanding jobs were also less prone as well. In Carl Cotman's work with beagles, the dogs who aged most successfully were the ones who were given both an enriched diet and an enriched environment—more toys, more stimulation, more exercise, more playmates. If it was right—and obviously there were individual counterexamples everywhere—the theory of cognitive reserve encompassed Michael Merzenich's early work on brain plasticity and, possibly, Scott Small's findings on neurogenesis. It was the metatheory, the story of stories, though for anyone who wanted to know what, specifically, he or she could do, or should do, to stay mentally fit, it might have been a distraction.

It was safe to say that no one sitting in the first-floor auditorium at Columbia University's Neurological Institute on a chill day in November 2004 where Yaakov Stern was holding grand rounds thought so. Most were white coats—neurologists and psychiatrists for the most part. Stern, a psychologist, with an easygoing, almost

slack manner, had been thinking through the question he raised
from the podium—"Why can some people tolerate more brain damage, more pathology like plaques and tangles than others?"—for
more than two decades. His work had taken him from the
conventional—pencil-and-paper tests—to the high-tech: he used
functional brain imaging to see cognitive reserve in action.

"How does the brain behave differently during a task as a function of cognitive reserve?" he asked. "How is cognitive reserve im-
plemented?" Stern projected a slide on the screen that, he said,
showed how a brain with more reserves had to work less hard than a
brain with fewer reserves. "Cognitive reserve is malleable," Stern
told the group. "It is influenced by aspects of experience in every
stage of life."

THERE ARE certain questions that fall maddeningly into the
chicken-egg category, and cognitive reserve is one of them. The evidence was clear, as a quick glance of headlines suggested: "Risk of
Mild Cognitive Impairment Increases with Less Education,"
"Childhood Environment Important in Staving Off Cognitive Decline," "Learning Slows Physical Progress of Alzheimer's." Even so,
how did the chicken get into the egg? Did people with higher IQs
(also protective, according to Stern) do better in school and therefore go farther with their education? In this case, cognitive reserve,
while not a function of standard measures of intelligence, would be
dependent on it. Were those people also more likely to continue to
stay intellectually stimulated? Were people with greater innate intelligence more likely to seek out mental challenges, even if denied
the benefit of a formal education?

Yaakov Stern's message that the not-as-bright could hoist themselves by their mental bootstraps if they were so inclined was later

reinforced in the mouse lab at the Massachusetts Institute of Technology in the spring of 2007, when researchers found that mentally impaired mice given lots of colorful toys and playmates and exercise equipment sprouted new neurons as well as new synapses and were, in the words of one of the scientists, "able to re-establish access to long-term memories after significant brain atrophy and neuronal loss had already occurred." What was most significant about the MIT finding, however, was not that happy brains do better than, in the words of Michael Merzenich, "crappy brains," but that the researchers believed they had identified a new drug that had the same effect as all that enrichment. (Maybe there would be no need to take up ballroom dancing after all.) The chances of that drug ever getting to market, of course, were slim to none, and in the interim ballroom was a better bet, though any aerobic activity would do. New neurons grow, the brain gets a second, a third, a fourth chance. They grow in the dentate gyrus, the part of the brain that suffers most from aging, both in people with Alzheimer's and in those who will never get it.

We were never meant to live as long as we do. We were not meant to be sedentary, or to get the bulk of our calories from simple carbohydrates, or to spend our intellectual capital on *American Idol*. How many times had we heard that sermon? (How many times had we flipped the channel?) If there was, as there almost surely had to be, a first cause that explained why a good brain went bad—if, for instance, a single dysfunctional molecule like the one Scott Small had found in the retromer complex could trigger a disease as massively devastating as Alzheimer's—could there also be an uncomplicated reason for the inevitable graying of the mind? Maybe. Maybe the answer lay in the RBAP48 molecule that Scott Small had found to be diminished in older brains. Maybe it lay in the signal-to-noise problem described by Mike Merzenich. Maybe it had to do with decreased neurogenesis. All of these things—and more—conspired to compromise memory and attention in the human brain. The fact was that a disease like Alzheimer's was, in the end, less complex than growing older. Not less devastating, just less complex. If there was a race to the cure, it seemed destined to win. But memory improved in humans who exercised. That was now known. Wasn't that a way of winning, too?

*Chapter Nine*

# Input, Output

WINNING WAS MOST DEFINITELY on the minds of the twenty-six or so people pacing the hall of the nineteenth floor of the Consolidated Edison building on Fourteenth Street in Manhattan, or sitting folded forward in plastic chairs (as if waiting for Rodin) in a high-ceilinged, once-gilded auditorium, or standing within reach of the bagels and Danish laid out on a side table along the auditorium wall. They were high school kids in church clothes, housewives sipping energy drinks, casual-Friday businessmen, and college students who carried briefcases. They were black and white and Asian and Indian, a Noah's ark of humanity, or what you might see on a city bus, especially if the city bus was going to the Eighth Annual United States Memory Championships. There were a handful of spectators, too: the odd "memory mom" or "memory dad," a couple of reporters, and a few curious onlookers who had seen a teaser for the event on the local news and had gotten up early on a Saturday morning to check it out. People are attracted to genius, but they're also drawn to freaks and sideshows, and it wasn't obvious which of these had brought them to this room with exactly zero natural light, with no affiliation with or reference to the world of sun and breeze and trees and clouds. Around the corner, at Washington Irving High School, students were taking their college entrance exams, and I wondered, had there been a spectators' gallery there, too, if some of its seats would have been filled as well. As for me, attending the U.S. Memory Championships was a way to see neural plasticity in action, since, for the most part, these "geniuses" were made, not born. Whether it also offered a bead on cognitive reserve was yet to be determined.

It was a little after nine in the morning and Ed Pinson, a man with a rich baritone and a powerful microphone, who had spent more than a few years as a United States Marine Corps drill sergeant, announced the first event: memory for names and faces. Some of us are naturally good at this—we actually remember the people to whom we are introduced at parties—and some of us are not, and typically being good or bad, if we've always been good or bad, is not an arbiter of what memory will be in the future. In real life (which, no doubt, the memory competitors but few others would have said this was), memory for names and faces was often an "issue"—which is to say, a problem. In books devoted to helping people improve their memory, there almost always was a chapter on the name-face dilemma, which seemed to be causing widespread social and workplace anxiety. (Invariably, these books instructed readers to construct a mental picture for each new person they met that somehow corresponded to his or her name. Robin Cooper, for instance, would be a bird on a barrel, and Tom Lindberg could be a turkey flying a plane. Cute, but what about a biologist I'd met recently named Agnieszka Staniszewski?) Being able to remember a client's name, according to Dr. Cynthia Green, the author of one of those books, was, at the very least, a perceived business advantage.

Still, being good at remembering names and faces was not what these "mental athletes," as they were being called, were. Nor were they great. Rather, to steal a word from the SAT-takers around the corner, they were preternatural ("beyond or different from what is natural, or according to the regular course of things, but not clearly supernatural or miraculous"). They had learned tricks. They had studied. They had trained, the way a violinist or a poker player might train, and in doing so had altered the neural neighborhoods where the affinity for matching names to faces resided. Could anyone do this? The answer was both yes and no. Unless there was a structural reason hindering learning, anyone could get better at remembering. Could anyone get great at it—same thing. Could anyone be preternatural—possibly, but less likely, though Wilma Rudolph won three Olympic gold medals in track despite having polio as a kid and wearing leg braces till she was twelve.

The contestants moved from the periphery to the center of the room where tables were set up café style, with a chair on either side, one for the athlete, the other for a proctor, who would hand over the material at Ed Pinson's instruction. The competitors were, to a person, grim-faced, though with lips pulled tight across their teeth, a few might have been thought to have been smiling. Orange foam plugs came out of pockets and were jammed into ears. Suit jackets were hung on the backs of chairs. There was little talking, a certain amount of stretching. A world-ranked competitor from Vienna, who was at the American championships for fun, taking time off from his job "inventing a new color," yawned. It was 9:35. Ed Pinson (whose face I cannot recall in any way) said a single word, "begin," precisely and loudly, and the proctors handed the contestants a stack of what looked like yearbook pages (without the pithy epigraphs or the endless strings of extracurriculars). The clock was in play. Competitors would have fifteen minutes to learn ninety-nine name-face pairs, after which they'd have twenty minutes not to forget them. To an observer, it seemed like an impossible task.

But so did running a six-minute mile, which ordinary people did every day.

The mental athletes hunkered down, looked for and found their game face, concentrated so hard they seemed to shrink. Boys pulled absently on their ties, girls twirled their hair. A competitor with a backward baseball cap who had spent the better part of the previous night into the morning in a bar, lowered his head incrementally by inches till his nose was a breath above the tabletop, which was either a learning style or a covert way of napping. All over the room legs were shaking—right legs, mostly. A young woman moved her index finger along the page like a blind person reading Braille. A man in his twenties mouthed the names to himself silently. He'd look down, say the name, look up, say the name. I knew this trick. By talking to himself, even without sound, he was hearing the name in his head, thereby giving his brain two sensory pathways, eyes and ears, to take it in.

"Five more minutes," Ed Pinson barked, cutting through the silence like a dog on a windless night. The mental athletes didn't stir. The five minutes ticked by, then ended. The proctors took back the stack of papers. The legs stopped shaking. The foam inserts were removed. The guy with the hangover put his head to the table at last, resting it in his crossed arms like a kid at school. People stood up, game faces gone, and moved to the front of the room where a middle-aged man was tapping on a microphone. He launched into a brief history of the memory championships, pointed out some of the luminaries who were competing, and asked them to join him on the stage. If this wasn't a bald attempt to separate the mental athletes from the names and faces they'd just been studying, that might have been the effect anyhow. His presence, his words, his friendliness were not unlike the intentional distracters built into neuropsychological tests. Memory, to stick, needed practice. He was interfering with that.

And then the twenty minutes were up. The man walked off the stage, the mental athletes went back to their tables and were told again to begin. The proctors passed out a new stack of yearbook pages. These pages had faces but no names, and the faces were in a different order than they had been before, so it was a whole new ball game. The room reclaimed some of its old silence, though it was underscored this time by the scratch of pens on paper. Ninety-nine faces and 198 names, since just knowing someone's surname or first name was not enough. And it was confusing by design: some of the faces belonged to people with the same first or last name— Christopher Foster and Christopher Post and William Post and Foster Williams. For the spectators there was little to watch. Heads bent over paper bobbed now and then. A teenager bit his lip. A woman stared into space. The five-minute warning sounded, but almost no one was still writing. The mental athletes had completed the task, or some part of it, in less than ten minutes. Before Pinson called time, they were all done.

The proctors collected the papers and retreated to the back of the room to tally the results while a writer and memory coach named Rhonda Hess, from Hershey, Pennsylvania, took to the stage to talk about "creative intelligence." Children, she was claiming, used much more of their brain than older people. For a moment I thought she meant this metaphorically, since older people tended to recruit more parts of their brain than younger people to accomplish the same task, a compensatory strategy as the brain became less efficient, but then she tossed out some figures—75 to 90 percent (the percentage of their "creative brain" used by children) and 5 to 15 percent (the percentage used by adults)—that sounded both official (though she did not cite sources) and officially like something one might hear on talk radio right before an ad for ginseng. Hess's overall message seemed to be that most grown-ups were not using their innate creative intelligence, which, from my perspective as a spectator at this event, seemed like an odd—or even subversive—message to offer a room full of memorizers. It was possible that the message was lost on them anyway, since they were nervously awaiting the verdict of the judges. After about fifteen minutes, it came. The first-place winner was Ram Kolli, a twenty-four-year-old financial analyst from Virginia, who scored a near perfect 96. It was Kolli who had been double-dipping during the exercise, mouthing the names while looking at the faces, giving his hippocampus two ways to take in the information. While it wasn't necessarily a winning strategy, it did have that obvious advantage.

On the numerous websites touting the memory championships owned by Tony Buzan, the British memory entrepreneur whose brainchild they were, the contests were often referred to as the Memory Olympics or the Memory Olympiad or the World Memoriad, and just like the decathlon in the other Olympics, this one had many events. After the names-and-faces hurdle, there was the poetry recall, where participants were handed a poem they'd never seen before (because it was unpublished) and given a quarter of an hour to commit it to memory. Not only that—they had to get the line breaks right, and the punctuation, and the spelling. One mistake in any line and the score for that line was a take-no-prisoners zero.

The poem for this day was called "The Tapestry of Me" and it was written by someone named Jeannine Marie Weaver, whose obscurity was key. It was fifty-three lines and 413 words long, the first ones being: "Within the tightly woven weaves of this tapestry of life / there runs a thread of compassion, a stitch of humanity / which has become the sheltering shroud of my heart." The night after the competition it was posted online on the Echoes of My Soul poetry forum (where, three years later, when I checked, it had been viewed a total of thirty-three times), but right then, in the Con Ed nineteenth-floor auditorium, it was getting its first public reading, though not out loud. While the memory challengers studied the poem, I took the opportunity to duck out of the room and into what appeared to be a hallway closet, where Tony Buzan, who was wearing a sporty, hand-tailored blue blazer over a collarless white linen shirt, had dragged two chairs and was conducting interviews, in hushed tones, away from the central arena.

What the nineteenth-century Frenchman Pierre de Coubertin was to the modern Olympics, the twenty-first-century Englishman Tony Buzan is to the modern memory Olympics. They were his idea—he used to work for Mensa, the organization for people who like to point out that they have genius-range IQs—and it was his corporation, the Buzan Company, that conceived, inaugurated, and ran the memory competitions worldwide, which could also be viewed, if one were feeling a little cranky, as one big infomercial for Buzan's memory-minded businesses. These included, among other things, Buzan Centers all over the world, where memory techniques were taught, as well as Buzan's lucrative consultancy, which counseled CEOs and their minions how to "unleash their genius." His genius, clearly, was making money. He had elevated a method of visualizing information, what he called Mind Mapping, into a marketable and desirable and somewhat proprietary "system." In corporate seminars, on iMindMap software, and in nearly one hundred books (*The Mind Map Book, Mind Maps at Work, The Illustrated Mind Map Book, Mind Maps for Kids*) Buzan had taught people to remember more of what they were hearing or reading by organizing the information into a nonlinear drawing that looked surprisingly like the branching axons and dendrites in the brain. "It's a brain-friendly way of controlling masses of information," the organizer of the U.S.

championship, Tony Dottino, a self-styled follower of Buzan's principles, explained. Later, by way of example, he told the story of a man named Henry, whom he put in the middle of the map, and from there drew separate lines, like sun rays, for Henry's occupation (attorney), age (39), and marital status (married, 1992, to Sheila). Poor Sheila got her own branch, from which hung news of their divorce, in 1995, from which hung a new shoot with the name of Henry's current girlfriend, Amber, and her occupation (exotic dancer). Dottino's point was that if someone told you the story of hapless Henry, you likely would not remember much of it (except for the Amber part), but if you Mind-Mapped Henry's life, more of the details would stick. When Dottino told me this, I had my doubts, but months later, when I was listening to Schantel Williams, the neuropsychological tester at NYU, tell me a story whose details I would be asked to recall, I applied the Mind Map and it actually worked. Not only did I remember almost every detail of the story the first time Williams asked me to recall it, I remembered it after half an hour, too. (In fact, years later, I remember it still.)

"We have to train our memory," Buzan said as we sat in the closet, explaining the rationale for his various businesses, which sounded missionary, the money part being a kind of irrelevant detail. "Instead, what we do to our memory is like having an Olympic athlete train by drinking twenty cans of beer a day, smoking one hundred cigarettes a day, watching four hours of telly a day, ordering him not to work out, making him sit in a car half the day, and eat white bread and fat and grease and sugar and cookies, and then wonder why you've ended up with an obese person who can't even walk a hundred meters.

"You need to train your memory like you train for any sport. We assume you either have a good memory or you don't. The fact is, everyone is born with a potentially fabulous memory."

Stop right there, mister, I wanted to say, but did not. This was Buzan's stump speech—it was bound to have excesses. And I knew what he meant. It was the entrepreneur's interpretation of Yaakov Stern's cognitive reserve and Michael Merzenich's neural plasticity. In fact, the more Buzan spoke, the more he sounded like Dr. Mike, though slicker, and with an Oxbridge accent (though he was educated at the University of British Columbia).

"In a well-used brain, the number of connections grows every year," he was saying. "If it's well used. If it is not—if it's subjected to drugs and bad food—like any other part of the body it will disengage. You'll have a flabby brain." (Okay, it was not exactly like Dr. Mike.) "The human brain was designed for activity. It wasn't designed to sit in a chair and watch TV."

Back in the big room, a former third-grade teacher and stay-at-home mom had just won the poetry contest, memorizing "The Tapestry of Me" in the allotted time in its entirety. (The winner, Tatiana Cooley-Marquardt, had a particular knack for remembering poems. In college at Monmouth University in New Jersey, she said, she got an A in English because she could recite Wordsworth's "Tintern Abbey." She also said she started reading at the age of two.) Now the contestants were on to the speed number competition, where they had five minutes to study pages of random numbers that had forty rows across and twenty rows down. For every correct row they'd get forty points. For every row where they made one mistake, twenty. For every row where they made more than two mistakes, zero. The foam plugs went back in the ears. Ram Kolli looked down at the paper and up at the ceiling, down at the paper, up at the ceiling. The leg shakers started up again, slow at first, then steady, like lawn mowers on a Saturday morning. A radio reporter held up her microphone to record a few minutes of sound. At that very moment this was probably the quietest place in all of Manhattan, in all of New York.

The competition wore on. For a spectator, there still was not much to look at. I read over "The Tapestry of Me" a few times, not hoping to commit it to memory—why would I want it there—and the thing that I kept on thinking about, and to which I kept on coming back, was that being good at memorizing a poem—no, being great at it—was not the same thing as being able to write a great or a good or any kind of poem at all. The ability to look at a page of eight hundred random numbers and recall large chunks of them would not make you a better mathematician, or any kind of mathematician, just as remembering long lists of random words (another event) would not make you a fine writer or a sensitive reader. At its extreme—what this was—a highly trained memory was entertaining and even admirable, but also beside the point, if the point was creating something of value, or if the point was success outside this airless room, or getting into a competitive college, or being analytical, or thinking out of or into the box. Memory was not intelligence, though it sometimes looked like it, especially on a certain kind of history exam. True, memory was a component of the standard IQ test, which said less about memory than about the limits of intelligence testing, which was bound to things that could be quantified and measured.

"There's a section on the Wechsler IQ test where you are asked to remember sequences of numbers," Tony Buzan told me when we were talking in the closet. "This is obviously a trainable skill. If you are normally able to remember seven digits, and you train your memory, you could remember 115 digits easily. Then your IQ would be in the three-hundred range." (An IQ of 300, as far as I can tell, has never been recorded.) But would you, with your 300 IQ, be any wiser or more insightful, let alone curious and inventive, than you were before?

"Everyone has strategies for remembering," Susan De Santi, the psychologist at the NYU Center for Brain Health, had told me, whether it is making lists, or rehearsing driving directions to yourself over and over again, or following Simonides around the bedroom dropping words on pillows and in hampers and on bookshelves. As people age, those strategies may become more necessary, but it would be wrong to consider them cheating, any more than it would be wrong to think that the winners of the memory championships event that required participants to remember the order of a deck of cards in less than a minute were cheating when they assigned each card a visual analog—Queen Elizabeth for the ace of diamonds, say, or the painting *American Gothic* for the two of spades. Why it would be easier to remember *American Gothic* than the two of spades has in part to do with the fact that it automatically halves the number of variables one has to remember, since it's no longer about suit *and* number. The other reason has to do with something Tony Buzan told the small crowd at the memory championships when he took the stage between the random numbers and random words competitions. "Philosophers have assumed that your basic language is your basic language," he said, with a hint of contempt in his voice, "and they are wrong. It's images. That is the language of memory. "'Orange words' trigger orange images. Memory takes information and throws back pictures."

At the time, I could *see* what he meant—when I thought of the words *traffic cone*, I envisioned one of those plastic orange dunce caps that line the highway, and when I thought of the word *orange*, I saw a piece of fruit, not an abstract splash of color. But Buzan only got it right halfway. It's not just images, it's images with a context, images with words, which was why I had done especially well on every word list I'd been asked to remember and recall—not only because I could see an elephant or a sock or a bowling ball but because I knew to put them somewhere and give them perspective. And I constructed stories about them, which required words (and an imagination). This may explain why asking someone to name all the animals she can think of in a minute that begin with the letter *L*, for instance (lion, lemur, leopard, lizard, llama, lark, Lorax . . . ), is a better window on impairment than asking her to remember a simple word list: because in a word list test you are given the words, while in the naming test you need to find the words. The words precede and invoke the image. Without words, without language, the image is inchoate. We see in images, true, but we know what we see because we have words. When words depart us, it is we, not them, who are lost.

AFTER A few hours of watching people try to remember things that had no meaning for them, things that, if they were lucky, they'd forget just as soon as they stepped out onto Fourteenth Street and rejoined the elemental world, the memory championships got boring; they couldn't hold my attention. Attention, of course, is a crucial component of memory, and if I hadn't been writing everything down and recording it, very little of it would have stayed with me. But that is why, in general, we take notes. They give us the opportunity to remember again. I did hang in long enough to see Ram Kolli win an airline ticket to London to represent the United States in the World Memory Championship, and for Samuel Gompers High School, a technical school in the Bronx, edge out Bergen Academy, a prep school in suburban New Jersey, by a single point to capture the high school division. I had come that morning wondering if the participants would be noticeably different from me and my friends—smarter, more facile, more successful, more articulate, more . . . something. I left thinking no, thinking that, in the Harvard neuroscientist Randy Buckner's words, while I knew what memory was for, I was not at all sure what a really, really, really good memory was good for, except for entertainment (and possibly not ending a sentence with a preposition). Was there an evolutionary benefit to being able to remember the order of a deck of cards in less than a minute?

Sitting there, watching a bunch of people try to commit a bunch of numbers to memory, I sketched out the questions I hoped these sixteen- and twenty-three- and thirty-seven-year-olds could answer in the future, if anyone bothered to ask them: Did acquiring a phenomenal capacity for recall by spending time training for the memory championships have the kind of protective effect that Yaakov Stern attributed to cognitive reserve? Was the ability to learn "Tintern Abbey" at twenty and "The Tapestry of Me" at thirty-three enough to overcome a family history of late-onset Alzheimer's or a personal genetic history that included either the *APOE4* gene or the *sorLA* mutation? Did intense mental exercise spur neurogenesis the way not-so-intense physical exercise did? (Probably not, but who knew?) Science was so good at suggesting story lines, but scientists, I'd come to see, were unlikely to spin them out. Not enough money. Not enough rigor. Not enough mystery. Not enough return. If this were a rule, though, it had been thoroughly broken by a neural engineer at the University of Southern California named Theodore Berger.

EVERYTHING I knew about Dr. Berger I learned from reading about him: that he had gone to Union College in upstate New York, that he was the son of an IBM engineer, that at Harvard, where he received a doctorate in 1976 in physiological psychology at the age of twenty-six, he was something of a boy wonder, with ten publications, including one in the prestigious journal *Science*, by graduation. I knew, too, that he had worked at the Salk Institute and the University of Pittsburgh before moving to USC, where he was the director of neural engineering; that he had won numerous awards, including the AARP's Man of the Year, and now had nearly two hundred papers on his résumé; that he had longish gray hair, slicked back; and that he drove a yellow Jaguar convertible and owned a company called Sentri that supplied police departments with a device that could distinguish between gunshots and a backfiring car, which was useful in places that were short of beat cops and had turned to webcam patrolling. It was all interesting in the disembodied, voyeuristic way the details of anyone's life are to someone else, but the real reason I was peering into Ted Berger's window was that he was on a quest to construct the world's first artificial hippocampus, a microchip that could be implanted in the cortex and take over the functions of a damaged one. By the time I showed up at his fourth-floor wet lab at USC's Viterbi School of Engineering, he and a team of postdoctoral fellows and graduate students were ten years into what they were envisioning as a twenty-year project. The "chip" had gone from the size of an overnight bag to that of a writing tablet to something as small as a piece of sheet cake, and it was going to have to get a whole lot smaller if it was ever going to fit in the brain. And shrinking was only one of Berger's challenges, which was why he was spending so much time at another USC facility, thirty miles away in Marina del Rey, working out the math of it.

"The hippocampus is like a jelly roll," said Dong Song, one of a trio of Berger's team who was showing me around the lab. In talks, I had heard Professor Berger refer to it as a banana, too, but the jelly-roll analogy seemed more apt: slice it anywhere and each piece looked the same. "We put slices of live rat hippocampus into a bath of artificial cerebral spinal fluid," Dong Song continued. "They can live for about twenty-four hours." Another member of the team pointed to what looked like a miniature guillotine on the lab bench. It had a sharp blade suspended above a cutting surface with a small cutout for the head. I guessed that the rat neck went in there. (I guessed right.) After that, the brain was dissected; the hippocampus was removed and sectioned. Dong Song pointed to a very thin, almost transparent slice about as big as a kernel of rice resting in a petri dish. The dish was set on a base made of glass, through which wires ran in and out. Those wires were connected to the oversize chip, which itself was connected to a signal box. Dong Song toggled a switch and a wave began to flow across a computer screen. It reminded me of seventh grade science lab, when we made a circuit out of wires and a battery and a bell, which rang every time the circuit was complete. This one was just like that—only many millions of dollars more complicated. "This is it," Song said, flipping the switch again. "So far. Ten years." When he said that, I remembered a plaintive comment someone had left after reading about the artificial hippocampus on a neuroscience website. "As someone who has had part of her hippocampus removed, I've been waiting anxiously for this since I began reading about it in 2001. Come on, Dr. Berger, come on!"

The obvious question to ask when someone has shown you an electric current running through a live piece of rat brain and coming out the other side, is how does it work? "We don't know," Dong Song said when I inquired. "We don't know, and it doesn't matter. This is an input-output model." As long as the signal that came out of the chip looked like what came out of a living hippocampus, that was all that counted. They had reduced the hippocampus to a series of algorithms. The brain slice sitting in the bath of spinal fluid seemed to prove it.

Still, willful ignorance, while efficient, seemed a strange posture for a scientist, especially a scientist whose primary study site was the cortex. "A basketball player doesn't need to know rocket science to launch a ball on a perfect trajectory, so why should a neuroscientist need to know all the nuances of the brain?" Ted Berger had reasoned before going forward with the project. I had also heard him give a lecture in which he described neurons, dismissively, as "little sacks of salt."

"The brain encodes things in terms of spatial-temporal patterns," he also said that day. "That's what's there, and even though I'd like to understand it in terms of memory, and I hope I will, here we're trying to replace the function of neurons."

"[Other scientists] tell me I don't know what memory is, which is true," Berger told a journalist from *Popular Science*. "And they ask how I can replace something that I don't understand?"

It's an interesting question, and not just about engineering or about neuroscience or about epistemology but, rather, about how it is possible to understand the brain and the body and all of life mechanistically, as a chain of chemical reactions, and so avoid questions of selfhood and personality and identity. So much of who we know ourselves to be comes from what we remember. It is not just that the brain codes in terms of spatial-temporal patterns, it's that our memory is what places us, as individuals, in space and time. It's through our memory that we know where we are, and where we are going, and who we are, and who we believe others know us to be. Without memory, living in a constantly refreshed present, we are absent both self-knowledge and history. A signal goes in, and a signal comes out, but what does it mean for our essence?

"GREAT, GREAT news!" Scott Small said, hanging up the phone, tapping on his computer keyboard, and pushing aside a pile of papers in one continuous motion as I crossed the transom into his office. It was spring 2007, and boats were moving easily along the East River, toy boats from the height and distance of Scott's office, shaded by toy trees. I took an automatic inventory of the room: in the two and a half years I had been visiting, the carpet had gotten a little worn, and the walls had yellowed, and the stack of journal articles heaped on the small metal table, near the small metal desk, had grown maybe half a foot a year, in a kind of rushed orogenesis that could be a metaphor for the expansion of knowledge. I took stock of Scott Small, too: milk-chocolate-colored shirt, no tie, dark-chocolate-colored pants, dark wavy brown hair, no gray, his posture relaxed, an obvious playfulness shingled over ambition.

I looked at him expectantly. "Great, great news" sounded like a novel, efficacious, safe drug, like the discovery of a new Alzheimer's gene, like the probable end to whatever unarticulated anxiety most of us have sequestered about a future where memory has faded, and like the end of every articulated anxiety, too.

"As of yesterday we not only have a mouse model of retromer dysfunction, we have a fly model, too!" he said enthusiastically.

Now it was his turn to look expectant, so I said something congratulatory but wan, like "great," or "terrific," but the truth was, from where I was standing, on the promontory of middle age, with a vast ocean of unknowing ahead, and the unpromising land of memory decline in the distance, a fly model of retromer dysfunction didn't quite do it. It wasn't big enough or splashy enough or dramatic enough. It wasn't enough. Unlike novelists or playwrights or poets, scientists don't start the story in medias res, but that's where they do most of their work. For those of us who listen—because we're innately interested or because we have a vested interest or both—the middle is only a bridge to the end, and we're impatient. Science, which invented geologic time, moves inexorably.

Still, in the years I had been coming to the old Presbyterian Hospital building or to the Neurological Institute to visit Scott Small, a tremendous number of discoveries had been made, and breakthroughs confirmed, and knowledge advanced. The sorLA gene discovered by Richard Mayeux and his collaborators had finally been revealed and published. Amyloid plaques could now be seen in a living brain thanks, especially, to a new imaging technique

developed by a chemist and physician at the University of Pittsburgh. There was a growing, open-source Alzheimer's gene bank.
Preliminary data from the Mayo Clinic–USC study of the Posit Science program showed that people who completed the training had
significant improvements in auditory memory, scoring much higher
than the control group on ten- and fifteen-word-list tests, even
though list-learning itself hadn't been part of the eight-week program. (According to Dr. Liz Zelinski at USC, "By doing the training, people got back up to ten years of memory, so that a
seventy-five-year-old now looks like a sixty-five-year-old.") Biomarkers in the blood and in cerebral spinal fluid could show
Alzheimer's nearly a decade before there were symptoms. So could
certain pencil-and-paper tests. Exercise had been shown to cause
new brain cells to grow in old brains, and that process, neurogenesis,
had been shown to improve memory. A diagnosis of mild cognitive
impairment was not, perforce, a sentence to die from Alzheimer's;
some people went from MCI back to normal. Memory loss as people
got older *was* normal. There was an observable, parseable, physiological difference between that kind of memory impairment and
Alzheimer's disease. The first neural prosthesis, an artificial hippocampus, was then just weeks away from being tested in living animals. The first round of immunizations for AD had been completed,
no one had gotten sick, and the method of delivery, if not the
method itself, had worked. So far, it was true, no drug, either for
Alzheimer's or for age-related memory loss (which was a condition,
not a disease), had made it through the pharmacological pipeline,
but not for want of trying, and almost every failure helped refine the
search. If, even two years before, the majority of researchers were
looking for ways to rid the brain of the sticky plaques that had defined Alzheimer's for the better part of a century, now they were
working from a newly revised all-points bulletin that suggested

those plaques were not the bad guys, but that the bad guy was soluble beta-amyloid, which Alzheimer's patients had in toxic excess.
And while no one yet knew why that was, the retromer theory put
forth by Scott Small and his associates offered a plausible explanation. The fly model that they had just created would get them closer
to the answer, and then, possibly, to a cure. "It's a lot easier to treat
a sick cell than a dead cell," Scott Small liked to say.

Scott picked up his computer and carried it to the back of his
office and motioned for me to sit down. A couple of weeks before he
had given a talk about his work to undergraduates at Columbia College, and when I couldn't go to that one, he had invited me to the
same lecture—what he was now calling his Campbell's soup talk because it was "canned"—at Cornell Medical School, but I couldn't
be there, either.

"So this is the lecture you refused to attend," he said, scrolling
past the title page, "Zooming in on Alzheimer's," advancing directly
to the next slide, which showed a flow chart, with the words *Gross
Anatomy, Microanatomy, Cells,* and *Molecules,* one atop the other,
with downward arrows in between. By gross anatomy, he explained,
he meant a specific place in the brain, like the hippocampus. By microanatomy, he meant a specific place in the hippocampus, such as
the entorhinal cortex or the dentate gyrus. By cells he meant the cells
in those regions. By molecules, he meant the molecules in those cells.
"The thing is," Small said, slipping invisibly into his professorial skin,
"you have to recognize that all the cells and molecules in the brain
are interconnected. You have to look at all of them simultaneously.
It's amazing how many people violate that first principle.

"In Alzheimer's you have synaptic dysfunction before you have
cell loss, and cell loss before you have plaques and tangles. So what
do you want to use as your indicator of dysfunction?" What he
meant was, if it was plaques and tangles, you would not simply have

come late to the party, but that the band would have packed up and the festivities would be over.

Scott tapped on the computer screen. "This," he said, "is how we found the retromer. By doing this kind of analysis. Now that we've found it, we can begin to zoom back up." He changed slides, to one where the arrows were pointing to the ceiling, which, I noticed, could use a good coat of paint, too. "That's the ultimate goal: correct the molecule, correct the cell, correct the microanatomy, correct the gross anatomy."

"Does that 'correct' the patient?" I asked.

He stopped and regarded me for a minute. I had clearly broken into his flow. It was as though he had momentarily forgotten this was an audience of one. "Well, yes," he said after a minute. "Knowing the mechanism is nice, but ultimately it's about curing the disease.

"If you correct the retromer, can the cells operate better?" he asked himself. "So far we've done that in the inverse. We've shown that if you manipulate retromer molecules you cause cell dysfunction, you cause hippocampal dysfunction, and in mice you cause memory problems. We still have to show that if you fix the retromer, memory improves. It's not like we can take you and knock down your retromer. We'd have to kill you to do that. But I think that if you come back here in five years, we'll have drugs for retromer dysfunction."

Though it was static, the longer I looked at Small's chart, the more dynamic it appeared. It was a kind of linear Mind Map to Scott Small's universe, his unified field theory and professional cosmology, even though brain science was not, as he also liked to say, rocket science. Small had started with a single assumption—that certain kinds of memory problems began in the hippocampus—and from there found a particular region, the entorhinal cortex, where something was amiss for people with Alzheimer's disease, and a completely different place in the hippocampus, the dentate gyrus, that went awry as people aged. From there the road diverged. When Small and his colleagues traveled down the path of the entorhinal cortex, they found the retromer. When they went down the path of the dentate gyrus, they found both the RBAP48 molecule (which, when he said it, sounded like R Baby 48) and neurogenesis. It was a bit like the Choose Your Own Adventure series, where the reader got to decide which story arc to follow, except in Small's case, he was following them both.

"Once we found the dentate gyrus, other research groups, completely independent from ours, found that neurogenesis occurs there, and also that neurogenesis declines as we age. Neurogenesis is now being studied in thousands of labs all over the world. It's the fastest-growing area of neuroscience. In our case, we found the dentate gyrus, and we also found the RBAP48 molecule there. It regulates how a cell produces new proteins. There's a lot less of it as we get older. It fits with memory decline. But you can find any molecule and tell a *Just So* story. Is it related to neurogenesis? We don't know yet. Is exercise a cure for age-related memory decline? Arguably, yes. I can tell you what I believe, not what I know or what anyone else knows. I believe that age-related decline in neurogenesis contributes to age-related memory decline. Therefore, I think that anything that induces neurogenesis will improve memory. Will it cure Alzheimer's disease? No, because that's happening in a different piece of real estate."

Small stopped to catch his breath. "You're getting the whole lecture anyway, even if you were boycotting it," he said. "Just not in order."

But there was an order. I could see that, clearly, for the first time. Everything in his universe did fit. It made sense that he studied Alzheimer's *and* normal memory decline simultaneously. It made sense that he was doing cell biology and electrophysiology and molecular biology and neuropharmacology at the same time *and* seeing patients. It was his way of abiding by that first principle of looking at everything at once.

A graduate student knocked on the door—it was almost time for a lab meeting—so Small flipped through the remaining slides too quickly for either of us to focus. While "Zooming in on Alzheimer's" was intended to be an introduction to his work, for me it was a summation. When he was finished, Scott asked me if I had any questions, and for the first time in more than two years I did not. "We're done then," he said, and though he meant it as a question, I took it as a statement, as both valediction and three-word commencement address.

"I'll walk you down," Scott said, and I gathered my things and took one last look out the window, across the Throgs Neck Bridge, and into Long Island, where Scott Small had lived for a while during high school, before moving back to Tel Aviv, before becoming a commando and fighting in a war, before college and medical school and everything he had learned since.

We made our way down the stairs and down the elevator and out of the dim hospital lobby where there was always someone sitting with her eyes closed and her head riding limply on her chest, and no one who thought she was dead. On the street we fell in with the people pulling intravenous lines and leaning on walkers, the ones in white coats, those in blue scrubs, surgeons with paper shower caps on their heads, tired medical students, babies in strollers, children in wheelchairs—every one of them, potentially, a patient of Scott Small's. The funny thing was that if, later in the day, any of them showed up in his examining room at the Neurological Institute, and he asked them to remember the words *apple, penny, table,* and to draw a cube in all its dimensions, and to touch a finger to their nose, and if on the basis of that test, and of symptoms observed, he made a diagnosis of Alzheimer's, the best he could offer was a prescription for drugs that did not work very well, and a referral to social services, and good wishes. All that work in his lab and, so far, in the clinic, not a lot to show for it. Still, it seemed that what let him send his patients into a future they would not know was knowing himself that the future would soon make good on the promise of science.

"When I first started out I was truly pessimistic," Small said. "I didn't believe in what I call 'the five-year plan'—that's when you ask someone when there's going to be a drug for memory loss and they always say 'in five years.' Even ten years ago I knew that was inaccurate. But over the past few years I've changed—I'm more optimistic now. We are really getting at the core defects of both Alzheimer's and age-related memory loss. To understand something to the point of being able to fix it you have to get down to the molecular level. And that's where we're at. The goal is to take a person with mild forgetfulness and prevent him or her from developing dementia. If we could do that, it would be an incredible success. We've entered the era where that's plausible to predict. My optimism speaks to that.

"On strict scientific grounds we should all be students of Occam's razor. Occam said that if you truly understand something, there will be singularity, and elegance. The blooming, buzzing world of biomedical science may not be as elegant as we think, but I have to believe that history is on Occam's side."

We reached the falafel cart where he was going to get lunch, and as we stood there, about to say good-bye, a tall, lanky man in jeans and a plaid shirt with unruly hair walking down 168th Street called out a greeting to Scott Small, who turned to see who it was.

"Did you see that guy?" Small asked, nodding in the direction of the man, who was disappearing into the pedestrian tide. "That guy is incredibly smart. No, I really mean it. He has a very big brain."

"You should talk," I said.

# Afterword

WRITERS AND SCIENTISTS share a vocational habit: They both ask a lot of questions. As for the answers, writers expect them right away. Scientists know better. Even if a single experiment suggests ten additional lines of exploration, it's crucial for them not to jump the intellectual queue or else the whole enterprise becomes muddled and hard to sort out. When Dr. Scott Small, for instance, mentioned that he and his associates were studying the effect of aerobic exercise on memory function by putting a group of sedentary people through a twelve-week exercise regimen, I wanted to know what would happen if they took people who already had been exercising moderately and increased the intensity of their workouts. I wanted to know what would happen if the protocol was one month, not three, and if there would be any measurable differences if participants used a stationary bike, which supports one's weight, rather than a stair-climber or treadmill, which doesn't. I wanted to know if cells in the olfactory bulb, which are the same kind as in the dentate gyrus, also increased after the exercise protocol. I wanted to know if, after exercising, people were able to distinguish smells better. (In a different part of the hospital, a different research group was working on a scratch-and-sniff test to diagnose Alzheimer's, which appeared to impair the sense of smell well before there were other, more noticeable symptoms.)

The list of questions in my notebook was long. It was a reporter's notebook, and these were a reporter's questions. Small's response, after I had lobbed a few of them over his net, was to say "Whoa!" Each one of my questions could be its own research study, and would have to be if he and his colleagues were really (factually, accurately) to answer them, and that would take a lot of money and a lot of time and meanwhile there were patients sitting anxiously in his waiting room.

By far the biggest question in Alzheimer's research over the past two decades has had to do with the role that beta-amyloid peptides play in causing the disease. For most people, discussions about beta-amyloid, and the controversy that has surrounded the amyloid hypothesis are more "inside baseball" than they want to know until, unfortunately, they are not. Within the scientific community that studies Alzheimer's, the amyloid discussion has been constant and often contentious. When I began writing *Can't Remember What I Forgot,* the conventional wisdom said that clumps of beta-amyloid—the plaques that show up in an Alzheimer's brain like wads of gum and act like black holes—were the cause of memory loss. Even so, there were enough doubters that the word "beta-amyloid" could usually incite a bar brawl if it was used in a declarative sentence with the words "cause" and "Alzheimer's disease." Five years later, though, and no one bothered to get out of their seats. Amyloid was pretty much accepted as the villain in the Alzheimer's story, though the plaques themselves were now considered essentially benign and maybe even beneficial, and a soluble form of amyloid called beta-amyloid 42 was thought to be the bad guy. That was where the amyloid hypothesis stood by the time my manuscript went to press.

More than a year after it was published, researchers at Harvard Medical School were able to extract soluble beta-amyloid from donated human (after death) Alzheimer's brains, inject them into rodent brains, and show it compromising their memory. When they injected plaques, however, they had no effect on memory until the amyloid in them was put back into a soluble form.

For most of us, amyloid is only of interest in relation to drug development and how it might contribute to a cure for Alzheimer's. When I last checked, there were more than thirty Alzheimer's drugs near the end of the drug development pipeline, a good number of which were working off the idea that if Alzheimer's was caused by too much beta-amyloid circulating in the brain, the best way to arrest the disease would be to get rid of it. By the summer of 2008, two of the first anti-amyloid drugs had made it through the last of the FDA's hoops, the Phase 3 clinical trial, which is designed to determine whether a drug works or not, and another had made it out of Phase 2. To be accurate, the first of these wasn't precisely a drug, it was the "immunization" I wrote about in the book. Most people called it the "Alzheimer's vaccine," even though it wasn't actually that. In its first, much earlier incarnation, as I pointed out, the Alzheimer's "vaccine" had caused serious, life-threatening side effects, and the clinical trial had to be halted. In its second iteration the vaccine not only proved to be safe, it also, miraculously, appeared to eliminate amyloid plaques. The hope was that once they were gone, the disease would be, too. That did not happen: once the plaques were cleared, memory function did not come back. The brain was already, irrevocably, impaired.

Though this was not happy news, it was also not unexpected. The amyloid hypothesis had moved on since it was first proposed that the body's own defenses could be marshaled to get ride of plaques; in essence, the experiment was stuck working on a question that was no longer being asked. If nothing else, immunization demonstrated that the plaques found in an Alzheimer's brain are not the cause of the problem, but an effect. This was a useful outcome for science, though this was of little solace to those enrolled in the clinical trial and others who were counting on this therapy to be the answer to their prayers.

Right around this time, another amyloid drug, Flurizan, also crossed the Phase 3 finish line. To people who pay attention to such things—investors and those invested in a much more profound way, Flurizan was one of the better-known Alzheimer's drugs in development, much touted despite some early, unpromising results. Unlike the "vaccine," Flurizan was a genuine anti-amyloid drug. A few days before the results of Flurizan's Phase 3 eighteen-month trial of 1,684 Alzheimer's patients were to be announced, a Danish drug company paid $100 million for the drug's European distributing rights. The word on the street was that the Danes knew something, and the something they knew was that the drug actually worked—why else risk so much money so close to the results' release date? Then that day arrived, and that question was asked again, but in a different, incredulous, what-were-they-thinking kind of way because it turned out that the trial was a bust. Flurizan had not proved to have a significant effect on cognition. Nor did it appear to improve "the activities of daily living." The American drug company, Myriad, which had already invested some $200 million in Flurizan decided to cut its losses. It walked away from the drug.

With Flurizan out of the picture, attention turned to a drug with the strange, almost biblical name of bapineuzumab, another anti-amyloid agent. Though not yet through Phase 3, its makers, Elan and Wyeth (the same companies behind the failed immunization trial), were reporting some mildly promising yet less than knock-'em-out-of-the-park results. On the one hand, the drug was found to be ineffective for people who carried the *APOE4* gene variant. On the other, people without that variant did slightly better on the drug than those taking a placebo. This was good enough to prompt Elan and Wyeth to open up the trial to more than four thousand participants, keeping bapineuzumab in play. The hope is that bigger numbers will show bigger effects.

Still, in the summer of 2008, it wasn't uncommon to pick up a newspaper or magazine and see a headline like this one in *BusinessWeek*: "Alzheimer's Drugs: Investors' Impatience," or this one, in the *Wall Street Journal*: "Wyeth, Elan Tumble on Chilly Response to Alzheimer's Drug Data." In those publications and in others, too, there was a certain amount of grumbling about the amyloid hypothesis itself, and about the money that had been spent pursuing it, and how that had impeded scientific progress. Yet, as Dr. Sam Gandy, the director of the Alzheimer's Disease Research Center at Mount Sinai School of Medicine in New York City, cautioned, what happened with Flurizan or the Alzheimer's immunization or even bapineuzumab did not mean that "other amyloid-targeted therapies in the clinical trial pipeline aren't valid. We learn a great deal from every clinical study. There are many ways to impact amyloid and its role in Alzheimer's. There are other drugs in development that target amyloid with mechanisms of action that are different from [these]. One or more of these drugs may ultimately prove successful." And, as professor Rudy Tanzi of Harvard pointed out, "This was just the first wave of drugs and it would be terribly bad for the field and for patients to make quick assumptions. There are many other drugs in the pipeline, some of them a thousand times more potent."

Tanzi, who was being asked to speak to the failure of the amyloid hypothesis as one of its strongest advocates, was burying his lead. Researchers at Imperial College, London, were just about to report that in a preliminary test of a new anti-amyloid drug called PBT2 that Professor Tanzi helped develop, those taking 250 mg of the drug did significantly better on tests of executive function—organizing and planning—than did those on both the placebo and a lower dose of the drug. The researchers also found that the higher dose significantly reduced the amount of beta-amyloid in participants' cerebral spinal fluid. Earlier studies, in mice, had shown that PBT2 cleared amyloid, improved cognition, and reduced damage to brain cells. In the summer of 2008, PBT2 was also on the move, hustling through the FDA pipeline.

Another even brighter ray emerged, to the surprise of many, from the tau side of the aisle. Tau tangles are the other signature of an Alzheimer's brain, and just as there have been researchers pursuing amyloid, there have been those on the trail of tau, though fewer of them with fewer resources. One of them was a scientist from the University of Aberdeen, Dr. Claude Wischik. In 1988, while attempting to use an old malaria drug, methylene blue, to dye some tau proteins in order to see them better, Wischik found himself unable to see the tangles at all: the dye had dissolved the tau. Twenty years later, a company called TauRx, working off Wischik's serendipitous discovery, reported astonishing results with its tau-eating drug, Rember: It reduced mental decline in people with mild to moderate Alzheimer's by 81 percent over twelve months. Meanwhile, those taking a placebo continued to get worse. "We have demonstrated for the first time that it may be possible to arrest progression of the disease by targeting the tangles which are highly correlated with the disease," Claude Wischik told *The Times* of London. "This is the most significant development in the treatment of the tangles since Alois Alzheimer discovered them in 1907."

While it would be easy to mistake Dr. Wischik's exuberance for hubris—these, after all, were early results in 321 subjects—it's important to remember that his excitement was two decades in the making. Talk about patience.

With all this pharmaceutical activity, there is now even more reason to subscribe to the five-year plan, the one that says there will be an Alzheimer's drug in five years. (And this despite the fact that in real terms the amount of money allocated to Alzheimer's research has gone down.) Meanwhile, evidence that aerobic exercise is an effective therapy for slowing down age-related memory loss, continues to mount. Add to the studies by Fred Gage, Scott Small, Arthur Kramer, and Carl Cotman, one from Australia, of people who were already experiencing mild dementia, and another from Germany that shows exercising improving cognition in young people, too. Yet one more study, of more than 6,500 people, suggests another way, besides neurogenesis, that exercise aids memory: by reducing belly fat. It turns out that people who are overweight and have a large belly are more than twice as likely to develop dementia as those with normal weight and belly size, and those who are obese and have a large belly are nearly four times as likely. As scientists have long known, when belly fat—which disrupts body chemistry more than less reactive fat elsewhere on the body—increases, blood glucose rises along with it. Some of Scott Small's most recent animal studies showed that rising glucose levels in turn disrupt the function of the dentate gyrus. That didn't draw a straight and conclusive line between waistline and memory, but it did suggest one. "It's possible," Small told me, "that blood glucose, which tends to drift upward as we get older, is one of the main contributors to age-related memory decline in all of us."

NOT LONG AFTER I finished *Can't Remember What I Forgot*, I went to see Dr. Robert Levine, a former associate clinical professor of neurology at Yale and the author of two books, *Aging with Attitude* and *Defying Dementia*, who has been repeating the exercise mantra for years. I thought it was time to try to clear up some unfinished business.

Dr. Levine was my father's neurologist, the one who suggested that my dad have an MRI and take neuropsychological tests in order to better diagnose his progressive memory loss. He is the doctor my dad blew off. Maybe those tests would have been conclusive, maybe not, but in their absence, and then in his, I was left wondering: Was it Alzheimer's or not? It was that question that had sent me on the journey that became this book.

Because my father's medical records had been destroyed in the intervening years, it was up to me to present my father's case to Dr. Levine. I recalled his strokes, his hypertension, his prostate cancer, his bad heart. I mentioned his getting lost problem, his agitation at the aquarium problem, his what to do with the recycling problem. I recited the medications that had been taken, the therapies that had been tried. This was no substitute for the missing records, but even so, the doctor wasn't convinced that the records would have yielded very much. "Primary-care physicians misdiagnose dementia all the time," Dr. Levine said. He was not claiming superiority but explaining how one dementia often looks like another, and how normal memory loss, which happens to everyone as they age, can often be mistaken for a disease like Alzheimer's.

"It sounds to me like your father had vascular dementia, not Alzheimer's," he said after a while, but before I could get too comfortable with that idea and let go of the notion that my father's memory loss foretold my own, Dr. Levine added a codicil. "Was there some Alzheimer's component? Maybe. It's very unusual to have a clean dementia. In any case, the risk factors for vascular disease are risk factors for Alzheimer's disease."

The doctor excused himself. It was a glorious day and he was eager to get in his daily ten-mile walk.

"Here's something to think about," he said before he set out. "Knowing all you know now about how exercise and nutrition and lifestyle affect memory, would you do anything different to lower your risk?" It is the same question I'd like to ask you.

# Notes

## Chapter One: Anxious

4   Here are some numbers:
From a survey conducted by *Modern Maturity* magazine, reported by Mike Ivey, "Total Recall: Baby Boomers Worry Over Memory Loss," *Capital Times*, February 7, 2003; http://www.madison.com/archives/read.php?ref-/tct/2003/02/07/0302070234.php.

4   Lots of people—most people—have a memory that leaks:
Dr. Jelle Jolles, "The Aging Brain: Distinguishing Normal and Pathological Memory Loss," Irvine Health Foundation Lecture, Maastricht Brain and Behavior Institute, May 13, 1999.

5   According to a survey conducted in 2002:
Peter D. Hart Associates, "Alzheimer's Disease: A Look at Voter Support for Increased Funding for Medical Research," April 12–16, 2002.

5   Similarly, when the MetLife Foundation in 2006:
MetLife Foundation, "Americans Fear Alzheimer's More Than Heart Disease, Diabetes, or Stroke but Few Prepare," summary of "MetLife Alzheimer's Survey: What America Thinks," May 11, 2006.

7      most of us will not live to see eighty-five:
       National Institute of Mental Health, *The Numbers Count:*
       *Mental Disorders in America,* NIH Fact Sheet, 2006, and
       "Prevalence and Incidence of Alzheimer's Disease," http://www
       .wrongdiagnosis.com/a/alzheimers_disease/prevalence.htm.

8      an estimated 16 million Americans:
       Alzheimer's Association Fact Sheet.

8      Even this statistic, from a Danish study:
       Cited in University of California at Berkeley, *Wellness Letter,*
       November 2000.

17     At the Maastricht University Brain and Behavior Institute:
       J. Jolles, et al., "The Maastricht Aging Study: Determinants of
       Cognitive Aging," Neuropsych Publishers, Maastricht,
       Netherlands (1995).

17     Jolles's results dovetailed:
       Ian Deary, et al., "Cerebral White Matter Abnormalities and
       Lifetime Cognitive Change: A 67-Year Follow-up of the Scot-
       tish Mental Survey of 1932," *Psychology and Aging* 18, no.1
       (2003): 140–48.

## Chapter Two: Certainty

34     a neurobiologist named Adam Gazzaley:
       Adam Gazzaley, et al., "Top-Down Suppression Deficit Under-
       lies Working Memory Impairment in Normal Aging," *Nature*
       *Neuroscience* 8 (2005): 1298–1300.

40     researchers did a series of surveys:
       Cited in Ilan Yaniv, et al., "On Not Wanting to Know and Not
       Wanting to Inform Others: Choices Regarding Predictive Ge-
       netic Testing," *Risk Decision and Policy* 9 (2004): 317–36.

40     researchers in Israel:
       Ibid.

42     In a (peer-reviewed) paper:
       William R. Shankle, et al., "Methods to Improve the Detection

of Mild Cognitive Impairment," *PNAS* 102, no.13 (March 29, 2005): 4919–24.

43  At the University of Maastricht:
Merijn van de Laar, "Olfactory Functioning and Memory in Normal Aging Subjects: A Pilot Study," University of Maastricht, February 2002.

44  Scientists at Columbia:
ABC News Online, "Scratch and Sniff Test May Detect Alzheimer's," December 14, 2004.

## Chapter Three: Diagnosis

53  "One of the best ways":
Sadie Dingfelder, "Gateways to Memory," *Monitor on Psychology* 35, no.7 (July/August 2004): 22.

59  According to the psychologist Elizabeth Loftus:
Elizabeth Loftus, *Memory: Surprising New Insights into How We Remember and Why We Forget* (Reading, Mass.: Addison-Wesley, 1980), 64–65.

59  researchers asked a random group:
Raymond Nickerson and Marilyn Jager Adams, "Long-Term Memory for a Common Object," *Cognitive Psychology* 11 (1979): 287–307.

64  "Even under the best circumstances":
Charles A. Morgan III, "Accuracy of Eyewitness Memory for Persons Encountered During Exposure to Highly Intense Stress," *International Journal of Law and Psychiatry* 27, no. 3 (May–June 2004): 265–79; also, *CNN Live* transcript, "The Mystery of Memory," December 27, 2005.

66  three years later:
Ulric Neisser and Nicole Harsch, "Phantom Flashbulbs: False Recollections of Hearing the News About *Challenger*," in *Studies in Flashbulb Memories*, ed. Eugene Winograd and Ulric Neisser (Cambridge: Cambridge University Press, 1992), 9–31.

75     In a paper published in 1971:
       James H. Schwartz, et al., "Functioning of Identified Neurons and
       Synapses in Abdominal Ganglion of *Aplysia* in Absence of Pro-
       tein Synthesis," *Journal of Neurophysiology* 34 (1971): 939–53.

## Chapter Four: Normal

80     According to the authors:
       Peter V. Rabins and Simeon Margolis, *The Johns Hopkins White
       Papers: Memory* (2004): 4.

81     older adults who performed as well:
       Roberto Cabeza, "Aging Gracefully: Compensatory Brain Ac-
       tivity in High-Performing Older Adults," *NeuroImage* 17
       (2002): 1394–1402.

90     A collaborator of his:
       K. A. Kent, et al., "Combining Functional Imaging with Micro-
       array: The Transcriptional-Silencer RBAP48 Is Implicated in
       Cognitive Aging," *Neural Systems, Memory and Aging,* 2004.

## Chapter Five: Inheritance

117    This point, exactly, was illustrated:
       Julia Tsai, et al., "Fibrillar Amyloid Deposition Leads to Local
       Synaptic Abnormalities and Breakages of Neuronal Branches,"
       *Nature Neuroscience* 7 (2004): 1181–83.

123    That discovery suggested:
       Scott Small, et al., "Model-Guided Microarray Implicates the
       Retromer Complex in Alzheimer's Disease," *Annals of Neurol-
       ogy* 58, no. 6 (November 2005): 909–19.

128    But it didn't fizzle:
       Nicholas Wade, "Study Detects a Gene Linked to
       Alzheimer's," *New York Times,* January 15, 2007; and Ekaterina
       Rogaeva, et al., "The Neuronal Sortilin-Related Receptor
       SORL1 Is Genetically Associated with Alzheimer Disease,"
       *Nature Genetics* 39 (2007): 168–77.

## Chapter Six: The Five-Year Plan

134 Researchers in Germany:
Caterina Breitenstein, et al., "D-Amphetamine Boosts Language Learning Independent of Its Cardiovascular and Motor Arousing Effects," *Neuropsychopharmacology* 29 (2004): 1704–14.

134 Researchers looking to see if amphetamines:
Richelle Kirrane, et al., "Effects of Amphetamine on Visuospatial Working Memory Performance in Schizophrenia Spectrum Personality Disorder," *Neuropsychopharmacology* 22 (2000): 14–18.

137 An article in the February 2002:
Robert Langreth, "Viagra for the Brain," *Forbes,* February 4, 2002.

138 Though Roche:
B. P. Ramos, S. G. Birnbaum, I. Lindenmayer, S. S. Newton, R. S. Duman, and A. F. T. Arnsten, "Dysregulation of Protein Kinase A Signaling in the Aged Prefrontal Cortex: New Strategy for Treating Age-Related Cognitive Decline," *Neuron* 40 (2003): 835–45.

146 Some were given 1,000 milligrams:
Cortex Pharmaceuticals Press Release, "Top-Line Findings on CX717 from the DARPA-Sponsored Shift Work Simulation Will Be Presented at Sleep 2006 Meeting," June 21, 2006.

146 another Cortex ampakine—CX516:
"Cortex Ampakine Fails Test," Schizophrenia.com, December 23, 2004; and Cortex Pharmaceuticals Press Release, "Ampakine Fixed-Dose CX516 Cross National Study of MCI Fails to Meet Primary End Point," February 12, 2004.

148 In 2006, another big pharmaceutical:
E. R. Siemers, et al., "Effects of a Gamma Secretase Inhibitor in a Randomized Study of Patients with Alzheimer's Disease," *Neurology* 66 (February 2006): 602–4.

## Chapter Seven: Gone to Mars

154    if popularity was measured:
       According to Thompson Publications' website, In-Cites, which
       tracks the top ten researchers in each scientific discipline, as of
       2006, Gage's papers were cited more frequently than those
       of any other neuroscientist; www.in-cites.com/top/2006/
       fifth06-neu.html.

154    Gage and his collaborators:
       Peter S. Ericksson, et al., "Neurogenesis in the Adult Human
       Hippocampus," *Nature Medicine* 4 (1998): 1313–17.

157    a study of elderly Japanese men:
       Lon R. White, et al., "Brain Aging and Midlife Tofu Con-
       sumption," *Journal of the American College of Nutrition* 19, no. 2
       (2000): 242–55.

160    an article from the *New York Times Magazine*:
       Jon Gertner, "Eat Chocolate, Live Longer?" *New York Times
       Magazine*, October 10, 2004.

161    In a paper written by Hollenberg:
       Naomi Fisher and Norman Hollenberg, "Flavanols for Cardio-
       vascular Health: The Science Behind the Sweetness," *Journal
       of Hypertension* 23, no. 8 (August 2005): 1453–59.

162    And in a study where participants:
       Ying Wan, "Effects of Cocoa Powder and Dark Chocolate on
       LDL, Oxidative Susceptibility and Prostaglandin Concentra-
       tions in Humans," *American Journal of Clinical Nutrition* 74, no.
       5 (2001): 596–602.

163    I read about the first:
       Rémi Quirion, "Tea Leaves Alzheimer's Disease Behind," *Health-
       care Quarterly* 9, no. 3 (2006): 21–22; Stéphane Bastianetto and
       Rémi Quirion, "Natural Extracts as Possible Agents of Brain
       Aging," *Neurobiology of Aging* 23, no. 5 (2002): 891–97.

165    the large, double-blind study:
       P. R. Solomon, et al., "Ginkgo for Memory Enhancement: A

Randomized Controlled Trial," *Journal of the American Medical Association* 288, no. 7 (2002): 835–40.

166 According to an article in the October 2003:
S. Garrard, et al., "Variations in Product Choices of Frequently Purchased Herbs: Caveat Emptor," *Archives of Internal Medicine* 163 (2003): 2290–95.

166 In an earlier piece:
G. E. Roffman, "Herbal Remedy Ripoffs," *D Magazine* (April 2000), 39–44.

167 In a talk to the Good Housekeeping Institute:
Dr. David Kessler, "The Good Housekeeping Institute Consumer Safety Symposium on Dietary Supplements and Herbal Remedies," New York, New York, March 3, 1998.

168 My own motivation:
Angeles Garcia and Katherine Zanibbi, "Homocysteine and Cognitive Function in Elderly People," *CMAJ* 171, no. 8 (October 12, 2004): 897–904.

169 A large population-based study:
Martha Clare Morris, et al., "Dietary Intake of Antioxidant Nutrients and the Risk of Incident Alzheimer's Disease in a Biracial Community Study," *JAMA* 287 (2002): 3230–37. Also see Jae Hee Kang, "A Randomized Trial of Vitamin E Supplementation and Cognitive Function in Women," *Archives of Internal Medicine* 166, no. 22 (December 11–25, 2006): 2462–68.

169 no relief from vitamin E:
R. C. Petersen, et al., "Vitamin E and Donepezil for the Treatment of Mild Cognitive Impairment," *New England Journal of Medicine* 352, no. 23 (June 9, 2005): 2379–88.

169 When scientists at the University of Pennsylvania:
Judy West, "Vitamin E Today, More Memory Tomorrow," *The Penn Current Online*, April 2004, http://www.upenn.edu/pennnews/current/2004/040104/research.html.

171 In a letter:
Reported in Joseph Baca, Director, Office of Compliance, Center

for Food Safety and Applied Nutrition, annual report, fiscal
year 2006. U.S. Food and Drug Administration, May 31, 2006.

176    scientists at Baylor University:
Homer Black, "Mechanisms of Pro- and Antioxidation," *Journal of Nutrition* 134 (November 2004): 3169S–70S.

## Chapter Eight: Signal to Noise

181    a patent application:
Henriette Praag and Fred Gage, filed 6/10/2004, United
States Patent 20050004046; http://www.freepatentsonline
.com/20050004046.html.

184    in twenty separate studies:
J. Travis, "Ibuprofen Cuts Alzheimer Protein Build-up," *Science News*, August 12, 2000.

184    When Gregory Cole:
G. P. Lim, et al., "Ibuprofen Suppresses Plaque Pathology and
Inflammation in a Mouse Model for Alzheimer's," *Journal of Neuroscience* 20, no. 15 (August 1, 2000): 5709–14.

187    In a study of "previously sedentary":
Arthur Kramer, et al., "Ageing, Fitness and Neurocognitive
Function," *Nature* 400 (July 29, 1999): 418–19.

187    Kramer's subsequent imaging research:
Stanley J. Colcombe, et al., "Aerobic Exercise Training Increases Brain Volume in Aging Humans," *Journal of Gerontology Series A: Biological and Medical Sciences* 61 (2006): 116–70.

187    researchers from the Karolinska Institute:
Elizabeth Rosenthal, "Research Suggests Exercise May Keep
Senility at Bay," *International Herald Tribune*, October 11, 2005.

187    the walking studies:
"Two Studies Show Walking Keeps Your Brain Fit," *Tufts University Health and Nutrition Letter* 22, no. 10 (2004): 8.

201    Researchers at Albert Einstein College of Medicine:
Joe Verghese, et al., "Leisure Activities and the Rise of Dementia

in the Elderly," *New England Journal of Medicine* 348, no. 25 (June 19, 2003): 2508–16.

204 mouse lab:
Andre Fischer, et al., "Recovery of Learning and Memory Is Associated with Chromatin Remodelling," *Nature* 447 (May 10, 2007): 178–82.

## Chapter Nine: Input, Output

222 The *sorLA* gene:
Ekaterina Rogaeva, et al., "The Neuronal Sortilin-Related Receptor SORL1 Is Genetically Associated with Alzheimer Disease," *Nature Genetics* 39 (2007): 168–77.

222 Amyloid plaques could now be seen:
"Study Confirms Imaging Compound Identifies Amyloid Beta in Human Brain," Massachusetts General Hospital press release, March 12, 2007, reporting on study in the March 2007 *Archives of Neurology*.

223 Biomarkers in the blood:
Miroslaw Brys, et al., "Cerebrospinal Fluid Biomarkers for Mild Cognitive Impairment," *Aging Health* 2, no. 1 (February 2006): 111–21; Sandip Ray, et al., "Classification and Prediction of Clinical Alzheimer's Diagnosis Based on Plasma Signaling Proteins," *Nature Medicine* 13(2007): 1359–62.

223 Exercise had been shown:
G. M. McKhann, et al., "An In Vivo Correlate of Exercise-Induced Neurogenesis in Adult Dentate Gyrus," *PNAS* 104, no. 13 (2007): 5638–43.

# A Note on Sources

To WRITE ABOUT cutting-edge advances in neuroscience I have relied primarily on the papers of biologists, geneticists, biochemists, neurologists, psychologists, epidemiologists, and other researchers, published in a broad array of medical and scientific journals, and too numerous to list here. The publications have ranged from *Science* and *Nature*, to the *Archives of Neurology*, to the *American Journal of Clinical Nutrition*, to the *Neurobiology of Aging* and beyond. They were made immeasurably easier to comprehend through the introduction to neuroscience I received reading, among other books, Eric Kandel's intellectual autobiography *In Search of Memory* (Norton, 2006); Kandel and Larry Squire's felicitous brief on the molecular biology of cognition, *Memory: From Mind to Molecules* (Owl Books, 2000); the work of Daniel Schacter, especially *Searching for Memory* (Basic Books, 1997) and *The Seven Sins of Memory: How the Mind Forgets and Remembers* (Houghton, Mifflin, 2002), both of which combine engaging storytelling with hard (but not hard to read) science; Rudy Tanzi's compelling, personal account of the search for the first Alzheimer's genes, *Decoding Darkness* (with Ann Parson, Perseus Press, 2000); Steven Pinker's entertaining and masterful *How the Brain Works* (Penguin Books, 1999); and, of course, anything by Oliver Sacks.

I also found the encyclopedic *Dana Guide to Brain Health* (Free Press, 2003) invaluable for understanding a wide spectrum of memory disorders and both *Mapping the Mind* by Rita Carter (University of California Press, 1999) and *The Physiology of Cognitive Processes* by Andrew Parker, Andrew Derrington, and Colin Blakemore (Oxford University Press, 2003) helpful in being able to visualize where those disorders emanate and how they look from the inside out. The many "Brain Briefings" and "Brain Backgrounders" supplied by the Society for Neuroscience (*Adult Neurogenesis, CREB and Memory, How Do Nerve Cells Communicate, How Do Facts Stay in Our Mind*; www.sfn .org) almost always anticipated questions raised by more academic and arcane sources, and the online Alzheimer Research Forum (www .alzforum.org) kept me up to date on AD research, conferences, and drugs in development. While there is nothing similar to keep track of the science of normal memory loss, AlzForum, Alzheimer's Disease International (www.alz.co.uk), and the American Alzheimer's Association (www.alz.org) are, in addition to their prime function, repositories of information on cognitive aging more generally.

Two anthologies, *The Oxford Handbook of Memory* (edited by Endel Tulving and Fergus I. M. Craik, Oxford University Press, 2000) and *Memory* (edited by Patricia Fara and Karalyn Patterson, Cambridge University Press, 2006), capture something of the lay of the land, the land in the first being the science of memory around the turn of this century, and in the second, the more enduring questions raised by questions of mind. *Memory Change in the Aged* (David F. Hultsch, Christopher Hertzog, Roger A. Dixon, and Brent J. Small, Cambridge University Press, 1998) offers a trove of fascinating insights and data about the normal course of memory decline from the six-year Victoria Longitudinal Study.

Almost all of philosophy addresses memory in one way or another, especially in terms of perception, epistemology, language, physiology, and human nature. Though philosophy wasn't my subject here, I especially enjoyed reading the work of Aristotle (*On Memory and Reminiscence*), John Locke (*An Essay Concerning Human Understanding*), René Descartes (*Meditations on First Philosophy*—particularly the section on the pineal gland), Henri Bergson (*Matter and Memory*), and Bertrand Russell's lecture on memory (from *The Analysis of Mind*) in light of advances in memory science. To understand where that science (as we know it) began, there is no better place to look than Hermann Ebbinghaus's 1885 book, *Memory: A Contribution to Experimental Psychology* (English edition 1913, Teachers' College, Columbia University). To understand where that science is taking philosophy, Gerald Edelman's *Second Nature: Brain Science and Human Nature* (Yale University Press, 2006) and Michael Gazzaniga's *The Ethical Brain: The Science of Our Moral Dilemmas* (Dana Press, 2005) are both wonderfully illustrative.

A number of relatively more recent works of cognitive psychology also stand out: Elizabeth Loftus's *Memory: Surprising New Insights into How We Remember and Why We Forget* (Addison-Wesley, 1980), Ulric Neisser's *Memory Observed: Remembering in Natural Contexts* (Worth Publishers, 1999), Gillian Cohen's *Memory in the Real World* (Psychology Press, 1996), and Elkhonon Goldberg's *The Executive Brain: Frontal Lobes and the Civilized Mind* (Oxford, 2001). Add to these, David Shenk's terrific journalistic exploration of memory and memory loss, *The Forgetting* (Anchor, 2003).

In the time I was working on this book, the literature on living with memory loss, not surprisingly, has burgeoned. Almost without exception, it is moving and full of hard-won wisdom. It includes Elizabeth Cohen's *The House on Beartown Road* (Vermillion, 2004) and *The Family on Beartown Road* (Random House, 2004), Eleanor Cooney's *Death in Slow Motion* (Perennial, 2004), and Elinor Fuchs's *Making an Exit* (Owl, 2006), all of which concern dementia in a parent. Even more intimate and chilling are Thomas DeBaggio's accounts of his own mental decline, *Losing My Mind* (Free Press, 2002) and *When It Gets Dark* (Free Press, 2003).

The number of self-help and how-to books for improving memory and forestalling memory decline also grew exponentially in those years, to the point where they seemed to comprise their own industrial sector. I read many of them and found them to be inspirational, but not for the obvious reason: they made me want to understand why and how the cognitive exercises and lifestyle changes being promoted might be salutary or not, and if they had any scientific validity. I didn't start tying my shoes with my left hand or taking up meditation. Instead, I embarked on the journey that led to this book.

# Acknowledgments

THIS BOOK IS DEDICATED to Barbara Epstein, who got me thinking about memory science when she asked me to write about "pop neurology" for *The New York Review of Books* in 2002. Her encouragement over the years, her generosity, her friendship, and her pitch-perfect editing were crucial to me in many ways. Her death in June 2006 was not only devastating personally, it closed one of the most delightful chapters in American letters. Though I finished the last piece Barbara assigned to me a few weeks before she died, she never got to see it, and the task of editing it fell to her *NYRB* partner, Robert Silvers. His graciousness and perspicacity are legendary, and I am lucky, now, to know that firsthand.

I am fortunate, too, to have worked with Henry Finder at *The New Yorker*. His curiosity and intelligence were inspiring and magical—which is to say that I could never figure out how he always seemed to know more about my subject than I did, even though I was engaged in research and he, ostensibly, was putting out a magazine. Thanks, also, to Andrea Walker and Julia Ioffe at *The New Yorker*, who kept me on track, and David Remnick for his timely and wise counsel.

Scott Small has been my guide through much of the neuroscientific world, and I have relied on his good humor, patience, and pedagogy. He is a phenomenal teacher, in addition to being a brilliant scientist and compassionate doctor, and whatever mistakes I've made here speak only to my inadequacies as his student.

I am grateful to Richard Mayeux, at Columbia's Taub Institute for Research on Alzheimer's Disease and the Aging Brain, for introducing me to Scott, for inviting me to the Dominican Republic and trusting me with his group's genetics discovery, and for the access he allowed me to his staff and to patients. I have learned much from Yaakov Stern, Larry Honig, Karen Duff, Rafael Lantigua, Jennifer Williamson, Joe Lee, Vinny Santana, Angel Piriz, Rosarina Estevez, Jennifer Manly, and Christian Habeck.

At the New York University Center for Brain Health, director Mony de Leon also has been remarkably open and generous, qualities replicated by his colleagues Susan De Santi, Kenneth Rich, and Schantel Williams.

Many other academic scientists and researchers gave unstintingly of their time and knowledge—so many, in fact, that Simonides wouldn't have enough rooms in his house to sequester them all. They include Carl Cotman, Frank La Ferla, Elizabeth Loftus, Michael Rugg, and Gary Lynch at UCI; Susan Bookheimer, Andrea Kaplan, Karen Miller, and Gary Small at UCLA; Michael Merzenich at UCSF; Randy Buckner and Rudolph Tanzi at Harvard; Amy Arnsten at Yale; Skip Rizzo and Dong Song at USC; Carol Barnes at the University of Arizona; Lindsay Farrar at Boston University; Peter St. George–Hyslop at the University of Toronto; Jim Joseph at the USDA at Tufts; and Tony Phelps and Molly Wagster at the National Institutes of Health.

Thanks, too, to Chris Hanks and Jill Prunella at the Amen Clinics; Kari Stefansson and Edward Farmer at deCODE genetics in

Iceland; Mel Epstein and Steve Bergman at Sention; Peggy Jara at Posit Science; Marla Hastings, the executive director of The Heritage, and Heritage residents Zoe Brown, Elmer George, Gloria Learned, and Ralph Morse; Harold Schmitz at Mars; Harry Tracy, editor of *NeuroInvestments*; Bruce Friedman, CEO of My Brain-Trainer; the Memory Championship's Tony Buzan and Tony Dottino; Larry Minikes and Ruth Olmstead of MindSpa; and Cynthia Green, psychologist, memory trainer, and author of *The Total Memory Workout*.

The librarians at Middlebury College put up with my requests for obscure journal articles. I am grateful to them, and to Middlebury president Ron Liebowitz and vice president Alison Byerly for supporting my research, and to Susan Perkins for making sure they knew what they were supporting.

Numerous friends helped out in one way or another (or many others) in the years I was writing this book, stepping into breaches opened up by my travels and travails. Thanks to Barry and Warren King; Nicky Dawidoff; Doug Lasdon; Missy and Dick Foote; Sara Rimer; Lisa Saiman; David Goldfarb; Peggy McKibben; Bernice Halpern; Jane Mayer; Geraldine Brooks; Shawn Leary; Michael Considine; Laurel Kritkausky; Aaron Coburn; Sally and Alex Carver; Jacob Epstein; my fellow North Branch School Board members: Mia Allen, Donna Rutherford, Mike Hussey, Cindy Seligman, and Michael Seligman, and North Branch teachers Tal Birdsey, Rose Messner, and Eric Warren; Gary and Kathy Wilson; Nick and Jackie Avignon; Don Stratton; Helen Young; Ann M. Martin; Dayna Macy; Dan Frank; and Annik LaFarge.

John Glusman, the editor of this book, first at FSG and then at Harmony, has not only shared his tremendous editorial talent but his friendship. His loyalty to me and to this project has been vital and sustaining. Kim Witherspoon and her colleagues at Inkwell

Management, especially Rose Marie Morse and Julie Schilder, knew just what to do and how to do it and have been terrific. At Harmony, too, I have been guided and helped by Kate Kennedy, Annsley Rosner, Kira Walton, Shawn Nicholls, David Tran, Christine Tanigawa, Lauren Dong, and, of course, Shaye Areheart and Jenny Frost.

Both of the McKibbens I live with, my husband, Bill, and my daughter, Sophie, set a very high bar for diligence, creativity, and commitment to one's work. I cherish their example and their love.

# Index

# About the Author

Sue Halpern received her doctorate from Oxford University in 1985 and first began teaching at Columbia University's College of Physicians and Surgeons. She is the author of *Four Wings and a Prayer*, *Migrations to Solitude*, and two books of fiction. Her work has appeared in *The New Yorker*, the *New York Times*, *Rolling Stone*, *Condé Nast Traveler*, and *The New York Review of Books*, among other publications. She lives in Ripton, Vermont, with her husband, writer Bill McKibben, and their daughter, Sophie, and is a scholar-in-residence at Middlebury College.